Challenges and Applications of Data Analytics in Social Perspectives

V. Sathiyamoorthi
Sona College of Technology, India

Atilla Elci
Hasan Kalyoncu University, Turkey

A volume in the Advances in Data Mining and
Database Management (ADMDM) Book Series

Published in the United States of America by
  IGI Global
  Engineering Science Reference (an imprint of IGI Global)
  701 E. Chocolate Avenue
  Hershey PA, USA 17033
  Tel: 717-533-8845
  Fax: 717-533-8661
  E-mail: cust@igi-global.com
  Web site: http://www.igi-global.com

Library of Congress Cataloging-in-Publication Data

Names: Sathiyamoorthi, V., 1983- editor. | Elçi, Atilla, editor.
Title: Challenges and applications of data analytics in social perspectives
  / V. Sathiyamoorthi and Atilla Elci, editors.
Description: Hershey, PA : Engineering Science Reference, [2020] | Includes
  bibliographical references and index. | Summary: ""This book focuses on
  prevailing challenges in data analytics and its application on social
  media like Facebook, Twitter, blogs, e-commerce, and
  e-service"--Provided by publisher"-- Provided by publisher.
Identifiers: LCCN 2019042042 (print) | LCCN 2019042043 (ebook) | ISBN
  9781799825661 (hardcover) | ISBN 9781799825678 (paperback) | ISBN
  9781799825685 (ebook)
Subjects: LCSH: Data mining--Social aspects. | Quantitative research. |
  Social media.
Classification: LCC QA76.9.D343 C455 2020 (print) | LCC QA76.9.D343
  (ebook) | DDC 001.4/2--dc23
LC record available at https://lccn.loc.gov/2019042042
LC ebook record available at https://lccn.loc.gov/2019042043

This book is published in the IGI Global book series Advances in Data Mining and Database Management (ADMDM)
(ISSN: 2327-1981; eISSN: 2327-199X)

British Cataloguing in Publication Data
A Cataloguing in Publication record for this book is available from the British Library.

For electronic access to this publication, please contact: eresources@igi-global.com.

Advances in Data Mining and Database Management (ADMDM) Book Series

David Taniar
Monash University, Australia

ISSN:2327-1981
EISSN:2327-199X

MISSION

With the large amounts of information available to organizations in today's digital world, there is a need for continual research surrounding emerging methods and tools for collecting, analyzing, and storing data.

The **Advances in Data Mining & Database Management (ADMDM)** series aims to bring together research in information retrieval, data analysis, data warehousing, and related areas in order to become an ideal resource for those working and studying in these fields. IT professionals, software engineers, academicians and upper-level students will find titles within the ADMDM book series particularly useful for staying up-to-date on emerging research, theories, and applications in the fields of data mining and database management.

COVERAGE

- Cluster Analysis
- Information Extraction
- Web Mining
- Database Testing
- Customer Analytics
- Factor Analysis
- Profiling Practices
- Data Analysis
- Sequence analysis
- Enterprise Systems

IGI Global is currently accepting manuscripts for publication within this series. To submit a proposal for a volume in this series, please contact our Acquisition Editors at Acquisitions@igi-global.com or visit: http://www.igi-global.com/publish/.

Titles in this Series

Multidisciplinary Functions of Blockchain Technology in AI and IoT Applications
Niaz Chowdhury (The Open University, Milton Keynes, UK) and Ganesh Chandra Deka (Ministry of Skill Development and Entrepreneurship, New Delhi, India)
Engineering Science Reference • © 2021 • 255pp • H/C (ISBN: 9781799858768) • US $245.00

Handbook of Research on Engineering, Business, and Healthcare Applications of Data Science and Analytics
Bhushan Patil (Independent Researcher, India) and Manisha Vohra (Independent Researcher, India)
Engineering Science Reference • © 2021 • 583pp • H/C (ISBN: 9781799830535) • US $345.00

Advanced Deep Learning Applications in Big Data Analytics
Hadj Ahmed Bouarara (Tahar Moulay University of Saida, Algeria)
Engineering Science Reference • © 2021 • 351pp • H/C (ISBN: 9781799827917) • US $245.00

Opportunities and Challenges for Blockchain Technology in Autonomous Vehicles
Amit Kumar Tyagi (Vellore Institute of Technolgy, Chennai, India) Gillala Rekha (K. L. University, India) and N. Sreenath (Pondicherry Engineering College, India)
Engineering Science Reference • © 2021 • 316pp • H/C (ISBN: 9781799832959) • US $245.00

Cross-Industry Use of Blockchain Technology and Opportunities for the Future
Idongesit Williams (Aalborg University, Denmark)
Engineering Science Reference • © 2020 • 228pp • H/C (ISBN: 9781799836322) • US $225.00

Applications and Developments in Semantic Process Mining
Kingsley Okoye (University of East London, UK)
Engineering Science Reference • © 2020 • 248pp • H/C (ISBN: 9781799826682) • US $195.00

Handling Priority Inversion in Time-Constrained Distributed Databases
Udai Shanker (Madan Mohan Malaviya University of Technology, India) and Sarvesh Pandey (Madan Mohan Malaviya University of Technology, India)
Engineering Science Reference • © 2020 • 338pp • H/C (ISBN: 9781799824916) • US $225.00

IGI Global
PUBLISHER of TIMELY KNOWLEDGE

701 East Chocolate Avenue, Hershey, PA 17033, USA
Tel: 717-533-8845 x100 • Fax: 717-533-8661
E-Mail: cust@igi-global.com • www.igi-global.com

Table of Contents

Detailed Table of Contents

Chapter 1

Calin Constantinov, University of Craiova, Romania
Mihai L. Mocanu, University of Craiova, Romania

In their very beginnings, when social networks were solely used for leisure purposes, any action performed online had minimal effect on the real world lives of their members. This has very much changed in our modern world, where becoming an influencer on Instagram can substantially raise one's income, politics is done on Twitter, and an inappropriate video posted on YouTube can get one fired. Similarly, professional networks have changed the approach universities take to prepare their students, the mechanisms behind companies seeking expertise, and the way in which professionals land matching jobs. In the context of discussing the benefits and pitfalls of using such platforms, several points relating to data privacy are highlighted. Additionally, for a complete view of all analytics possibilities, a survey was conducted by looking over 24 research papers, summarising their findings, detailing the six generic research areas which were identified and speculating on what the future might hold.

Chapter 2

Durgadevi Mullaivanan, Pondicherry Engineering College, India
Kalpana R., Pondicherry Engineering College, India

In recent days, data mining has become very popular, and numerous research works have been carried out of using data mining techniques in the healthcare sector. The healthcare transactions generate a massive amount of data which are very voluminous and complex to be processed. Therefore, data mining techniques have been employed, which provides a practical methodology for transforming the massive amount of data into efficient knowledge for the process of decision making. Prediction and classification are the two forms of data analysis methods. However, it is still difficult to explore the complete literature in the healthcare domain. This chapter reviews the research overview that is done in the healthcare sector utilizing different data mining methodologies for prediction and classification of diverse diseases. Also, a detailed comparison of reviewed methods takes place for better understanding of the existing models. An extensive experimental study is also performed to analyze the performance of data mining algorithms.

The ever-rapid development of technology in today's world tends to provide us with a dramatic explosion of data, leading to its accumulation and thus data computation has amplified in comparison to the recent past. To manage such complex data, emerging new technologies are enabled specially to identify crime patterns, as crime-related data is escalating. These digital technologies have the potential to manipulate and also alter the pattern. To combat this, machine learning techniques are introduced which have the ability to analyse such voluminous data. In this work, the authors intend to understand and implement machine learning techniques in real time data analysis by means of Python. The detailed explanation in preparing the dataset, understanding, visualizing the data using pandas, and performance measure of algorithm is evaluated.

Chapter 4

The neural network is one of the best data mining techniques that have been used by researchers in different areas for the past 10 years. Analysis on Indian stock market prediction using deep learning models plays a very important role in today's economy. In this chapter, various deep learning architectures such as multilayer perceptron, recurrent neural networks, long short -term memory, and convolutional neural network help to predict the stock market prediction. There are two different stock market price companies, namely National Stock Exchange and New York Stock Exchange, are used for analyzing the day-wise closing price used for comparing different techniques such as neural network, multilayer perceptron, and so on. Both the NSE and NYSE share their common details, and they are compared with various existing models. When compared with the previous existing models, neural networks obtain higher accuracy, and their experimental result is shown in betterment compared with existing techniques.

Chapter 5

Data, which is available in abundance and in accessible forms, if analyzed in an efficient manner, unfolds many patterns and promising solutions. The present world is moving from the information age to the digital age, entering a new era of analytics. Whatever the end user does is recorded and stored. The purpose of data analytics is to make the "best out of waste." Analytics often employs advanced statistical techniques (logistic regression, multivariate regression, time series analysis, etc.) to derive meaning from data. There are essentially two kinds of analytics: 1) descriptive analytics and 2) predictive analytics. Descriptive analytics describes what has happened in the past. Predictive analytics predicts what will happen in the future.

Chapter 6

Namratha Birudaraju, Anurag University, India
Adiraju Prasanth Rao, Anurag University, India
Sathiyamoorthi V., Sona College of Technology, Salem, India

The main steps for agricultural practices include preparation of soil, sowing, adding manure, irrigation, harvesting, and storage. For this, one needs to develop modern tools and technologies that can improve production efficiency, product quality, schedule and monitoring the crops, fertilizer spraying, planting, which helps the farmers choose the suitable crop. Efficient techniques are used to analyze huge amount of data which provide real time information about emerging trends. Facilities like fertilizer requirement notifications, predictions on wind directions, satellite-based monitoring are sources of data. Analytics can be used to enable farmers to make decisions based on data. This chapter provides a review of existing work to study the impact of big data on the analysis of agriculture. Analytics creates many chances in the field of agriculture towards smart farming by using hardware, software. The emerging ability to use analytic methods for development promise to transform farming sector to facilitate the poverty reduction which helps to deal with humane crises and conflicts.

Chapter 7

Adiraju Prasanth Rao, Anurag Group of Institutions, India
K. Sudheer Reddy, Anurag Group of Institutions, India
Sathiyamoorthi V., Sona College of Technology, Salem, India

Cloud computing and internet of things (IoT) are playing a crucial role in the present era of technological, social, and economic development. The novel models where cloud and IoT are integrated together are foreseen as disruptive and enable a number of application scenarios. The e-smart is an application system designed by leveraging cloud, IoT, and several other technology frameworks that are deployed on the agricultural farm to collect the data from the farm fields. The application extracts and collects the information about the residue levels of soil and crop details and the same data will be hosted in the cloud environment. The proposed e-smart application system is to analyze, integrate, and correlate datasets and produce decision-oriented reports to the farmer by using several machine learning techniques.

Chapter 8

Rohit Rastogi, Dayalbagh Educational Institute, India & ABES Engineering College,
Ghaziabad, India
Devendra Kumar Chaturvedi, Dayalbagh Educational Institute, India
Sathiyamoorthi V., Sona College of Technology, Salem, India

Many apps and analyzers based on machine learning have been designed already to help and cure the stress issue, which is increasing. The project is based on an experimental research work that the authors have performed at Research Labs and Scientific Spirituality Centers of Dev Sanskriti VishwaVidyalaya, Haridwar and Patanjali Research Foundations, Uttarakhand. In the research work, the correctness and accuracy have been studied and compared for two biofeedback devices named as electromyography (EMG) and galvanic skin response (GSR), which can operate in three modes, audio, visual and audio-visual, with the help of data set of tension type headache (TTH) patients. The authors have realized by their research work that these days people have lot of stress in their life so they planned to make an effort for reducing the stress level of people by their technical knowledge of computer science. In the project they have a website that contains a closed set of questionnaires from SF-36, which have some weight associated with each question.

Chapter 9

D. Sudaroli Vijayakumar, PES University, Bangalore, India
Senbagavalli M., Alliance University, Bangalore, India
Jesudas Thangaraju, Mahendra Engineering College (Autonomous), Namakkal, India
Sathiyamoorthi V., Sona College of Technology, Salem, India

Today's wealth and value are data. Data, used sensibly, are making wonders to make wise decisions for individuals, corporates, etc. The era of spending time with an individual to understand them better is gone. Individual's interests, requirements are identified easily by observing the activities an individual performs in social media. Social media, started as a tool for interaction, has grown as a platform to make and promote business. Social media content is unavoidable as the data that are going to be dealt with is huge in volume, variety, and velocity. The demand for using machine learning in analysing social media content is increasing at a faster pace in identifying influencers, demands of individuals. However, the real complexity lies in making the data from social media suitable for analysis. The type of data from social media content may be audio, video, image. The chapter attempts to give a comprehensive overview of the various pre-processing methods involved in dealing the social media content and the usage of right algorithms at the right time with suitable case examples.

Chapter 10

Taushif Anwar, Pondicherry University, Pondicherry, India
V. Uma, Pondicherry University, Pondicherry, India
Md Imran Hussain, Pondicherry University, Pondicherry, India

E-commerce and online business are getting too much attention and popularity in this era. A significant challenge is helping a customer through the recommendation of a big list of items to find the one they will like the most efficiently. The most important task of a recommendation system is to improve user experience through the most relevant recommendation of items based on their past behaviour. In e-commerce, the main idea behind the recommender system is to establish the relationship between users and items to recommend the most relevant items to the particular user. Most of the e-commerce websites such as Amazon, Flipkart, E-Bay, etc. are already applying the recommender system to assist their users in finding appropriate items. The main objective of this chapter is to illustrate and examine the issues, attacks, and research applications related to the recommender system.

Chapter 11

Santhi Selvaraj, Mepco Schlenk Engineering College, India
Raja Sekar J., Mepco Schlenk Engineering College, India
Amutha S., Mepco Schlenk Engineering College, India

The main objective is to recognize the chat from social media as spoken language by using deep belief network (DBN). Currently, language classification is one of the main applications of natural language processing, artificial intelligence, and deep learning. Language classification is the process of ascertaining the information being presented in which natural language and recognizing a language from the audio sound. Presently, most language recognition systems are based on hidden Markov models and Gaussian mixture models that support both acoustic and sequential modeling. This chapter presents a DBN-based recognition system in three different languages, namely English, Hindi, and Tamil. The evaluation of languages is performed on the self built recorded database, which extracts the mel-frequency cepstral coefficients features from the speeches. These features are fed into the DBN with a back propagation learning algorithm for the recognition process. Accuracy of the recognition is efficient for the chosen languages and the system performance is assessed on three different languages.

Ayurveda medicines uses herbs for curing many ailments without side effects. The biggest concern related to Ayurveda medicine is extinction of many important medicinal herbs, which may be due to insufficient knowledge, weather conditions, and urbanization. Another reason consists of lack of online facts on Indian herbs because it is dependent on books and experts. This concern has motivated in utilizing the machine learning techniques to identify and reveal few details of Indian medicinal herbs because, until now, it is identified manually, which is cumbersome and may lead to errors. Many researchers have shown decent results in identifying and classifying plants with good accuracy and robustness. But no complete framework and strong evidence is projected on Indian medicinal herbs. Accordingly, the chapter aims to provide an outline on how machine learning techniques can be adopted to enrich the knowledge of Indian herbs, which advantages both common man and the domain experts with wide information on traditional herbs.

All these types of analytics have been answering business questions for a long time about the principal methods of investigating data warehouses. Especially data mining and business intelligence systems support decision makers to reach the information they want. Many existing systems are trying to keep up with a phenomenon that has changed the rules of the game in recent years. This is undoubtedly the undeniable attraction of 'big data'. In particular, the issue of evaluating the big data generated especially by social media is among the most up-to-date issues of business analytics, and this issue demonstrates the importance of integrating machine learning into business analytics. This section introduces the prominent machine learning algorithms that are increasingly used for business analytics and emphasizes their application areas.

Chapter 14

Arram Sriram, Anurag Group of Institutions, India
Prasanth Rao Adhiraju, Anurag Group of Institutions, India
Praveen Kumar Kalangi, Anurag Group of Institutions, India
Sathiyamoorthi V., Sona College of Technology, Salem, India

Social media websites enable users to create and share content or to participate in social networking. The main advantage of social media is the ability to communicate with different people to share their knowledge and discuss social events. The impact of social media on people and their behavior is enormous and also solves many problems if it works fine. But there may be negative aspects as well when they are exchange their ideas between people of very different cultures, religions, different age group, and misbehavior of a few users. These problems are addressed using data analytics, which takes people context into account, learns from it, and takes proactive steps according to their situation and expectations, avoiding user intervention as much as possible. This chapter presents all possible problems in social media and enabling those scenarios with effective solutions.

Chapter 15

Bollipelly PruthviRaj Goud, Anurag Group of Institutions, India
A. Prasanth Rao, Anurag Group of Institutions, India
Sravan kumar S., Anurag Group of Institutions, India
Sathiyamoorthi V., Sona College of Technology, Salem, India

IoT comprises billions of devices that can sense, communicate, compute, and potentially actuate. The data generated by the IoTs are valuable and have the potential to drive innovative and novel applications. IoT allows people and things to be connected anytime, anyplace and to anyone with the internet using tiny sensor. One of the best advantages of the IoT is the increasing number of low-cost sensors available along with its functionalities. A few standard sensors include linear accelerator, compass, light sensors, camera, and microphone, moisture, location, heart rate, and heart rate variability. The trend is multi-sensor platforms that incorporate several sensing elements. In such environment, discovering, identifying, connecting, and configuring sensor hardware are critical issues. The cloud-based IoT platforms can retrieve data from sensors IoT is an inter-disciplinary technology, encompassing multiple areas such as RTS, embedded systems. This chapter detailed investigation and presents highly innovative and revolutionary ideas in healthcare application are available.

Preface

Data Science is an extremely important domain in today's data-driven world where 90% of the data has been created in the last 2 years alone. Scientists examine large amounts of data to uncover hidden patterns, correlations, and insights. With today's technologies, it's possible to analyze a huge amount of data and get answers from it almost immediately. It is more efficient and faster compared to traditional business intelligence solutions. Thus, data science is booming, and so is data analytics. Data analyst is then assigned to help organization to make better business decisions. This can fall under the purview of cutting down costs, increasing the returns coming from marketing initiatives, advising corporate management on entering new geographies, make newer product launches, and so forth. A data analyst in a large organization can even play the role which is specific to what he does in the organization: so, a data analyst in a Fortune 500 company may go by the name of financial analyst, sales analyst, operations analyst, marketing analyst, chief data officer, and so on.

Social media is one such domain that has increased the growth rate of the data. Data available from social media is an example of how new digital technologies provide businesses with a more comprehensive understanding of the consumer. Social media has become embedded in nearly every sphere of life. News stories circulate social media channels side-by-side business promotions and everyday sentiments of users. Daily actions and interactions are recorded and collected so that one can discover information such as what the target audience is talking about and what the wider trends of the day are. More specifically, how are they interacting with the company? Are they sharing or liking or negative about what was posted?

Social media is just one field of digital disruption that is generating more data to draw intuition from. How economic transactions occur has been digitized to such an extent that one can analyze not only consumer's interaction with marketing and news but also how and when they act after liking or sharing a company's promotion, tracking of consumers, telling about who they are interacting with and what is attracting them. This list goes on.

With exponentially increasing amounts of data accumulating day-by-day in real-time, there may be no reason why one should not turn it to a competitive advantage. While machine learning, driven by advancements in artificial intelligence, has made great strides, it has not been able to surpass several challenges that still prevail in the way of better success. Such limitations as the lack of better methods, urge for deeper understanding of problems, and need for advanced tools are hindering progress. For example, memory-augmented neural networks require read/write access to a large working memory to discover facts, store, and avail them transparently. Similarly, achieving natural language processing and understanding content are still lacking drastically. Object detection, correct identification, localization and search, image classification and semantics, semantic segmentation, and enabling neural networks to learn using much fewer examples may as well be recounted.

Thus, the proposed title for this book focuses on prevailing challenges in data analytics and its application on social media like WWW, Facebook, Twitter, blogs, e-commerce, e-service, and similar social outlets. Social media involves various interactive Web 2.0 Internet-based applications, user-generated content, digital photos or videos, and data generated through all online interactions, user-created service-specific profiles created by users of websites or applications. Among all of the possible interactions, e-commerce, e-education, e-health and various other prevailing e-services have been identified as important domains for application of analytics techniques. So, this book focuses on various machine learning and deep learning techniques in improving practice and research in such e-X domains in social realm.

Prevailing knowledge and research issues in the following are being covered through contributed authors of specific field expertise:

- Introduction to data analytics,
- AI, deep learning, machine learning applications;
- Cloud computing, edge computing, and social media;
- Social media use cases for individuals and organizations;
- Challenges of Internet- and cloud-based IoT applications, and edge computing;
- (Social/) Big data issues: gathering, governance, GDPR, security, and privacy;
- Data analytics practice using tools & languages, Python, R, so on;
- Machine and deep learning techniques in IoT and cloud;
- Data cleaning, reduction, and visualization techniques and tools;
- Applications of data analytics in emerging fields;
- Emerging trends in data analytics: explainable AI, natural language processing (NLP), predictive and augmented analytics, dark data, continuous intelligence, data fabric, persistent memory servers …

With Regards

V. Sathiyamoorthi
Sona College of Technology, India

Atilla Elçi
Hasan Kalyoncu University, Turkey

Acknowledgment

We are very happy and thankful to IGI Global Inc., USA, for allowing us to produce this book entitled *Challenges and Applications of Data Analytics in Social Perspectives*, which is highly needed in the present data-driven internet world.

We express our deep sense of gratitude to Jan Travers, Lindsay Wertman, Michael Brehm, Jordan Tepper, Halle N. Frisco, Kayla Wolfe, Josh Christ, and other members of IGI Global who supported either directly or indirectly during book project development.

We are thankful to all authors who have contributed their valuable efforts and ideas in the form of chapters in our book. Also, we would like to express our sincere thanks to all our reviewers for their continuous support, guidance, and encouragement in bringing this book into success.

We are thankful to the management and faculty of our institutions for their support and kindness while completing this book.

Also, we are much thankful to our family members for their support and encouragement in achieving this target in our academic career goal.

With Regards

V. Sathiyamoorthi
Sona College of Technology, India

Atilla Elçi
Hasan Kalyoncu University, Turkey

Chapter 1
A Comprehensive Review of Professional Network Impact on Education and Career

Calin Constantinov
University of Craiova, Romania

Mihai L. Mocanu
University of Craiova, Romania

ABSTRACT

In their very beginnings, when social networks were solely used for leisure purposes, any action performed online had minimal effect on the real world lives of their members. This has very much changed in our modern world, where becoming an influencer on Instagram can substantially raise one's income, politics is done on Twitter, and an inappropriate video posted on YouTube can get one fired. Similarly, professional networks have changed the approach universities take to prepare their students, the mechanisms behind companies seeking expertise, and the way in which professionals land matching jobs. In the context of discussing the benefits and pitfalls of using such platforms, several points relating to data privacy are highlighted. Additionally, for a complete view of all analytics possibilities, a survey was conducted by looking over 24 research papers, summarising their findings, detailing the six generic research areas which were identified and speculating on what the future might hold.

INTRODUCTION

During the last decade, the emergence of Web 2.0 standards, aimed at electronically connecting people and easing their collaboration, has greatly facilitated the implementation and maintenance of various social networks, making them an integral part of our online presence (Dasgupta & Dasgupta, 2009). Along with the exponential growth of content being produced using these novel platforms, new endeavours, aiming to uncover the underlying aspects within massive amounts of interconnected information,

DOI: 10.4018/978-1-7998-2566-1.ch001

have also emerged. In turn, big data engineering, mining and analysis can now be distinguished as very prolific research areas.

In the context of these people-centric Web 2.0 techniques, many social platforms have rapidly become household names. They cover diverse specialised topics, such as LinkedIn helping professionals expose resumes, share knowledge or seek jobs or talent, or ResearchGate enabling academics to disseminate their work and collaborate. Of course, there is also the more generic effort of simply (re)connecting people, such as Facebook facilitates users keeping contact with friends and family. By eliminating various time and location barriers, social networks make it easier for people to engage. Some of these platforms are open for everybody, while others are closed-circle networks, as per the aforementioned ResearchGate, which only allows academics to enrol. The success of a social network greatly depends on how its members are motivated to contribute (Constantinov, Mocanu, Bărbulescu, Popescu, & Mocanu, 2017), meaning that only a number of them have achieved success, gathering a strong community of users that generate data.

In order to conduct relevant analytical studies, large amounts of information are required, reason for which only the most popular social networks are usually targeted by the scientific community. Typical academic research includes the effort of identifying patterns within the data which can then be used to predict social or economic behaviours. However, interest in the topic started to exponentially grow when the business angle of performing this analysis became obvious: Data insights can be leveraged by companies to better target their products to potential customers, by identifying those individuals which are more likely to have an interest in them.

Having Soryani and Minaei's (2011) research as a starting point, where these authors detailed the types of analytics that can be conducted over social platforms, this chapter gets more specific by looking over how data from a professional social network can be put to use. For supporting claims, this chapter references an arguably decent number of highly relevant papers. Discussions are first centred around topics such as the issues faced by universities when trying to assess and improve the degree to which their alumni are prepared for the job market. Similarly, it is debated that it is not sufficient for graduates to obtain an initial job for a university programme to be deemed successful, but they should further show a clear and thriving evolution. It is also argued that social networks have made job transitions happen easier, by enabling users to almost effortlessly find and even be found by companies having suitable job openings, facilitating their career progress. Lastly, it is evaluated how companies can leverage social network information for making sure that the right employees are given access to the right training programmes and courses, helping them reach their full potential and placing them in the right positions.

Throughout the discussion, the authors will highlight the fact that these are problems which can be more easily addressed by employing novel technologies, presenting concrete evidence regarding the ways in which social data analysis can help.

BACKGROUND

As the services LinkedIn provides have diversified over the years, seeing it as simply a tool people use when changing jobs is becoming an outdated perception. Nowadays, LinkedIn can be viewed as a complex platform that enables individuals to learn and grow, making companies to even encourage their employees to use it. This section will detail on what are the risks and benefits of using professional social networks, with a focus on LinkedIn. A brief introduction on the interest that the platform now holds for researchers also follows.

The Age of LinkedIn

Skeels and Grudin (2009) pointed out that, because in its early days Facebook was restricted to university students and then to the employees of a few companies, along with its typical use-case, this platform additionally had a clear professional role. Specifically, using it was seen as beneficial for people following a traditional educational trajectory, understanding that relationships can certainly provide a career edge. Perhaps because at the time of that study LinkedIn was much more static than it is today, the formation of groups being one of the few options for enabling interactions, only 4% of the people questioned by the authors reported using the platform on a daily basis. The prevailing attitude that the work highlights is that people used to visit the platform only when actively looking for a new job. During that period, just a handful of people who are called *Influencers* could write content on LinkedIn. In 2014, this feature was rolled out to all its members, allowing people to write articles (such as on a blog) and post updates directly on their profile (Roslansky, 2014). This was an incentive for contributors to become noticed and for members to return to the Web site often for consuming content. Time spent on the platform suddenly started to have a new connotation, as professionals could learn valuable, first-hand insights.

Another interesting observation is that, for reasons relating to awkwardly asking users to fill the *Current position* section of their profiles, LinkedIn did not initially market itself to students, leading them to believe that it is only addressed to mid-career professionals. This was, however, addressed over time, and, in 2016, the company released a new app conveniently called *LinkedIn Students* which aims to help young professionals start their career (Yu 2014). Appealing to younger generations has been a great move by LinkedIn, as Skeels and Grudin (2009) mention that most heavy LinkedIn users are fresh professionals, namely millennials around the age of 25. Many of them are at most at their second job, are known for not sticking with a company for too long and perceive constant job offers as a way to raise self-esteem. LinkedIn is also described as a way in which they can stay up-to-date with their peers' career trajectories (so-called *ambient awareness*) as the platform servers as a "self-updating address book." Conversely, many professionals aged between 36–45 feel that they have "maxed out" their networks, and, as no longer tending to grow their connection graph, start to use LinkedIn more rarely.

Following updates on a social network gives people a certain sense of knowing someone at a personal level and can reduce the anxiety associated with approaching other professionals. Thus, LinkedIn is also described as a possible ice-breaker: A connection invite is not regarded as imposing or intrusive and is an easy way to potentially build social capital. An interesting aspect relates to how organisations typically think of these disruptive technologies: Although some consider that they stand in the way of productivity, progressive-minded companies might, for instance, see how social networks can also strengthen ties between colleagues. More specifically, following a teammate on Facebook might reveal more sincere aspects of his/her daily life than can be seen at the workplace. Of course, this depends on whether or not employees find it non-boundary-crossing to become *friends* on the platform.

Historically, email services and instant messaging posed the same questions regarding productivity more than a decade and a half ago, but, as they were popular among students which later became managing employees, they soon were widely accepted in most workplaces. Similar attitudes surrounding social networks should be expected in the future: Activity on LinkedIn will probably no longer be solely viewed as a possible indicator for planning future career steps. Contrarily, by considering the learning opportunities, LinkedIn usage should be encouraged, as it can help professionals stay up to date with developments in their fields through written articles and group discussions. As this is an important aspect, one of the following sections will detail how the services LinkedIn offers have started to diverse over time.

Considering the vast information available, LinkedIn is now also making the traditional *CV* (Curriculum Vitae) obsolete. Candidates can now choose to "Easy Apply" for a job directly on the platform, using their profile data. This is also beneficial for LinkedIn, which can gather more data if playing an important part in managing the recruitment process. In recruiting, referrals are an asset, as individuals tend to be selective when recommending a peer, as this can affect their reputation. Even these recommendations can also happen within the platform. In other cases, however, the recruiter typically does a background investigation of the candidate. For instance, as people are commonly evaluated based on who they know, Caers and Castelyns (2011) sustained that a recruiter can easily make guilt-by-association errors when visualising the peers of a potential candidate. This became a strong point for why certain members chose to keep their connection network private.

Caers and Castelyns (2011) additionally mentioned that about 42% of their respondents stated that they look over the number of connections that a user has. This is a very surprising phenomenon considering that many people on LinkedIn rely on *growth hacking*. Specifically, this technique implies that members randomly send connection requests to many other members, hoping that some will respond. A possible reason for which such a metric is appealing might be the fact that this is not something that can be deduced from a traditional resume. Interestingly, when it comes to recommendations received on LinkedIn, 80% of the recruiters confirmed their importance, although they seem more aware of the temptation of *growth hacking*. As a response, recruiters typically try to look for "courtesy" recommendations in order to balance them out.

Zide, Elman, and Shahani-Denning (2014) indicated that, when it comes to usage, social networks are now just behind major search engines. As LinkedIn is becoming a primary tool used by recruiters, members need to learn how to market themselves, especially if considering that the extent to which they succeed in highlighting their skill set and talents can become critical for their future. This is one of the motivations behind this chapter, as, when comparing its high usage with the scarcity of literature regarding LinkedIn, it becomes obvious that more practical studies are desirable.

Although some might argue that, no matter the efforts done by LinkedIn, people are still using the platform solely during job transitions, there are undoubtable changes to this trend. It can be pointed out that, besides jobs, events such as meetups or workshops are now also being promoted on the platform, while certain members are gaining high notoriety through their knowledge-sharing posts and articles. Recently, LinkedIn has also rolled out a photo-tagging feature, similar to the one available for some time on Facebook, along with the option to "react" to content on the platform (Chen, 2019). While this stands to show that the major platforms are now converging towards a generic social network consisting of a set of common features, a positive side-effect is that studies which have been carried out over one network can easily be adapted to others as well.

Data Mining and Privacy Concerns

As Caers and Castelyns (2011) and Zide et al. (2014) observed, the extent to which professionals admit using Facebook data during the recruitment process can be labelled as troubling. Additionally, Skeels and Grudin (2009) reported how employees judge their coworkers or clients based on what they share on social media platforms. As for many of these sites the primary usage is leisure, members might sometimes choose not to bother with privacy concerns, when posting content. Even worse, tweets on Twitter and pictures on Instagram are typically public. As it can be expected that people will be judged more and more based on their digital footprint, it is never too early to think about the permanent consequences of the actions performed online.

For instance, students should be advised about the implications of their Facebook posts, as, from a professional point of view, these can lead to unwanted biases even during the prescreening phase. Additionally, people tend to also post religious and political believes on Facebook. While this should definitely not be regarded as negative behaviour, there are cases of easy-to-offend recruiters which do not remain impartial while navigating through this information. As Skeels and Grudin (2009) discussed, things are now becoming much more complicated as, given the popularity of generic social networking sites, people often connect with both genuine friends, but also with work colleagues, on Facebook. Ideally, members would tweak the security settings of their profiles and define custom audience lists for their content, keeping some posts as intimate as possible, in a carefully controlled fashion. Otherwise, individuals who should clearly be part of disjunctive audiences all get to "see the same thing." However, this is just one type of concern regarding data exposed on social networks; Soryani and Minaei (2011) highlighted many others.

Fortunately, in the last few years, people are becoming aware of the potential consequences and tend to control the amount of information that they share. This is similar to what happened to the younger generation of Facebook users that slowly saw the platform becoming popular among their parents. At that time, they were forced to search for alternatives that could be used for sole entertainment purposes without any worries. One example is the steep rise in popularity for apps such as Snapchat, which is both not that popular among adults and also commonly (and ignorantly) regarded as a platform that does not leave permanent traces of the shared content (Magid, 2013). More recently, TikTok made headlines due to similar issues (Perez, 2019).

Although in a grey area from an ethical point of view, analysing Facebook data for capturing job success predictors and personality indicators is now used as a complementary tool in recruiting. For instance, sentiment analysis can be deployed on the content shared online, in order to assess the overall attitude of an individual. A very basic example was seen on Twitter, which, in 2011, allowed users to search for positive or negative tweets (Peri & Ho, 2011). As mentioned in an earlier section, everyone can now post content on LinkedIn, which means that, as enough data is available, the same analysis techniques can be applied to this platform. Moreover, doing so might not raise the same ethical issues, as the professional purpose of LinkedIn is clear to all the parties involved.

Bradbury (2011) illustrated novel techniques which can be applied when doing big data analysis in the context of a social network. Specifically, it is now becoming common to model these networks by using graph structures which come with a set of dedicated metrics. Some examples include *closeness* and *degree*, which are related to how "important" or central a node is within the graph, *betweenness*, which models the number of times a node is part of the shortest path between two other nodes, and *structural cohesion*, which refers to the minimum number of individuals required to be removed in order to disconnect the graph. The last metric is strongly related to the idea of *weak ties*, which bears great importance within professional social networks.

The strength of a LinkedIn profile not only comes from maintaining connections with close friends or colleagues, but also from extending the network beyond these individuals. LinkedIn seems to intentionally rely on the concept of *weak ties*, allowing to view profiles and suggesting connections for people a degree or two outside the current user's network. These *weak ties*, otherwise known as acquaintances, provide bridges to new worlds of fresh information and ideas. *Bridge nodes* become bottlenecks as they connect network submodules and are vital for making sure information flows through the whole social structure. While research effort Bakshy, Rosenn, Marlow, and Adamic (2012) shows that *weak ties* are indeed responsible for propagating information on Facebook, Hwang, Kim, Ramanathan, and Zhang (2008) proposed a novel approach to assessing the critically of individual entities and relationships. By first defining a new concept, called *bridging coefficient*, which can be applied for both nodes and edges and combining it with *betweenness*, the authors introduced the *bridging centrality* metric. This metric can be used in a *bridge cut* algorithm which is showed to produce better cluster structures. Psychologically, in a professional context, the strength associated with acquaintances comes from the necessity of being more direct and sincere when reaching out to them, making interactions more efficient (Miller, 2016). Easley and Kleinberg (2010) discussed the fact that, as an individual tends to have access to the same information as his/her close friends, the best job leads are more likely to come from *weak ties*. Many LinkedIn members can thus act as intermediaries for passing messages (regarding job opportunities) along a network of *weak ties*.

Apart from the aforementioned metrics, performing data mining in order to learn about what individuals know exposes one of the hidden dangers of LinkedIn: Accidentally revealing sensitive corporate information. Bradbury's (2011) work gives an example of how, by innocently filling out the role description section on a LinkedIn profile, data regarding future services currently held secret can be exposed and leveraged by others for competitive intelligence. This phenomenon has since been coined *light-leakage*. This is also addressed in the authors' previous work (Constantinov, Iordache, Georgescu, Popescu, & Mocanu, 2018). A conflict of interests develops between companies protecting their trade secrets and employees who want to highlight their key job responsibilities in order to build a stronger and more attractive professional profile. This is thus a completely different problem, but which also relates to privacy.

When using the platform in the usual fashion, depending on user roles, there are various ways in which LinkedIn profiles can be searched and seen. Unauthenticated users can rely on public profiles, as also indexed by search engines, which, depending on each user's settings, contain a subset of the information available on their full profiles. Basic LinkedIn users normally see the full profile of any other member. *Premium* users are allowed to perform unlimited, specific searches returning a larger number of profiles.

In case of systems that want to gather as much data as possible, it is common to rely on a different workflow, based on using the public API (application programming interface) of a platform. In case of LinkedIn, authentication keys are obtained, allowing third-party apps to access various data entities. The typical scenario is that users authorise these apps, granting them a number of permissions which generally relate to different profile sections or types of activities that the app can "see" and use. Doing so should not pose any moral issues as the user is in full control of what information he/she allows to be disclosed.

Over time, after analysing various changelogs, it has been observed that social network security policies are constantly adjusting, particularly in the direction of restricting the amount of information exposed via public APIs. For instance, in case of Facebook, in 2014, by obtaining a user access token with appropriate permissions, an app could also access a great deal of information regarding the authorising user's friends, including their activity. One year later, even for simply checking whether two users were friends, both should have had authorised that app. As giving a user the power to grant access to the data of another user, without the second user's consent did seem inappropriate, this amendment was understandable. However, this happened too late, and abuses ultimately led to the Cambridge Analytica scandal (Meredith, 2018). Around the same time, LinkedIn decided that, except for its partners, it was not going to allow apps to get the full profile details of a user, even if he/she were to allow it (Trachtenberg, 2015). Prior to this point, much more information was available from the LinkedIn API. If looking over all the major social networks, LinkedIn seems to be having one of the most restrictive data access policies. Out of the many reasons for which this happens, it is worth mentioning that, if third-party companies were to mine all the data available on LinkedIn, they would be able to provide some of the same services for which LinkedIn charges *Premium* users.

A greater problem arises when using crawlers that can automatically parse profiles, especially if they use the credentials of a *Premium* member, thus having largely unrestricted access to the platform. As these kinds of actions violate LinkedIn's *User Agreement*, there were multiple cases of lawsuits resulting in such crawlers being taken down. Things are starting to take a different twist, as, in 2017, the result of a lawsuit (Rodriguez, 2017) stated that at least public profile data should be available for scraping for anyone interested. Related to this subject, Anabo and Albizuri (2017) argued that, in case of using data for research purposes, it should not be mandatory to ask for permission.

On the other hand, LinkedIn gave a good reason for wanting to stop tools from scraping, as there are companies which use profile data for predicting when an employee is likely to leave. Starting from 2014, members have the option of silently updating the profiles without broadcasting the changes to their network, by turning off LinkedIn *Broadcasts* (Oakley, 2014). However, by periodically mining profile data, these changes could still be detected. As LinkedIn understands that some people might be reluctant when searching for a job, as of 2016, members have to option of using the *Open Candidates* feature (Shapero, 2016). This enables job seekers to send a signal only to recruiters not believed by the platform to be linked with the seeker's current employer, keeping everything as secret as possible.

Considering this whole context, research efforts do not only deal with the unwillingness of users to authorise access to personal data but also face problems actually getting this data even when permission is given. For gathering information, some of the works that will be presented in a later section rely on public profiles, sometimes available through search engines, thus bypassing the permission of the users. While the legal status of doing so is not yet clear, this might still pose some moral questions. Other studies make use of data coming from surveys, which, as the authors will later describe, comes with another set of problems. In most cases, studies are carried out for a few hundred or thousand individuals. There are, however, privileged research efforts which have been granted unrestricted access to professional social network data. For instance, some of the works rely on very large sets of LinkedIn profiles. As expected, the experiments carried out in these papers are typically much more conclusive, as they have the advantage of being run over millions of users.

CURRENT STATE-OF-THE-ART

Information overload has driven the evolution of sophisticated computational tools capable of making associations between entities. While the lack of data was a common problem some time ago, thanks to wide Internet access and cheap storage solutions, many organisations face the problem of gathering data at a faster pace than actually being able to process it for uncovering hidden insights. As long as this is the case, this input remains raw information, with little explicit value. However, by surfacing otherwise invisible details, data mining can play a significant role in decision-making, driving the key transition from supposition to facts and creating a major competitive advantage. As a result, platforms, such as LinkedIn, that are generating large amounts of potentially interesting content, will always be targeted by complex experiments.

This section is the result of the authors analysing 24 papers by the means of a full-text review, drawing on Richthammer, Weber, and Pernul's (2017) procedure. The results show how diverse research carried over professional networks can be. Depending on what data source is used and on what the desired outcomes are, the authors organised the papers in a number of categories. Within a category, the works are chronologically ordered based on publication date. For papers which could have been included in more than one category, the authors chose the most relevant one.

On the other hand, for better expressing that articles typically dealt with more than one topic, the authors decided to build a system that would better express this visually. While conducting these thorough reviews, personal observations and annotations were attached to each paper. The authors thus decided to index all data produced for a research article along with the actual content of the paper itself to Elasticsearch. Additionally, for each of the topics, they manually defined dictionaries containing sets of significant terms. This allowed the automatic assessment of how well each paper actually covers every topic. For representing the results, a small application was then written that generated the radar charts that can be found in Table 1. Lastly, besides mentioning key aspects for each of these research efforts, Table 2 can be used for comparing papers which specifically target LinkedIn. Both these Tables can be found in the Annex at the very end of this chapter. In Table 2, the following abbreviations were used:

- U/A, standing for "unrestricted access" to data and generally used for papers where at least one author was associated with LinkedIn in some way. While in some cases the exact number of entities used is known, the authors decided to omit it from the Table, as it is usually at least five orders of magnitude higher than in case of papers not relying on this privilege.
- N/S, standing for "not specified" and used when either the population size is unknown or the means by which data was gathered was not explicitly mentioned.
- N/T, standing for "not tested" and manly used for preliminary works.

While some of the mentioned papers do not directly use professional network data, they still discuss topics that make them valuable to be referenced in this chapter. Although not exhaustive, this survey covers many of the most relevant efforts in their respective research area. Some of the papers include research conducted when the popularity of LinkedIn was not as great as it is today. Nevertheless, given their impact, they are still included for this analysis. In summary, the authors believe that all the papers in this section discuss topics that are now as pertinent as ever especially when keeping in mind the current impact of professional platforms. The identified categories follow below.

Aligning Universities' Curricula with Industry Demands

This topic covers the ways in which various data sources can be used to better describe and assess the syllabus or curriculum of a university programme. According to how data was obtained, two directions can be observed: A manual approach, which, for example, relies on sending questionnaires to students and alumni, hoping that they will respond, and an automated approach, which, for instance, can use publicly available data coming from professional networks.

One of the key aspects of performing alignment is to find a common language for expressing both course outcomes and industry requirements. Xun, Gottipati, and Shankararaman (2015) and Shankararaman and Gottipati (2016) described possible approaches and mentioned that little work had been published in this area. This alignment has a dual role in both providing a means to improve the curricula, by highlighting where it fails to meet industry expectations, and in helping students chose courses relevant for their career plan, by identifying the gaps between their current knowledge and the responsibilities a certain position within the job market requires.

Given the noisy, unstructured, and natural language description of both curricula outcomes and industry standards, this alignment process is often manual and thus overlooked. However, as one of the key success metrics of a university programme is employability, efficiently preparing a student for what the industry expects of him/her justifies extensive research on this topic.

Mining Social Data for Evaluating What Alumni Are Doing

This category includes several works performed by universities that use LinkedIn data to evaluate how the careers of their alumni have progressed. Along with providing more concrete insights on the outcomes of a programme, as Anabo and Albizuri (2017) pointed out, this information is also valuable for students wanting to attend a similar programme, as they can use the results of such a study for planning their careers. While the authors' previous work (Constantinov, Popescu, Poteraş, & Mocanu, 2015) does also partially relate to this topic, the papers included in this category are much more focused on the subject.

Performing Recommendations Using LinkedIn Data

Papers from this category provide a stronger focus on showing how both content and collaborative filtering can be done using LinkedIn profile information. For instance, Diaby, Viennet, and Launay's (2013) and Diaby and Viennet's (2014) papers show how users willing to authorise an application can benefit by receiving tailored job recommendations resulting from content-based analysis. Interestingly, most authors share a common message: Following the revelation surrounding its value, social network data has now become a trade good for many corporations operating over various domains.

A Closer Look on Skills and Competencies

As opposed to talking about the competencies of alumni, this category focuses on the problem of defining and assessing competency levels for a given skill, as certain job positions require. Similarly, efforts to identify people who show great proficiency with a given skill are also included.

An important component of LinkedIn is represented by endorsements which allow users to validate each other's expertise in a certain skill that they claim to know. As already discussed, although this metric should have an indisputable weight when trying to identify talent, it is typical that endorsements are commonly-exchanged amiabilities, and, in some cases, strongly abused. This makes the process of simply counting them either insufficiently relevant or even meaningless.

As for more advanced approaches, Alvarez-Rodríguez and Colomo-Palacios (2014) detailed how an analysis leveraging the power of graphs can be carried out over professional data, while Ha-Thuc et al.'s (2015) work, benefiting from unrestricted access to the LinkedIn dataset, performed multidimensional computations which have a high probability of being accurate. Alternatively, possible solutions for assessing the competence level of each skill a member showcases can be developed by adapting other graph-based approaches, such as the maximum flow model (Levien, 2009), as a solution for estimating confidence levels for nodes. More recently, in 2016, LinkedIn introduced a new way of identifying relevant endorsements, by a not-fully-disclosed machine learning based approach (Yeh, 2016).

Identifying Similarities Using Professional Network Data

This topic includes a number of research papers that leverage the tightly-connected, graph-like structure of social network data for identifying people (or companies) deemed to be similar using various criteria. For instance, when used in conjunction with assigning expertise scores for people, such an effort can prove very valuable in the effort of identifying individuals who are highly likely to fill a job opening.

General Analysis of Jobs and Job Posts

As social networks are now largely popular, job offerings can reach a wide audience when they are promoted through them. For this reason, ads for specific vacancies are not only found on LinkedIn, but also on Facebook and even ResearchGate. This makes gathering a comprehensive list of active openings relatively easy, enabling the highlighting of various insights on the current state of the job market. This last group includes two works that perform these kinds of analysis on job offerings.

FUTURE RESEARCH DIRECTIONS

Up to this point, the authors discussed the very wide range of topics that professional networks have fundamentally changed. In this section, after grasping all popular current trends, they try and anticipate the next ones to follow, speculating how various stakeholders, such as educational institutions, companies and professionals, are likely going to be further impacted in the next few years.

Universities: Greater Possibilities for Reconnecting with Alumni

A problem which is typically expressed in some of the above-mentioned works describes the difficulty of gathering feedback from students and alumni. In many cases, especially up until a few years ago, researchers largely relied on surveys as the only viable option. However, many papers, such as Gonçalves, Ferreira, de Assis, and Tavares's (2014) work, detail that these questionnaires do not achieve good response rates from alumni, concluding that using them is not optimal. One reason is that, as time passes, people slowly lose contact with their universities, especially in case they relocate. In our current fast-paced world, traditional reconnection methods, such as sending a periodic newsletter or relying on alumni to occasionally check the institution's Web site or even attending dedicated events, are simply not enough. Luckily, some more up-to-date alternatives, which the authors will explore in the remainder of this section, are more likely to be successful.

Large-Scale Usage of Social Media for Tracking Alumni

Given people's modern habit of constantly checking social media, the small effort of liking the Facebook page of a former university can have a much greater impact than one might expect. Anabo and Albizuri (2017) believe that educational institutions should start to think prospectively and recommend the creation of a social media strategy for keeping alumni engaged. The ideal outcome is that the user has the chance to see updates from the institution every other few times he/she checks his/her feed. It is now often the case that educational organisations assign a dedicated person in charge of their social media presence. This person can easily interact with comments and inquiries on the official page of the institution, providing publicly visible responses. Given the inherent "snowball effect" of social networks, such interactions can further generate more contributions as they raise the university page's visibility. More specifically, Facebook uses an applied machine learning (Dunn, 2016) approach for ranking stories on the user's feed, which boosts pages that generate engaging content. Something similar is also happening on the LinkedIn feed (Jurka, 2014). Psychologically, this can have the effect of helping users perceive that the bond with their universities was reestablished, making them more willing to participate in various activities and studies which the institution might carry out.

Another important point is represented by the fact that information filled in traditional questionnaires cannot be regarded with high confidence, as there is no direct accountability for supplying false or exaggerated data. A means to determine people to provide sincere and accurate answers would be to implement a mechanism that could directly impact their reputation. One alternative is making responses public or, at the very least, expose them to each user's peers for validation. Undoubtedly, it can safely be expected that such a measure would cause the response rates to drop even further. Fortunately, social networks can again provide a feasible solution to this problem. Instead of relying on alumni to manually fill responses, researchers now have the possibility to build applications which, upon being authorised using the LinkedIn account of a user, can gather this data automatically. Of course, profile information cannot be viewed as undeniably exact, as it is common for disadvantageous information to be skipped, while other positive facts to get enhanced. However, as everyone has access to this data, heavily lying about job experience and skills on a public resume has a great chance of affecting reputation. Taking this into consideration, using data which is publicly visible on LinkedIn can be assumed to raise the probability for an experiment to provide accurate results. In turn, such an approach arises data privacy concerns, which the authors detailed throughout this chapter.

On the bright side, when aiming for higher response rates, it can reasonably be assumed that an alumnus might be more willing to authorise an application with his/her public information, instead of spending time to answer a survey. While this strategy is clearly advantageous, unfortunately, there are limitations to the kind of information that can be obtained from a LinkedIn profile, especially if attempting to use the official APIs. There are also hybrid approaches, similar to what Anabo and Albizuri (2017) described, where manually entered answers are combined with LinkedIn data. This can ease the effort for the users, requiring them to fill in less information.

Another point is that certain responses coming from fresh alumni, who are still transitioning the difficult period of switching from an academic life to a job within the industry, are likely to be negatively biased. This leads to another advantage that systems performing automated data gathering have: In case of traditional surveys, periodically and excessively asking the same individuals for feedback is likely to irritate participants and make them less likely to further respond. However, modern approaches can unmeddlingly gather data multiple times and even try to detect when the career of an individual starts to stabilise.

Apart from participating in studies, alumni can play a much more active role by providing highly valuable input to the current students of their *Alma Mater* universities. Many educational institutions have implemented an alumni mentoring programme which fosters strong connections, enabling students to seek career guidance and job-search advice from former students who are now well-established professionals. As social networks are perfect for breaking all sorts of barriers between people, it can be expected that such platforms will play an important role in helping mentees and mentors bond. As the authors pointed out above, people are already on Facebook, scrolling through their news feed and interacting with posts by liking them or adding comments. As most often a news feed blends friend-related, work-related and hobby-related data, casually contributing to a post in a group of alumni can still be felt like a leisure activity, rather than a responsibility. Thus, networking and collaboration might be more likely to happen in the Facebook ecosystem. Nevertheless, some of these points are also valid for LinkedIn as well.

Lastly, an important change related to all these interactions is that, as the impact of professional networks is becoming hard to ignore, novel ways for evaluating an educational institution, solely based on social media information, are likely to become popular. Thus, it is highly likely to sense a disruption in the way the best universities are evaluated and perceived in the years to follow.

How LinkedIn is Helping Directly

As a response to the clear interest in better understanding what alumni were doing professionally, LinkedIn launched the *Classmates* (Allen, 2011) tool in 2011. Originally, this module was meant to allow former students to search and connect with fellow graduates, catching up with how their careers had evolved and seeing what connections, skills or groups they ended up sharing. In 2013, this was followed by *University Pages* (Allen, 2013b), which officially allowed universities to share news and promote activities while bringing all their alumni together. Over time, functionalities were combined and transformed into the *Higher Education* programme, which includes an enhanced *Alumni Tool* (Allen, 2013a) for every educational institution. Insights are provided for each generation of alumni, including details such as their current location and industry, the programme they have studied, and general statistics surrounding their skills. This not only aims to benefit educational institutions in their efforts to understand the progress of their graduates but also aids students in choosing the right university, given their desired career goal, taking successful professionals as an example. In a similar fashion, since 2016, *Premium Insights* (Kamil, 2016) has allowed paying users to see details regarding a company, including information such as employee count, new hires breakdowns, and employee distribution by function. A list of notable alumni, comprised of most impressive former employees, is also presented.

As the digital revolution has brought very fast-paced changes to the job market, many universities are now looking into providing lifelong learning programmes, which can help professionals remain up-to-date with major developments. At an extreme, as the retirement age is constantly increasing, workshops aimed at the older population (Seals, Clanton, Agarwal, Doswell, & Thomas, 2008) need to become widely adopted. LinkedIn has also acknowledged the importance of continuous learning for a successful long-term career path, in a way becoming a direct competitor with universities in this area. Thus, in 2016, the *LinkedIn Learning* (Roslansky, 2016) programme was launched. By analysing the profile of a member, this system is able to compute *Learning Paths* and recommend courses that can be taken to increase proficiency in different skills which would make a profile more attractive.

Companies: Social Data in Human Capital Management

Although arguably invasive, constantly looking over what employees are doing on social networks is part of the new people analytics movement, which is expected to gain significant momentum in the following years. The reason behind this is a paradigm shift in which human resources departments are being transformed into human capital management divisions. This is a recognition that people are indeed the greatest asset for a company, often having the most significant and direct influence on revenue. Information and communication technologies is one of the industry sectors where this is easiest to observe.

Employees are becoming the "ambassadors" of a company, even unknowingly, whenever exposing information to the outside world by either detailing their jobs on a LinkedIn profile (Constantinov et al., 2018) or by anonymously posting reviews and even salaries on Glassdoor. They are the ones sharing stories regarding their work and potentially attracting new people when participating to ever more popular international conferences.

Talent Management

While it is with every right to frown upon the invasion of employee privacy, there are clear benefits to performing analysis on their data, when this is done for the right reasons. For instance, all this information can be used in talent management. By integrating various input streams, such as articles written on LinkedIn, affinities expressed on various social media, group memberships or even blog posts, these novel tools seek to uncover skills in which people might be qualified. It is often that the company is not aware of them and is thus not capitalising properly. Similarly, finding hidden potential might lead to identifying existing employees who are a good fit for promoting to a certain key position, avoiding spending resources in staffing external people who are not aligned with the organisation's culture. Such analytics can be applied to both technical and soft skills, given that personality traits can have a major impact on the outcome of a project.

Based on identifying key indicators for great potential, the right path for growing their career can be suggested to promising employees. Ideally, for top talented people, analytics can be run in order to forecast their role fit over the next few years. These individuals could then get recommendations on the right courses and trainings to take while the organisation attempts to make sure that their future jobs positions will be requiring these new skills. Such a strategy proves to be quite important as, in case of ambitious employees, positions keeping them from learning new things can lead to frustration, which, over time, lowers productiveness or, even worse, makes them leave the organisation. Thus, using novel technologies that produce data-driven judgements will become the norm when investing in employee professional development as a way in which to keep them motivated and happy. As a more concrete example, Bersin (2016) reported how a software company was able to find career trajectories that produced top leaders, leading to changes in the organisation's planning programmes. Positive *influencers* can also be identified and promoted. These people can become talent attractors by their simple presence and attitude, dragging people to the company and pushing things forward.

Of course, performing complex people analytics which can back-up decision-making requires very large amounts of meaningful and heterogeneous data. In order to, on one hand, limit or avoid any privacy-related issues and, on the other hand, create a reliable source for generating this data, many companies are even trying to implement internal social networks. Usually, these kinds of systems are integrated with source control tools and company wiki systems. This opens up endless data mining opportunities (Guzman, Azócar, & Li, 2014), such as the case where sentiment analysis was performed on GitHub commit messages in order to surface various insights. As with any such platform, its success largely depends on how widely it is adopted by its target users. This is why other companies alternatively chose to use *Workplace by Facebook* ("Introducing workplace by Facebook," 2016). By having the same simple and convenient look and feel as the most popular social platform while keeping personal user information separated from the corporate account, this solution has proven effective for many organisations. As, besides creating data, social networks are based on the idea of collaboration between members, it can be expected that such platforms will become a main productivity tool for employees.

Talent does sometimes need to be imported from outside the organisation. Coming back to LinkedIn, an example on how to leverage platform data is found in Bersin's (2016) study, which mentioned the use-case of a company that successfully attracts talent from their competitors by only focusing on engineering candidates with certain characteristics within their profiles.

Other interesting tools being developed, but which can arguably be considered too invasive, include various systems that are trying to predict retention by determining which individuals are most likely to leave, based on their social activity on various public platforms. While full details were not disclosed, the existence and very high accuracy of such systems were confirmed by IBM, which can now easily figure out the next employee to leave the organisation (Rosenbaum, 2019).

Lastly, companies do not only want to grow their teams but sometimes also need to reduce their operations. Thus, by using more complex methods related to sentiment analysis, toxic leaders which demotivate their teams can be surfaced.

Building Great Teams

Given the understanding that people need to be placed in the right context in order for them to thrive and become fully productive, as opposed to focusing on individual accomplishments, efficiency and performance should be instead evaluated on a per-team basis. While there is no silver bullet to what actually makes a team productive, it becomes important to understand that members should not only be chosen based on how their technical skills complement each other but also based on their personalities. As Mårtensson and Bild (2016) detailed, this is already common in education, where business schools are known to engineer study groups so that they foster long-term tight bonds.

A relevant example can be found in Gorla and Lam's (2004) work, which talks about how team composition in software project units is one of the main factors that influence the effectiveness of a project's delivery. In their research, the authors attempted to determine if personality analysis can help create high-functioning software development teams. For the experiments, they defined personality using a four-dimensional model based on the Myers-Briggs type indicator model (McCrae &, Costa, 1989): Social interaction (extrovert or introvert), information gathering (sensing or intuitive), decision-making (thinking or feeling), and dealing with the external world (judging or perceiving).

If attempting to perform such computations in a more automated manner, software companies can use internal data, such as velocity trends, budget burn rates or the number of issues reported, in order to evaluate how well a project is going. Simple team temperature feedback forms could additionally be used. Assessing personality through specialised tools can also be done with minimal human intervention, by processing large amounts of input from various information sources. Of course, LinkedIn data might be insufficient to compute personality, but, as the authors already mentioned, some companies look over what their employees publicly do on multiple social networks. Moral concerns are undoubtedly valid, however, there are also positive sides: Building great teams as well as finding the best ways in which to bolster an individual's professional evolution are now becoming less of a guesswork.

Employees: The Future of Job Searching

Solis, Li, and Szymanski's (2014) report stated that 88% of the surveyed companies were, at the time of that study, undergoing some form of digital transformation. This suggests that the high demand for technical experts should not be expected to drop in the following years. As real talent is scarce and jobs are becoming increasingly specialised, companies often find themselves competing for employees, leading to increasingly better work conditions as a response to candidates having higher expectations.

Millennials now make up a significant percentage of the employed professionals. This, along with the proliferation of online networking, has completely reshaped the job market. For instance, successfully attracting talent is now significantly dependent on how well a company uses social media to tell its story (White, 2015). Being absent from social media might mean that an employer remains mostly unknown to this age group. This aspect is confirmed by Ha-Thuc et al. (2015), who mentioned that, because everything seems to be happening online, companies are investing significant capital in using platforms like LinkedIn for recruiting. More often, especially for experienced candidates, jobs "find" people, instead of the other way around. Highly skilled professionals are already setting the trend for not looking for a job per se, but rather pursuing the right company culture or, at an even finer grain, the right team within a larger organisation. In case of a fit, their exact role inside the organisation is sometimes tailored to individual skill sets.

As the authors discussed several times in this chapter, there now is an abundance of tools recruiters can use to find talent, while recommender systems are becoming more precise in guessing which job to recommend and when. This is also backed-up by systems that are likely to correctly assess the skills of an individual in an automatic manner and to direct him/her to the most suitable position within a certain company. All these trends are making pursuing a new opportunity less of a taboo subject. Although counter-intuitive at first glance, it is now increasingly uncommon for companies to actually support their employees when looking into outside opportunities (Bonnici, 2018). Thus, in a dynamic job market dominated by freelancers or by employees sticking around for the length of a single project, very rapid job changes are to be expected (Berger, 2016).

Since a future where the majority of job hops happen due and by the means of social media is foreseeable, LinkedIn is already starting to have major competitors. For instance, at the beginning of 2017, Google launched an artificial intelligence powered job-search service within its Google Search engine (Zakrasek, 2017). By integrating data from various platforms and Web sites including social networks, this service allows users to look for available openings within their current area, as well as provide estimates on commute times and even salaries. Lastly, Facebook is slowly entering this market as well, allowing small business post jobs on the platform.

CONCLUSION

In the end, over the years, the release of various features has transformed LinkedIn from a social network for specialists to a gigantic platform covering various angles of the professional life. In turn, this has raised interest in developing the right tools for understanding vast and interconnected data in order to highlight extremely valuable aspects.

As proof for the varied amount of research that can be carried over professional network information, during the study behind this chapter, the authors analysed 24 representative works. Based on the most representative issue that they covered, the researchers defined a way in which to group them, ending up with six major topics: Curricula alignment, alumni outcome, recommendations, skill assessment, professional similarity, job post analysis. The results reported in these representative works are already impressive; nevertheless, the complexity and diversity of future analysis efforts should be expected to grow.

REFERENCES

Allen, C. (2011, October 19). *LinkedIn Classmates: Explore possibilities by connecting with fellow alumni*. Retrieved from https://blog.linkedin.com/2011/10/19/linkedin-classmates

Allen, C. (2013a, January 30). *Start mapping your career with LinkedIn alumni*. Retrieved from https://blog.linkedin.com/2013/01/30/start-mapping-your-career-with-linkedin-alumni

Allen, C. (2013b, August 19). *Introducing LinkedIn university pages*. Retrieved from https://blog.linkedin.com/2013/08/19/introducing-linkedin-university-pages

Alvarez-Rodríguez, J. M., & Colomo-Palacios, R. (2014). Assessing professional skills in a multi-scale environment by means of graph-based algorithms. In *Proceedings of the 2014 European Network Intelligence Conference (ENIC), IEEE* (pp. 106-113). 10.1109/ENIC.2014.12

Anabo, I. F., & Albizuri, I. E. (2017). Linkedin as a tool for higher education programme evaluation. *Revista de Educación a Distancia, 1*(53), 1–17.

Bakshy, E., Rosenn, I., Marlow, C., & Adamic, L. (2012). The role of social networks in information diffusion. In *Proceedings of the 21st International Conference on World Wide Web, ACM* (pp. 519-528). 10.1145/2187836.2187907

Berger, G. (2016, April 12). *Will this year's college grads job-hop more than previous grads?* Retrieved from https://blog.linkedin.com/2016/04/12/will-this-year_s-college-grads-job-hop-more-than-previous-grads

Bersin, J. (2016). *Predictions for 2016: A bold new world of talent, learning, leadership, and HR technology ahead*. Deloitte Consulting LLP.

Bonnici, R. (2018, September 11). *Why I Encourage My Best Employees to Consider Outside Job Offers*. Retrieved from https://hbr.org/2018/09/why-i-encourage-my-best-employees-to-consider-outside-job-offers

Bradbury, D. (2011). Data mining with Linkedin. *Computer Fraud & Security, 10*, 5–8.

Caers, R., & Castelyns, V. (2011). Linkedin and Facebook in Belgium: The influences and biases of social network sites in recruitment and selection procedures. *Social Science Computer Review, 29*(4), 437–448. doi:10.1177/0894439310386567

Caldeira, D. C., Correia, R. C., Spadon, G., Eler, D. M., Olivete-Jr, C., & Garcia, R. E. (2017). Data mining on Linkedin data to define professional profile via MineraSkill methodology. In *Proceedings of the 2017 12th Iberian Conference on Information Systems and Technologies (CISTI), IEEE* (pp. 1-6). 10.23919/CISTI.2017.7975730

Case, T., Gardiner, A., Rutner, P., & Dyer, J. (2013). A Linkedin analysis of career paths of information systems alumni. *Journal of the Southern Association for Information Systems, 1*(1), 1–13. doi:10.3998/jsais.11880084.0001.102

Cetintas, S., Rogati, M., Si, L., & Fang, Y. (2011). Identifying similar people in professional social networks with discriminative probabilistic models. In *Proceedings of the 34th International ACM SIGIR Conference on Research and Development in Information Retrieval* (pp. 1209-1210). 10.1145/2009916.2010123

Chen, C. (2019, April 11). *Introducing LinkedIn reactions: More ways to express yourself*. Retrieved from https://blog.linkedin.com/2019/april-/11/introducing-linkedin-reactions-more-ways-to-express-yourself

Cheng, Y., Xie, Y., Chen, Z., Agrawal, A., Choudhary, A., & Guo, S. (2013). Jobminer: A real-time system for mining job-related patterns from social media. In *Proceedings of the 19th ACM SIGKDD International Conference on Knowledge Discovery and Data Mining* (pp. 1450-1453). 10.1145/2487575.2487704

Colomo-Palacios, R., Tovar-Caro, E., García-Crespo, Á., & Gómez-Berbís, J. M. (2010). Identifying technical competences of it professionals: The case of software engineers. *International Journal of Human Capital and Information Technology Professionals*, *1*(1), 31–43. doi:10.4018/jhcitp.2010091103

Constantinov, C., Iordache, L., Georgescu, A., Popescu, P.-Ş., & Mocanu, M. (2018). Performing social data analysis with neo4j: Workforce trends & corporate information leakage. In *Proceeding of the 2018 22nd International Conference on System Theory, Control and Computing (ICSTCC), IEEE* (pp. 403-406). 10.1109/ICSTCC.2018.8540645

Constantinov, C., Mocanu, M., Bărbulescu, N., Popescu, E., & Mocanu, A. (2017). Movierate: Considerations on applying a custom social reputation engine for movie reviews. In *Proceedings of the 18th International Carpathian Control Conference (ICCC), IEEE* (pp. 183-188). 10.1109/CarpathianCC.2017.7970394

Constantinov, C., Popescu, P. Ş., Poteraş, C. M., & Mocanu, M. L. (2015). Preliminary results of a curriculum adjuster based on professional network analysis. In *Proceedings of the 2015 19th International Conference on System Theory, Control, and Computing (ICSTCC), IEEE* (pp. 860-865). 10.1109/ICSTCC.2015.7321402

Dasgupta, D., & Dasgupta, R. (2009). *Social networks using Web 2.0*. IBM Corporation.

Diaby, M., & Viennet, E. (2014). Taxonomy-based job recommender systems on Facebook and Linkedin profiles. In *Proceedings of the 2014 IEEE Eighth International Conference on Research Challenges in Information Science (RCIS)* (pp. 1-6). 10.1109/RCIS.2014.6861048

Diaby, M., Viennet, E., & Launay, T. (2013). Toward the next generation of recruitment tools: an online social network-based job recommender system. In *Proceedings of the 2013 IEEE/ACM International Conference on Advances in Social Networks Analysis and Mining, ACM* (pp. 821-828). 10.1145/2492517.2500266

Dunn, J. (2016, May 9). *Introducing FBLearner Flow: Facebook's AI backbone*. Retrieved from https://code.facebook.com/posts/1072626246134461/introducing-fblearner-flow-facebook-s-ai-backbone

Easley, D., & Kleinberg, J. (2010). *Networks, crowds, and markets: Reasoning about a highly connected world*. Cambridge University Press. doi:10.1017/CBO9780511761942

Garg, P., Rani, R., & Miglani, S. (2015). Mining professional's data from Linkedin. In *Proceedings of the 2015 Fifth International Conference on Advances in Computing and Communications (ICACC), IEEE* (pp. 98-101). 10.1109/ICACC.2015.35

Gonçalves, G. R., Ferreira, A. A., de Assis, G. T., & Tavares, A. I. (2014). Gathering alumni information from a web social network. In *Proceedings of the Web Congress (LA-WEB), 2014 9th Latin American, IEEE* (pp. 100-108). 10.1109/LAWeb.2014.17

Gorla, N., & Lam, Y. W. (2004). Who should work with whom? Building effective software project teams. *Communications of the ACM, 47*(6), 79–82. doi:10.1145/990680.990684

Guzman, E., Azócar, D., & Li, Y. (2014). Sentiment analysis of commit comments in github: An empirical study. In *Proceedings of the 11th Working Conference on Mining Software Repositories, ACM* (pp. 352-355). 10.1145/2597073.2597118

Ha-Thuc, V., Venkataraman, G., Rodriguez, M., Sinha, S., Sundaram, S., & Guo, L. (2015). Personalized expertise search at linkedin. In *Proceedings of the 2015 IEEE International Conference on Big Data (Big Data)* (pp. 1238-1247). 10.1109/BigData.2015.7363878

Ha-Thuc, V., Xu, Y., Kanduri, S. P., Wu, X., Dialani, V., & Yan, Y., … Sinha, S. (2016). Search by ideal candidates: Next generation of talent search at Linkedin. In *Proceedings of the 25th International Conference Companion on World Wide Web, International World Wide Web Conferences Steering Committee* (pp. 195-198). 10.1145/2872518.2890549

Hwang, W., Kim, T., Ramanathan, M., & Zhang, A. (2008). Bridging centrality: Graph mining from element level to group level. In *Proceedings of the 14th ACM SIGKDD International Conference on Knowledge Discovery and Data Mining, ACM* (pp. 336-344). 10.1145/1401890.1401934

Introducing workplace by Facebook. (2016, October 10). Retrieved from https://newsroom.fb.com/news/2016/10/introducing-workplace-by-facebook

Jurka, T. (2018, March 29). *A Look Behind the AI that Powers LinkedIn's Feed: Sifting through Billions of Conversations to Create Personalized News Feeds for Hundreds of Millions of Members.* Retrieved from https://engineering.linkedin.com/blog/2018/03/a-look-behind-the-ai-that-powers-linkedins-feed-sifting-through

Kamil, M. (2016, June 3). *Introducing Premium Insights: Keeping you in the know on companies you care about.* Retrieved from https://blog.linkedin.com/2016/06/02/introducing-premium-insights-keeping-you-in-the-know

Levien, R. (2009). Attack-resistant trust metrics. In *Computing with Social Trust* (pp. 121–132). Springer. doi:10.1007/978-1-84800-356-9_5

Li, L., Zheng, G., Peltsverger, S., & Zhang, C. (2016). Career trajectory analysis of information technology alumni: A Linkedin perspective. In *Proceedings of the 17th Annual Conference on Information Technology Education, ACM* (pp. 2-6). 10.1145/2978192.2978221

Lops, P., De Gemmis, M., Semeraro, G., Narducci, F., & Musto, C. (2011). Leveraging the Linkedin social network data for extracting content-based user profiles. In *Proceedings of the fifth ACM Conference on Recommender Systems* (pp. 293-296). 10.1145/2043932.2043986

Magid, L. (2013, May 1). *What is snapchat and why do kids love it and parents fear it? (Updated)*. Retrieved from https://www.forbes.com/sites/larrymagid/2013/05/01/what-is-snapchat-and-why-do-kids-love-it-and-parents-fear-it

Mårtensson, P., & Bild, M. (2016). *Teaching and learning at business schools: Transforming business education*. Taylor & Francis. doi:10.4324/9781315611907

McCrae, R. R., & Costa, P. T. Jr. (1989). Reinterpreting the Myers-Briggs type indicator from the perspective of the five-factor model of personality. *Journal of Personality, 57*(1), 17–40. doi:10.1111/j.1467-6494.1989. tb00759.x PMID:2709300

Meredith, S. (2018, April 10). *Facebook-Cambridge Analytica: A timeline of the data hijacking scandal*. Retrieved from https://www.cnbc.com/2018/04/10/facebook-cambridge-analytica-a-timeline-of-the-data-hijacking-scandal.html

Miller, M. (2016, August 17). *To get a job, use your weak ties*. Retrieved from https://www.forbes.com/sites/nextavenue/2016/08/17/to-get-a-job-use-your-weak-ties

Oakley, P. (2014, July 13). *Turn off LinkedIn Broadcasts when you change your profile and other automatic updates*. Retrieved from https://www.linkedin.com/pulse/20140713162507-3188984-turn-off-linkedin-broadcasts-when-you-change-your-profile-and-other-automatic-updates/

Perez, S. (2019, January 30). *It's time to pay serious attention to TikTok*. Retrieved from https://techcrunch.com/2019/01/29/its-time-to-pay-serious-attention-to-tiktok

Peri, C., & Ho, B. (2011). *Sams teach yourself the Twitter API in 24 hours*. Pearson Education.

Richthammer, C., Weber, M., & Pernul, G. (2017). Reputation-enhanced recommender systems. In *Proceedings of the IFIP International Conference on Trust Management*, (pp. 163-179). Springer.

Rodriguez, S. (2017, August 14). *U.S. judge says LinkedIn cannot block startup from public profile data*. Retrieved from https://www.reuters.com/article/us-microsoft-linkedin-ruling-idUSKCN1AU2BV

Rosenbaum, E. (2019, April 3). *IBM artificial intelligence can predict with 95% accuracy which workers are about to quit their jobs*. https://www.cnbc.com/2019/04/03/ibm-ai-can-predict-with-95-percent-accuracy-which-employees-will-quit.html

Roslansky, R. (2014, February 19). *The definitive professional publishing platform*. Retrieved from https://blog.linkedin.com/2014/02/19/the-definitive-professional-publishing-platform

Roslansky, R. (2016, September 22). *Introducing LinkedIn Learning, a better way to develop skills and talent*. Retrieved from https://learning.linkedin.com/blog/whats-new/launching-linkedin-learning

Santos, A. C. S. G., Menezes, T. P., & Hora, H. R. M. (2014). Análise do perfil de aluno e egresso de cursos técnicos por meio de data mining: Estudo de caso no Instituto Federal Fluminense. *Tear: Revista de Educação. Ciência e Tecnologia, 3*(1), 1–24. doi:10.35819/tear.v3.n1.a1828

Seals, C. D., Clanton, K., Agarwal, R., Doswell, F., & Thomas, C. M. (2008). Lifelong learning: Becoming computer savvy at a later age. *Educational Gerontology, 34*(12), 1055–1069. doi:10.1080/03601270802290185

Shankararaman, V., & Gottipati, S. (2016). Mapping information systems student skills to industry skills framework. In *Proceedings of the Global Engineering Education Conference (EDUCON), IEEE* (pp. 248-253). 10.1109/EDUCON.2016.7474561

Shapero, D. (2016, October 6). *Now you Can Privately Signal to Recruiters You're Open to New Job Opportunities*. Retrieved from https://blog.linkedin.com/2016/10/06/now-you-can-privately-signal-to-recruiters-youre-open-to-new-job

Silva, P. R., & Brandão, W. C. (2015). Arppa: Mining professional profiles from Linkedin using association rules. In *Proceedings of the 7th International Conference on Information, Process, and Knowledge Management (eKnow 2015), Lisbon, Portugal, February 22, 2015, International Academy, Research, and Industry Association* (pp. 72-77). Academic Press.

Skeels, M. M., & Grudin, J. (2009). When social networks cross boundaries: A case study of workplace use of Facebook and Linkedin. In *Proceedings of the ACM 2009 International Conference on Supporting Group Work, ACM* (pp. 95-104). 10.1145/1531674.1531689

Solis, B., Li, C., & Szymanski, J. (2014). The 2014 state of digital transformation. *Altimeter Group*, *1*(1), 1–33.

Soryani, M., & Minaei, B. (2011). Social networks research aspects: A vast and fast survey focused on the issue of privacy in social network sites. *International Journal of Computational Science*, *8*(3), 363–373.

Tajbakhsh, M. S., & Solouk, V. (2014). Semantic geolocation friend recommendation system: Linkedin user case. In *Proceedings of the 2014 6th Conference on Information and Knowledge Technology (IKT), IEEE* (pp. 158-162). 10.1109/IKT.2014.7030351

Tantawy, R. Y., Farouk, Z., Mohamed, S., & Yousef, A. H. (2014). *Using professional social networking as an innovative method for data extraction: The ICT Alumni Index case study*. arXiv preprint arXiv:1410.1348.

Trachtenberg, A. (2015, February 12). *Changes to our developer program*. Retrieved from https://developer.linkedin.com/blog/posts/2015/developer-program-changes

Wang, J., Zhang, Y., Posse, C., & Bhasin, A. (2013). Is it time for a career switch? In *Proceedings of the 22nd international conference on World Wide Web, ACM* (pp. 1377-1388). 10.1145/2488388.2488509

White, C. (2015, June 25). *Don't knock millennials until you try their recruiting ideas*. Retrieved from https://business.linkedin.com/talent-solutions/blog/2015/06/dont-knock-millennials-until-you-try-their-recruiting-ideas

Xu, Y., Li, Z., Gupta, A., Bugdayci, A., & Bhasin, A. (2014). Modeling professional similarity by mining professional career trajectories. In *Proceedings of the 20th ACM SIGKDD international conference on Knowledge discovery and data mining* (pp. 1945-1954). 10.1145/2623330.2623368

Xun, L. S., Gottipati, S., & Shankararaman, V. (2015). Text-mining approach for verifying alignment of information systems curriculum with industry skills. In *Proceedings of the 2015 International Conference on Information Technology Based Higher Education and Training (ITHET), IEEE* (pp. 1-6). IEEE.

Yeh, Y. (2016, October 19). *Rethinking endorsements so you always look your best*. Retrieved from https://blog.linkedin.com/2016/10/19/rethinking-endorsements-LinkedIn-features

Yu, A. (2016, April 18). *Introducing the LinkedIn Students App: Helping Soon-to-Be College Graduates Conquer Their Job Search*. Retrieved from https://blog.linkedin.com/2016/04/18/introducing-the-linkedin-students-app--helping-soon-to-be-colleg

Zakrasek, N. (2017, November 15). *New tools to make your job search simpler*. Retrieved from https://www.blog.google/products/search/new-tools-make-your-job-search-simpler

Zide, J., Elman, B., & Shahani-Denning, C. (2014). Linkedin and recruitment: How profiles differ across occupations. *Employee Relations, 36*(5), 583–604. doi:10.1108/ER-07-2013-0086

ADDITIONAL READING

Arnedillo-Sánchez, I., De Aldama, C., & Tseloudi, C. (2018). rESSuME: Employability Skills Social Media SurvEy. *International Journal of Manpower, 39*(8), 1080–1095. doi:10.1108/IJM-10-2018-0333

Bastian, M., Hayes, M., Vaughan, W., Shah, S., Skomoroch, P., Kim, H., ... Lloyd, C. (2014, October). Linkedin skills: large-scale topic extraction and inference. In *Proceedings of the 8th ACM Conference on Recommender systems* (pp. 1-8). 10.1145/2645710.2645729

Kutlu, B., Rabea, A., & Udeozor, C. R. (2018). *LINKEDIN for Recruitment: An Examination of Recruiters Use of "Apply" and "Easy Apply"*. Features.

Land, S. F., Willemsen, L. M., & Unkel, S. A. (2015, August). Are spectacles the female equivalent of beards for men? How wearing spectacles in a LinkedIn profile picture influences impressions of perceived credibility and job interview likelihood. In *International Conference on HCI in Business (pp. 175-184)*. Springer, Cham.

Malherbe, E., Diaby, M., Cataldi, M., Viennet, E., & Aufaure, M. A. (2014, August). Field selection for job categorization and recommendation to social network users. In *2014 IEEE/ACM International Conference on Advances in Social Networks Analysis and Mining (ASONAM 2014)* (pp. 588-595). IEEE. 10.1109/ASONAM.2014.6921646

Parkavi, A., & Lakshmi, K. (2017, August). Predicting the course knowledge level of students using data mining techniques. In *2017 IEEE International Conference on Smart Technologies and Management for Computing, Communication, Controls, Energy and Materials (ICSTM)* (pp. 128-133). IEEE. 10.1109/ICSTM.2017.8089138

Unkelos-Shpigel, N., Sherman, S., & Hadar, I. (2015, May). Finding the missing link to industry: LinkedIn professional groups as facilitators of empirical research. In *2015 IEEE/ACM 3rd International Workshop on Conducting Empirical Studies in Industry* (pp. 43-46). IEEE.

Wu, L., Shah, S., Choi, S., Tiwari, M., & Posse, C. (2014, October). The Browsemaps: Collaborative Filtering at LinkedIn. In RSWeb@ RecSys.

APPENDIX

Table 1. Radar charts for all featured research

Ref.	Radar Chart	Ref.	Radar Chart
Santos, Menezes, & Hora, 2014		Constantinov et al., 2015	
Xun et al., 2015		Shankararaman & Gottipati, 2016	
Case, Gardiner, Rutner, & Dyer, 2013		Gonçalves et al., 2014	
Tantawy, et al., 2014		Silva & Brandão, 2015	
Garg, Rani, & Miglani, 2015		Li, Zheng, Peltsverger, & Zhang, 2016	
Anabo & Albizuri, 2017		Lops, De Gemmis, Semeraro, Narducci, & Musto, 2011	

continues on following page

22

Table 1. Continued

Wang, Zhang, Posse, & Bhasin, 2013		Diaby et al., 2013	
Diaby & Viennet, 2014		Tajbakhsh & Solouk, 2014	
Colomo-Palacios et al., 2010		Alvarez-Rodríguez & Colomo-Palacios, 2014	
Ha-Thuc et al., 2015		Cetintas, Rogati, Si, & Fang, 2011	
Xu, Li, Gupta, Bugdayci, & Bhasin, 2014		Ha-Thuc et al., 2016	
Cheng et al., 2013		Caldeira et al., 2017	

Table 2. Summaries of papers using LinkedIn data

Ref.	Year	Data Src.	Pop. Size	Data Gat.	Methodology	Outcome
Aligning Universities' Curricula with Industry Demands						
Constantinov et al., 2015	2015	University Courses, LinkedIn	258	Manual	Gathering skills from LinkedIn alumni profiles, including partially extracting them from free-text sections.	Comparison between university programme outcomes and common LinkedIn skills.
Shankararaman & Gottipati, 2016	2016	University Courses, SFIA, Skills Matrix, LinkedIn.	70	LinkedIn API	Preprocessing data, modelling it as vector, indexing with Lucene.	Enhancing SFIA modelled curriculum with SFIA modelled LinkedIn profiles, generating individual student reports and recommending SFIA modelled job roles.
Mining Social Data for Evaluating What Alumni Are Doing						
Case et al., 2013	2013	LinkedIn	175	Manual	Gathering historical job title information from profile pages. Evaluating the willingness of alumni to give direct feedback through a LinkedIn group.	Assessing the balance between technical and nontechnical job titles of alumni after graduation, 5, 10, and 15 years later.
Gonçalves et al., 2014	2014	LinkedIn	457	Google Custom Search Engine	Starting from a set of positive examples of LinkedIn alumni profiles, using Cosine Similarity to detect more profiles than a Naïve Bayes approach.	Methodology for identifying LinkedIn alumni profiles from alumni lists. Graphical representation of geographic distribution of alumni.
Tantawy et al., 2014	2014	LinkedIn	16561	Manual	Looking over current country of residence, graduating university and current employer for multiple alumni.	Estimating the percentage of alumni that have a LinkedIn profile. Computing the geographic distribution of the alumni. Computing their per-company distribution.
Silva & Brandão, 2015	2015	LinkedIn	1847	Semi-automatic	Using LinkedIn Search to identify alumni. Feeding profiles to a crawler for additional data gathering.	Statistics regarding top cities, industries, specialisations and positions, by the number of employees. Computing association rules with Apriori.
Garg et al., 2015	2015	LinkedIn	255	LinkedIn API	Gathering and normalising basic profile information.	Visual representations of Greedy, Hierarchical and K-means clusters computed based on job, company or location similarity.
Li et al., 2016	2016	LinkedIn	635	Manual	Modelling Bachelor of Science and Master of Science alumni job-related data using an SQL solution.	Improving curricula based on insights regarding common jobs alumni land after graduation as well as 5 and 10 years later. Showing how Master's alumni have a broader career perspective.

continues on following page

Table 2. Continued

Ref.	Year	Data Src.	Pop. Size	Data Gat.	Methodology	Outcome
Anabo & Albizuri, 2017	2017	LinkedIn	75	Manual	Employing a hybrid approach by looking over LinkedIn profile fields as well as organic responses in a LinkedIn group forum. Gathering quantitative and qualitative alumni data regarding the outcomes of a higher education programme.	Evaluation of an Erasmus Mundus Master's programme with regards to the impact on mobility and employability as well as perceived interculturality for its graduates.
Performing Recommendations Using LinkedIn Data						
Lops et al., 2011	2011	Research papers dump, LinkedIn	22	LinkedIn API	Modelling user profiles and research papers in a Vector Space Model by using TF-IDF.	Suggesting research papers to users based on their profiles and the profiles of their closest connections.
Wang et al., 2013	2013	LinkedIn	U/A	U/A	Modelling job transitions using a hierarchical proportional hazards model enhanced with a hierarchical Bayesian framework.	Using tenure-based decision probabilities for determining the right time to perform job recommendations.
Diaby et al., 2013	2013	Facebook, LinkedIn	N/S, Work4 app users	N/S, LinkedIn API most likely	Using a number of user profile attributes with differently associated weights for modelling TF-IDF vectors used for a linear SVM approach. Modelling jobs within the same vector space.	Performing job recommendations over an in-house set of job posts.
Diaby & Viennet, 2014	2014	O*NET-SOC, Facebook, LinkedIn	N/S, Work4 app users	N/S, LinkedIn API most likely	Indexing O*NET-SOC with Elasticsearch for obtaining occupation-to-relevancy vector representa-tions for user profiles and jobs. Using these vectors to show the superiority of a linear SVM approach over various similarity measures.	Representing user profiles and jobs using a common taxonomy. Performing job recommendations over an in-house set of job posts.
Tajbakhsh & Solouk, 2014	2014	LinkedIn	532	LinkedIn API	Computing various similarity degrees between nearby users, including semantic similarity. Using Analytical Hierarchy Process to weight similarity terms.	Building communities of experts having similar skills by performing connection recommendations to users.
A Closer Look on Skills and Competencies						
Alvarez-Rodríguez & Colomo-Palacios, 2014	2014	LinkedIn	10 test users, 30-50 connec-tions	Manually enhanced LinkedIn API data	Considering temporal ordering of endorsements when proposing a novel graph-based analysis algorithm for raking expertise. Building on top of well-known algorithms such as SPEAR and HITS.	Assessing competency levels for skills on LinkedIn profiles according to a 4- and 5-level scale.

continues on following page

Table 2. Continued

Ref.	Year	Data Src.	Pop. Size	Data Gat.	Methodology	Outcome
Ha-Thuc et al., 2015	2015	LinkedIn	U/A	U/A	Predicting expertise scores on both explicit and cooccurrence inferred LinkedIn skills starting from a training set. Using a logistic regression approach, factoring in various LinkedIn signals. Deploying a matrix factorisation algorithm using Apache Hadoop.	Improving the precision and ranking of results for personalised, exploratory search queries containing one or more LinkedIn skills.
Identifying Similarities Using Professional Network Data						
Cetintas, Rogati, Si, & Fang, 2011	2011	LinkedIn	U/A	U/A	Using heterogeneous data sources for each user for building a probabilistic discriminative model that identifies latent content and graph classes. Learning a specialised similarity model for each latent class.	Identifying similar people with a higher degree of accuracy than a baseline logistic regression approach.
Xu et al., 2014	2014	LinkedIn	U/A	U/A	Modelling career paths using a time-series model. Learning node level similarity using a logistic regression approach. Alignment and matching on career sequences.	An improved accuracy when identifying similar people.
Ha-Thuc et al., 2016	2016	LinkedIn	N/T	N/T	Combining the efforts of Xu et al.'s (2014) and Ha-Thuc et al.'s (2015) works, along with an algorithm for determining similar companies. Normalising job titles for building interactive queries in order to identify and rank similar people.	A proposition of a query-by-example search engine for talent.
General Analysis of Jobs and Job Posts						
Cheng et al., 2013	2013	LinkedIn	U/A	U/A	Modelling job-hops as a series of temporal graphs. Performing graph-specific computations for discovering influential companies while accounting for temporal information. Analysing graph structure evolution for detecting communities of related companies.	Discovering influential and similar companies. Demonstrating a system that stays up-to-date with all developments within the job market by using social network data.
Caldeira et al., 2017	2017	LinkedIn	4113 job posts	Job API	Modelling job posts as documents. Using data cleansing, tokenisation, stemming, n-gram identification and TF-IDF for extracting keywords and Apriori for identifying associations.	Identifying language and location-specific attractive competencies for the job market. Identifying common associations between competencies which could be used for recommending learning activities.

Chapter 2
A Comprehensive Survey of Data Mining Techniques in Disease Prediction

Durgadevi Mullaivanan
Pondicherry Engineering College, India

Kalpana R.
Pondicherry Engineering College, India

ABSTRACT

In recent days, data mining has become very popular, and numerous research works have been carried out of using data mining techniques in the healthcare sector. The healthcare transactions generate a massive amount of data which are very voluminous and complex to be processed. Therefore, data mining techniques have been employed, which provides a practical methodology for transforming the massive amount of data into efficient knowledge for the process of decision making. Prediction and classification are the two forms of data analysis methods. However, it is still difficult to explore the complete literature in the healthcare domain. This chapter reviews the research overview that is done in the healthcare sector utilizing different data mining methodologies for prediction and classification of diverse diseases. Also, a detailed comparison of reviewed methods takes place for better understanding of the existing models. An extensive experimental study is also performed to analyze the performance of data mining algorithms.

1. INTRODUCTION

Data mining is a procedure of discovering knowledge from massive databases to uncover trends and patterns exist in data. The vast amount of data present in the information industry has to be converted to extract useful information from it (Neesha Jothi, et.al, 2015). Data mining also perform several other processes like cleaning, integration, transformation, mining, evaluation, and presentation. The different stages included in data mining are demonstrated in Fig. 1. There are two categories exist in the data mining patterns such as Descriptive, Classification and Prediction (G. E. Vlahos, et.al, 2004). The descriptive

DOI: 10.4018/978-1-7998-2566-1.ch002

function deals with the general properties of data whereas the classification and prediction deal with the concepts of data. The descriptive function involves summarization and mapping of data which is commonly known as data characterization and data discrimination. Predictive analytics is a combination of historical data, machine learning, and artificial intelligence. Predictive analytics helps to analyze the state of the current data to determine the future outcome. It becomes much more prevalent in areas like finance, marketing, healthcare, social networking, and other areas. The implementation of predictive analytics is a complex process as it comes with many challenges. The ultimate aim of predictive analytics in the digital world is to get better revenue and profit at reduced cost and risk. The problem of every prediction must come with a "remedy." Predictive analytics can be applied to any type of mysterious data in the past, present or future (Chandamona and Ponperisasmy, 2016).

In the healthcare sector, data mining becomes more familiar. Numerous factors have been inspired by the usage of data mining in healthcare (Salim A. Dewani and Zaipuna O. Yonah, 2017). The subsistence of medical insurance abuse and fraud makes numerous healthcare insurers to utilize data mining approaches to decrease their losses by identifying and tracking offenders. Fraud identification utilizes the applications of data mining in the profitable globe, for instance, the identification of false transactions in credit card. The massive sum of data generated through the healthcare sector is very complicated and huge to be processed and investigated through the conventional approaches.

Figure 1. Data mining stages

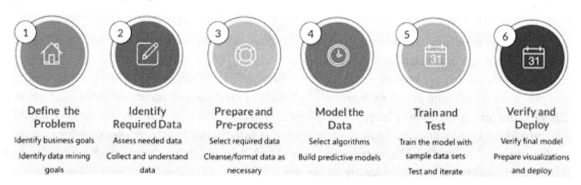

Define the Problem	Identify Required Data	Prepare and Pre-process	Model the Data	Train and Test	Verify and Deploy
Identify business goals	Assess needed data	Select required data	Select algorithms	Train the model with	Verify final model
Identify data mining goals	Collect and understand data	Cleanse/format data as necessary	Build predictive models	sample data sets Test and iterate	Prepare visualizations and deploy

Data mining enhances the procedure of decision-making through exploring patterns and tendency in a massive quantity of composite data. The investigation has become very important since economical pressure has enhanced the requirement of healthcare sectors to create decisions using the investigation of medical as well as financial data. The healthcare organizations which make use of data mining techniques that are highly positioned to meet its long-term requirements (I. Witten, et.al, 2011). Number of applications related to healthcare is existed by the use of data mining techniques. In general, they can be integrated as the examination of treatment efficiency, healthcare management, management of customer relationship, and discovery of abuse and fraud. Applications of data mining are employed for validating the efficiency of medical treatments. Using the symptoms, causes, and treatments courses, data mining techniques offer an investigation of the patient status. Numerous dedicated medical data mining like predictive analysis and medicine of DNA micro-arrays are also developed. The primary use of predictive analytics in medical decision aiding systems is to predict the percentage of risk of developing certain diseases like diabetes, heart disease or other complications.

In the fast growing world, a number of disease existences tend to increase drastically and data mining applications find useful in assisting it. Since numerous disease prediction models exists, it is difficult to explore the precious review in the area of health care. This chapter makes a review of the present research overview that is performed in the healthcare sector utilizing different data mining methodologies for prediction and classification of diverse diseases. In addition, a detailed comparison of reviewed methods also takes place for better understanding the existing models. An experimental study is also done to analyze the performance of data mining algorithms.

The rest of the chapter is arranged as below — section 2 provides the overview of data mining process. Section 3 reviews the existing data mining techniques in an elaborate way. Section 4 performs the validation of the reviewed methods and Section 5 concludes the extensive survey.

2. BACKGROUND INFORMATION

We discuss a few basic concepts relative to the process of data mining and various stages involved in it.

Data Preprocessing: The data in the real world is inconsistent and incomplete with lots of error. The data preprocessing step transforms the raw data into certain behavior or trends which is understandable. The preprocessing involves cleaning, integration, transformation, reduction, and discretization. The irrelevant and redundant information frequently results in rates that exceed the range. For instance, Salary (-100) and unfeasible data combinations, E.g.: (Gender: Male Pregnant: Yes).

Data Cleaning: Data cleaning removes the incomplete (no attribute values), noisy (errors/outliers) and inconsistent (difference in codes/names) data. It fills the missing values using the attribute mean and also predicts the missing values with a learning algorithm. It also identifies the outliers by binning (sorting the attributes), clustering (grouping the attributes) and regression (predicting the attributes).

Data Integration: The data from various sources are combined together from multiple databases, data cubes or flat files. Metadata is a process which holds data about the data which helps to solve the problem of redundancy during the integration of data.

Data Transformation: Data transformation is the procedure of transforming the data from one form to another for appropriate mining. The data transformation includes normalization, generalization, aggregation, and construction of attributes.

Data Reduction: Data reduction is the process of reducing the voluminous data (reducing the number of attributes or their respective values) for efficient storage.

Data Discretization: The process of converting a continuous attribute to an ordinal attribute by supervised and unsupervised techniques.

Datasets: A dataset is a set of data comprising of rows and columns, where each row corresponds to one or more members, and every column represents a specific variable for each member. The field of healthcare analytics highly depends on the dataset. The HIPPA (1996) and HITECH (2009) acts provides standards for the disclosure of personal health information to improve the quality, safety, and efficiency of the health information exchange. There are lots of data available across the WWW that can be useful for healthcare analytics in data mining.Healthdata.gov, WHO, data.gov, HMD, openFDA, medicare.gov are some of the best standardized freely available healthcare datasets employed in data mining. The UCI machine learning repository is one of the primary sources of all machine learning datasets widely used by students and researchers. Every dataset holds an attribute value pair and its corresponding class. For example consider the PIMA Indian Diabetes Dataset from the UCI repository holds eight attributes, 768 samples, and 2 class values. In data mining, the attributes and instances are considered to be the input (individual patient's records with their medical values) and the class value as output (diseased/not diseased).

3. DATA MINING TECHNIQUES IN THE HEALTHCARE SECTION

In this section, we discuss the applications of different data mining methods in the healthcare sector. Some of them are anomaly detection, association rule mining, clustering, classification, the hybrid system, and other approaches. A classification hierarchy is shown in Fig. 2. A comparison of the reviewed approaches is given in Table 1.

Figure 2. Classification of data mining approaches

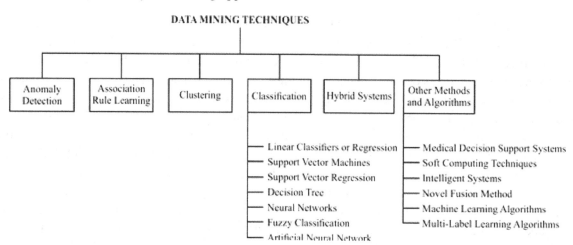

Anomaly Detection Techniques

The term anomaly generally defines something which diverges from what is normal, standard or expected. In the field of data mining, anomaly detection is popularly known as the outlier detection, noise removal or novelty detection. The presence of anomalies in datasets may or may not be detrimental. Though anomaly detection was proposed as an application to data security for intrusion detection systems, it can be used for inductive learning and soft computing approaches. The three broad types of anomaly detection methods are: Unsupervised, supervised, and semi supervised anomaly detection techniques. The outlier analysis can be described as a collection of 'd' data points with 'o' outliers. The problem of anomaly detection is to find the peak 'o' data points that are entirely dissimilar to the existing data. Therefore the ultimate aim of anomaly detection is to find the inconsistent data from the dataset and an efficient method to eliminate the outliers. In healthcare applications, the data collected from a variety of medical devices like magnetic resonance imaging (MRI), electrocardiograms (ECG) may contain unusual patterns of data reflecting disease conditions.

Table 1. Comparison of reviewed approaches

Technique	Disease predicted	Name of the Preprocessing Technique	Dataset Name&Source	No of&Type of Attributes [Instances]	Performance Evaluation Factors and Tool used
Anomaly Detection (Saba Bashir et al, 2016)					
	Heart, Breast Cancer, Liver, Diabetes, Parkinson's Disease and Hepatitis	Grubb's test for Outlier Elimination and Detection [2016]	Medical Dataset [PIMS]	1 Continuous value	ACC
Association Rule Learning					
Rule-based Classification (J.Jabez Christopher et al, 2015)	Liver Disorder, Heart, hepatitis, diabetes, breast cancer	WSO [2015]	Liver Disorder, cleveland, hepatitis, pima, Wisconsin [UCI]	7,14,20,9,10 [303,768]	ACC
Clustering					
	Lymphoma (J.Jabez Christopher et al, 2015)	WSO [2015]	Lymphoma dataset [UCI]	18[148]	
	Heart, Breast Cancer, Liver, Diabetes, Parkinson's Disease and Hepatitis (Saba Bashir et al, 2016)	K-means Clustering [2016]	Medical Dataset [PIMS]	2[2] Binary, Numerical and Categorical Attributes	ACC
Classifications					
Linear Classifiers or Regression	Type II Diabetes (Bum Ju Lee and Jong Yeol Kim, 2016)	Naïve Bayes andLR [2016]	Real Life Dataset Men - 4906, Women -7031[Korean Health and Genome Epidemiology]	21	AUC [WEKA TOOL]
	Liver Cancer Prediction model for Type II Diabetes (Hsiao-Hsien Rau et al, 2016)	LR [2016]	Training Group (1442 cases) and Test Group (618 cases) Real Life Dataset[NHIRD of Taiwan]	10 Value Attribute	SN,SP,AUC
	Diabetes (Xue-Hui et al, 2013)	LR [2013]	Training Data set (1031 cases) and Testing Data set (456 cases) Original Dataset[Guangzhou,China]	12	ACC,SN,SP SPSS Statistical Program Version 130 and SPSS Modeler Version 141
	Kidney Disease (M. Diciolla et al, 2015)	SVM [2015]	Clinical Datasets 1174 Records[Italy, Norway and Japan]	Numeric Value	ACC,PR,RC,FM
Support Vector Machines (SVM)	Cancer, Type 1 Diabetes, Type 2 Diabetes Ageing genes (Jiahao Sun et al, 2009)	SVM [2009]	Cancer Genome, GenAgedatabase[Welcome Trust Sanger Institute, Public and Private Resources, Human Ageing Genomic	Numeric	ACC,PR,RC[SVM Toolbox]
	Diabetes (Kemal Polat et al, 2008)	Least Square (LS-SVM) and Generalized Discriminant Analysis (GDA-LS-SVM)[2008]	Pima Indian Diabetes Dataset[UCI]	8	ACC,SN,SP
	Breast Cancer, Diabetes and Heart Diseases (Baek Hwan Cho et al, 2008)	SVM-RBF kernels [2008]	UCI	[500]	WEKA and LIBSVM

continues on following page

31

Table 1. Continued

Technique	Disease predicted	Name of the Preprocessing Technique	Dataset Name&Source	No of&Type of Attributes [Instances]	Performance Evaluation Factors and Tool used
Support Vector Regression (SVR)	Type I Diabetes (Eleni I. Georga et al, 2013)	SVR [2013]	27 Patients in free living condition[METABO]		ACC
DTs	Kidney Disease (M. Diciolla et al, 2015)	DT with 13 rules [2015]	Clinical Datasets 1174 Records [Italy, Norway and Japan]	Numeric Value	ACC,PR,RC,FM
	Heart Failure (Peter C. Austin et al, 2013)	Classification and Regression Trees, Bagging, Random Forests, Boosting and SVMs [2013]	Real Life Dataset[Hospitals in Ontario, Canada]	34 Variables	SN,SP,AUC
	Diabetes (Xue-Hui et al, 2013)	DT C50 [2013]	Training Data set (1031 cases) and Testing Data set (456 cases) Original Dataset[Guangzhou, China]	12	ACC,SN,SP SPSS Statistical Program Version 130 and SPSS Modeler Version 141
	Diabetic Retinopathy, Diabetic Nephropathy, Diabetic Neuropathy (Foot Problem) (Chien-Lung Chan et al, 2008)	C50 [2008]	Real time Dataset (8736 Diabetic Patients)[Northern Taiwan]		SN,SP
	Type-2 Diabetes (Yang Guo et al, 2012)	Bayes Network [2012]	Pima Indian Diabetes Dataset[UCI]	9[768] Numeric and Nominal	ACC, WEKA Tool
Neural Networks	Diabetes Mellitus (Chiara Zecchin et al, 2012)	NN [2012]	20 simulated datasets and on 9 real Abbott FreeStyle Navigator datasets[Abbott Diabetes Care, Alameda, CA]		MATLAB
	Diabetic Retinopathy, Diabetic Nephropathy, Diabetic Neuropathy (Foot Problem) (Chien-Lung Chan et al, 2008)	NN [2008]	Real time Dataset (8736 Diabetic Patients)[Northern Taiwan]		PR,RC
	End Stage Kidney Disease (ESKD) (M. Diciolla et al, 2015)	Neuro Fuzzy Systems [2015]	Clinical Datasets 1174 Records[Italy, Norway and Japan]	Numeric Value	ACC,PR,RC,FM
Fuzzy Classification	Diabetes (Mostafa and Mohammad, 2011)	FCS-ANTMINER [2011]	Pima Indian Diabetes Dataset[UCI]	8[768] Integer Value	ACC,PR,RC,FM WEKA Tool
	Diabetes (Esin at al, 2010)	LDA and ANFIS [2010]	Pima Indian Women Diabetes Dataset[Phoenix, Arizona, USA]	8768 (Class 0 - 500 and Class 1 - 268)	ACC,SN,SP

continues on following page

Table 1. Continued

Technique	Disease predicted	Name of the Preprocessing Technique	Dataset Name&Source	No of&Type of Attributes [Instances]	Performance Evaluation Factors and Tool used
ANN	Liver Cancer Prediction model for Type II Diabetes (Hsiao-Hsien Rau et al, 2016)	Artificial Neural Network (ANN) [2016]	Training Group (1442 cases) and Test Group (618 cases) Real Life Dataset[NHIRD of Taiwan]	10 Value Attribute	SN,SP,AU WEKA Tool C
	Kidney Disease (M. Diciolla et al, 2015)	Artificial Neural Network (ANN) [2016]	Clinical Datasets 1174 Records[Italy, Norway and Japan]	Numeric Value	ACC,PR,RC,FM
	Diabetes (Xue-Hui et al, 2013)	ANN [2013]	Training Data set (1031 cases) and Testing Data set (456 cases) Original Dataset[Guangzhou, China]	12	ACC,SN,SP SPSS Statistical Program Version 130 and SPSS Modeler Version 141
5Hybrid Systems					
	Parkinson's (Hui-Ling Chen et al, 2016)	ELM and KELM [2016]	Parkinson's Dataset[UCI]	22	ACC,SN,SP,AUC WEKA Tool, MATLAB
	Liver Disorder,Breastcancer,Hepatitis,Diabetes, (Mohammad HosseinZangooei et al, 2014),	Support Vector Regression (SVR) using NSGA-II - Disease Diagnosis [2014],	Liver Disorder, Wisconsin, Hepatitis,Pima[UCI]	7,32,19,8 Numeric Value	ACC,PR,RC,FM
	End Stage Renal Disease (ESRD) (Xue-Hui et al, 2013)	Hybrid Classification Model Based on Rough Set (RS) Classifiers [2013]	Real Word ESRD Dataset[Clinic or Medical Center in Taiwan]	27[1227] Numeric, Symbolic, Continuous, Nominal and Categorical	ACC,PR,RC,FM
	Diabetes,HeartDisease (Humar and Novruz, 2008)	Hybrid Neural Network (ANN and FNN) [2008]	Pima Indian Diabetes and Cleveland Heart[UCI]	9,13	ACC,SN,SP
6Other Methods and Algorithms					
Medical Decision Support System (MDSS)	Heart, Breast cancer, Diabetes, Liver, parkinsons [6]	HMV Ensemble [2016]	Cleveland,Statlog, UMC and WBC, PIDD and BDD, ILPD and BUPA, PIMS blood CP Dataset UCI, Pakistan Institute of Medical Sciences (PIMS) Hospital	13,13,13,13,11[2] Test Attribute, Unit Attribute	ACC,SN,SP,FM
Soft Computing Techniques	Type II Diabetes (ArunaPavate and Nazneen Ansari, 2015)	KNN-GA, WKNN-GA and DWKNN-GA [2015]	140 Non-Diabetes, 95 Diabetes(235 Patients) Real Life Dataset Maharashtra	15	ACC,SN,SP
Extreme Learning Machines	Type II Diabetes (Eleni I. Georga et al, 2015)	ELM kernels (KOS-ELM) [2015]	15 - Type I Diabetes Patients (3F, 12M) Real Life Dataset Parma and University Hospital Motol, Prague	9	Lynx MATLAB

continues on following page

Table 1. Continued

Technique	Disease predicted	Name of the Preprocessing Technique	Dataset Name&Source	No of&Type of Attributes [Instances]	Performance Evaluation Factors and Tool used
Intelligent System	Diabetes (ZhilbertTafa et al, 2015)	SVM and Naïve Bayes [2015]	Real Life Dataset (CDCP), US	8[402]	PR,RC [MATLAB]
Novel Fusion Method (Fusing based classifier)	Cancer, Diabetes, Anemia (Abdulaziz Yousef and Nasrollah Moghadam Charkari, 2015)	Sequence Fusion Method [2015]	52 Prostate Cancer, 83 Diabetes, 72 Anemia disease genes OMIM Database	10000 instances (5000 – Positive, 5000 - Negative)	PR,RC,FM,AUC
Machine Leaning Algorithm	Parkinson's Disease (PD) (Conrad S. Tucker et al. 2015)	Data Mining Driven Methodology [2015]	Real Life Datasets (Adherent and Non-Adherent patients) [Clinic or Hospital]	10[163, 232, 186, 335, 194, 102, 229] Numeric Values	ER,PR,RC,FM [WEKA Tool]
Multi-Label Learning Algorithms	Chronic Diseases (Damien Zufferey et al, 2015)	ML-kNN, AdaBoostMH, Binary Relevance, Classifier Chains, HOMER and RAkEL [2015]	Real Life Datasets (19773 Families of Chronic Diseases)| MIMIC-II Database]	Quantitative Values and Categorical Values	PR Java librarieshavebeenused:Mulan (version14)andWeka (version 376) OS: Ubuntu Linux 1204 LTS 64 bits)

The traditional medical decision support systems generally depend on individual classifier; otherwise an effortless integration of these classifiers tends to exhibit average results. In (Saba Bashir et al, 2016), a multi-layer classifier ensemble model is developed depending upon the optimum integration of different classifiers. The presented model is called as "HMV" which resolve the difficulties present in the traditional performance bottlenecks using a set of 7 different classifiers. This model is validated on two breast cancer dataset, two diverse heart disease dataset, two diabetes dataset, two liver disease dataset, hepatitis dataset and Parkinson's disease dataset attained from open access repository. The efficiency of the presented model is analyzed by comparing with different familiar classifiers as well as ensemble models. The experimentation part depicts that the presented model deals with every attribute type and attained better prediction accuracy. This study also included a case study using a real time medical dataset for depicting better results.

Association Rule Learning

The association rule learning aims at extracting the interesting relations between the data stored in large databases by frequent pattern matching. The association rule learning establishes the correlation between the attribute value pairs of the dataset in the form of if-then rules. The 'if' part called as the rule antecedent and the 'then' part known as the rule consequent, which states the degree of the vagueness of the rule (do not have any values in common).The association rule learning has been extensively used in the process of effective decision making. For instance, the Apriori algorithm for finding the frequent item sets. Association rules generally depend on the criteria of support, confidence and lift. Support is the process of measuring the degree of frequent item sets. Confidence determines the number of valid if then statements ('true' value).The input and output values of confidence can be compared with the help of a lift.

Rule-based classification is a classical data mining process which is employed in diverse medical diagnosis systems. The rules will be saved in the rule base which strongly influences the classification efficiency. The filtered rule sets using data mining approaches will undergo optimization by the use of heuristic or meta-heuristic methods for improving the rule base quality. In (J.Jabez Christopher et al, 2015), a Wind-driven Swarm Optimization (WSO) algorithm is employed. The novelty of the study remains in the bio-inspired feature of the algorithm. Here, the rule extraction takes place using DTs and the optimal rule set fulfills the need of the application which can be used for prediction purposes. The results of WSO have undergone a comparison with the classical Particle Swarm Optimization. The experimentation has been done on 6 different benchmark medical dataset, and WSO proves its efficiency on all the applied dataset. For instance, conventional C4.5 algorithm produces 62.89% accuracy using 43 rules for liver disorders dataset whereas as WSO achieves 64.60% using 19 rules. The WSO offers precise and concise rule set compared to the other one.

Clustering

Clustering is the procedure of combining abstract elements into related elements. In other words, it is the method of segregating objects based on their common characteristics. Similar and dissimilar objects are grouped in two different clusters. Clustering is one of the unsupervised machine learning (ML) technique which has no pre defined classes. The closeness of data can be evaluated using data typology. Consider a collection of 'X' data points. Clustering segregates the data into 'Y' disjoint groups a_1, a_2, a$_3$,... such that the union of these groups returns the original data point 'X' whereas the intersection is empty. The partitioned and hierarchical are the two broad categories of clustering methods. The partition method considers an input parameter of 'K' clusters. The partition method is based on the mechanism of greedy heuristics which performs the relocation of data points from one cluster to another based on the input parameters. The hierarchical model generates a tree structure for representing the relationship between the data. The hierarchical clustering can be performed in two ways: 1.Top down or divisive which divides each cluster into smaller groups. 2. Bottom up or agglomerative which merges similar groups of clusters into larger groups.

In (Saba Bashir et al, 2013), the k-means clustering process is employed in the presented HMV model to remove noise from the applied medical dataset. The unwanted, as well as noise in the dataset, can also be removed by the use of the clustering process. The K-means clustering process initially clusters the data into K clusters or groups which have identical features. Next, every cluster centroid is determined and the distance to every point from the specific centroid is determined. A threshold rate is employed to eliminate the noise and forms clusters. When the distance is higher than the threshold, then a specific point considered as noise and gets eliminated.

Classification

The process of predicting the outcome based on the set of a given input is known as classification. The classification of the data mining system can be categorized based on different kinds of data sources, database included, type of knowledge to be explored and mining methods employed. Classification assigns class labels to each of the elements in the dataset. These class labels are grouped into a training set to build a model for classifying a new set of objects. Today's world of big data comprises of extensive databases that are difficult to be categorized or organized. The best example is Facebook which crunches a terabyte of data every day. The healthcare systems can make use of classification to predict whether the patient will be prone to a particular disease or not.

Linear Classifiers or Regression

The linear classifiers or regression are both supervised ML techniques whose goal is to forecast a target class or a value. A linear classifier predicts the target class (Yes/No) with the help of a linear combination of characteristics known as the feature values which are represented in a feature vector. Linear classifiers can handle both binary classification and multi classification problems. For example, in clinical decision support systems, consider a patient profile to predict whether the particular patient is diabetic or not (binary classification). Similarly, all the patients in a hospital database are considered to predict which patient has the highest risk of developing diabetes (multi classification). Linear regression predicts the discrete or continuous value which establishes the relationship among two parameters. The parameter to be predicted is known as the dependent variable and the variable employed for predicting the value of the other variable is known as the independent variable. These variables can fit into a straight line or a linear equation that minimizes the inconsistencies among the actual and predicted values.

In (Xue-Hui et al, 2013), the efficiency of different classifiers like logistic regression (LR), ANNs and DT model to predict diabetes or prediabetes are analyzed by the use of general risk factors. A set of 735 patients tested positive under diabetes or prediabetes whereas 752 persons under normal level in Guangzhou, China. A set of the questionnaire is provided to gather details related to the demographic features, heredity, lifestyle risk, and anthropometric measurements factors. Next, a set of 3 predictive methods are developed by the use of one output variable and 12 input variables from the questionnaire details. These three models are validated, and the results confirmed that the DT attains maximum results followed by LR and ANN.

In (Hsiao-Hsien Rau et al, 2016), data mining methods are employed to design the prediction model for liver cancer in 6 years of analysis from type II diabetes. Data collection takes place from the National Health Insurance Research Database (NHIRD) of Taiwan involving a total of 22 million people. Here, patients who were recently identified with type II diabetes are chosen from 2000 to 2003, with no previous cancer identification. The encrypted personal ID is used to carry out the data connectivity with the cancer database for identifying the presence of liver cancer. In the end, a group of 2060 patients are identified as test positive and allocated to a control group for carrying out data linkage with the cancer registry database for recognition whereas the patients were identified with liver cancer.

Support Vector Machines (SVM)

SVM or the support vector networks are supervised ML techniques which combine classification and regression analysis for analyzing the data given. The SVM creates a hyperplane which divides the data into classes. In this method, in 'n' dimensional space, every data item is given as a point. Here 'n' represents the sum of features where the rate of every feature corresponds to the rate of a specific coordinate and a hyperplane segregates the classes (set of features).The SVM can handle both continuous and categorical variables. The SVM is very resilient to handle the problem of over fitting.

In (Baek Hwan Cho et al, 2008), a new visualization system for risk factor analysis (VRIFA), new nonlinear kernel and localized radial basis function (LRBF) kernel is employed on an LRBF kernel and nomogram for visualizing the performance of nonlinear SVMs and enhance the results interpretability when controlling tremendous accuracy during prediction. Three representative medical dataset from the UCI repository are employed to validate the results. The experimental values indicated that the classifier results of the LRBF are alike the RBF, and the LRBF is easier to envision through a nomogram. The experimental values indicated that the LRBF kernel is less receptive to noise features when compared to the RBF kernel, whereas the LRBF kernel reduces the classifier accuracy significantly and needed features are removed. (Kemal Polat et al, 2008) intends to the identification of diabetes disease by the use of Least Square SVM (LS-SVM) and Generalized Discriminant Analysis (GDA). Also, a novel cascade learning system LS-SVM and GDA is also used.

Support Vector Regression (SVR)

The support vectors are data points near to the boundary in which the distance between the points is minimum or least. In simple regression, the rate of error is minimized whereas, in SVR, the error rate is mapped to an absolute value of the threshold. SVR is an efficient tool for the evaluation of real valued functions.

In (Eleni I. Georga et al, 2013), subcutaneous (s.c) glucose prediction is considered as a multi-variate regression issue that is resolved by the use of SVR. It depends on the following characteristics namely s.c.Plasma insulin concentration, glucose profile, the appearance of meal-derived glucose in the complete movement and energy expenses while in physical actions. A set of 6 cases respective to a diverse combination of the previously mentioned parameters are employed to analyze the impact of the input on each day glucose prediction. In free-living conditions, it is validated on a set of 27 patients.10-fold cross validation is employed to every dataset separately for optimizing and testing the model. The experimental values depicted that the presented model will considerably enhance performance.

DTs

Classification trees are often employed for classifying the patients based on the existence and non-existence of diseases. However, they have the constraint of low accuracy. The other tree approaches like bootstrap aggregation (bagging), random forests, boosting, and SVM are used. In (Peter C. Austin et al, 2013), a comparison is made with the traditional classification trees for classifying heart failure (HF) patients based on the below sub-kinds: HF with reduced ejection fraction and HF with preserved ejection fraction (HFPEF). The application of tree-based approaches provides enhanced results over the traditional model for identifying HF types.

Neural Networks (NN)

NN process the data as same as the human brain. NN contains a massive number of highly interlinked processing elements (neurons) which operates concurrently for solving particular issue. They learn from the example and carry out a particular process. (Chiara Zecchin et al, 2012) presented a method for predicting short-time glucose by the use of previous CGM sensor readings and details related to the intake of carbohydrate. The predictor integrates a first-order polynomial extrapolation and NN model algorithm for the linear and nonlinear elements of glucose dynamics. This model is tested on 20 experimented dataset and nine real Abbott FreeStyle Navigator dataset. A comparison is made with the latest NN glucose predictor. The experimental values recommended that the usage of meal details enhances the performance of the prediction process.

Fuzzy Classification

In (Mostafa and Mohammad, 2011), an Ant Colony-based classifier model is presented for extracting a collection of fuzzy rules to diagnose the diabetes disease called FCS-ANTMINER. Here, few latest approaches have been reviewed and then derived a novel method that results in significantly better performance on the applied problem. It exhibits advanced features which makes it distinguishable from other ones. The attained classifier accuracy is 84.24%, and it revealed that the presented model is better than the compared ones.

In (Esin et al, 2010), an Adaptive Network Based Fuzzy Inference System (ANFIS) and intellectual diagnosis system for diabetes on LDA called LDA-ANFIS is introduced. The process involves two stages: LDA and ANFIS. The former stage is employed for separating the features parameters among patient and healthy (diabetes) data. The latter phase gives extracted features and provided to the ANFIS classifier. The accurate diagnosis presentation of the LDA-ANFIS model is determined by the use of sensitivity as well as specificity. The presented model achieves a maximum classifier accuracy of 84.61%.

Artificial Neural Network (ANN)

(Hsiao-Hsien Rau et al, 2016) aims to apply different data mining techniques to develop type II diabetes mellitus patient prediction model for liver cancer. Since diabetes patients are not often visiting the doctors, offering decision support for earlier identification concerning the possibility of cancer will be highly helpful for diabetes patients. Then, detection about the cancer probability is critical for patients with diabetes. A set of training and testing process is carried out to build ANN and LR. A set of ten variables are applied to build the ANN and LR models. Once the optimum prediction method is developed, a web-based application system for predicting liver cancer offers support to doctors during the consultation of diabetes patients. The performance revealed that the model could be employed as an efficient predictor model for predicting liver cancer. It also agreed that the model could help the doctors to recommend possible liver cancer patients and useful to reduce the upcoming cost incur on cancer treatment.

Hybrid Systems

In (Humar and Novruz, 2008), an efficient classifier model for medical data is presented. Also, a hybrid NN comprising of fuzzy neural network (FNN) and ANN is introduced. Two practical problem data are analyzed to decide about the usability of the presented model. The data is gathered from the UCI repository. The datasets are Cleveland heart disease and Pima Indians diabetes. For validating the results of the presented model, a set of measures and k-fold cross-validation are employed. The presented model attained accuracy rates of 86.8% and 84.24% for the applied dataset, correspondingly. In (Xue-Hui et al, 2013), a hybrid model for evaluating HD is presented to study the therapeutic things and to discover the relationship among coverage and accuracy for attracted parties. The presented model exhibited high performance with maximum accuracy and minimum standard deviation using fewer variables.

Other Methods and Algorithms

Medical Decision Support Systems

In (Hsiao-Hsien Rau et al, 2016), data mining methods are employed to design the prediction model for liver cancer in 6 years of analysis from type II diabetes. Data collection takes place from the NHIRD of Taiwan involving a total of 22 million people. Here, patients who were recently identified with type II diabetes are chosen from 2000 to 2003, with no previous cancer identification. Then, encrypted personal ID is used to carry out the data connectivity with the cancer database for identifying the presence of liver cancer. In the end, a group of 2060 patients is identified as test positive and allocated to a control group to assist in carrying out data association process using the database of cancer registry to recognize whether the patients were detected with liver cancer.

Soft Computing Techniques

An adequate system is produced (ArunaPavate and Nazneen Ansari, 2015) to predict diabetes and with the difficulties of the risk level. To offer a precise prediction, techniques like a nearest neighbor, fuzzy rule-based system and genetic algorithm are employed. A set of 235 individual's data were gathered in this method. The optimal feature subset produced through the executed method comprises the highest general risk factors like family history, weight, alcohol habit, other difficulties relating with diabetes, BMI, smoking habit are assumed for the disease predication. The proposed method offers 95.50% accuracy, 86.95% specificity and 95.83% sensitivity that aid to effectively predict the disease.

Extreme Learning Techniques

In type I diabetes, an online machine-learning system to the nonlinear glucose time sequence issue is projected. For the single hidden layer feed-forward NN, an extreme learning machine (ELM) recently projected (Eleni I. Georga et al, 2015). The rapid learning speed and enhanced accuracy of ELM tend to examine the applicability towards the issue of glucose prediction. Online sequential ELM kernels (KOS-ELM) and online sequential ELM (OS-ELM) is intended to provide self-monitoring data of diabetes patients. By focusing at carbohydrates intake, subcutaneous glucose, physical activity, and insulin therapy, a set of multivariate feature is used. The simulation results given that KOS-ELM produces better results when compared with OS-ELM using temporal gain, regularity and prediction error.

Intelligent systems

With the combined Implication of Naïve Bayes statistical modeling and SVM (ZhilbertTafa et al, 2015) this paper aims to enhance the computer-aided diagnosis trustworthiness using the 402 patient's medical examinations. Few parameters which are not used in prior computer-aid examinations are used in this dataset. The entire reliability is improved by the combining execution of the methods which is helpful in computer-aided diagnosis of diabetes.

Novel Fusion Method

To recognize the genes of the disease, a new Sequence-based fusion method (SFM) is projected (Abdulaziz Yousef and Nasrollah Moghadam Charkari, 2015). The amino acid series of protein are used that are global data despite employing incomplete and noisy prior-knowledge to represent the genes to four various feature vectors. The intersection collection of four negative sets that are produced using distance method is assumed to choose the negative data from candidate genes. To merge the four independent standard predictors' outcome depending on the SVM method, the DT (C4.5) had been used as the combining technique. Through a few state-of-art measures, the simulation outcomes of the projected technique are verified. The simulation results denote that F-measure, precision, and recall of 84%, 82.6%, and 85.6% correspondingly. The outcomes show the efficacy of the projected technique.

Machine Learning Algorithm

Depending on the gain variations, a data mining technique is introduced which employs non-wearable multimodal sensors to model, low cost, and predict patient's adherence (Conrad S. Tucker et al, 2015). A study has been conducted including Parkinson's disease patients who are "off" and "on" medication to decide the method's statistical validity. When they are far from the clinic, the data gained can be employed to enumerate patients' adherence. With regard to patient safety, the data-driven system might enable for prior warnings. The authors shown the ability to differentiate among PD patients off and on medication using entire body movement with precision higher than 97% for few patients and precision of 78% for common model that comprised of multi-patient data.

Multilabel Learning Algorithms

The intention of (Damien Zufferey et al, 2015) is to offer comparative results of the existing multi-label learning approaches for investigating the multivariate series of medical data from patient's data affected by chronic diseases. This model seems to be better for defining merged medical conditions, particular to constantly ill patients.

By the availability of comparative analysis, validation of new techniques has to be improved. Based on the method, a summary of statistics method is chosen to process the sequential clinical data.

4. PERFORMANCE VALIDATION MEASURES

In this section, the set of measures used to validate the results are explained below. The performance of the data mining technique has to be evaluated to examine the efficiency and performance of any developed model. The computational complexity and comprehensibility can be attained by evaluating the data mining model across several performance measures such as accuracy, precision, F measure, recall, sensitivity, specificity, positive prediction, negative prediction and error rate. The performance of the algorithm can be visualized as a table which is popularly known as the confusion matrix (supervised learning) or the matching matrix (unsupervised learning).

The matrix comprised the contingency table (rows and columns) represented in two dimensions as an actual class and predicted class. E.g. In the field of medicine, consider a blood sample analysis taken to determine if the patient has a particular disease or not. i.e., there are two possible outcomes - positive or negative which can be represented as a 2×2 matrix with four possible outcomes as shown in Table 2. In medical testing, the false positive and false negatives are reported as an error in diagnosis which is commonly known as the 'false alarm.' The measures are illustrated in Fig. 3 and a sample Diagnostic Test Evaluation Calculator is shown in Fig. 4.

Figure 3. Classification measures

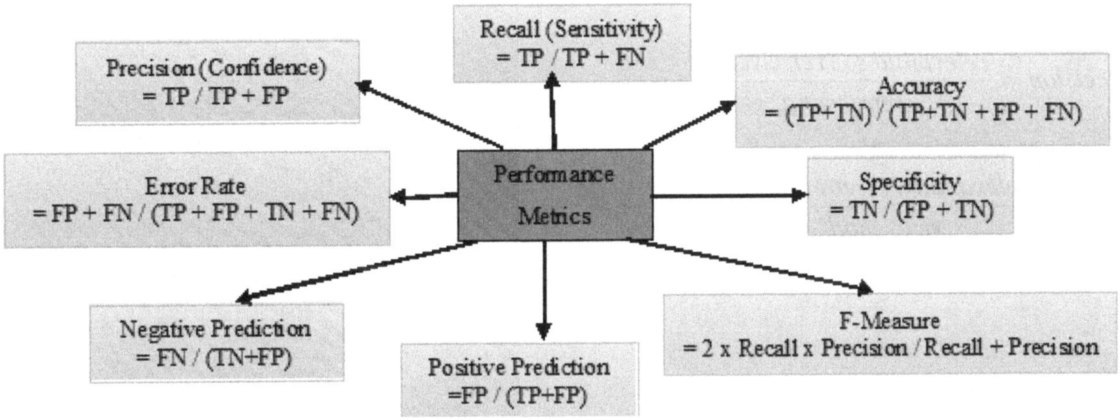

$$\text{Recall (Sensitivity)} = TP / TP + FN$$

$$\text{Precision (Confidence)} = TP / TP + FP$$

$$\text{Accuracy} = (TP+TN) / (TP+TN + FP + FN)$$

$$\text{Error Rate} = FP + FN / (TP + FP + TN + FN)$$

Performance Metrics

$$\text{Specificity} = TN / (FP + TN)$$

$$\text{Negative Prediction} = FN / (TN+FP)$$

$$\text{Positive Prediction} = FP / (TP+FP)$$

$$\text{F-Measure} = 2 \times \text{Recall} \times \text{Precision} / \text{Recall} + \text{Precision}$$

Table 2. Confusion matrix

	Actual Values	
	Positive(1)	Negative(0)
Positive(1)	True Positive	False Positive
Negative(0)	False Negative	True Negative

Figure 4. Diagnostic test evaluation calculator

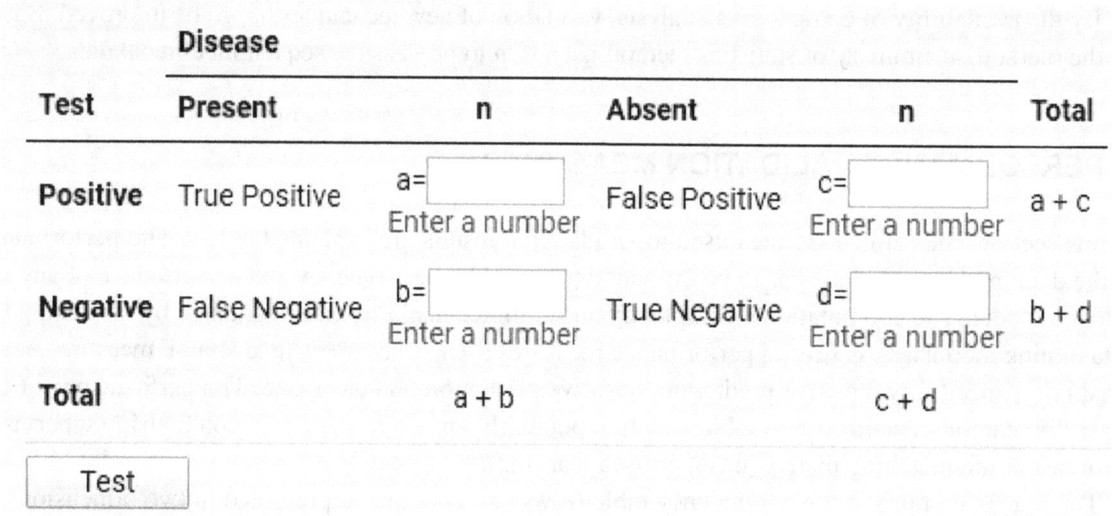

Test	Disease Present	n	Absent	n	Total
Positive	True Positive	a= [Enter a number]	False Positive	c= [Enter a number]	a + c
Negative	False Negative	b= [Enter a number]	True Negative	d= [Enter a number]	b + d
Total		a + b		c + d	

Test

Performance Analysis w.r.t Precision and Recall

Precision and recall are a measure of relevance in order to the retrieved instances. For instance, in an automated information retrieval system, the mission is to return a set of ID's which can be either relevant or not relevant to the search. In this scenario, the precision is estimated by segmenting the relevant ID's by the total number of retrieved ID's and the recall is estimated by segmenting the sum of relevant ID's by the sum of ID's which are true. To simplify this, the precision and recall can be equated as follows

$$Precision = \frac{relevantid's \cap retreivedId's}{retreivedid's}$$

$$recall = \frac{relevantid's \cap retreivedId's}{relevantid's}.$$

Table 3. Comparative result of different methods under several measures

Method	Precision %	Recall %	F-Measure %	AUC %	Accuracy %	Sensitivity %	Specificity %
RelifF Linear				0.833	0.764	0.876	0.558
RelifF RBF				0.835	0.763	0.882	0.543
RelifF LRBF				**0.843**	0.773	0.886	0.566
Sensitivity Analysis Linear				0.833	0.770	0.887	0.549
Sensitivity Analysis RBF				0.835	0.755	0.853	0.574
Sensitivity Analysis LRBF				**0.845**	0.772	0.881	0.571
SVM-RFE Linear				0.832	0.778	0.891	0.563
Nomogram-RFE Linear				0.832	0.766	0.884	0.547
Nomogram-RFE LRBF				**0.847**	0.776	0.887	0.568
C5.0 (Neuropathy)						64.71	83.48
NN (Neuropathy)						**67.63**	**99.70**
C5.0 (Nepropathy)						69.44	81.36
NN (Nepropathy)						**74.44**	**98.55**
C5.0 (Retinopathy)						58.62	74.73
NN (Retinopathy)						**59.48**	**99.86**
Hybrid (ANN and FNN)				**84.24**	80.3	87.3
LS-SVM					78.21	73.91	80
GDA-LS-SVM					**82.05**	**79.16**	**83.33**
MLP (T1D)	74.77	57.24			68.50		
FLANN (T1D)	73.06	59.41			68.44		
SVM (T1D)	78.68	56.61			**70.49**		
MLP (T2D)	78.24	55.96			69.91		
FLANN (T2D)	75.13	55.96			67.45		
SVM (T2D)	84.41	55.93			**72.18**		
LDA-ANFIS					**84.61**	83.33	85.18
FCS-ANTMINER	85.86	84.13	84.98		**84.24**		
Naïve Bayes Network					71.5		
Byes Network					**72.3**		
LR					76.13	79.59	72.74
ANN					73.23	82.18	64.49
DT C5.0					**77.87**	64.49	75.15
SVM-NGA-II	90.48	85.60	87.97		84.61		
SVR-NGA-II	91.40	87.20	89.25		**86.13**		
Smalter's method	63.5	73.2	68				
ProDiGe	72.6	60	66				
PUDI	75.3	80.7	77.9				
SFM	77.3	79.9	78.5				

continues on following page

Table 3. Continued

Method	Precision %	Recall %	F-Measure %	AUC %	Accuracy %	Sensitivity %	Specificity %
WSO					82.03		
C4.5					83.07		
SVM					95.52		
NB					94.53		
SVM (Class YES)	0.892	0.868					
SVM (Class NO)	0.97	0.975					
NB (Class YES)	0.814	0.921					
NB (Class NO)	0.981	0.951					
KNN (GA-version 1)					90.50	85.70	80.25
WKNN (GA-version 2)					92.87	90.25	84.45
DWKNN (GA-version 3)					95.50	95.83	86.95
ANN (Sub-Model 1)				**0.837**		0.757	0.755
LR (Sub-Model 1)				0.778		0.666	0.790
ANN (Sub-Model 2)				**0.700**		0.751	0.605
LR(Sub-Model 2)				0.604		0.765	0.564
ANN (Sub-Model 3)				**0.828**		0.737	0.776
LR (Sub-Model 3)				0.778		0.666	0.876
NB (PIDD)			81.64		75.52	79.77	83.60
LR (PIDD)			82.12		75.78	79.07	85.40
SVM (PIDD)			83.25		76.95	78.99	88.00
HMV (PIDD)			83.40		77.08	78.93	88.40
NB (BDD)			94.91		91.32	94.77	95.04
LR (BDD)			95.35		91.81	92.35	98.54
SVM (BDD)			95.10		91.56	94.02	96.21
HMV (BDD)			96.00		**93.05**	94.12	97.96
NB (waist-to-hip ratio+TG in men)				0.653			
LR (waist-to-hip ratio + TG in men)				**0.661**			
NB (rib-to-hip ratio+ TG in women)				0.73			
LR (rib-to-hip ratio+ TG in women)				**0.735**			

Performance Analysis w.r.t F-Measure

The F measure is also known as the F_1 score or F score has been used extensively for data retrieval in the machine learning domain and natural language processing. F- Score is a measure of testing the accuracy computing the harmonic average of precision and recall. F-Measure helps to determine the robustness (high precision and low recall) of the classifier.

Performance Analysis w.r.t Area Under Curve (AUC)

The graphical plotting of the true positive rate against the false positive rate at a range of thresholds is known as the receiver operating characteristic curve (ROC).Here; the true positive rate indicates the probability of detection whereas the false positive rate indicates the probability of false alarm. The ROC helps in diagnostic decision making by generating a cumulative distribution function. Consider the area of a graph y=f(x) with x- axis representing the definite integral $\int_{b}^{a} f(x) dx$ .This formula results in positive value above the x-axis and negative below the x-axis. Therefore the ultimate aim is to determine the area between the two curves (above and below) by calculating the definite integral between the two values of independent variables.

Performance Analysis w.r.t Accuracy

Accuracy is described as the proportion of the sum of correctly classified samples and to the sum of input samples taken. Accuracy is calculated by computing all the possible terms of positives and negatives (TP, TN, FP, FN) with any class of imbalanced datasets. Calculation of accuracy in machine learning models acts a significant role in making practical decisions as it mitigates the cost by reducing the error. E.g. in medical decision support systems, consider a false positive diabetes diagnosis which increases the cost of the analysis and stress in the patient.

Performance Analysis w.r.t Sensitivity and Specificity

The sensitivity and specificity measure eliminates false negatives and false positives. A predictor is said to be ideal if it is 100 percent sensitive. Consider the scenario of identifying healthy and sick patients in clinical decision support systems. When all the sick patients are correctly classified as sick, the system is said to be highly sensitive. Similarly, when no healthy individuals are recognized incorrectly as sick, the system is said to be highly specific. Therefore sensitivity can be described as the proportion of the sum of true positives to the sum of sick individuals in the population (probability of tested –positive result indicating that the patient has the disease).Specificity can be described as the proportion of the sum of true negatives to the total number of healthy individuals in the population (Probability of a tested negative result indicating that the patient is well).

Performance Analysis w.r.t Error Rate

In a binary classification problem, the error rate is defined as the percentage of error in prediction which can be determined with the help of a confusion matrix. There are two types of errors in statistical hypothesis testing – type I and type II errors. The type I error is also known as the false positive and type II as false negative. These types of errors are based on the fact of accepting or rejecting an alternative hypothesis based on the results. Here hypothesis is the method of testing the random relationship between two sample distributions. E.g. in clinical decision support systems, consider the hypothesis and null hypothesis as following,

Hypothesis: The symptoms of the patient may improve after treatment X more rapidly than after placebo. Null hypothesis: The symptoms of the patient after treatment X are impossible to differentiate from placebo.

Here the Type I error resulting in false positive indicates that the treatment X is helpful than the placebo whereas the Type II error indicating false negative fails to state that treatment X is helpful than the placebo even when it is really helpful. The third kind of error (Type III error) was also found by Mosteller which involves rejecting the phenomenon of the null hypothesis for the incorrect reason. The error rate of numerical models can be evaluated in terms of mean squared error (average of square differences between the actual and predicted values), mean absolute error (uses absolute values instead of squares) and bias (average of prediction between actual and predicted values).

Performance Analysis w.r.t Positive and Negative Prediction

The positive predictive value is described as the proportion of the sum of true positives to the ratio of the sum of false positives and true positive whereas, the negative predictive value is described as the proportion of true negatives to the sum of a number of false negatives and true negatives. The positive and negative predictions are often to be confused with the rate of sensitivity and specificity. The positive prediction can genuinely predict the ratio of patients who are prone to the disease and the negative prediction can truly predict the ratio of patients who are healthy in clinical decision support systems. The diagnostic test evaluation calculator indicating the diseased and non diseased cases are represented in Fig. 4.

Results and Discussion

In this section, we made a comparative analysis of different reviewed methods under different evaluation parameters as mentioned above. The results attained by the reviewed methods are provided in Table 3.

Results Analysis Interms of Precision and Recall

Fig. 5 shows the comparative analysis of different methods interms of precision and recall. From all the compared methods, it is noted that the NB (Class NO) achieves a maximum precision value of 98.1 and recall value of 95.1. At the same time, SVM (Class NO) attains almost higher precision and recall values of 97 and 97.5 respectively. In line with, SVR-NGA-II offers higher performance with the precision and recall values of 91.8 and 87.2 respectively. Though these values seem higher, it is not superior to NB and SVM (Class NO). Similarly, the SVM-NGA-II attains slightly lower performance than SVR-NGA-II with the precision and recall values of 90.48 and 85.6 respectively. Likewise, SVM (Class YES) shows somewhat better results with the precision and recall values of 89.2 and 86.8 respectively. At the same time, the NB (Class YES) also performs well with the precision and recall values of 81.4 and 92.1 respectively. In the same way, the SVM (T2D) manages to perform will with the precision and recall values of 84.41 and 55.93 respectively.

The other methods namely FLANN (T1D), SVM (T1D), MLP (T2D) and FLANN (T2D) achieves a lower precision and recall values of 73.06 and 59.41, 78.68 and 56.61, 78.24 and 55.96, and 75.13 and 55.96 respectively. In line with, some of the other methods such as Smalter's method, ProDiGe, PUDI

Figure 5. Results analysis interms of precision and recall

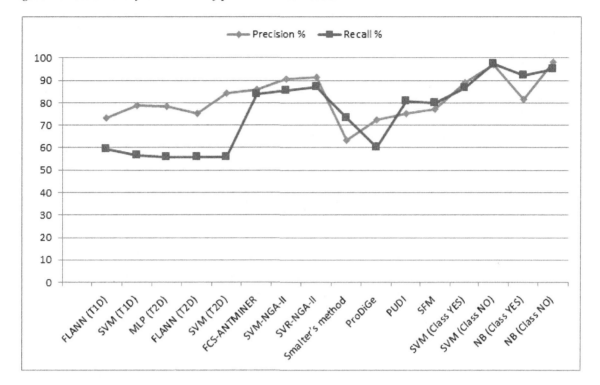

and SFM also fail to show better results with the precision and recall values of 63.5 and 73.2, 72.6 and 60, 75.3 and 80.7, 77.3 and 79.9, respectively. From the above tables and figure, it is evident that the NB (Class NO) method shows effective results with the precision value of 98.1 and recall value of 95.1.

Results Analysis Interms of Accuracy

Fig. 6 investigates the results attained by various methods interms of accuracy. The value of accuracy should be maximum for better performance. From the figure, it is clear that the two methods namely SVM and DWKNN (GA-version 3) obtains maximum accuracy of 95.52 and 95.5 respectively. In addition, NB method also tries to depict maximum performance with the accuracy of 94.53.

At the same time, WKNN (GA-version 2) and HMV (BDD) also shows competitive results with the accuracy values of 92.87 and 93.05 respectively. And, three methods namely NB (BDD), LR (BDD) and SVM (BDD) showed near identical results with the accuracy values of 91.32, 91.81 and 91.56 respectively. The KNN (GA-version 1) also shows better results with the high accuracy of 90.5. Unfortunately, these various methods attains higher values, but not than SVM and DWKNN (GA-version 3). And, some of the methods namely RelifF LRBF, Sensitivity Analysis Linear, Sensitivity Analysis LRBF, SVM-RFE Linear Nomogram-RFE LRBF, DT C5.0 and HMV (PIDD) showed near identical results with the accuracy values of 77.3, 77, 77.2, 77.8, 77.6, 77.87 and 77.08 respectively. Among the compared ones, Naïve Bayes Network shows minimum accuracy of 71.5 whereas SVM shows maximum classification accuracy of 95.52.

Figure 6. Results analysis interms of accuracy

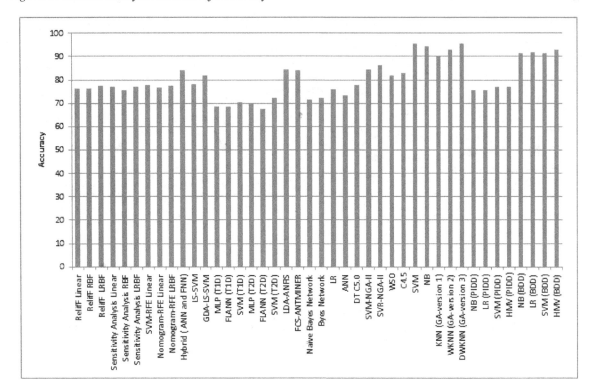

Results Analysis Interms of Sensitivity and Specificity

Fig. 7 shows the comparative analysis of different methods interms of sensitivity and specificity. From all the compared methods, it is noted that the DWKNN (GA-version 3) achieves a maximum sensitivity value of 95.83 and maximum specificity value of 99.7 is attained by NN (Neuropathy). At the same time, HMV (BDD) attains almost higher specificity and sensitivity rates of 94.12 and 97.96 respectively. In line with, NB (BDD) offers higher performance with the sensitivity and specificity values of 94.77 and 95.04 respectively. Though these values seem higher, it is not superior to DWKNN and NN. Similarly, the SVM (BDD) attains slightly lower performance than DWKNN and NN with the sensitivity and specificity values of 94.02 and 96.21 respectively. Likewise, SVM (PIDD) shows somewhat better results with the sensitivity and specificity values of 78.99 and 88 respectively. At the same time, the LR (BD) also performs well with the sensitivity and specificity values of 92.35 and 98.54 respectively. In the same way, the HMV (PIDD) manages to perform with the sensitivity and specificity values of 78.93 and 88.4 respectively.

The other methods namely RelifF RBF, NN, DT C5.0 and ANN achieves a lower sensitivity and sensitivity values of 88.2 and 54.3, 74.44 and 98.55, 64.49 and 75.15, and 75.7 and 75.7 respectively. In line with, some of the other methods such as Sensitivity analysis Linear, Nomogram-RFELRBF, Hybrid and LDA-ANFIS also fail to show better results with the sensitivity and specificity values of 88.7 and 54.9, 88.7 and 56.8, 80.3 and 87.3, 83.33 and 85.18, respectively. From the above tables and figure, it is evident that the DWKNN (Class NO) and NN method shows effective results with the sensitivity value of 95.83 and specificity value of 99.7.

Figure 7. Results analysis interms of sensitivity and specificity

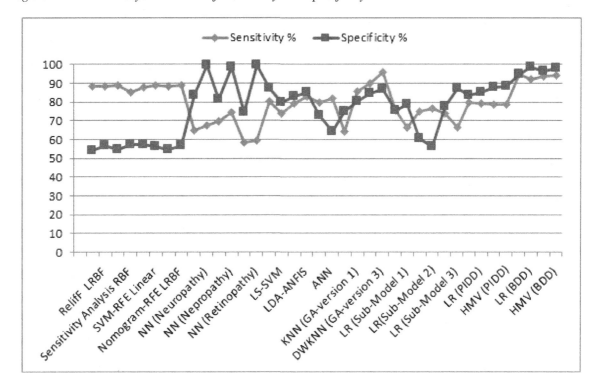

Results Analysis Interms of F-measure

Fig. 8 investigates the results attained by various methods interms of F-measure. From the figure, it is clear that the two methods namely SVM and HMV obtain maximum F-measure of 95.1 and 96 respectively. In addition, LR method also tries to depict maximum performance with the F-measure of 95.35. At the same time, SVM and HMV (PIDD) also show competitive results with the F-measure values of 83.25 and 83.4 respectively. And, three methods namely NB (PIDD), and LR (PIDD) showed near identical results with the F-measure values of 81.64, and 82.12 respectively. The SVR NGA-II also shows better results with the high F-measure of 89.25. Unfortunately, these various methods attains higher values, but not than SVM and HMV. And, some of the methods namely SVM-NGA II, Smalter's method, PUDI, SFM, ProDiGe showed results with the F-measure values of 87.97, 68, 77.9, 78.5, and 66 respectively. Among the compared ones, ProDiGe shows minimum accuracy of 66 whereas HMV shows maximum classification accuracy of 96.

Results Analysis Interms of AUC

Fig. 9 investigates the results attained by various methods interms of AUC. From the figure, it is clear that the two methods namely Nomogram-RFE Linear and Sensitivity analysis LRBF methods obtain maximum AUC of 0.847 and 0.845 respectively. In addition, RelifF LRBF method also tries to depict maximum performance with the AUC of 0.843. At the same time, Sensitivity analysis Linear and Sensitivity analysis RBF also shows competitive results with the AUC values of 0.833 and 0.835 respectively.

Figure 8. Results analysis interms of F-measure

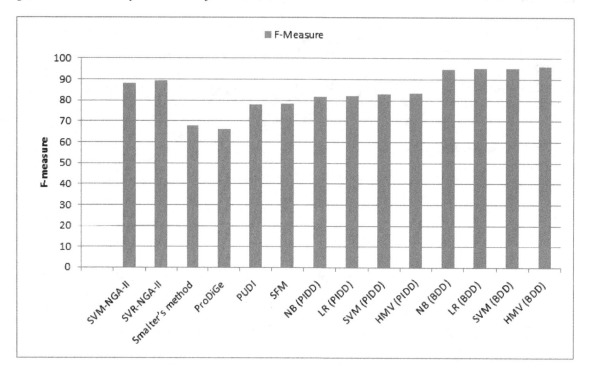

And, two methods namely RelifF RBF and Sensitivity analysis RBF showed identical results with the AUC values of 910.835 and other two methods named as SVM-RFE Linear and Nomogram-RFE Linear shows similar outcomes of 0.832 AUC. The ANN (Sub-Model 1) also shows better results with the high AUC of 0.837. Unfortunately, these various methods attains higher values, but not than Nomogram-RFE Linear. And, some of the methods namely RelifF LRBF, LR(Sub-Model 1), ANN (Sub-Model 2), LR(Sub-Model 2), ANN (Sub-Model 3), LR (Sub-Model 3), NB (waist-to-hip ratio+TG in men), LR (waist-to-hip ratio + TG in men), NB (rib-to-hip ratio+ TG in women), LR (rib-to-hip ratio+ TG in women) showed results with the AUC values of 0.843, 0.778, 0.7, 0.604, 0.828, 0.778, 0.653, 0.661, 0.73 and 0.735 respectively. Among the compared ones, LR (Sub-Model 2) shows minimum AUC of 0.604 whereas Nomogram-RFE Linear shows maximum classification AUC of 0.847.

CONCLUSION

In the fast growing world, a number of disease existences tend to increase drastically and data mining applications find useful in assisting it. Since numerous disease prediction models have been developed, it is difficult to explore the valuable literature in the health care domain. This chapter has reviewed the present overview of research that is done in the healthcare sector utilizing different data mining methodologies for prediction and classification of diverse diseases. Also, a detailed comparison of reviewed methods also takes place to better understanding the existing models. An experimental study is also done to analyze the performance of data mining algorithms.

Figure 9. Results analysis interms of AUC

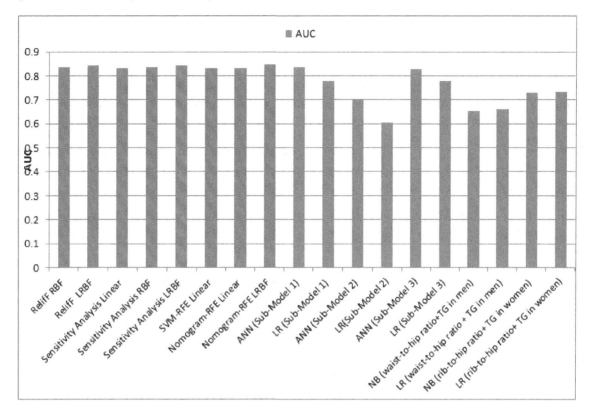

REFERENCES

Austin. (2013). Using methods from the data- mining and machine-learning literature for disease classification and prediction: a case study examining classification of heart failure subtypes. *Journal of Clinical Epidemiology, 66,* 398-407.

Bashir, S., Qamar, U., Khan, F. H., & Naseem, L. (2016). HMV: A Medical Decision Support Framework Using Multi-Layer Classifiers For Disease Prediction. *Journal of Computational Science, 13,* 10–25. doi:10.1016/j.jocs.2016.01.001

Chan, C.-L. (2008). Investigation of Diabetic Microvascular Complication using Data Mining Techniques. *International Joint Conference on Neural Networks (IJCNN 2008).*

Chandamona, P. (2016). Improved analysis of data mining techniques on medical data. *Int. J. Nano Corr Sci and Eng., 3*(3), 85–90.

Chen. (2016). An efficient hybrid kernel extreme learning machine approach for early diagnosis of Parkinson's disease. *Neurocomputing, 184,* 131–144.

Cho. (2008). Nonlinear Support Vector Machine Visualization for Risk Factor Analysis Using Nomograms and Localized Radial Basis Function Kernels. *IEEE Transactions on Information Technology in Biomedicine, 12*(2).

Christopher. (2015). A Swarm Optimization approach for clinical knowledge mining. *Computer Methods and Programs in Biomedicine, 121*, 137–148.

Dewani & Yonah. (2017). A novel holistic disease prediction tool using best fit data mining techniques. *Int. J. Com. Dig. Sys., 6*(2).

Diciolla, M., Binetti, G., Di Noia, T., Pesce, F., Schena, F. P., Vågane, A. M., Bjørneklett, R., Suzuki, H., Tomino, Y., & Naso, D. (2015). Patient classification and outcome prediction in IgA nephropathy. *Computers in Biology and Medicine, 66*, 278–286. doi:10.1016/j.compbiomed.2015.09.003 PMID:26453758

Dogantekin, E., Dogantekin, A., Avci, D., & Avci, L. (2010). An intelligent diagnosis system for diabetes on Linear Discriminant Analysis and Adaptive Network Based Fuzzy Inference System: LDA-ANFIS. *Digital Signal Processing, 20*(4), 1248–1255. doi:10.1016/j.dsp.2009.10.021

Ganji, M. F., & Abadeh, M. S. (2011). A fuzzy classification system based on Ant Colony Optimization for diabetes disease diagnosis. *Expert Systems with Applications, 38*(12), 14650–14659. doi:10.1016/j.eswa.2011.05.018

Georga. (2013). Multivariate Prediction of Subcutaneous Glucose Concentration in Type 1 Diabetes Patients Based on Support Vector Regression. *IEEE Journal of Biomedical and Health Informatics, 17*(1).

Georga, E. I. (2015). Online Prediction of Glucose Concentration in Type 1 Diabetes Using Extreme Learning Machines. *International Conference*, 3262-3265. 10.1109/EMBC.2015.7319088

Guo, Y. (2012). Using Bayes Network for Prediction of Type-2 Diabetes. *The 7th International Conference for Internet Technology and Secured Transactions (ICITST-2012)*.

Jothi, N. (2015). Data mining in healthcare. *Procedia Computer Science, 72*, 306–313. doi:10.1016/j.procs.2015.12.145

Kahramanli, H., & Allahverdi, N. (2008). Design of a hybrid system for the diabetes and heart diseases. *Expert Systems with Applications, 35*(1-2), 82–89. doi:10.1016/j.eswa.2007.06.004

Lee & Kim. (2016). Identification of Type 2 Diabetes Risk Factors Using Phenotypes Consisting of Anthropometry and Triglycerides based on Machine Learning. *IEEE Journal of Biomedical and Health Informatics, 20*(1).

Pavate & Ansari. (2015). Risk Prediction of Disease Complications in Type 2 Diabetes Patients Using Soft Computing Techniques. *Fifth International Conference on Advances in Computing and Communications*.

Polat, K., Güneş, S., & Arslan, A. (2008). A cascade learning system for classification of diabetes disease: Generalized Discriminant Analysis and Least Square Support Vector Machine. *Expert Systems with Applications, 34*(1), 482–487. doi:10.1016/j.eswa.2006.09.012

Rau. (2016). Development of a web-based liver cancer prediction model for type II diabetes patients by using an artificial neural network. *Computer Methods and Programs in Biomedicine, 125*, 58–65.

Sun, J. (2009). Functional Link Artificial Neural Network-based Disease Gene Prediction. *Proceedings of International Joint Conference on Neural Networks*. 10.1109/IJCNN.2009.5178639

Tucker, C. S., Behoora, I., Nembhard, H. B., Lewis, M., Sterling, N. W., & Huang, X. (2015). Machine Learning Classification Of Medication Adherence In Patients With Movement Disorders Using Non-Wearable Sensors. *Computers in Biology and Medicine, 66*, 120–134. doi:10.1016/j.compbiomed.2015.08.012 PMID:26406881

Vlahos, G. E. (2004). Ferratt and Knoepfle, The use of computer based information systems by German managers to support decision-making, inf. *Manage, 41*(6), 763–779.

Witten & Hall. (2011). *Data mining: Practical machine learning tools & techniques*. Google.

Xue-Hui. (2013). Comparison of three data mining models for predicting diabetes or prediabetes by risk factors. *Kaohsiung Journal of Medical Sciences, 29*, 93-99.

Yousef, A., & Charkari, N. M. (2015). SFM: A Novel Sequence-Based Fusion Method For Disease Genes Identification And Prioritization. *Journal of Theoretical Biology, 383*, 12–19. doi:10.1016/j.jtbi.2015.07.010 PMID:26209022

Zangooei, M. H., Habibi, J., & Alizadehsani, R. (2014). Disease Diagnosis with a hybrid method SVR using NSGA-II. *Neurocomputing, 136*, 14–29. doi:10.1016/j.neucom.2014.01.042

Zecchin. (2012). Neural Network Incorporating Meal Information Improves Accuracy of Short-Time Prediction of Glucose Concentration. *IEEE Transactions on Biomedical Engineering, 59*(6).

ZhilbertTafa. (2015). An Intelligent System for Diabetes Prediction. *4th Mediterranean Conference on Embedded Computing MECO – 2015*, 378-382.

Zufferey, D., Hofer, T., Hennebert, J., Schumacher, M., Ingold, R., & Bromuri, S. (2015). Performance Comparison Of Multi-Label Learning Algorithms On Clinical Data For Chronic Diseases. *Computers in Biology and Medicine, 65*, 34–43. doi:10.1016/j.compbiomed.2015.07.017 PMID:26275389

Chapter 3
Analysis of Crime Report by Data Analytics Using Python

G. Maria Jones
Saveetha Engineering College, India

S. Godfrey Winster
SRM Institute of Science and Technology, India

ABSTRACT

The ever-rapid development of technology in today's world tends to provide us with a dramatic explosion of data, leading to its accumulation and thus data computation has amplified in comparison to the recent past. To manage such complex data, emerging new technologies are enabled specially to identify crime patterns, as crime-related data is escalating. These digital technologies have the potential to manipulate and also alter the pattern. To combat this, machine learning techniques are introduced which have the ability to analyse such voluminous data. In this work, the authors intend to understand and implement machine learning techniques in real time data analysis by means of Python. The detailed explanation in preparing the dataset, understanding, visualizing the data using pandas, and performance measure of algorithm is evaluated.

INTRODUCTION

According to FBI (Federal Bureau of Investigation), crimes are defined as an offensive which involves threat of forces. The violent crimes are comprised with main four forms: murder, rape, robbery and aggravated followed by a property crimes ("Violent Crime - Crime in the United States 2009," n.d.). From traditional days to modern days, crimes have been evolved in various forms like computer crime, computer- related crimes, cyber-crimes and digital crimes. Computer crimes are defined as any crime act committed via computers and when computer involved in criminal act it is known as computer-related crimes. Cybercrime encompassed of criminal act including misuse of computers which are connected to internet. Finally, a relatively new and advanced crime called digital crime where attacks includes un-authorized network access, manipulation and dissemination of sensitive information, theft of data, child

DOI: 10.4018/978-1-7998-2566-1.ch003

pornography, narcotics traffickers and many more. As more number of digital devices evolved when compared to olden days, the data stored on digital gadgets are massive. Initially, hacking was coined by Massachusetts Institute of Technology (USA) in 1960s.

Computer Criminal activities have existed for decades and came to forefront in mid-80's which exposed the vulnerability of system data. In 1986, a German hacker used personal computer and modem for exploiting sensitive information by tapping into a military database (Britz, n.d.). In 1988, a student crippled over 6000 computers and damaged millions of computers by Morris Worm which infected 10% of computers connected in a network by exploiting UNIX operating system security holes. In mid-80's, many Phreakers were involved in manipulation of telecommunication system (Britz, n.d.). The following table.1 showcases the evolution of cyber-attacks starting from 1960. Industrial Big data, Mobile Devices, Internet of Things, Network connected devices and data-driven techniques are enabled and accessed through networks (LAN,WAN, etc.) to accumulate the enormous amount of information from connected machines and turn the big machinery data into actionable information (Zhao et al., 2019). The automation of systems has immense impact as it is proficient in detecting fraudulent activities from huge volumes of data, to design and develop machine learning algorithms to detect fraud. The growing addiction to technology in the present setup is an invitation to attempt cyber-crime and so counter measures are essential to tackle such criminal activities. With the accessibility of latest smartphones with 2G, 3G, 4G and upcoming 5G technologies, the user has the opportunity to communicate and exchange every piece of information using e-services which includes social networks, e-mails, blogs, etc (Méndez, Cotos-yañez, & Ruano-ordás, 2019).

The availability of data sets is enormous and since there is huge volume of data, storage and sophisticated software are at hand, the potential threat incidents are very likely to occur and so data analysis aids in preventing and detecting the crime. Further, collaborative efforts among investigation departments, researchers, and businesses has led to the development of data analytical techniques which have effective accompanying tools, such as variety of programming languages, software programs, applications, etc. To extract useful information from raw data and make appropriate decisions from this data, machine learning techniques have been recognized as a powerful solution. As a branch of Artificial Intelligence (AI), Machine Learning (ML) and deep learning models provide a platform to represent the data, classify and predict data patterns of information processing. About 93,000 fraud cases had been registered in China regarding mobile phones in the form of mails, messages, live chats, calls, social networking posts etc.(Wei, Sunny, & Liu, 2019).

The machine learning algorithms are classified into three types. They are supervised learning, unsupervised learning and reinforcement learning. Since machine learning is an advanced technique, it has the capacity to detect the crime with highest accuracy. In this chapter, the author offers techniques of data analytics methodologies to detect the criminal pattern which can be advantageous for criminal investigation to be effective and also to prevent crime. There are many facts that can allow law enforcement departments to provide and use their sources in crime scene to prevent from manipulating of original data and also helps to monitor the crime. These measures can efficiently prevent and respond quickly to criminal activities (Catlett, Cesario, Talia, & Vinci, 2019). The chapter considered a case study of Chicago, San Francisco and India crime report for analysing and visualizing. All the crime report has been gathered from online repository with more than 70 thousand crime event details including X and Y axis co-ordinates. The experimental results show the effectiveness of achieving great accuracy in ML algorithms.

The main goal of this work comprised of developing data visualization methods which can address the visualization and ML techniques to various form of crime. Thus, the main focus is to help the common person to understand the crime rate which has been increasing and also for police department in detecting crime patterns and perform crime analysis to formulate strategies for crime prevention and reduction. The present work proposes the use of data visualization techniques with a common goal of developing analysis tool. For this aim, the following objectives were formulated.

- To analyse and develop a data cleaning algorithm which cleans and remove unwanted data from 3 city crime dataset for ML algorithm.
- To enhance ML algorithms to identify crime patterns from historical data.
- To explore and enhance supervised algorithms to predict future crime behaviour based on previous crime trends.
- To identify and analyse common crime patterns to reduce further occurrences of similar incidence.
- To develop anomalies detection algorithms to identify change in crime patterns.
- To analyse the crime incident based on social media content by sentimental analysis.

The rest of the chapter is organized as follows. Section 2 provides a brief literature survey of data analytics and their application used ML. Section 3 gives the basic introduction to data visualization technique, Section 4 provides the approaches to solve problems in cyber security using ML. Section 5 presents the detailed methodology of the system. Section 6, 7 and 8 gives visualization process using data analytics and describes the experimental evaluation of Chicago, San Francisco and India crime dataset, Section 9 provides how sentiment analysis used for crime data and Finally, Section 10 concludes with future directions.

REALTED WORK

There are many applications from various fields are used by machine learning approaches. The work of (Karie, Kebande, & Venter, 2019) proposed a new concept of deep learning cyber-forensics framework to bring out the efficiency into cyber forensics field for managing and helping the investigation process. The future work mentioned as to work with the help of deep learning algorithms. A hybrid approach done by (Carcillo, Borgne, Caelen, & Kessaci, 2019) to analyse supervised learning and unsupervised learning for detecting fraud with promising result through cluster approach for AUC-PR. The author (Catlett et al., 2019) presented an approach based on spatio temporal and auto regression model for detecting crime in the cities of Chicago and New York yielding higher accuracy than earlier research. The work of (Liew et al., 2019) proposed a security alert mechanism for identifying phishing URLs of twitter user by using random forest algorithm with 11 classification class of twitter which acquired the accuracy of 97.50% effectively. The work presented by (Saeid, Rezvan, & Barekatain, 2018)about various machine learning algorithms with the challenges of IoT by considering smart cities wherein they explained how techniques are applied to retrieve the information.

The author (Comput, Kozik, Choraś, Ficco, & Palmieri, 2018) proposed an attack detection by using extreme learning machine algorithm from edge computing. The survey presented by (Ryman-tubb, Krause, & Garn, 2018) on payment fraud detection by Artificial Intelligence and Machine Learning with challenges and also mentioned that the future direction for research would be cognitive computing. The

Long Short-Term Memory (LSTM) (Jurgovsky et al., 2018) was employed to detect credit card fraud during the transactions. The author introduced (Ghiassi & Lee, 2018) n-gram and statistics approach for sentimental analysis to estimate the accurate tweet sentiments from twitter. A Method developed by authors (Nami & Shajari, 2018) for detecting fraudulent transactions with cardholder spending behaviour and achieved 23% of prevention of damage with proposed method. A scalable real-time fraud finder (SCARFF) method (Carcillo et al., 2018) presented which is integrated with Machine Learning for identifying credit card fraud with real time data set. The author (Méndez et al., 2019) introduced a feature selection method for detecting spams and compared the results with information gain and latent dirichlet allocation. The work was disclosed with the aim of identifying the adversaries by performing closed and open set experiments with correctly identified performance ranges from 82.2% to 97.9% and 73.8% to 77.6% respectively (Mondal & Bours, 2018).

The model's robustness score were evaluated by an author using two machine learning algorithms, where the first algorithm was to select the features and the second algorithm is used to find the malware detection with highest accuracy in classifying malware executable (Katzir & Elovici, 2018)(Jones, Geoferla, & Winster, 2020). The main objective of the research was to detect suspicious call log activities from mobile phones by using machine learning algorithm for improving cyber-resilience activities (Nguyen, Minh, Tran, & Hluchy, 2018). The machine learning and deep learning approaches are reviewed by (Gbenga, Stephen, Chiroma, Olusola, & Emmanuel, 2019) for spam filtering application where the mails are classified into spam and ham from publically available dataset with evaluating performance metrics. To identify criminal networks (Qazi & William, 2019) proposed a method to find crime places, objects of crime using spatial temporal method and also demonstrated it with burglary dataset. The work of (Wei et al., 2019) examined the vulnerability on mobile internet especially in social networking sites and also evolved the pattern of fraud, suspicious messages. The author (Das & Das, 2019) proposed a graph based clustering in crime report of United states of America, United Arab Emirates and India by using ML techniques especially with supervised and unsupervised learning. Behavioural Evidence Analysis(BEA) analysed and evaluated (Al, Bryce, Franqueira, Marrington, & Read, 2019) 5 real time cases on Dubai police report where investigators can get better understanding of victims and offenders.

The Chicago hotspot crime map data (Mohler, 2014) had taken from online publically available for analysing short and long term pattern by using EM algorithm and also mentioned that future work is aimed to improve the accuracy of the system. This work had given the challenges, roles for detecting text based cyber-stalking by using machine learning methods and also discussed about Anti cyber stalking text based system framework (Frommholz, Martin, Zinnar, Mitul, & Emma, 2016). The article gives the importance of mobile forensics and also retrieving and reconstructing the information from terrorist for investigation purpose (Dwi et al., 2016) (Jones & Winster, 2017). The author investigated and demonstrated the technique used for forensics investigation and concluded that no other technique can recover all data from mobile devices (Grispos, Storer, & Bradley, 2011) (Maria Jones, Godfrey Winster, & Santhosh Kumar, 2019) . The cyber bullying and low level drug dealing criminal activities pattern are identified by using neural and neurofuzzy techniques on an original dataset (Barmpatsalou, Cruz, & Member, 2018). The work describes identifying malicious call activity on network over 9 billion records by using machine learning approach (Li, Xu, Liu, Ren, & Wu, n.d.). The author proposed two algorithms for removing identifying image forgery and also the source of image which was developed for strengthen the mobile forensics approach (Javier et al., 2017).

The authors (K K & Vinod, 2018) approached the crime detection process using Data Mining technique which consist of pre-processing, clustering, classification and visualization for providing good result.

The authors also used RF (Random forest) and NN (Neural networks) algorithms for crime classification whereas for clustering the crime, they used K-means algorithm. The WEKA tool has been used for analysing the crime data in India during the period of 2001 to 2012. The another authors (Yadav, Timbadia, Yadav, Vishwakarma, & Yadav, 2017) used India crime data during 2001 to 2014 for analysing the crime rate by using supervised, unsupervised and semi-supervised learning. The proposed work is analysed by feeding the historical data for training the data by using WEKA tool.

APPROACHES TO SOLVE MACHINE LEARNING TASKS

There are three types of learning algorithms are used to solve complex problems. They are as follows:

Machine Learning Algorithms in Cyber-Security

Let's analyse the different methods of machine learning techniques to solve the cyber security problems in real time scenario.

1. Supervised Learning

The supervised learning is defined as, the input and target data which is labelled/ known. For analysing, it should contain a greater number of training data with input and corresponding output. For example, consider a basket with 3 different types of fruits say apple, banana and cherry which have their own unique features. The algorithm will learn about their physical characters (size, colour, shape and fruit name) by training. During the testing process, the algorithm will be able to classify the fruit based on the size, colour, shape and Fruit name learned during training. Here, the author can assume that input variable is P and the output variable is X and the supervised learning mapping function from input to output variable is as follows:

$$X = f(P) \tag{1}$$

Generally, supervised learning is classified into two types. They are classification and regression. The algorithms included in supervised learning are: Liner Regression, Logistic Regression, Naïve Bayes, Decision Tree, Random Forest and Support Vector Machine.

a. Regression

Regression is also known as prediction which is used to predict the task. The best example for regression is the prediction of prices of the house, age, weather etc. In cyber security field, it can be applied to predict fraud detection. The feature in cyber security (e.g., the total amount of suspicious transaction, ID, location, etc.) is to determine and analyse the probability of fraudulent actions. The following algorithms can be applied for regression tasks.

i.   Liner Regression
ii. Polynomial Regression

iii. Decision Trees
iv. SVR (Support Vector Regression)
v. Random Forest

b. Classification

Classification consists of classifying the output variable with either or choices, such as, white or black; spam or ham, etc. In terms of cyber security domain, it means filtering of spam or ham emails, classifying fraudulent and authorized transaction data. The supervised learning approaches are suitable for classification where examples of certain groups are known. All classes should be defined in the beginning. Below mentioned algorithms are used for classification tasks.

i. Logistic Regression
ii. K-Nearest Neighbors (K-NN)
iii. Support Vector Machine (SVM)
iv. Kernel SVM
v. Naïve Bayes
vi. Decision Tree
vii. Random Forest

2. Unsupervised Learning

The next learning algorithm is unsupervised learning in which input is known whereas output is unlabelled/ unknown. From the example of the fruit, the output is not known. So, it should be categorized based on physical characters. The unsupervised learning is represented X as the input.

The unsupervised algorithms are clustering and association. The input variable P is given but no corresponding output will be present. Some algorithms in unsupervised algorithms are K-means clustering, dimensionality reduction, Principle Component Analysis (PCA) and Independent Component Analysis (ICA).

a. Clustering

Clustering is an unsupervised learning. In simple words, it can be described as grouping of same data points and which are used to find the groups in the particular data set. Social network analyses, pattern recognition, medical imaging, etc. are the applications of clustering algorithm. Identifying criminal activity by analysing GPS data logs, and to detect the fraudulent activities is one of its applications in cyber security domain. The following algorithms are used for clustering

i. K-means Cluster
ii. Bayesian Network
iii. Gaussian Mixture Model

b. Dimensionality Reduction

Dimensionality Reduction is mostly used in classification task and also for predictive modelling. When there are more data features, it's harder and difficult for data visualization. In the domain of cyber security tasks, face detection from crime scene, IoT botnet detection, etc.

i.   Principal Component Analysis
ii. Linear Discriminant Analysis

3. Reinforcement Learning

Reinforcement learning is all about decision making and it is known as semi-supervised learning. It can be used in neural network. Some applications of reinforcement learning are game programming, information retrieval, traffic system, etc. Reinforcement learning is comprised with many software's and machines to find out the better behavioural in a particular situation. It is different from supervised learning where supervised learning is trained with the correct answer but reinforcement and unsupervised learning are not trained with the correct answer. It will learn from it experience from the absence of answer model. So, the decision is dependent. The best example for reinforcement learning is chess game. The following are the applications of reinforcement learning.

i.   This type of learning model can be used in robotics for industrial automation.
ii.   To be used for automobile, aircraft control.
iii. Can be used for business planning and for data pre-processing in Machine Learning.

Figure 1. Architecture diagram of the system

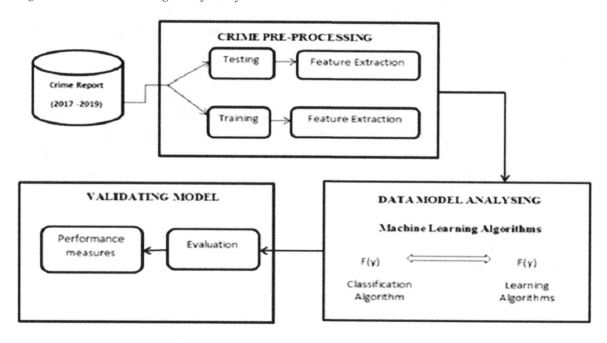

METHODOLOGY

In this session, a detailed proposed architecture is explained in figure.1. Once the report has been collected in CSV format, the noise has to be removed and report is pre-processed into training, testing and feature selection. Here, supervised learning is used for the implementation. Finally, the validation model is implemented with accuracy, precision, recall and F1* score.

ANALYSIS OF CHICAGO CRIME DATA

In the following sections, the authors describe the steps carried out in our analysis in Chicago data: (i) dataset preparation (ii) visualization and detection of crime occurrence (iii) algorithm analysis and (iv) training and evaluation of models.

Dataset Preparation

The data visualization technique is carried out with the help of python language and real time crime dataset is used for analysis. Most of the crime dataset is collected from UCI, Kaggle, Data.gov, Github repository. In this chapter, Chicago Crime Report has been gathered from the 'Chicago Data Portal' police department where crime reports from 2001 to the present with all the necessary details are reported. The full survey of Chicago crime is showed in figure 2. The authors have taken the crime report from 2017 to 2019 for analysis. All statistics data are stored in comma separated value (.CSV) file format. A detailed representation of crime dataset is found below:

Tuples = {Date, Block, IUCR, Primary Type, Description, Location, Arrest, Domestic, Beat, District, Ward, Community Ward, FBI Code, X Coordinates, Y Coordinates, Year, Latitude, Longitude, Location, Zip Code, Community Area, Wards, Police District and Police Beats }

Figure 2. Crime Rate report from 2001 to 2019 (till July 22 2019)

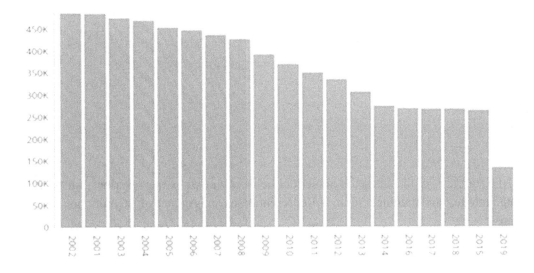

After importing the library, we read the dataset using function read_csv() function as shown in figure 3 to read the comma separated file for analysing in python.

Figure 3. Importing libraries and dataset

```
In [6]: import pandas as pd
        import numpy as np
        import matplotlib as plt
        %matplotlib inline
        df =pd.read_csv('C:\\Users\\USER\\Desktop\\Crime.csv')
```

Once the Crime dataset has been read, the author can view a few instances from corresponding data set. So, head() function is used to view the five rows from dataset which is shown in figure 4. The commands like head(5), tail (5) are used to display the first 5 rows and last 5 rows respectively from dataset.

Figure 4. Displaying output for head( )

	Date	Block	IUCR	Primary Type	Description	Location Description	Arrest	Domestic	Beat	District	...	Longitude	Location	Historical Wards 2003-2015	Zip Codes
0	07/15/2019 11:58:00 PM	047XX N MELVINA AVE	486	BATTERY	DOMESTIC BATTERY SIMPLE	RESIDENCE	False	True	1622.0	16.0	...	-87.781963	(41.967040741, -87.781963169)	25.0	21869.0
2	07/15/2019 11:54:00 PM	033XX W MONROE ST	1310	CRIMINAL DAMAGE	TO PROPERTY	APARTMENT	False	False	1124.0	11.0	...	-87.709674	(41.879607443, -87.709674313)	11.0	215572.0
3	07/15/2019 11:50:00 PM	012XX S UNION AVE	430	BATTERY	AGGRAVATED: OTHER DANG WEAPON	STREET	False	False	1232.0	12.0	...	-87.645069	(41.865819053, -87.645069093)	8.0	149170
4	07/15/2019 11:48:00 PM	079XX S DAMEN AVE	470	PUBLIC PEACE VIOLATION	RECKLESS CONDUCT	STREET	True	False	611.0	6.0	...	-87.673126	(41.750005014, -87.673125651)	6.0	215564.0
5	07/15/2019 11:45:00 PM	036XX N CLARK ST	810	THEFT	OVER $500	SIDEWALK	False	False	1923.0	19.0	...	-87.656854	(41.947626023, -87.656853521)	38.0	211860

5 rows × 27 columns

Next, the summary of the dataset in numerical fields is viewed by the describe() function. The data is separated into test and training. Figure 5. Representation can is done by hist() function where the size can by bins.

Figure 5. Shows the histogram of crime report

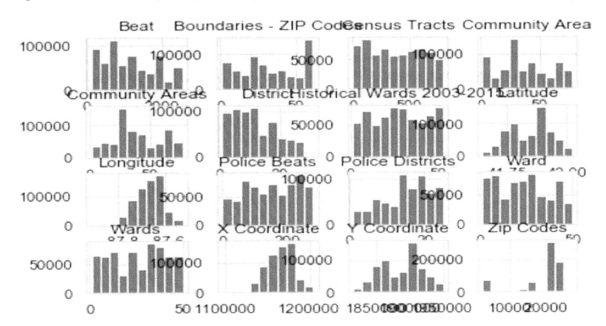

One of the finest visualization techniques is Heapmap which is handy to compare variables with respective to the values. Seaborn are based on matplotlib library. From seaborn library, this function creates a grid for all the instances with 2D input matrix with certain data and values to the heatmap and it exactly displays the output plot in the shape of a matrix as shown in figure 6.

Figure 6. Represents the heap map of testing set

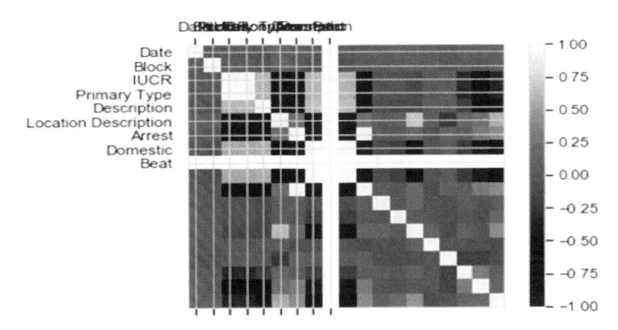

Visualization Crime Occurrence Detection

The authors are set to analyse crime report of Chicago data from 2017-2019. In figure 7, the authors grouped the crime report by year and plotted the crime occurrence from 2017 to 2019. To reduce processing time in analysing huge amount of data, a data analytics method is considered to visualize number of crimes occurred in three years as shown in figure 7. Each year, the crime rate had been increased.

Figure 7. Shows the total crime rate taken place in 3 years

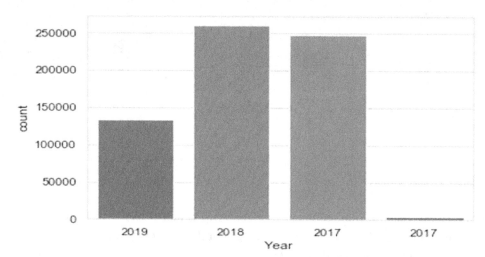

This work takes into consideration the analysis of arrest data and years from crime dataset. Figure 8 gives the detailed understanding of arrest rate with labels of true and false. The four years arrest data are taken into consideration to analysis the true and false data of crime report.

Figure 8. Displays the arrest data corresponding to year

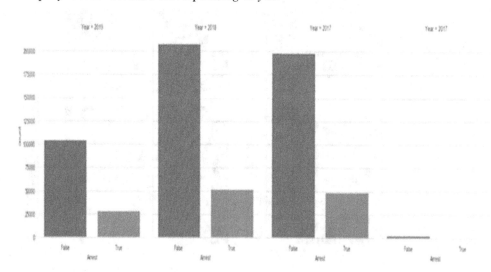

This analysis evidently provides the understanding of crimes committed by criminals where "Theft" & "Battery" have a highest committed count as shown in figure 9. However, the other crime types are also taken into considerations for analysing. Figure.9 gives pictorial representation of crime types from highest to lowest order.

Figure 9. Shows the number of crimes happened

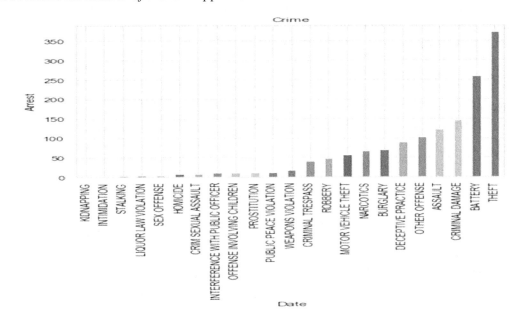

Algorithm Analysis

In this chapter, the authors have used classification algorithms from supervised learning. The detailed explanations of these algorithms are explained as follows:

1. Logistic Regression

Generally, logistics regression is statistical method for analysing the data with more independent variable. In a classification problem, the target variable y, can take only discrete values for given dataset of features x. The simple Logistic regression models can be calculated using the sigmoid function as shown in equation (2):

$$P(z) = \frac{1}{1 + e^{-y}} \tag{2}$$

In machine learning, it is used to identify the classification problem. Some examples of binary classification problems include:

- To identify Spam or ham email
- Fraudulent activities (yes/no)
- To Diagnosis a disease malignant or benign.

2. K-NN

K nearest neighbors or KNN Algorithm is also used for classification and regression task. In KNN, it classifies the data points based on the distance function and if the points of nearest neighbours increases, the accuracy of the system might be increases. The distance can be calculated by using Euclidean, Manhattan and Hamming distances,

3. Naïve Bayes

Naïve bayes algorithm is based on conditional probability where the best hypothesis (h) is selected from data set (c). It works based on assumption of independent variables and it be calculated by following equation (3):

$$P(h \mid c) = \frac{P(c \mid h) \times P(h)}{P(c)} \tag{3}$$

Where,
P(h|c) = The probability of h (hypothesis) given that c (crime rate) has occurred.
P(c|h) = The probability of crime occurring given that h has occurred
P(h) = The probability of hypothesis h occurring.
P(c) = The probability of crime event has occurring.

4. SVM

A Support Vector Machine is used for both classification and regression problems generally differentiating the classes by separating hyper plane. Hyper plane helps to classify the data points. SVM can be implemented by using kernel which can be calculated as shown in equation (4).

$$g(y) = B_i + \sum_{i=1}^{n} (x_0 \times (y \times y_i)) \tag{4}$$

However, there are three different types of kernels that are commonly used in support vector machine and they are as following equations (5), (6) and (7).
Liner Kernel

$$g(y,y_i) = \Sigma(y \times y_i) \tag{5}$$

Polynomial Kernel

$$k(y,y_i) = 1 + \Sigma(y \times y_i)^d \tag{6}$$

Radial Kernel

$$K(y, y_i) = e^{-gamma \times \sum (y - y_i^2)} \tag{7}$$

5. Decision Tree

A decision is also known as classifier in the form of tree where it has root node, children node and a leaf node. So it is called as tree structured classifier. In decision tree, initial starting condition goes with root node, based on the test, the next decision branch will be taken and it goes on till the leaf node. Here classification, regression and probability examples can be predicted.

6. Random Forest

Random Forest Algorithm can be used to solve both classification and regression problems. It is similar to decision tree working nature. The accuracy gets higher when more number of trees is in forest. Some applications in random forest algorithm are banking sector, e-commerce, Medicine, cyber security, etc.

Training and Evaluation of Models

The evaluation model of Chicago dataset is initially trained on 60% of dataset and 40% has been performed on the test dataset, which consists of the last three years of data (i.e., years 2017–2019). The cross-validation method is used to divide the data into k fields and it has to be repeated k times. Each time the k data will be taken for training and k-1 times for testing where k can be either 5 or 10 depending on datasets. Figure 10 observes the performance measure of evaluation. To this end, performance measures have been evaluated using accuracy, precision, recall and F1*score which is given in following equations (8), (9), (10) and (11). The evaluation metrics are used to calculate the accuracy of the crime detection and verify the efficiency of the algorithm by using TP (True Positive), FN (False Negative), TN (True Negative) and FP (False Positive). The percentage of accuracy is calculated by the ratio of correctly identified TP rate in crime rate over the total amount of crime sample as shown in the equation (8). The precision rate is calculated by the ratio of correctly identified crime rate by total sum of TP and FP as shown in the equation (9). The recall sample is calculated same like precision with the difference of ratio of TP over the sum of TP and FN as given in equation (10) and finally F1* Score is calculated with the prediction accuracy by using P and R as per the equation (11).

$$Accuracy = \left\langle \frac{TP_n + TN_n}{TP_n + FP_n + TN_n + FN_n} \right\rangle \tag{8}$$

$$\Pr ecision = \left\langle \frac{TP_n}{TP_n + FP_n} \right\rangle \tag{9}$$

$$\mathrm{Re}\,call = \left\langle \frac{TP_n}{TP_n + FN_n} \right\rangle \qquad (10)$$

$$F1 * Score = 2 * PR / (P + R) \qquad (11)$$

After collected the crime data from official website of Chicago police department, the data are pre-processed and analysed the pattern by using ML algorithms. Here, we used six supervised algorithm. Such as, logistic regression, K-NN, Support vector machine, decision tree and random forest. The evaluation result shows the logistic regression, SVM and random forest performs good with higher accuracy of 94 whereas KNN, Naïve Bayes and Decision tree gives the accuracy of 93, 39 and 85 respectively as shown in fig.10.

Figure 10. Present the final output for evaluation metrics

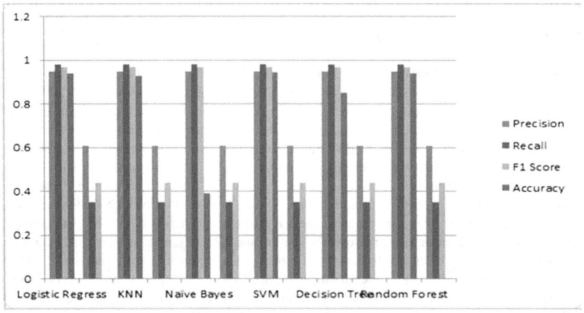

Analysing San-Francisco Crime Data

San Francisco was first evolved in the year 1849 during Gold Rush of California when the city expanded both in terms of land area and population. Since, the population were increasing rapidly; the social problems and crime rate are also increasing highly. Analysing and predicting the crime is one of the important factors to reduce the threat for people and also essential task for police department to find out the occurrence of crime. In this section, different approaches of data visualization have been used for analysing the San Francisco crime report for clear understanding about crime. Data visualization is the act of representing the information in visual formats for understanding the patterns and relationship between each data with visual images. Since data are increasing, human interpretation becomes tough and requires more time. So, machine learning task makes it easier to analyse the prediction and detection process. Predictive analysis provides the best evaluation of what comes in future.

Based on the historical data, the predictive analysis works to predict the unknown events of future. Some techniques like data mining, statistics, Artificial intelligence and machine learning modelling are used to analyse and predict the future. Generally, data visualization is not only essential for data scientists, it is important and necessary for all fields like marketing, industries, finance, institutions and so on. Detecting and predicting the crime rate is an essential task for improving the police department. So that, the threat ratio might be reduce. Here, the San Francisco crime data is analysed which is collected from kaggle repository. We have collected about 80,000 with 8 variables from 2003 to 2015 occurred crimes. The data set comprised with following observing features:

- Time and date
- Crime Incident
- Description of crime
- Week
- District
- Resolved Cases
- Address
- X and Y – Latitude and Longitude

From San Francisco dataset, there are about 25 varieties of crimes where murder, theft, assault, drug dealing are most frequent crimes. We concluded from Figure 11 that the top 15 crimes occurred in San Francisco city. So it is necessary to allocate more number of law enforcement resources to dealing with these types of crimes as they are more likely to occur. As part of our visualization analysis, we also analysed how the occurrences of crimes in districts wise as shown in figure 12. From analysis of figure 12, we could see that district of southern police department handled more cases than park police department.

Figure 11. Present the major crimes in San Francisco

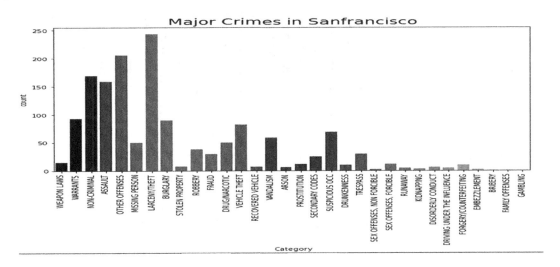

Figure 12. Present the final output for evaluation metrics

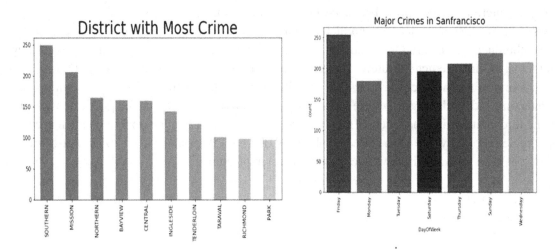

The crime distribution may be categarized as major crime occurred, hour, distict, week days and so on. Meanwhile, we were interested in analysing the when the crimes are occurring in and district and week days. For that, we have used matlabplot library. As shown in figure 12, southern police department has handled many cases whereas the most occurrence of crime has appeared on Friday when compared to other days.

The comparison between district and crime occurrence is categorized as shown in figure 13. Using panda crosstab library, the visualization is made and we can easily analysis the category of crime in district wise. The San Francisco crime seems to have top 5 crimes occurs as 66% of world records by statistical report (Abouelnaga, 2016).

Figure 13. The occurrence of crime in district and day wise

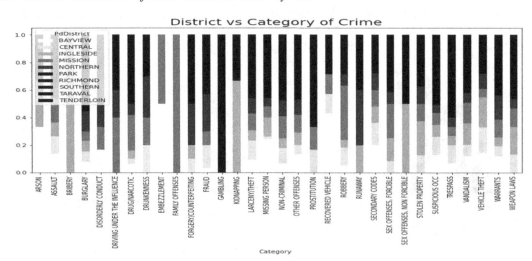

Analysing India Crime Data

There is a huge amount of violent and property crimes are readily increasing around the world. In this section, the effort is taken to analyse and represent the crime rate in India between the time intervals of 2001 to 2012. A comparison were done on IPC crimes for 1999 and 2006 committed crimes by (Dutta, Mousumi and Husain, 2009) . From analysing result, it shows that both violent and property related crimes are highly dominant when compared to others crimes in both years.

The crimes against person which includes like murder, kidnapping, homicide etc. are largely increasing and also economic crimes also get increasing. Meanwhile, crimes against women, property and public are fallen down by 2%. Due to challenges in crime, the law enforcement, justice, courts and other legal processing should incorporate the novel methods, techniques to prove the guilt. An analysis of crime will tend to provide essential policies implications and also this analysis will help to improve the understanding of Indian crime rate. Since, effective usage of communication technology, the illicit drug marketing also plays a major role in crime analysis which globally affects the ratio of crime rate.

Based on the report given by National Crime Records Bureau (NCRB), in India the crimes like burglary and robbery are reduced a period of 53 years with the percentage of 79.8 and 29 respectively whereas the other crimes like murder and kidnapping has been increased by 7% and 48% respectively. Crime analysis is defined as the identification of crime task and behavioural relationship with criminals. Some popular crimes in India are listed as: murder case that happened during 2005 at Uttar Pradesh, Terrorist attack during 2008 at Mumbai and many more (K K & Vinod, 2018). The Intelligence Bureau of India has published the annual crime report occurred in India during 1953. This intelligence system continuously collected the crime report and published the national crime report till 1986. The NCRB took over and started publishing systematic report with statistics for all states, union territories for six violent crimes. In this section, again data visualization technique is used with the help of python language and real time crime dataset is used for analysis. For analysing Indian crime, the real time dataset is collected from Kaggle. Indian Crime Report has been gathered from 2001 to the 2012 with all the necessary details are reported. All statistics data are stored in comma separated value (.CSV) file format. A detailed representation of crime dataset is found below:

Tuples = {state, district, year, murder, homicide, rape, kidnapping, cheating, burglary, auto theft, arson, cheating, dacoity, robbery, theft and so on}

From 2001 to 2012 the highest occurrence of crime is visualized in a line graph using matlapplot. From figure 14, we can understand that theft placed in higher degree where as many other crimes placed at lower degree. Almost all types of crimes are taken under consideration which will be useful for public to stay aware of criminals and for police department to find out the criminals.

The figure 15 represents the crime categorized based on the highest crime rate appeared in state wise in India. From figure 15, we can see that Madhya Pradesh has the highest range of crime occurred from 2001 to 2012 and also Lakshadweep is lowest range among all state.

The figure 16 represents the heapmap of crime appeared in state wise in India. The correlation concept represents covariance matrix.

Figure 14. Crime committed in India from 2001 to 2012

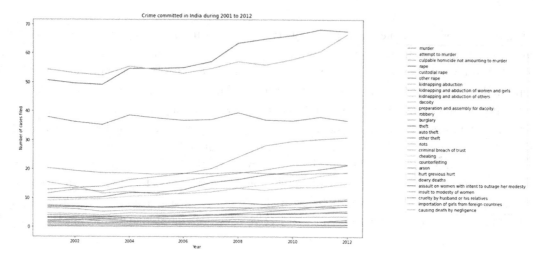

Figure 15. Highest crime states in India

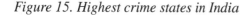

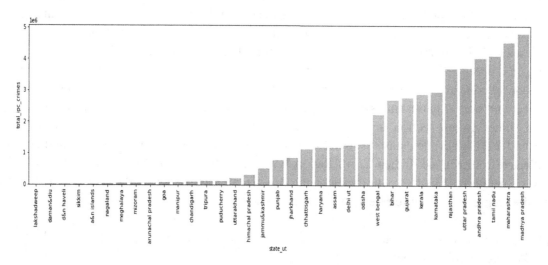

Figure 17 represents the crime categorized based year regarding the frequencies of crime on each year rate appeared in state wise in India and also represents the percentage of murder which is evaluates from 2001 to 2012. We can see that the percentage of murder cases has got highest peak in the year 2009. From frequency of crime rate figure 17, we can understand that each year the ratio of crime is increasing not have any evidences of slowing down.

ANALYSING SOCIAL MEDIA CONTENT

Over past few years, the social media has reached dramatic popularity for personal communication which makes people more convenient in sharing, posting their opinions, views and so on. The most popular sites are Facebook, YouTube, Instagram, Twitter and so on. Each social medial platform has millions of users which not only makes convenient to people but also allows user to connect the people around the globe with the help of internet facilities. These platforms are also useful for advertising, recruiting new employees, and so on. Social media provides a platform for good and bad means of communication. Sometimes, social media provides a way for cybercrime unlike traditional crimes and also used to prevent the crime from happening. Regardless of gender, age, many people are having account in social media networks to connect with people across the globe in virtually. Some people are having ten thousands of followers with multiple same account but at the same time, there is a chance of fake profiles also which is spam and with illegal content. These fake profilers are anonymous who probably commit the crimes like online threats, cyber harassments, cyber stalking, hacking, illegal transactions and many more.

Figure 16. Heap map of crimes occurred in India

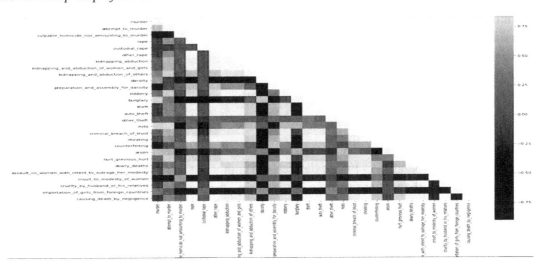

Figure 17. Frequency of crime occurred and percentage of murder case

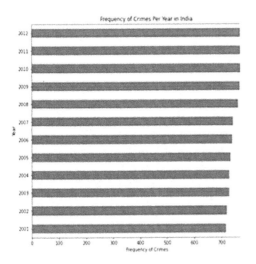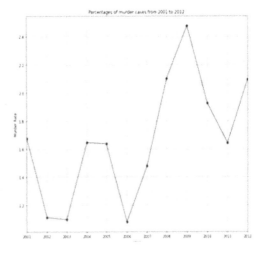

In this section, the author has introduced sentimental analysis for crime dataset in which it helps to determine the expression of the sentences, whether the text has positive, negative or neural about the specific topic. Sentimental analysis helps to monitor the social media activities to gain the knowledge about public, media opinion on specific events. In many social media network, sentimental analysis played an important role of analysing the events. The best example is twitter data by analysing users tweets on large scale events like election, pandemic outbreaks, national breaking news and so on. This analysis helps us to gain the knowledge about the unusual events in particular place and also able to understand the clear form of public opinion as information is collected from them. That's why sentimental analysis is also known as opinion mining. The social media content is always unstructured which are comprised with more noise like Hashtags, symbols, grammars, Emoji's and so on. For analysing social media content, we have used twitter data through sentimental analysis. Before the process starts, the pre-processing is the major step to eliminate the unnecessary noises. The following are the basic steps to remove the noises from text dat.

- Eliminating Stop Words
- Eliminating Punctuations
- Eliminating URLS
- Eliminating Hashtags
- Eliminating Symbols like (!, @, $, <, & and so on)
- Eliminating space, Emotions.

The author has collected the twitter data about 6000 data from UCI and kaggle repository. For identifying the sentence polarity in twitter dataset, the author has used positive and negative polarity. To identify and classify the twitter text based on polarity, the sentimental analysis is used. Figure 18 represents the number of data tweets placed in the dataset.

Figure 18. Number of Tweet data

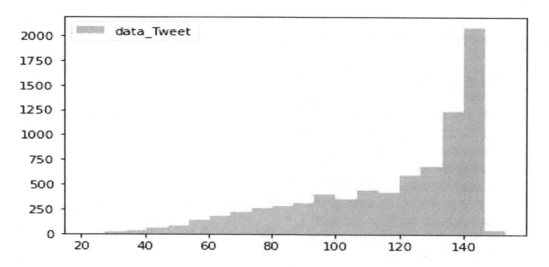

In figure.19 the twitter dataset is classified into two region like positive and negative polarity which represents the data is highly unbalanced due to positive polarity has 31.07% whereas negative polarity has 68.9%.

Figure 19. Tweet Classification based on positive and negative polarity

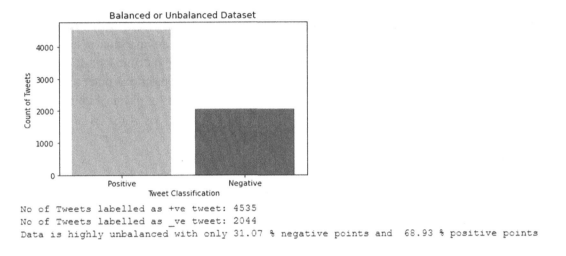

```
No of Tweets labelled as +ve tweet: 4535
No of Tweets labelled as _ve tweet: 2044
Data is highly unbalanced with only 31.07 % negative points and  68.93 % positive points
```

Figure 20 represents the top word frequencies from dataset. The wordcloud helps to identify the most used words where the size of each word represents their frequency. It can be replaced by score called TF-IDF to filter the common words from the text. The higher frequency words can arrange in cluster or cloud form in any type of arrangement based on programmer design.

Figure 20. Wordcloud based on top words

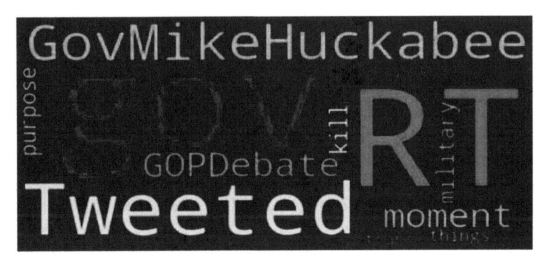

CONCLUSION AND FUTURE WORK

This chapter presents data analytics with general visualization and analysis of Crime Prediction in real world dataset of Chicago, San Francisco and India. Experimental evaluation and performance metrics were performed on training and testing data related to the crime report which showed that the methodology is presented with significant accuracy for Chicago data set. A literature review gives the detailed review of ML algorithms which were applied to different applications. Another deep learning approach called Time series analysis might be useful to predict the future occurrence of crime. In future, we intend to investigate forensics with machine learning technique which also plays an important role in identifying the future based on the historical data. As forensics plays a major role in crime identification, the accuracy evaluation is important to prove a law investigation case. A forensics examiner aims to identify the criminals who leave the traces of crime either as digital finger prints or physical items.

ACKNOWLEDGMENT

This research received no specific grant from any funding agency in the public, commercial, or not-for-profit sectors.

REFERENCES

Abouelnaga, Y. (2016). *San Francisco Crime Classification*. Retrieved from https://arxiv.org/abs/1607.03626

Al, N., Bryce, J., Franqueira, V. N. L., Marrington, A., & Read, J. C. (2019). Behavioural Digital Forensics Model : Embedding Behavioural Evidence Analysis into the Investigation of Digital Crimes. *Digital Investigation, 28*, 70–82. doi:10.1016/j.diin.2018.12.003

Barmpatsalou, K., Cruz, T., & Member, S. (2018). Mobile Forensic Data Analysis : Suspicious Pattern Detection in Mobile Evidence. *IEEE Access: Practical Innovations, Open Solutions, 6*, 59705–59727. doi:10.1109/ACCESS.2018.2875068

Britz, M. T. (n.d.). Computer Forensics and Cyber Crime (3rd ed.). Academic Press.

Carcillo, F., Borgne, Y. Le, Caelen, O., & Kessaci, Y. (2019). Combining unsupervised and supervised learning in credit card fraud detection. *Information Sciences*. doi:10.1016/j.ins.2019.05.042

Carcillo, F., Dal, A., Borgne, Y. Le, Caelen, O., Mazzer, Y., & Bontempi, G. (2018). *SCARFF : A scalable framework for streaming credit card fraud detection with spark*. doi:10.1016/j.inffus.2017.09.005

Catlett, C., Cesario, E., Talia, D., & Vinci, A. (2019). Spatio-temporal crime predictions in smart cities : A data-driven approach and experiments. *Pervasive and Mobile Computing, 53*, 62–74. doi:10.1016/j.pmcj.2019.01.003

Comput, J. P. D., Kozik, R., Choraś, M., Ficco, M., & Palmieri, F. (2018). A scalable distributed machine learning approach for attack detection in edge computing environments. *Journal of Parallel and Distributed Computing*, *119*, 18–26. doi:10.1016/j.jpdc.2018.03.006

Das, P., & Das, A. K. (2019). Knowledge-Based Systems Graph-based clustering of extracted paraphrases for labelling crime. *Knowledge-Based Systems*, *179*, 55–76. doi:10.1016/j.knosys.2019.05.004

Dutta, M., & Husain, Z. (2009). *Munich Personal RePEc Archive Determinants of crime rates : Crime Deterrence and Growth*. Academic Press.

Dwi, N., Cahyani, W., Hidayah, N., Rahman, A., Glisson, W. B., & Choo, K. R. (2016). The Role of Mobile Forensics in Terrorism Investigations Involving the Use of Cloud Storage Service and Communication Apps. *Mobile Networks and Applications*. Advance online publication. doi:10.100711036-016-0791-8

Frommholz, I., Martin, H. M., Zinnar, P., Mitul, G., & Emma, S. (2016). *On Textual Analysis and Machine Learning for Cyberstalking Detection*. doi:10.100713222-016-0221-x

Gbenga, E., Stephen, J., Chiroma, H., Olusola, A., & Emmanuel, O. (2019). *Heliyon Machine learning for email spam filtering : review, approaches and open research problems*. doi:10.1016/j.heliyon.2019. e01802

Ghiassi, M., & Lee, S. (2018). A domain transferable lexicon set for Twitter sentiment analysis using a supervised machine learning approach. *Expert Systems with Applications*, *106*, 197–216. doi:10.1016/j. eswa.2018.04.006

Grispos, G., Storer, T., & Bradley, W. (2011). A comparison of forensic evidence recovery techniques for a windows mobile smart phone. *Digital Investigation*, *8*(1), 23–36. doi:10.1016/j.diin.2011.05.016

Javier, L., Villalba, G., Lucila, A., Orozco, S., Rosales, J., & Hernandez-castro, J. (2017). A PRNU-based counter-forensic method to manipulate smartphone image source identification techniques. *Future Generation Computer Systems*, *76*, 418–427. doi:10.1016/j.future.2016.11.007

Jones, G. M., Geoferla, L. A., & Winster, S. G. (2020). *A Heuristic Research on Detecting Suspicious Malware Pattern in Mobile Environment*. Academic Press.

Jones, G. M., & Winster, S. G. (2017). Forensics Analysis On Smart Phones Using Mobile Forensics Tools. *International Journal of Computational Intelligence Research*, *13*(8), 1859–1869.

Jurgovsky, J., Granitzer, M., Ziegler, K., Calabretto, S., Portier, P., He-guelton, L., & Caelen, O. (2018). Sequence classification for credit-card fraud detection. *Expert Systems with Applications*, *100*, 234–245. doi:10.1016/j.eswa.2018.01.037

K. K., D., & Vinod, S. (2018). Crime analysis in India using data mining techniques. *International Journal of Engineering & Technology, 7*(2.6), 253. doi:10.14419/ijet.v7i2.6.10779

Karie, N. M., Kebande, V. R., & Venter, H. S. (2019). Forensic Science International : Synergy Diverging deep learning cognitive computing techniques into cyber forensics. *Forensic Science International: Synergy*, *1*, 61–67. doi:10.1016/j.fsisyn.2019.03.006 PMID:32411955

Katzir, Z., & Elovici, Y. (2018). *Quantifying the resilience of machine learning classifiers used for cyber security.* doi:10.1016/j.eswa.2017.09.053

Li, H., Xu, X., Liu, C., Ren, T., & Wu, K. (n.d.). *A Machine Learning Approach To Prevent Malicious Calls Over Telephony Networks.* Academic Press.

Liew, S. W., Fazlida, N., Sani, M., Abdullah, M. T., Yaakob, R., & Sharum, M. Y. (2019). An effective security alert mechanism for real-time phishing tweet detection on Twitter. *Computers & Security, 83,* 201–207. doi:10.1016/j.cose.2019.02.004

Maria Jones, G., Godfrey Winster, S., & Santhosh Kumar, S. V. N. (2019). *Analysis of mobile environment for ensuring cyber-security in IoT-based digital forensics* (Vol. 900). Advances in Intelligent Systems and Computing. doi:10.1007/978-981-13-3600-3_14

Méndez, J. R., Cotos-yañez, T. R., & Ruano-ordás, D. (2019). A new semantic-based feature selection method for spam filtering. *Applied Soft Computing, 76,* 89–104. doi:10.1016/j.asoc.2018.12.008

Mohler, G. (2014). Marked point process hotspot maps for homicide and gun crime prediction in Chicago . *International Journal of Forecasting, 30*(3), 491–497. doi:10.1016/j.ijforecast.2014.01.004

Mondal, S., & Bours, P. (2018). Journal of Information Security and Applications A continuous combination of security & forensics for mobile devices. *Journal of Information Security and Applications, 40,* 63–77. doi:10.1016/j.jisa.2018.03.001

Nami, S., & Shajari, M. (2018). Cost-sensitive payment card fraud detection based on dynamic random forest and k -nearest neighbors. *Expert Systems with Applications, 110,* 381–392. doi:10.1016/j.eswa.2018.06.011

Nguyen, G., Minh, B., Tran, D., & Hluchy, L. (2018). Data & Knowledge Engineering A heuristics approach to mine behavioural data logs in mobile malware detection system. *Data & Knowledge Engineering, 115*(January), 129–151. doi:10.1016/j.datak.2018.03.002

Qazi, N., & William, W. B. L. (2019). *An interactive human centered data science approach towards crime pattern analysis.* doi:10.1016/j.ipm.2019.102066

Ryman-tubb, N. F., Krause, P., & Garn, W. (2018). Engineering Applications of Artificial Intelligence How Artificial Intelligence and machine learning research impacts payment card fraud detection : A survey and industry benchmark. *Engineering Applications of Artificial Intelligence, 76*(November), 130–157. doi:10.1016/j.engappai.2018.07.008

Saeid, M., Rezvan, M., & Barekatain, M. (2018). Machine learning for internet of things data analysis : A survey. *Digital Communications and Networks, 4*(3), 161–175. doi:10.1016/j.dcan.2017.10.002

Violent Crime - Crime in the United States 2009. (n.d.). Retrieved March 14, 2020, from https://www2.fbi.gov/ucr/cius2009/offenses/violent_crime/index.html

Wei, R., Sunny, X., & Liu, X. (2019). Telematics and Informatics Examining the perceptual and behavioral effects of mobile internet fraud : A social network approach. *Telematics and Informatics, 41*(April), 103–113. doi:10.1016/j.tele.2019.04.002

Yadav, S., Timbadia, M., Yadav, A., Vishwakarma, R., & Yadav, N. (2017). Crime pattern detection, analysis & prediction. *Proceedings of the International Conference on Electronics, Communication and Aerospace Technology, ICECA 2017,* 225–230. 10.1109/ICECA.2017.8203676

Zhao, R., Yan, R., Chen, Z., Mao, K., Wang, P., & Gao, R. X. (2019). Deep learning and its applications to machine health monitoring. *Mechanical Systems and Signal Processing, 115,* 213–237. doi:10.1016/j.ymssp.2018.05.050

Chapter 4
Analysis on Indian Stock Market Prediction Using Deep Learning Models

Kalaivani Karuppiah

PSNA College of Engineering and Technology, India

Umamaheswari N.

PSNA College of Engineering and Technology, India

Venkatesh R.

PSNA College of Engineering and Technology, India

ABSTRACT

The neural network is one of the best data mining techniques that have been used by researchers in different areas for the past 10 years. Analysis on Indian stock market prediction using deep learning models plays a very important role in today's economy. In this chapter, various deep learning architectures such as multilayer perceptron, recurrent neural networks, long short -term memory, and convolutional neural network help to predict the stock market prediction. There are two different stock market price companies, namely National Stock Exchange and New York Stock Exchange, are used for analyzing the day-wise closing price used for comparing different techniques such as neural network, multilayer perceptron, and so on. Both the NSE and NYSE share their common details, and they are compared with various existing models. When compared with the previous existing models, neural networks obtain higher accuracy, and their experimental result is shown in betterment compared with existing techniques.

INTRODUCTION

Stock marketplace is an area in which publicly-held corporations share their shopping for and promoting of stocks takes location. Those percentage markets may be defined in kinds consisting of number one & secondary market. Number one marketplace is the markets wherein new problems are brought

DOI: 10.4018/978-1-7998-2566-1.ch004

thru preliminary public services. Secondary marketplace is nothing however in which investors change their securities on their own. Inventory market couldn't are expecting also they have non-linear time collection statistics. At a selected series of time the contemporary reputation of proportion market are diagnosed due to high fluctuation (Hamzaebi et al., 2009). Linear models such as automobile regression, car regressive moving average, car regressive integrated transferring common, convolutional neural network and so forth (Zhang, 2003)[3].the principle problems with those models are that they paintings only for precise time association records; i.e the version identified for a particular corporation might not perform nicely for another. Due to the difficult to understand and unforeseeable nature of financial alternate, securities trade estimating is going for broke contrasted with specific areas. Its miles a standout amongst the greatest motives in the back of the problem in securities alternate forecast. Right here is the area the usage of profound learning fashions in budgetary (Heaton et al., 2017) looking ahead to comes in. Profound neural gadget was given its name because of the usage of neural machine engineering in dl fashions. It is likewise referred to as ann. Anns are tremendous approximators and they are suit to take in and sum up for a truth. Beneficial use of ann in figuring out problems is extraordinarily fruitful because of the accompanying attributes.

For the beyond few a long term, ANN has been used for inventory marketplace prediction. Contrast examine of diverse DL fashions of stock marketplace prediction has already been completed as we're capable of see in (Selvin et al., 2017). Coskun Hamzacebi has experimented forecasting the use of iterative and directive strategies (Hamzaebi et al., 2009). Ajith Kumar Rout et.Al made use of a low complexity recurrent neural network for inventory marketplace prediction (Rout et al., 2015).Yunus Yetis et.Al carried out ANN to predict NASDAQ's (country wide affiliation of Securities dealers automatic Quotations) inventory price with given input parameter of stock market (Yetis et al., 2014). Roman et.Al completed an evaluation on more than one stock marketplace goes returned using lower returned propagation and RNN (Roman & Jameel, 1996). Neini et.Al con- ducted a assessment look at amongst Feed forward MLP an Elman Recurrent network for predicting inventory charge of organization (Jia, 2016). Mizuno et.Al performed neural networks to technical assessment as a prediction model (Mizuno et al., 1998). Guresen in 2011 had finished a examine to recognize approximately the effectiveness of ANN in stock market forecasting (). In (), they explored the interdependency among inventory extent and inventory rate on a wonderful form of nifty 50 indexed companies. In (), Batres-Estrada explains about distinct applications of DL fashions on time collection assessment. X Ding et.Al in () con- ducted a take a look at on aggregate of herbal language processing (NLP) and financial time collection assessment. In (), they used ML algorithms like least rectangular help Vector tool (LSSVM) and Particle Swarm Optimization (PSO) for stock marketplace prediction. In (), deals with multi-level fuzzy inference and wavelet rework for forecasting stock trends. Right here the quick-term capabilities present in the stock style are described the use of wavelet redecorate.

ARTIFICIAL NEURAL NETWORK

ANN (Wang et al., 2011) is a computational shape which performs alongside these lines to that of organic neurons (Moghaddam et al., 2016). Its miles intended to differentiate a hidden sample from information and to sum up from it. ANN's are taken into consideration as non-direct real records equipment (Rather et al., 2015). The complex connection amongst yields and records resources may be proven utilizing ANN. The primary favorable role of ANN is its potential to take within the hidden examples from the statistics, where the more part of the ordinary techniques comes up brief (Zhang et al., 1998). Normally, ANN incorporates of three layers especially enter layer, shrouded layer and yield layer. Non-direct enactment capacities are applied in every one of the hubs in protected up just as yield layers barring enter layer. Every hub inside the records layer is associated with every neuron in the succeeding concealed layer pursued by using yield layer.

Figure 1. Artificial neuron

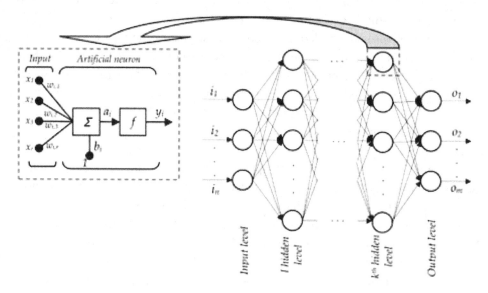

The above figure demonstrates a fake neuron which is a basic preparing unit propelled from the organic neuron (Moghaddam et al., 2016) (Menon et al., 2016). The neuron has 'm' inputs (xi) and each information is associated with the neuron by weighted connection (wi) . Here the neuron wholes up the sources of info increased by the loads utilizing the underneath condition

$$NN = \Sigma\, x_i w_i + C$$

Where NN is the net sum and C is the threshold value. Activation Function is nothing but finding a function with the help of net sum.

Artificial Neuron = F(A) (Activation Function)

The given inputs are real number. The value C sometimes considered as an imaginary input such as x0 = +1 and a connection weight w0 for the simplicity of computation.

FEED FORWARD NETWORK

Feed forward machine (Moghaddam et al., 2016) otherwise called MLP is a case of an essential neural gadget. Every statistics neuron is hooked up to the succeeding concealed layer neurons thru a weighted matrix wiki. A community has three locations of layers enter, protected up and yield layers (Roman & Jameel, 1996). Fake neurons are the ones which can be available inside the covered up and yield layer (Roman & Jameel, 1996) that's in any other case known as (Vatsal, 2007). Every any such neurons get contributions from a past layer. Neurons within the gadget are not related to the neurons in a similar layer but they're related to neurons inside the following layer. Condition for initiation artwork (Wang et al., 2011) of an ith hid neuron is given by way of

$$h_i = f(u_i) = f\left(\sum_{k=0}^{K} w_{ki} x_k \right)$$

FNNs are a sort of NN in which associations among units don't travel in a circle but in a single co-ordinated way. Ordinarily, an FNN comprises of an input layer of neurons (hubs), one or more covered up layers of neurons, and a yield layer of neurons. The input layer and yield layer frame bookends for covered up layers of neurons. Signals are proliferated from the input layer to hidden neurons and after that onto yield neurons, which output responses of the arrange to exterior clients. That's, signals as it were move in a forward course on a layer-by-layer premise.

Figure 2. Recurrent neural networks

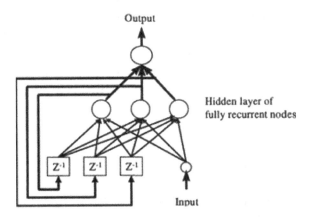

RECURRENT NEURAL NETWORK

Diverse to MLP, RNN (Jia, 2016) takes contribution from two resources; one is from the present and the other from an earlier time. Statistics from these two resources are utilized to pick out how they reply to the new association of facts. That is completed with the assistance of a complaint circle where yield at every second is a contribution to the following minute. Here we can say that the repetitive neural device has memory. Every records arrangement has plenty of data and these records are positioned away in the concealed circumstance of repetitive structures. This concealed facts is recursively applied within the machine as it clears ahead to manipulate every other precedent. Fig 2.2 demonstrates a pictorial portrayal of repetitive neural networks.

Contribution to concealed layer condition is given as:

$$h_t = g_n(W_{xh} + W_{hh}h_{t-1} + b_h)$$

LONG SHORT TERM MEMORY

Because of their adequacy in expansive all the way down to earth applications, LSTM systems are becoming an abundance of inclusion in logical diaries, specialized internet web sites, and usage publications. Be that as it can, in plenty of articles, the derivation recipes for the LSTM machine and its parent, RNN, are expressed aphoristically, on the equal time as the practice equations are ignored thru and via. Moreover, the method of "unrolling" a RNN is automatically brought without avocation in the course of the writing. The goal of this paper is to make clear the simple RNN and LSTM necessities in a solitary archive. Attracting from mind sign getting ready, we officially infer the equal antique RNN detailing from differential situations. We at that component suggest and know-how an genuine articulation, which yields the RNN unrolling approach. We likewise audit the troubles with getting ready the same old RNN and cope with them via using converting the RNN into the "Vanilla LSTM" set up via a improvement of wise contentions. We provide all conditions regarding the LSTM framework together with genuine depictions of its constituent substances. Even though flighty, our selection of documentation and the approach for introducing the LSTM framework underlines simplicity of comprehension. As an detail of the exam, we distinguish new possibilities to improve the LSTM framework and consolidate these augmentations into the Vanilla LSTM put together, turning in the most massive LSTM version thus far. The intention peruse has truly been supplied to rnns and LSTM arranges through numerous reachable property and is available to a desire academic approach. A machine analyzing expert looking for path for executing our new multiplied LSTM model in programming for experimentation and studies will discover the bits of bdd5b54adb3c84011c7516ef3ab47e54 and determinations on this educational exercising widespread also.

METHODOLOGY

Dataset is taken from notably exchanged hundreds of 3 wonderful regions which might be automobile, Banking and IT divisions from NSE. The concerning stocks from these divisions are Maruti, Axis bank, and Hcltech. Each carries records like stock photograph, stock arrangement, inventory date and beyond shutting, beginning, excessive, low, closing, shutting and ordinary charges, all out exchanged quantity, turnover and number of exchanges. From those datasets, we dispose of just the day-wise shutting price of each inventory for the reason that day smart inventory cost is preferred on account that financial experts determine choice on purchasing which inventory or relinquishing which stock depending on the give up fee of the market. This normalized statistics changed into given as the center to the community in a window length of two hundred to are waiting for 10 days in future. And the output from the network turned into subjected to a De-normalization manner for acquiring authentic anticipated values. The train-

Figure 3. Long short-term memory

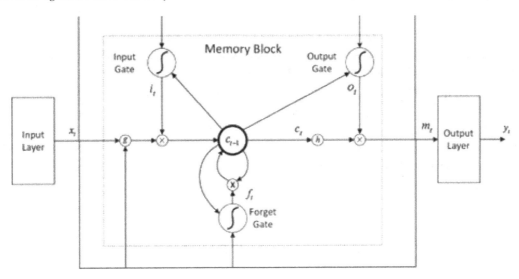

ing of community changed into completed for a thousand epochs. The window length became constant thru acting blunders calculation on each window length which varies from 50 to 250. Among this, the window length of 200 resulted minimum error than exclusive window sizes.

WINDOW size fixing. The desk 1 shows the MAPE (imply Absolute percentage blunders) obtained for distinctive window size and prediction days. The topmost row with values 100, 200, a hundred, two hundred and 500 represents window size and 15, 25, 35, forty inside the first column represents the prediction days. From the desk, it's far clear that minimal MAPE is obtained with window size 200 for 10 days prediction. So here we restore our window size as two hundred with 10 days prediction.

Table 1. Table elaborating window size and interval of prediction days

Pred:days	100	200	300	400	500
10	4.0	4.34	4.62	4.32	4.18
20	6.53	6.05	5.88	5.61	5.16
30	6.49	7.84	6.97	5.11	5.86
40	9.65	9.4	6.84	5.86	7.06

Predicted output changed into subjected to intend absolute percentage error for calculating the error within the anticipated output. Equation for calculating MAPE is given under

$$\frac{1}{n}\sum\left(\frac{|\,Actual - Forecast\,|}{|\,Actual\,|}\right)$$

Therefore through the 'Actual' values are the labels and 'Forecast' values are the predicted values.

RESULTS AND DISCUSSION

Here we have carried out the analysis on two stock markets information and they are NSE and NYSE. For this, we had used 4 forms of deep neural networks named MLP, RNN, LSTM, and CNN. All those networks had been skilled with NSE facts of Tata cars which belong to the automobile quarter. And those networks subjected to test using the facts from NSE and NYSE. For NSE we pick statistics from automobile, monetary, IT sectors and for NYSE we select financial and petroleum sectors. For the comparison among linear and non-linear fashions, we've used ARIMA model which is a linear version.

On these paintings we've got taken into consideration four hundred days prediction for ARIMA and neural community. The motive at the back of this was to examine the overall performance of ARIMA and neural network for a particular time period. The consequences acquired are tabulated in table 2 which is given below,

Table 2. MAPE incurred during the prediction of MARUTI, HCL and AXIS BANK NSE values using ARIMA model for the duration of 450 days

COMPANY	MAPE
MARUTI	11.77
HCL	15.70
AXIS BANK	10.75

Table 3 indicates the MAPE received via the neural community for four hundred days prediction. Evaluating table 2 and table three results indicates that the overall performance of neural network architecture is higher than that of ARIMA. This will be due to the cause that ARIMA fails to become aware of the non-linearity current with within the facts, wherein as neural network architectures can pick out the non-linear trends present with within the data.

Table 3. MAPE incurred during the prediction of MARUTI, HCL and AXIS BANK NSE values using DL network for the duration of 450 days

COMPANY	RNN	LSTM	CNN	MLP
MARUTI	5.92	6.13	4.05	4.91
HCL	5.50	5.62	4.50	3.95
AXIS BANK	11.74	4.98	5.32	5.6

Table 4. MAPE incurred during the prediction of MARUTI, HCL and AXIS BANK NSE values using DL network

COMPANY	RNN	LSTM	CNN	MLP
MARUTI	7.96	6.47	5.46	6.39
HCL	9.63	7.07	7.52	8.48
AXIS BANK	10.37	9.23	8.04	9.20

In case of Maruti, fig (4a) shows the MLP network which becomes successful in taking pictures the sample because it makes use of the cutting-edge window facts for the prediction. However in case of fig(4b) and fig(5a) among the length of 1500 and 2300 days RNN and LSTM didn't pick out the seasonal pattern which may be considered as trade in conduct of device. In fig(5b) CNN nearly captured the sample since it debts best the information in a selected window.

Figure 4. (a) Real and Predicted values of MARUTI stock using MLP;(b) Real and Predicted values of MARUTI stock using RNN

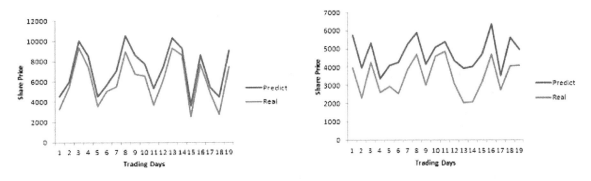

Figure 5. (a) Real and Predicted values of MARUTI stock using LSTM ; (b) Real and Predicted values of MARUTI stock using CNN

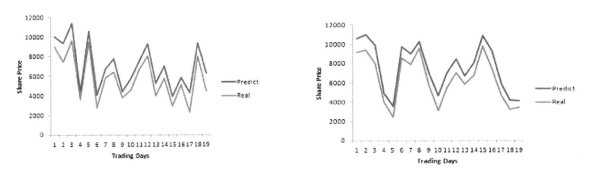

In case of AXIS financial institution, from fig(4a), MLP community identified the pattern at the beginning but on attaining the term among 1400 and 1700 days it did not seize the sample. Similar results may be discovered in fig(5b) where RNN captured the sample at the preliminary degree but on accomplishing the term among 1300 and 1600 it fails to identify the sample. From fig(5a) and fig(5b), LSTM and CNN, LSTM community isn't figuring out the sample for time intervals between 200 and 500 days in which as CNN almost captured the sample besides at the period among 1600 and 1800 days.

Figure 6. (a) Real and Predicted values of HCLTECH stock using MLP;(b) Real and Predicted values of HCLTECH stock using RNN

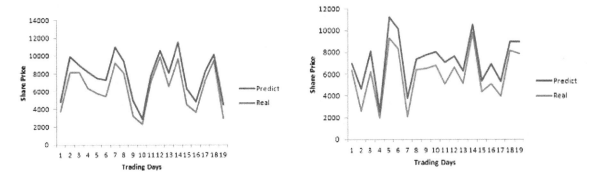

In case of HCLTECH, fig (6a), MLP network is a hit in shooting the seasonal sample however between the term 1600 and 1900 days it did not seize the pattern. In fig(6b) RNN was almost a success in identifying the pattern where as fig(7a) and fig(7b) indicates that LSTM and CNN fail to capture change in device among the duration 1400 and 1800 days.

Figure 7. (a) Real and Predicted values of HCLTECH stock using LSTM; (b) Real and Predicted values of HCLTECH stock using CNN

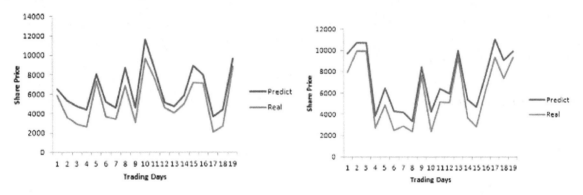

CONCLUSION

In this proposed work we used four DL architectures for the inventory rate prediction of NSE and NYSE, which is probably exceptional important inventory markets inside the worldwide. Right here we knowledgeable 4 networks MLP, RNN, LSTM and CNN with the inventory charge of TATA cars from NSE. The models acquired have been used for predicting the inventory price of MARUTI, HCL and AXIS economic group from NSE inventory marketplace and additionally for predicting the stock rate of financial group OF America (BAC) and CHESAPEAK energy (CHK) from NYSE. From the end result acquired, its miles clear that the models are able to identifying the patterns present in every the inventory markets. This shows that there exist an underlying dynamics, not unusual to every the inventory markets. Linear fashions like ARIMA are a univariate time collection prediction and as a end result they may be not capable of figuring out underlying dynamics internal numerous time collections. From the end result, we are in a position to complete that DL models are outperforming ARIMA model. Within the proposed paintings, CNN has achieved better than distinctive 3 networks as its miles capable of taking photographs the abrupt modifications in the device due to the fact a selected window is used for predicting the subsequent immediately. This painting hasn't explored the gain of the use of a hybrid community which mixes networks to make a version for prediction.

REFERENCES

Glorot, X., Bordes, A., & Bengio, Y. (2011, June). Deep sparse rectifier neural networks. In *Proceedings of the Fourteenth International Conference on Artificial Intelligence and Statistics* (pp. 315-323). Academic Press.

Hamzaebi, C., Akay, D., & Kutay, F. (2009). Comparison of direct and iterative artificial neural network forecast approachesin multi-periodic time series forecasting. *Expert Systems with Applications*, *36*(2), 3839–3844. doi:10.1016/j.eswa.2008.02.042

Heaton, J. B., Polson, N. G., & Witte, J. H. (2017). Deep learning for finance: Deep portfolios. *Applied Stochastic Models in Business and Industry*, *33*(1), 3–12. doi:10.1002/asmb.2209

Jia, H. (2016). *Investigation into the effectiveness of long short term memory networks for stock price prediction.* arXiv preprint arXiv:1603.07893

Menon, V. K., Vasireddy, N. C., Jami, S. A., Pedamallu, V. T. N., Sureshkumar, V., & Soman, K. P. (2016, June). Bulk Price ForecastingUsing Spark over NSE Data Set. *International Conference on Data Mining and Big Data*, 137-146. 10.1007/978-3-319-40973-3_13

Mizuno, H., Kosaka, M., Yajima, H., & Komoda, N. (1998). Application of neural network to technical analysis of stock market prediction. *Studies in Informatics and Control*, *7*(3), 111–120.

Moghaddam, A. H., Moghaddam, M. H., & Esfandyari, M. (2016). Stock market index prediction using artificial neural network. *Journal of Economics, Finance and Administrative Science*, *21*(41), 89–93. doi:10.1016/j.jefas.2016.07.002

Rather, A. M., Agarwal, A., & Sastry, V. N. (2015). Recurrent neural network and a hybrid model for prediction of stock returns. *Expert Systems with Applications*, *42*(6), 3234–3241. doi:10.1016/j. eswa.2014.12.003

Roman, J., & Jameel, A. (1996). Backpropagation and recurrent neural networks in financial analysis of multiple stock market returns. *Twenty-Ninth Hawaii International Conference on System Sciences*, *2*, 454-460.

Rout, A. K., Dash, P. K., Dash, R., & Bisoi, R. (2015). Forecasting financial time series using a low complexity recurrent neural network and evolutionary learning approach. *Journal of King Saud University-Computer and Information Sciences*, *29*(4), 536–552. doi:10.1016/j.jksuci.2015.06.002

Selvin, S., Vinayakumar, R., Gopalakrishnan, E. A., Menon, V. K., & Soman, K. P. (2017). Stock price prediction using LSTM, RNN and CNN-sliding window model. *International Conference on Advances in Computing, Communications and Informatics*, 1643-1647. 10.1109/ICACCI.2017.8126078

Sen, J. (2018). *Stock Price Prediction Using Machine Learning and Deep Learning Frameworks.* . doi:10.13140/RG.2.2.35704.49923

Vatsal, H. S. (2007). *Machine learning techniques for stock prediction.* www.vatsals.com

Wang, J. Z., Wang, J. J., Zhang, Z. G., & Guo, S. P. (2011). Forecasting stock indices with back propagation neural network. *Expert Systems with Applications*, *38*(11), 14346–14355. doi:10.1016/j.eswa.2011.04.222

Yetis, Y., Kaplan, H., & Jamshidi, M. (2014). Stock market prediction by using artificial neural network. *World Automation Congress (WAC)*, 718-722. 10.1109/WAC.2014.6936118

Zhang, G., Patuwo, B. E., & Hu, M. Y. (1998). Forecasting with artificial neural networks: The state of the art. *International Journal of Forecasting*, *14*(1), 35–62. doi:10.1016/S0169-2070(97)00044-7

Zhang, G. P. (2003). Time series forecasting using a hybrid ARIMA and neural network model. *Neurocomputing*, *50*, 159–175. doi:10.1016/S0925-2312(01)00702-0

Chapter 5
Application of Data Analytics in Emerging Fields

Sujaritha M.
Sri Krishna College of Engineering and Technology, India

Kavitha M.
Sri Krishna College of Engineering and Technology, India

Fenila Naomi J.
Sri Krishna College of Engineering and Technology, India

ABSTRACT

Data, which is available in abundance and in accessible forms, if analyzed in an efficient manner, unfolds many patterns and promising solutions. The present world is moving from the information age to the digital age, entering a new era of analytics. Whatever the end user does is recorded and stored. The purpose of data analytics is to make the "best out of waste." Analytics often employs advanced statistical techniques (logistic regression, multivariate regression, time series analysis, etc.) to derive meaning from data. There are essentially two kinds of analytics: 1) descriptive analytics and 2) predictive analytics. Descriptive analytics describes what has happened in the past. Predictive analytics predicts what will happen in the future.

INTRODUCTION

IDC predicts that by 2025, the total amount of digital data created worldwide will rise to 175 zettabytes (from approximately 40 zettabytes in 2019), ballooned by the growing number of devices and sensors. The mission of this chapter is to make a clear understanding of why Analytics? Where to use Analytics? Outcome of Analytics?

This Chapter provides in-depth foundation level knowledge that enables reader of this chapter to efficiently provide grounding in basic and advanced methods to Analytics and tools, including MapReduce and Hadoop in different field of study. The rate in which data is exponentially growing has

DOI: 10.4018/978-1-7998-2566-1.ch005

led to the evolvement of many technologies to better utilize this data for timely and accurate decision making with the help of Analytics. This chapter adds a comprehensive coverage of Analytic algorithms specially meant for analyzing data at an in-depth level. Decision trees, Support Vector machines and Neural networks are considered to be highly effective in analyzing complex data for different domain. Variety of solutions can be provided for storing, managing, accessing, protecting, securing, sharing and optimizing the information once analytics are properly fitted. Different Analytics tools are used some are open source and some are paid. Paid Tools such as SAS, WPS, MS Excel, Tableau, Pentaho, Statistica, Qlikview, KISSmetrics KISSmetrics,WeKa, BigML. Free Tools such as R, Google Analytics, Hadoop, Python, Spotfire can be used for Analyzing the data.

The following subsection deals with different emerging trends in various fields, along with dataset, tools for processing the data and Analytical methods used. Some source of dataset are kaggle, catalog, etc which is available for public for research.

Information Analytics has a key job in improving your business. Here are 4 primary variables which imply the requirement for Data Analytics:

- **Accumulate Hidden Insights:** Hidden bits of knowledge from information are assembled and after that broke down as for business necessities.
- **Create Reports**: Reports are produced from the information and are passed on to the separate groups and people to manage further activities for a skyscraper in business.
- **Perform Market Analysis:** Market Analysis can be performed to comprehend the qualities and the shortcomings of contenders.
- **Improve Business Requirement:** Analysis of Data enables improving Business to client prerequisites and experience.

LITERATURE REVIEW

The term "Enormous Data" or "Big Data" has as of late been applied to datasets that develop so huge that they become abnormal to work with utilizing customary database the board frameworks. They are informational collections whose size is past the capacity of regularly utilized programming instruments and capacity frameworks to catch, store, oversee, just as procedure the information inside a tolera-ble passed time. Enormous information sizes are continually expanding, as of now running from a couple dozen tera-bytes (TB) to numerous petabytes (PB)(Baltrusaitis et al., 2018; Bent et al., 2001; Bose & Cocke, 2003) of information in a solitary informational collection. Subsequently, a portion of the troubles identified with large information incorporate catch, stockpiling, search, sharing, investigation, and picturing. Today, endeavors are investigating huge volumes of exceptionally nitty gritty information in order to find realities they didn't know before. Consequently, enormous information investigation is the place progressed systematic strategies are applied on large informational indexes. Examination dependent on huge information tests uncovers and uses business change. Be that as it may, the bigger the arrangement of information, the more troublesome it becomes to oversee. In this segment, we will begin by talking about the qualities of large information, just as its significance. Normally, business advantage can ordinarily be gotten from examining bigger and progressively complex informational indexes that require ongoing or close constant abilities; nonetheless, this prompts a requirement for new information designs, expository strategies, and instruments. In this manner the progressive area will expand the enormous information examination instruments and me-thods, specifically, beginning with the large information stockpiling and the executives, at that point proceeding onward to the huge information scientific preparing. It at that point finishes up with a portion of the different enormous information examinations which have developed in utilization with large information.

Characteristics of Big Data

We have to understand the characteristics of Big Data before getting into tools. figure 1 depicts the different Vs of big data.

Figure 1. 5Vs of BigData

Volume

- The name 'Big Data' itself is related to a size which is enormous.
- Volume is a huge amount of data.
- To determine the value of data, size of data plays a very crucial role. If the volume of data is very large then it is actually considered as a 'Big Data'. This means whether a particular data can actually be considered as a Big Data or not, is dependent upon the volume of data.
- Hence while dealing with Big Data it is necessary to consider a characteristic 'Volume'.

Example: In the year 2016, the estimated global mobile traffic was 6.2 Exabytes(6.2 billion GB) per month. Also, by the year 2020 we will have almost 40000 ExaBytes of data.

Velocity

- Velocity refers to the high speed of accumulation of data.
- In Big Data velocity data flows in from sources like machines, networks, social media, mobile phones etc.

- There is a massive and continuous flow of data. This determines the potential of data that how fast the data is generated and processed to meet the demands.
- Sampling data can help in dealing with the issue like 'velocity'.

Example: There are more than 3.5 billion searches per day are made on Google. Also, FaceBook users are increasing by 22%(Approx.) year by year.

Variety

- It refers to nature of data that is structured, semi-structured and unstructured data.
- It also refers to heterogeneous sources.
- Variety is basically the arrival of data from new sources that are both inside and outside of an enterprise. It can be structured, semi-structured and unstructured.
- **Structured data**: This data is basically an organized data. It generally refers to data that has defined the length and format of data.
- **Semi- Structured data**: This data is basically a semi-organised data. It is generally a form of data that do not conform to the formal structure of data. Log files are the examples of this type of data.
- **Unstructured data**: This data basically refers to unorganized data. It generally refers to data that doesn't fit neatly into the traditional row and column structure of the relational database. Texts, pictures, videos etc. are the examples of unstructured data which can't be stored in the form of rows and columns.

Veracity

- It refers to inconsistencies and uncertainty in data, that is data which is available can sometimes get messy and quality and accuracy are difficult to control.
- Big Data is also variable because of the multitude of data dimensions resulting from multiple disparate data types and sources.

Example: Data in bulk could create confusion whereas less amount of data could convey half or Incomplete Information.

Value

- After having the 4 V's into account there comes one more V which stands for Value!. The bulk of Data having no Value is of no good to the company, unless you turn it into something useful.
- Data in itself is of no use or importance but it needs to be converted into something valuable to extract Information. Hence, you can state that Value! is the most important V of all the 5V's.

DATA ANALYTICS IN RETAIL

Information Analytics understand their customer's necessities all the more effectively, while in like manner helping them to get a more prominent measure(Baltrusaitis et al., 2018) of the right kind of customers by answering the following questions.

How to assemble edges at a thing level?

- Insights into your customer profile that helps answer tends to like their personality and why they make certain purchases (Market Basket assessment)
- Identify things that are most likely going to be gotten together.

Which exhibiting approaches work better than other individuals?

- ROI of exhibiting spend
- Optimal Pricing

What progressions and offers to use in each store?

- Store adroit thing mix
- Personalized offers
- Efficient stock procedure

DATA ANALYTICS IN INTERNET BUSINESS

Securing - how your guests and clients found and got together at your site.

- Shopping and securing conduct: how clients draw in with your site, which things they see, which ones they fuse or expel from shopping receptacles; near to starting, surrendering, and finishing exchanges.
- Economic Performance – what number of things the common exchange intertwines, the run of the mill requesting respect, restrains you expected to issue.
- Money-Hazard examination: Working capital administration, Fraud identification and counteractive action, Shareholder metric investigation

Innovation is the thing that puts the shrewd in brilliant cultivating and the accompanying make up the system:

- Global situating frameworks and differential worldwide situating frameworks for better exactness
- Geographical data frameworks
- Remote detecting innovations like information sensors, RADARS, information transmitters, automatons, cameras, and other associated gadgets
- Cloud design
- The Internet of Things, where gadgets are fit for speaking with one another and convey ongoing updates and warnings to ranchers on harvest statuses, water levels, dampness content, crop yield, and that's only the tip of the iceberg.

Advances like Machine Learning, Data Analytics, and Big Data for the whole procedure and arrangement to bode well. Issue isn't when there are no mechanical answers for cultivating concerns, however not having a legitimate utilization of them is a greater concern.

OVERVIEW OF TOOLS USED IN DATA ANALYTICS

SAS

SAS stands for Statistical Analysis Software. It was created in the year 1960 by the SAS Institute. From 1st January 1960, SAS was used for data management, business intelligence, Predictive Analysis, Descriptive and Prescriptive Analysis etc.(Lakshmiprabha & Govindaraju, 2019; Salgueiro & Kivshar, 2016)

SAS is basically worked on large datasets. With the help of SAS software you can perform various operations on the data like –

- Data Management
- Statistical Analysis
- Report formation with perfect graphics
- Business Planning
- Operations Research and project Management
- Quality Improvement
- Application Development
- Data extraction
- Data transformation
- Data updation and modification

WPS

The World Programming System, also known as WPS Analytics or WPS, is a software product developed by a company called World Programming. WPS Analytics supports users of mixed ability to access and process data and to perform data science tasks. It has interactive visual programming tools using data workflows, and it has coding tools supporting the use of the SAS language mixed with Python, R and SQL(Kalyoncu & Toygar, 2015; Mainetti et al., 2016)

Microsoft Excel is one of the most used software applications of all time. Hundreds of millions of people around the world use Microsoft Excel. You can use Excel to enter all sorts of data and perform financial, mathematical or statistical calculations.

This section illustrates the powerful features Excel has to offer to analyze data.

- Sort: You can sort your Excel data on one column or multiple columns. You can sort in ascending or descending order.
- Filter: Filter your Excel data if you only want to display records that meet certain criteria.
- Conditional Formatting: Conditional formatting in Excel enables you to highlight cells with a certain color, depending on the cell's value.
- Charts: A simple Excel chart can say more than a sheet full of numbers. As you'll see, creating charts is very easy.
- Pivot Tables: Pivot tables are one of Excel's most powerful features. A pivot table allows you to extract the significance from a large, detailed data set.
- Tables: Tables allow you to analyze your data in Excel quickly and easily.

- What-If Analysis: What-If Analysis in Excel allows you to try out different values (scenarios) for formulas.
- Solver: Excel includes a tool called solver that uses techniques from the operations research to find optimal solutions for all kind of decision problems.
- Analysis ToolPak: The Analysis ToolPak is an Excel add-in program that provides data analysis tools for financial, statistical and engineering data analysis.

Tableau

Tableau is a Data Visualization tool that is widely used for Business Intelligence but is not limited to it. It helps create interactive graphs and charts in the form of dashboards and worksheets to gain business insights. And all of this is made possible with gestures as simple as drag and drop. Table 1 depicts the different types of Tableau available in market.

Table 1. Types of Tableau available in market

	Key Features	Other Features	Operating environment	license
Tableau Desktop	Creating dashboards and stories locally	Tableau personal – limited data sources, non connectivity to tableau server Tableau Professional – full enterprise capabilities	Windows, mac	Personal - $999 Professional - $1999
Tableau Public	A massive, public, non-commercial Tableau server	All data published in public	-	free
Tableau online	Creating dashboards and stories on the cloud	Live connections	-	$500 per year
Tableau Reader	View Dashboards and sheets locally	cannot modify workbooks or connect to the server	Windows, mac	free
Tableau	Connect to data source	Users can directly interact with dashboards via browser	windows	Core Licensing

Note:- The above table depicts different Tableau available in market as on dated.

Pentaho

Pentaho Reporting is a suite (collection of tools) for creating relational and analytical reporting. Using Pentaho, we can transform complex data into meaningful reports and draw information out of them. Pentaho supports creating reports in various formats such as HTML, Excel, PDF, Text, CSV, and xml.

Pentaho can accept data from different data sources including SQL databases, OLAP data sources, and even the Pentaho Data Integration ETL tool.

Features of Pentaho

Pentaho Reporting primarily includes a Reporting Engine, a Report Designer, a Business Intelligence (BI) Server. It comes loaded with the following features –

- **Report Designer**: Used for creating pixel perfect report.
- **Metadata Editor:** Allows to add user-friendly metadata domain to a data source.
- **Report Designer and Design Studio:** Used for fine-tuning of reports and ad-hoc reporting.
- **Pentaho user Console Web Interface:** Used for easily managing reports and analyzing views.
- **Ad-Hoc Reporting Interface:** Offers a step-by-step wizard for designing simple reports. Output formats include PDF, RTF, HTML, and XLS.
- **A Complex Scheduling Sub-System**: Allows users to execute reports at given intervals.
- **Mailing:** Users can email a published report to other users.
- **Connectivity:** Connectivity between the reporting tools and the BI server, which allows to publish the content directly to the BI server.

QlikView

QlikView is a leading Business Discovery Platform. It is unique in many ways as compared to the traditional BI platforms. As a data analysis tool, it always maintains the relationship between the data and this relationship can be seen visually using colors. It also shows the data that are not related. It provides both direct and indirect searches by using individual searches in the list boxes.QlikView's core and patented technology has the feature of in-memory data processing, which gives superfast result to the users. It calculates aggregations on the fly and compresses data to 10% of original size. Neither users nor developers of QlikView applications manage the relationship between data. It is managed automatically.

Features of QlikView

QlikView has patented technology, which enables it to have many features that are useful in creating advanced reports from multiple data sources quickly. Following is a list of features that makes QlikView very unique.

- **Data Association is Maintained Automatically:** QlikView automatically recognizes the relationship between each piece of data that is present in a dataset. Users need not preconfigure the relationship between different data entities.
- **Data is Held in Memory for Multiple Users, for a Super-Fast User Experience:** The structure, data and calculations of a report are all held in the memory (RAM) of the server.
- **Aggregations are Calculated on the fly as Needed:** As the data is held in memory, calculations are done on the fly. No need of storing pre-calculated aggregate values.
- **Data is Compressed to 10% of its Original Size:** QlikView heavily uses data dictionary. Only essential bits of data in memory is required for any analysis. Hence, it compresses the original data to a very small size.

- **Visual Relationship Using Colors:** The relationship between data is not shown by arrow or lines but by colors. Selecting a piece of data gives specific colors to the related data and another color to unrelated data.
- **Direct and Indirect Searches:** Instead of giving the direct value a user is looking for, they can input some related data and get the exact result because of the data association. Of course, they can also search for a value directly.

KISSmetrics

KISSmetrics is a powerful web analytics tool that delivers key insights and user interaction on your website. It defines a clear picture of users' activities on your website and collects acquisition data of every visitor.

You can use this service free for a month. After that, you can switch on to a paid plan that suits you. KISSmetrics helps in improving sales by knowing cart-abandoned products. It helps you to know exactly when to follow up your customers by tracking the repeat buyers activity slot.

KISSmetrics helps you identify the following –

- Cart size
- Landing page conversion rate
- Customer activity on your portal
- Customer bounce points
- Cart abandoned products
- Customer occurrence before making a purchase
- Customer lifetime value, etc.

Best Features of KISSmetrics

- Ability to track effective marketing channels.
- Figure out how much time a user takes to convert.
- Determine a degree of which user was engaged with your site.
- A convenient dashboard. You do not need to run around searching for figures.

WEKA

Waikato Environment for Knowledge Analysis, It is a data mining / machine learning tool developed by department of computer science, university of Waikato, New Zealand. WEKA is also a bird found only on the island of New Zealand. Table 2 depicts the important features of WEKA.

DATA ANALYTICS IN AGRICULTURE DEVELOPMENT IN INDIA

Precision farming gives farmers the ability to make more profitable use of crop inputs along with manures, pesticides, crops and irrigating systems.Spreading shrewd sensors with compelling data analytics investigation will lead us a step forward to free farmers from uncertain weather constraints. This section deals with Sample dataset, tools for processing data and possible Analytical methods used for finding a pattern or valuable insights for agriculture sector. Dataset like "KBS037-001 Geo-referenced Annual Crop Yields - Raw Data" for agriculture sector will be discussed further, understanding the dataset and performing analytical methods will be discussed in detail.

This datatable is part of the Precision Agriculture Yield Monitoring in Row Crop Agriculture dataset. The LTER annual crops (corn, soy and wheat), treatments 1-4, are harvested annually using a combine equipped with a GPS and precision agriculture software to allow detailed yield measurements with coincident GPS latitude and longitude data. Table 3 and Table 4 depicts the sample attributes of KBS037-001.

Table 2. Features of WEKA

S.No	Features	Purpose
1	Explorer	Graphical interface to perform the data mining tasks on raw data
2	Experimenter	Allows users to execute different experimental variations on data sets
3	Knowledge flow	Explorer with drag and drop functionality. Supports incremental learning from previous results
4	Simple CLI	Command line interface. Simple interface for executing commands from a terminal.
5	Workbench	Combines all GUI interfaces into one.

Note: WEKA- Waikato Environment for Knowledge Analysis, CLI- command-line interface

Table 3. Sample attributes

Variate	Description	Units
longitude	longitude of monitor at time of reading	degree
latitude	latitude of monitor at time of reading	degree
crop flow lb s	flow rate of grain passing the sensor	lb/s
datetime	date and time of the sampling	
duration	number of seconds since the last reading	second
distance in	length of sampled area	inch
swth wdth in	width of sampled area (swath)	inch
moisture	gravimetric moisture of grain	%
status	header status (up or down)	
pass num	an number that is incremented on each pass of the field	number
serial number	serial number of yield monitoring device	number
field	user-assigned designation for sampled field	
dataset	user-assigned designation for load within a field	
product	user-assigned designation for crop being sampled	
elevation ft	altitude of GPS system	foot

Note: some conversion units are to be followed for specific variate

Table 4. Sample dataset

longitude	latitude	crop_flow_lb_s	datetime	duration_s	distance_in	swth_wdth_in	moisture	status	pass_num	serial_num	field	dataset	product	elevation_ft
-85.372824	42.408276	3.29	2013-07-24 19:20:04+00	1.0	56.0	180.0	6.6	0	141	5648	F1: Lysimeter	L1:	Wheat (Sft Rd Wtr)	953.5
-85.372838	42.408288	2.89	2013-07-24 19:20:03+00	1.0	47.0	180.0	6.6	0	141	5648	F1: Lysimeter	L1:	Wheat (Sft Rd Wtr)	953.5
-85.372847	42.408296	2.89	2013-07-24 19:20:02+00	1.0	38.0	180.0	6.6	0	141	5648	F1: Lysimeter	L1:	Wheat (Sft Rd Wtr)	953.5
-85.372855	42.408301	3.69	2013-07-24 19:20:01+00	1.0	18.0	180.0	6.6	0	141	5648	F1: Lysimeter	L1:	Wheat (Sft Rd Wtr)	953.5
-85.372855	42.408304	3.39	2013-07-24 19:20:00+00	1.0	39.0	180.0	6.6	0	141	5648	F1: Lysimeter	L1:	Wheat (Sft Rd Wtr)	

Note: The table include sample data collected from GPS tracking system

BIG DATA IN MUSIC INDUSTRY

Spotify has announced their first music streaming analytics tool, also known as Publishing Analytics. It would give music publishing companies daily streaming statistics for recordings, such as data about the songwriters and how many albums they have sold since their debut.Google's AI Duet is a demo using Magenta, a sound processing AI project that runs Tensorflow under the hood to perform machine learning on audio. AI duet acts as a virtual piano that we will play and an AI will attempt to accompany.

Magenta, Google's research arm that finds ways of using AI to help people's creativity, has developed an instrument it calls NSynth Super. It is based on the NSynth algorithm which uses a deep neural network technique to generate sound. NSynth was released by Google a few months ago. Rather than generating music notes, NSynth replicates the sound of an instrument. What makes the algorithm unique is that it continuously learns the core qualities of what makes up an individual sound and is able to combine various sounds to generate something completely new.

NSynth Super is an open source experimental instrument. It gives musicians (and deep learning followers) the ability to explore completely new sounds generated by the NSynth machine learning algorithm. It has been built using open source libraries like TensorFlow and openFrameworks.

The instrument can be played via any MIDI source, like a keyboard or a sequencer. Figure 2 shows how data analytics is performed in music industry.

Figure 2. Data analytics in music

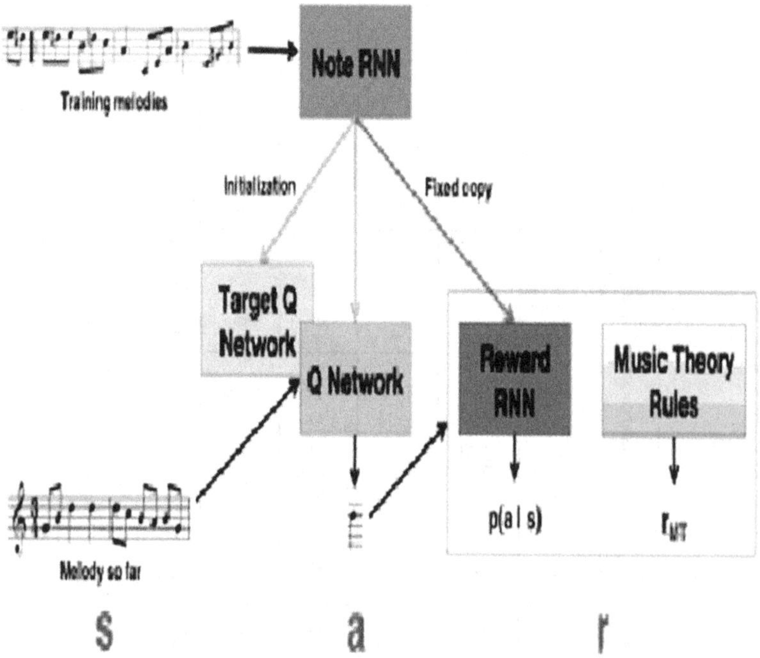

DATA ANALYTICS IN SPORTS

sports analytics can be roughly translated to the use of data related to sports such as statistics of players, Weather conditions, pitch information etc. to create predictive models to make informed decisions. The primary objective of sports analysis is to improve the team performance. Sports analytics is also used to understand and maintain the fan-base of big teams.

The Sports Analytics was brought to the public eyes in 2011 by a movie called "Money ball" featuring attempts of Oakland Athletics Baseball team's 2002 season. The coach, Billy Beane restored the team using empirical data and statistical analyses on players' performance. He used trials with sabermetrics to improve his team and ended up finishing at the first place American League West on that season. Today with the advancement in Big Data technology every sports team are crunching data to gain a competitive advantage.

Sports organizations can detect patterns in digital engagement, such as online sports viewing, to understand what and when fans are watching via app logins and online video views. They are creating more immersive experiences via augmented reality. They can mine sentiment from social media streams to understand what fans are thinking and can use analytics to engage those fans via social channels. Social media is proving to be a great marketing ground for university teams to connect with millennials and market tickets using data-driven campaigns.

Wearables, for example, can help monitor players on the field and are becoming increasingly advanced as time goes on, even becoming integrated in players' uniforms! Coaches can already check on players' fatigue and hydration levels. As these devices become smarter, player safety and performance will also be tracked, analyzed and improved.Data from fans will continue to influence marketing efforts and decisions about sporting events, such as when to schedule games and how to cater to fan preferences. Advances in big data can even lead to career opportunities for avid fans with a talent for numbers. The possibilities are endless for coaches, players and fans – and we'll only continue to see data playing a larger role in sports moving forward. Keep an eye out for big data advancements with your favorite team!

Football, also called soccer, is one of the most popular sports in the world, if one considers the number of fans as well as the number of players. However, footballers face serious injuries during the match and even during training. Concussion, hypoglycemia, swallowing the tongue and shortness of breath are examples of the health problems footballers face, and in extreme cases, may lead to death. In addition, many sport clubs and sport academies spend millions of dollars contracting new professional footballers or even developing new professional footballers. The Internet of Things (IoT) is a new paradigm that combines various technologies to enhance our lives. Today's technology can protect footballers by diagnosing any health problems, which may occur during the match or training session, which, if detected early, may prevent any adverse effects on their long-term health. This paper proposes an IoT-based architecture for the sport of football, called IoT Football. Our proposal aims to embed sensing devices (e.g. sensors and RFID), telecommunication technologies (e.g. ZigBee) and cloud computing in the sport of football in order monitor the health of footballers and reduce the occurrence of adverse health conditions.

DATA ANALYTICS IN EDUCATION

Imagine if you could proactively identify students needing additional support and coordinate the additional resources necessary to improve performance and contribute to a higher academic rating for the school. Also, imagine if you could provide students the means to effectively plan, connect, collaborate, research, and gain insight from others whether physically or virtually on campus. Schools and education systems face complexity in preparing diverse students for a dynamic future. Part of monitoring and evaluating their progress is collecting data on student learning and system performance. As these datasets have grown larger and more complex, the tools and capacity to leverage data for improved outcomes has not always kept pace.

Tools like Power BI and Azure Machine Learning give educators and school leaders powerful self-serve capabilities to view, analyse, and make predictions from data, thus turning the cost of data into advantage. In addition to reports on past and current performance viewed dynamically using Power BI, Azure Machine Learning includes data models that conduct predictive analytics that show likelihood of specific outcomes for students while there is time to make changes in school programs that improve outcomes. The analytics can include recommended interventions and can calculate cos

The advantages of data visualization, analysis, and prediction benefit: - Students get feedback on their pattern of performance in learning systems, and who may be assessed more frequently in ways that better guide progress and give them a personalized learning experience - Parents get detailed reports on student progress Education Analytics white paper I March 2017 16 - Teachers get detailed reports on all students, as well as relative effectiveness of lessons and content, freeing them from low-order assessments to focus on more complex feedback - Content designers and curriculum managers get data on content usage and relationships between content and learning - School leaders get student progress data, teacher effectiveness data, and school-level outcomes. Facility factors like busing, buildings, schedules, and activities can be factored into learning. Staff factors like professional learning and credentials can be analysed - School system leaders get data across campuses year to year - Policymakers get outcomes associated with different school and community conditions - Education researchers who will get ongoing insights into impacts of practices and conditions at large scale

Casestudy: Tacoma public schools In the U.S., 1.2 million students drop out of high school annually. Student dropout rates can contribute to societal issues, for example those without high school diplomas have an average $200,000 of unrealized income, and 75% of crimes in the U.S. are committed by high school dropouts. Just a few years ago, Tacoma Public School System in the U.S. had a school graduation rate of 55%. By adopting a Whole Child approach to education powered by predictive analytics, Tacoma raised its graduation rate to over 83%. Using advanced analytics and a dynamic business intelligence dashboard, Tacoma leaders get early warnings for each student who is identified as at risk for not graduating, and school staff can intervene quickly. Shaun Taylor, Tacoma Public Schools CIO, said, "With Azure Machine Learning, we proved that we have the right tool to get us where we want to go in terms of predicting student success. It's a tool our educators will be able to use to start tackling the problem of student disengagement. " Benefits of cloud-based advanced analytics for Tacoma include: - Both static data, such as student characteristics and past performance, and dynamic data such as formative assessments and usage of learning systems can be accommodated by cloud-based advanced analytics, making the results far more useful in guiding student learning - The full range of descriptive, diagnostic, predictive, and prescriptive analytics are possible - The data models can be built once and then run as needed, making the reports more easily and frequently accessible by educators - Analysis and reporting are done at system, school, and individual student levels, enabling personalization of learning and broader insights about what works - Each student's progress can be viewed in the Power BI displays, as well as on-demand aggregated views of data accessed using natural language query. This capability enables greater use of data with fewer specialized skills and less time needed - At-risk prediction allowed early identification of students needing additional supports.

DATA ANALYTICS IN IOT APPLICATIONS

The Internet of Things (IoT) envisions a world-wide, interconnected network of smart physical entities. These physical entities generate a large amount of data in operation and as the IoT gains momentum in terms of deployment, the combined scale of those data seems destined to continue to grow. Increasingly, applications for the IoT involve analytics.

When machines are connected to internet, we start getting real-time data in large amount. That real-time data is not only helpful in the Descriptive analysis but also helpful in understanding the behavioral patterns to get predictive and prescriptive analysis which means what will happen and actions we have to take. In short, with the emergence of IoT, the whole equation has transformed. Now we can leverage this data in our daily job to get best possible outcomes and also understand where their time and money are spent. So that we can use the resources in an effective manner hence wastage can be minimized.

Data Analytics is defined as a process which identifies all data sets with variable data properties to extract meaningful conclusions. The conclusions we get are in the form of trends, patterns, and statistics that is helpful for the organization to take effective decisions. Data Analytics has a vital role in the growth and success of IoT applications and investments. Analytics tools will allow the business units to make effective use of their following below datasets:

- **Volume:** IoT applications make use of the huge collection of data sets. The organizations need to manage these large volumes of data and to analyze the same for extracting appropriate patterns. With data analytics these datasets along with real-time can be analyzed easily and effectively.
- **Structure:** IoT applications involve all types of datasets that may be structured, semi-structured and unstructured. There are chances that there can be a significant difference in the data formats and types. Hence, it allows the business executive to analyze all these varying datasets using automated tools and software.
- **Driving Revenue**: The data analytics in IoT investments will allow the business units to gain insights about customer's preferences and choices. This will lead to the development of services and offers the customer demands and expectations. And this in return leads to the organizations revenue and growth.
- **Competitive Edge:** IoT is a buzzword in the current era of technology and there are lot of IoT application developers and providers in the market. The businesses will offer better services with the help of data analytics and in return this will help them to gain the competitive edge in the market.

Following are the different types of data analytics that can be used and applied in the IoT investments:

Streaming Analytics: This form of data analytics is also referred as event stream processing and it analyzes huge in-motion data sets. Real-time data streams are analyzed in this process to detect urgent situations and immediate actions. IoT applications based on financial transactions, air fleet tracking, traffic analysis etc. can benefit from this method.

Spatial Analytics: This is the data analytics method that is used to analyze geographic patterns to determine the spatial relationship between the physical objects. Location-based IoT applications, such as smart parking applications can benefit from this form of data analytics.

Time Series Analytics: As the name suggests, this form of data analytics is based upon the time-based data which is analyzed to reveal associated trends and patterns. IoT applications, such as weather forecasting applications and health monitoring systems can benefit from this form of data analytics method.

Prescriptive Analysis: This form of data analytics is the combination of descriptive and predictive analysis. It is applied to understand the best steps of action that can be taken in a particular situation. Commercial IoT applications can make use of this form of data analytics to gain better conclusion.

DATA ANALYTICS IN AUGMENTATION TECHNOLOGY

Augmented analytics, which uses machine learning (ML) and artificial intelligence (AI) techniques to automate multiple aspects of data work will change how analytics content is prepared, discovered and shared.the Augmented Analytics process enables the extraction of intelligence through built-in trend recognition and pattern recognition tools. For obtaining improved data insights, augmented analytics will recast big Data into smart data. Being an advanced data processing tool, augmented analytics is able to derive the real essence of insights from big data. Many businesses are already focused on evolving smart data analytics solutions to obtain valuable insights from their big data sets.

Smart data will assist many businesses in reducing the threat of losing data. It will also improve a series of activities such as product development, operations, consumer experience, predictive maintenance, and innovation.

DATA ANALYTICS IN NLP

By 2020, Gartner reported, half of queries will be generated via search, natural language processing (NLP) or voice — or are expected to be generated automatically. This trend is being driven by the need to make analytics accessible to more people in the organization and will allow users to use analytics tools as easily as they speak with virtual assistants now. Sentiment Analysis is a broad range of subjective analysis which uses Natural Language processing techniques to perform tasks such as identifying the sentiment of a customer review, positive or negative feeling in a sentence, judging mood via voice analysis or written text analysis etc. For example-

"I did not like the chocolate ice-cream" – is a negative experience of ice-cream.

"I did not hate the chocolate ice-cream" – may be considered as a neutral experience

Language identification is the task of identifying the language in which the content is in. It makes use of statistical as well as syntactical properties of the language to perform this task. It may also be considered as a special case of text classification.

To get started in natural language processing we will start with some very simple text parsing. Tokenization is the process of taking a stream of text like a sentence and breaking it down to its most basic words. For instance take the following sentence: "The red fox jumps over the moon." Each word would represent a token of which there are seven.

To Tokenize a sentence using python:

```
myText = 'The red fox jumps over the moon.'
myLowerText = myText.lower()
myTextList = myLowerText.split()
print(myTextList)
OUTPUT:
['the', 'red', 'fox', 'jumps', 'over', 'the', 'moon']
```

Table 5. Chart suggestion for different data set

Purpose	Static / Dynamic	Variables	Suggested chart
comparison	Among items	Two variables per item	Variable width column chart
		One variable per item	Many Category – Embedded chart Few category, many Items – Bar Chart Few category, few items – column chart
	Over time	Many Periods	Cyclical data – Circular Area chart Non-Cyclical data – Line Chart
		Few Periods	Few category- Column chart Many Category – Line Chart
Relationship	Two variables		Scatter chart
	Three variables		Bubble chart
Distribution	Single variable	Few data points Many Data points	Column Histogram Line Histogram
	Two Variable		Scatter chart
	Three Variable		3D Area Chart
composition	Changing over time	Few Periods	Only relative difference matter- stacked 100% column matter Relative and absolute difference matter – Stacked column chart
		Many periods	Only relative differences matter- stacked 100% Area matter Relative and absolute difference matter – Stacked Area chart
	static	Simple share of Total	Pie chart
		Accumulation or subtraction to total	Waterfall chart
		Components of components	Stacked 100% column chart with subcomponents

Note: 3D- 3 Dimension

VISUALIZING DATA IN TERMS OF DIAGRAM

Here sample suggestion Table 5 of charts are mentioned for more clarity in visualizing data.

FREE SOFTWARE

R

R is an open-source programming language that was created by Roass Ihaka and Robert Gentleman in 1995. The purpose of developing this language was to focus on delivering a more user-friendly and better way to perform statistics, data analysis, and graphical modules. R is the only programming language that allows statisticians to perform the most complicated and intricate analyses without getting into too much of details. With so many benefits for data science, R has gradually mounted heights among professionals of big data.

Hadoop

The Apache Hadoop software library is a framework that allows for the distributed processing of large data sets across clusters of computers using simple programming models. It is designed to scale up from single servers to thousands of machines, each offering local computation and storage. Rather than rely on hardware to deliver high-availability, the library itself is designed to detect and handle failures at the application layer, so delivering a highly-available service on top of a cluster of computers, each of which may be prone to failures.

Why is Hadoop important?

- *Ability to store and process huge amounts of any kind of data, quickly.* With data volumes and varieties constantly increasing, especially from social media and the Internet of Things (IoT), that's a key consideration.
- *Computing power:* Hadoop's distributed computing model processes big data fast. The more computing nodes you use, the more processing power you have.
- *Fault tolerance.* Data and application processing are protected against hardware failure. If a node goes down, jobs are automatically redirected to other nodes to make sure the distributed computing does not fail. Multiple copies of all data are stored automatically.
- *Flexibility.* Unlike traditional relational databases, you don't have to preprocess data before storing it. You can store as much data as you want and decide how to use it later. That includes unstructured data like text, images and videos.
- *Low cost.* The open-source framework is free and uses commodity hardware to store large quantities of data.
- *Scalability.* You can easily grow your system to handle more data simply by adding nodes. Little administration is required.

The project includes these modules:

- **Hadoop Common**: The common utilities that support the other Hadoop modules.
- **Hadoop Distributed File System (HDFS)**: A distributed file system that provides high-through-put access to application data.
- **Hadoop YARN**: A framework for job scheduling and cluster resource management.
- **Hadoop MapReduce**: A YARN-based system for parallel processing of large data sets.
- **Hadoop Ozone**: An object store for Hadoop.
- **Hadoop Submarine:** A machine learning engine for Hadoop

Google Analytics

Google Analytics is a free Web analytics service that provides statistics and basic analytical tools for search engine optimization (SEO) and marketing purposes. The service is available to anyone with a Google account.

Google Analytics features include:

- Data visualization tools including a dashboard, scorecards and motion charts, which display changes in data over time.
- Segmentation for analysis of subsets, such as conversions.
- Custom reports.
- Email-based sharing and communication.
- Integration with other Google products, such as AdWords, Public Data Explorer and Website Optimizer.

Python

Python is already used by some of the biggest names in tech, along with some less likely but equally-impressive users.

Uber, PayPal, Google, Facebook, Instagram, Netflix, Dropbox, and Reddit all use Python in their development and testing. Moreover, Python is also used extensively in robotics and embedded systems (it can even be used to control Arduinos). Even legacy systems written in C and C++ are easy to interface with Python. Anywhere that data analysis is required, Python and its assorted libraries shine. Goldman Sachs is one of several large financial institutions using Python to express the massive amounts of data they generate. This alone is an area Python is well suited to, and increasingly this field is making use of machine learning.

Spotfire

Spotfire allows users to combine data in a single analysis and get a holistic view of the same with an interactive visualization. Spotfire software makes businesses smart, delivers AI-driven analytics, and makes it easier to plot interactive data on maps. The platform helps businesses transform their data into powerful insights with ease and in less time. It speeds up data analysis across an organization for faster, confident, and much accurate decision-making.

CONCLUSION

This chapter aims to increase the level of awareness of the intellectual and technical issues surrounding the analysis of massive data. This is not the first report written on massive data, and it will not be the last, but here given the major attention currently being paid to massive data in science, with difference appropriate tools. The purpose of data analytics is clearly explained with opensource tools and paid tools. The selection of data set and analytic tools is very important in any data analytics.

REFERENCES

Baltrusaitis, T., Ahuja, C., & Morency, L.-P. (2018). Multimodal machine learning: A survey and taxonomy. *IEEE Transactions on Pattern Analysis and Machine Intelligence*, 1–1. PMID:29994351

Bent, D., Hughes, D. W., Provine, R. C., Rastall, R., Kilmer, A., Hiley, D., Szendrei, J., Payne, T. B., Bent, M., & Chew, G. (2001). *Notation. In Grove Music Online*. Oxford University Press.

Bose, L., & Cocke, J. (2003). Visualizing Boolean Construction of Decision Supporting System for Monitoring Function in Sports Training. *Proceedings of PODC*.

Kalyoncu, C., & Toygar, Ö. (2015). Geometric leaf classification. *Computer Vision and Image Understanding*, *133*, 102–109. doi:10.1016/j.cviu.2014.11.001

Lakshmiprabha, K. E., & Govindaraju, C. (2019). Hydroponic-based smart irrigation system using Internet of Things. *International Journal of Communication Systems*, e4071. doi:10.1002/dac.4071

Mainetti, L., Patrono, L., & Stefanizzi, M. L. (2016). An Internet of sport architecture based on emerging enabling technologies. *Computer and Energy Science (SpliTech) International Multidisciplinary Conference on*, 1-6. 10.1109/SpliTech.2016.7555928

Salgueiro, J. R., & Kivshar, Y. S. (2016). Optimization of Biased PT-Symmetric Plasmonic Directional Couplers. *Selected Topics in Quantum Electronics IEEE Journal of*, *22*(5), 60–66. doi:10.1109/JSTQE.2016.2555283

Chapter 6
Architecture for Analyzing Agriculture Data Using Data Analytics

Namratha Birudaraju
Anurag University, India

Adiraju Prasanth Rao
https://orcid.org/0000-0002-5119-3987
Anurag University, India

Sathiyamoorthi V.
https://orcid.org/0000-0002-7012-3941
Sona College of Technology, Salem, India

ABSTRACT

The main steps for agricultural practices include preparation of soil, sowing, adding manure, irrigation, harvesting, and storage. For this, one needs to develop modern tools and technologies that can improve production efficiency, product quality, schedule and monitoring the crops, fertilizer spraying, planting, which helps the farmers choose the suitable crop. Efficient techniques are used to analyze huge amount of data which provide real time information about emerging trends. Facilities like fertilizer requirement notifications, predictions on wind directions, satellite-based monitoring are sources of data. Analytics can be used to enable farmers to make decisions based on data. This chapter provides a review of existing work to study the impact of big data on the analysis of agriculture. Analytics creates many chances in the field of agriculture towards smart farming by using hardware, software. The emerging ability to use analytic methods for development promise to transform farming sector to facilitate the poverty reduction which helps to deal with humane crises and conflicts.

DOI: 10.4018/978-1-7998-2566-1.ch006

INTRODUCTION

Agriculture is the backbone for most of the countries around the world. But it is facing many problems in the developing countries where farmers cannot afford modern technologies and tools.

In farming sector, there has been a digital revolution. Big Data is playing a vital role in the development where the machines are equipped with various kinds of sensors which measures data in their environment which is used for predicting machines behaviour.

It promises a level of precision, information storage, processing and analyzing which was not possible previously due to limitations in the technology.The use of information sets and latest digital tools for collecting, aggregating and analyzing is done by Big Data. Information is gathered based on agricultural equipments and farmers using data from large datasets and analytics to make farming decisions.

Big Data in agriculture is Electronic Farm Records which contains dampness content information, pH level information, soil temperatures maps and information, electrical conductivity maps and information, online networking posts, protection and yield related data.

Big Data addresses the problems in the society which includes the need of consumers, producers, business analysts, marketing agents and decision making. Generally, analysis is done on large volumes of data and used in decision making process.

At present, agricultural sector is at the initial phase of rendering Big Data services. Farmers must join data systems and share farm data. Various applications and techniques can be used to enhance the farms productivity along with reducing their use of inputs.

Smart Farming is a emerging concept towards farm management using modern technology to increase the quantity and quality of product using the required human labor.

The technologies available for farmers today are:

- Sensors are used to monitor and optimize the soil, water, light, humidity, temperature management
- Cell phones are used by farmers to remotely monitor their equipment, crops, and livestock.
- Data analytics is applied which enable monitoring and supervision of growth rate and nutrient requirements of a plant and can be used to make data-based decisions like which crops to plant for their next .

Figure 1. Why Agriculture needs Big Data?

BACKGROUND

Coble et al. (2016) proposed "large, diverse, complex, longitudinal, and distributed data sets generated by click-through streams, email, instruments, online transactions, satellites, sensors, video, and all other sources digital available today and in the future. This method is supported by describing data in terms of volume, velocity, variability, and accuracy, with "volume" referring to the size of the data, "velocity" measuring data flow, "variability" indicating the lack of structure and finally "veracity" accuracy and reliability of data.

Stubbs suggests big data as it is used in agriculture is small in terms of data size and more with the combination of technology and advanced analytics that creates a new way of processing data in a very useful and timely manner.

Woodard and Verteramo - Chiu 2017 mentioned that the use of geo-spatial techniques could improve crop harvesting models and the price of plant insurance products. We expect the sector to find the use of these methods in a number of areas including environmental economics. Agricultural information policies are analyzed and modified with various latest analytical tools and techniques. Decisions based on data collected from accurate agricultural technologies are applied at the farm level and to inputs and equipment manufacturers. There is an impact of management processes on production outcomes and on the management of farm managers.

Fountas et al., 2006 stated that Precision Agriculture is a knowledgeable work that can be categorized by data collection, data analysis and decision-making. It helps to differentiate decisions according to the planning and strategic boundaries.

Data fl q, 2015 outlined Big Data tools that will help farmers improve productivity and increase business efficiency. Big Data differs in the collection of historical information in terms of volume and analytical power embedded in modern digital technology. Big Data is collected from a variety of sources and is used to interpret past events and predict the behavior and process of future events.

Similarly, Monsanto's IFS described online as integrating 'innovations in seed science, agronomy, data analysis, precision farming equipment and hybrid messaging services and flexible planting techniques to improve maize harvesting potential' (Monsanto, 2014) . They contribute to the long-standing pairing between good health and the effective use of new technology in the workforce (Marx and Roe-Smith, 1994).

Tremblay (2017) states that agricultural research should extend beyond Fisher's experimental design and apply analytical methods that can learn from mechanical and sensory data, i.e., it must rely on visual production data from controlled trials.

Banbure et al. (2011) concluded that a good or effective broadcast model should take into account both previous behavior of the series and easily recognizable symptoms of the same period.

TRADITIONAL METHODS OF FARMING

For a long time, farmers relied on traditional farming methods. Though there are many agricultural machines, major agricultural operations are done by farmers using simple and traditional tools like wooden plough, sickle, etc. Machines are mostly not used in ploughing, sowing, irrigating, harvesting threshing, transporting the crops by small and marginal farmers. It results in large amounts of human labor and in low yields per capita labor force.

Organic farming relies mostly on natural methods such as animal manure, crop residues, crop rotation, off-farm organic waste, use of the biological system of plant protection and nutritional mobilization. Organic farming is a unique method of farming which promotes agro-ecosystem health such as soil biological activity, biological cycle, and biodiversity.Organic agriculture is capable of contributing to socio-economic and ecologically sustainable development.

There is a need to mechanize the agricultural operations so that wastage of labor force is avoided and farming is made convenient and efficient. Agricultural implementation and machinery are vital for efficient and effective agricultural operations which facilitates multiple cropping and by increasing production.

Figure 2. Generations of farming methods

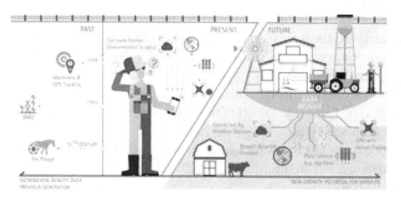

For the optimization of crop yield and quality there is an ongoing development in improving crop management advice to cope up with the spatial variability of the growth process, caused by local variations in soil composition, moisture and nutrition content. To achieve this reliable information is required on the actual status of the vegetation and the expected development and yield given different management scenarios. In order to determine this cause, the observations must be integrated and analyzed with other models and observations. To achieve this data driven approach can be followed to determine the relation between the multiple observations .Correlation, regression and histogram techniques can be used to analyze the data.

Management Information Systems is a repository where data from multiple sensors and resources are gathered, stored, analyzed, and retrieved for actions. The repository gives information on: (a) Crops (b) Climate (c) Devices (d) Global positioning systems

The initial step is collection of data. Data is continually collected, analyzed, and simulated to understand and predict crop growth and its behavior under various circumstances and analyzed to find spatial and temporal relationships and they results are visualized.

Many data-intensive technologies are available to help farmers monitor and control weeds and pests. Big Data analytics and tools can be used to analyze that provide improved crop management decisions for weed control and crop protection.

Figure 3. Usage of information technology in agriculture

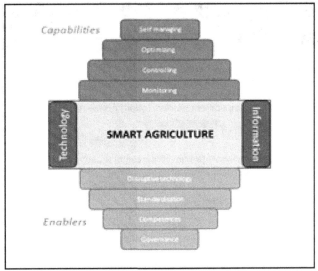

Figure 4. Data insight to farmers

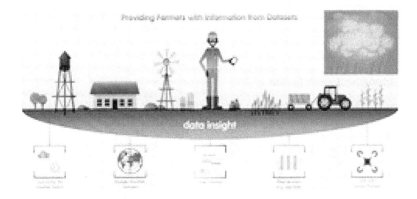

BIG DATA OPPORTUNITIES AND BENEFITS IN FARMING

In farming sector, big data can be seen as a combination of technology and analytics that collects and compile novel data and process it in a more useful and timely way to assist decision making.

According to agriculture experts, big data collects data from multiple sources and translates it into information which improves business processes and solve problems at larger scale and speed.

Keeping the crop and meeting the food needs of the growing community while also protecting the necessary natural resources, making additional changes and data tools can help determine what these changes should be.

The end result of gathering data is to analyze it and come up with actionable solutions with better results. For example, a satellite image of a land has many layers of data embedded into a single spectrum which gives us a lot of information to analyze. Decision making for farmers has become easy with the geospatial approach and satellite monitoring of farms.

Figure 5. Process of big data in agriculture

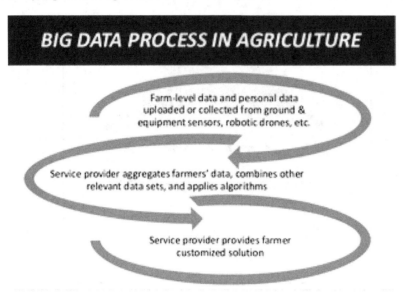

Data analysis not only creates greater awareness and more accurate knowledge, but it can fill the gap in the supply and marketing chain of the industry which helps farmers, insurance agencies, loan banks, seed companies, machine industry.

Figure 6. Big data opportunities in farming

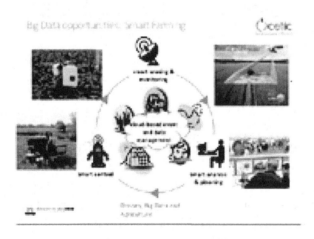

Ways in which data analysis can help farming:

- Development of new seed traits
- Precision farming
- Food tracking
- Effect on supply chains

Some of the more prominent Uses of Big Data in farming include:

Yield Prediction

Yield prediction uses mathematical models to analyze data around yield, weather, chemicals, leaf and biomass index etc with machine learning for decision making. Predicting yields help farmer to get insight on what, where and when to plant.

Risk Management

Farmers can leverage a web of big data to evaluate the chances of events like crop failure and improve feed efficiency within the production of livestock.

Food Safety and Spoilage Prevention

The collection of data like humidity, temperature and chemicals will give an image of health around smart agricultural businesses allowing instant detection of microbes and incidents of contamination.

Equipment Management

Equipment manufacturers like John Deere have already made a good start by fitting of sensors around vehicles to aid their providing of data. Farmers can then log into special portals to manage maintenance of equipment in order to reduce downtime and keep everything productive. As many companies provide solutions to aid areas of equipment management and supply chain optimization, we can expect a much smoother delivery of crops to the market.

CONCEPTUAL FRAMEWORK FOR BIG DATA IN AGRICULTURE

Various phases of the framework for big data analytics in agriculture are:

Data Acquisition

The initial step of data analytics is data collection. It will capture various types of data such as structured, semi structured and unstructured data. The data is collected from various sources. For agricultural data it is collected from government database, GPS etc and that raw data is filtered, the necessary data is stored and unnecessary data is ignored.

Information Extraction

This phase extracts the data required for analysis by integrating, interpreting, mining and analyzing. It is done based on daily activity data, weather prediction, crop information etc and finally extracts required structured data.

Figure 7. Conceptual framework for big data analytics in agriculture

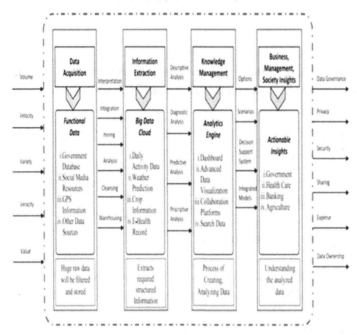

Conceptual framework for Big Data analytics in agriculture.

Knowledge Management

Big Data generates large statistical samples which increases the accuracy of the results. It involves descriptive, diagnostic, predictive analytics etc. It is done at collaboration platforms, dashboards etc. Finally the analyzing data is created.

Business management and society insights

This is the last phase where the data is turned into insights such as agriculture, banking etc. the information captured from sensors on the farm is used for improving the risk of crop failure and increase feed effectively.

FUTURE SCOPE

In adopting latest technologies the agricultural sector is slow as it requires large scale of operations and the cost of initial investment is high. Implementation of new technologies has a major impact on the future of farmers. With the help of various visualization and analysis tools, producers, farmers, and consultants can connect and simplify their data management at a less cost. The shift towards new technologies is possible by research and development in both hardware and software services. In recent years, agricultural innovation has resulted in new methods to improve productivity.

In the future, technology plays vital role in agriculture. Several operations will be automated, from planting to harvesting. The main challenges are lack of digital skills, poor telecommunication infrastructures, and concerns on data ownership and use must be carefully addressed.

The factors associated and which still need further attention are:

- Sustainable Agriculture: Though technology is used in increasing the productivity of the agriculture, environmental and social factors are not considered
- Technological Constraint: Standardization of technology is important in improving the communication between farm equipment as it provides more precision, accuracy, speed, and reliability by reducing future cost. Research and open source projects should be encouraged more to improve the quality of technological solutions.
- End-User Oriented: Solution providers should make products and solutions easy, readable, and understandable. Technological solutions should always be user-friendly. It should suit local contexts and needs.
- Multidiscipline Collaboration: Many issues in the agriculture can be approached from various other disciplines. They provide better solutions, improves productivity. Collaboration and cooperation among experts from different fields will improve the agricultural industry.

Figure 8. Agriculture in future

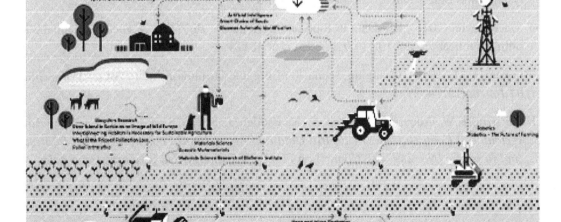

CONCLUSION

Currently, there is a need for every farmer to adopt new and modern tools and techniques to balance food demand and supply concerns. Present environmental conditions are not favorable, making it harder for farmers to predict rainfall, soil conditions, and even the groundwater level. . If the latest technology is easily available and user-friendly, it can support millions of farmers. There is a need for dedicated research in the field of Big Data in agriculture and access to data sources is important for researchers to practice, innovate, and create other platforms. Companies must provide balance between confidential farms data and data that can be used to enhance their work. These factors will fill the gap between both Big Data and agricultural space in the future coming years.

Before implementation of big data in farming it was not possible to predict Pest and crop diseases and natural disasters. Big data and monitoring technologies can track such events and even predict them completely. By giving past and present data into a system and extracting insights through valid algorithms, data science can effectively boost future yields. This can save farmers and supply chain stakeholders a lot of money as well as help to facilitate distribution patterns and supply. Big data drives the incorporation of modern technology into the field. UAVs or drones can be used to fly over and assess land patterns. Alternatively, Internet of Things sensors can track and monitor croplands and plants remotely. Hence, Big data analytics will become the future technology to analyze the agricultural data.

REFERENCES

Ashok, K. (2018). Big Data in Agriculture: A Challenge for the Future. *Applied Economic Perspectives and Policy*, *40*(1), 79–96. doi:10.1093/aepp/ppx056

Basnet & Bang. (n.d.). The State-of-the-Art of Knowledge-Intensive Agriculture: A Review on Applied Sensing Systems and Data Analytics. *Journal of Sensors*.

Bronson & Knezevic. (2016). Big Data in food and agriculture. *Big Data & Society*, (January-June). Advance online publication. doi:10.1177/2053951716648174

Chandrashekar, H. M. (2010). Changing, scenario of organic farming in India: An overview. *International NGO Journal*, *5*, 34–39.

Coble, K., Griffin, T. W., Ahearn, M., Ferrell, S., McFadden, J., Sonka, S., & Fulton, J. (2016). *Advancing U.S. Agricultural Competitiveness with Big Data and Agricultural Economic Market Information, Analysis, and Research (No. 249847)*. Council on Food, Agricultural, and Resource Economics.

Diebold, F. X. (2012). *A Personal Perspective on the Origin(s) and Development of "Big Data": The Phenomenon, the Term, and the Discipline, Second Version*. University of Pennsylvania, Penn Institute for Economic Research, Working PaperNo.13-003.

Dyer, J. (2016). *The Data Farm: An Investigation of the Implications of Collecting Data on the Farm*. Nuffield Australia Project No 1506.

Fan, J., Han, F., & Liu, H. (2014). Challenges of Big Data Analysis. *National Science Review*, *1*(2), 293–314. doi:10.1093/nsr/nwt032 PMID:25419469

Garnett, T., Appleby, M. C., Balmford, A., Bateman, I. J., Benton, T. G., Bloomer, P., Burlingame, B., Dawkins, M., Dolan, L., Fraser, D., Herrero, M., Hoffmann, I., Smith, P., Thornton, P. K., Toulmin, C., Vermeulen, S. J., & Godfray, H. C. J. (2013). Sustainable intensification in agriculture: Premises and policies. *Science*, *341*(6141), 33–34. doi:10.1126cience.1234485 PMID:23828927

Kellengere Shankarnarayan, V., & Ramakrishna, H. (2020, September). Paradigm change in Indian agricultural practices using Big Data: Challenges and opportunities from field to plate. *Information Processing in Agriculture*, *7*(3), 355–368. Advance online publication. doi:10.1016/j.inpa.2020.01.001

Kramer, S. B., Reganold, J. P., Glover, J. D., Bohannan, B. J. M., & Mooney, H. A. (2006). Reduced Nitrate Leaching and Enhanced Denitrifier Activity and Efficiency in Organically Fertilised Soils. *Proceedings of the National Academy of Sciences of the United States of America*, *103*(12), 4522–4527. doi:10.1073/pnas.0600359103 PMID:16537377

Lan, Y., Chen, S., & Bradley, K. F. (2017). Current status and future trends of precision agricultural aviation technologies. *International Journal of Agricultural and Biological Engineering*, *10*(3), 1–17.

Mariappan & Zhou. (n.d.). A Threat of Farmers' Suicide and the Opportunity in Organic Farming for Sustainable Agricultural Development in India. *Sustainability 2019*. doi:10.3390u11082400

Mishra, B. B., & Nayak, K. C. (2004). Organic farming for sustainable agriculture. *Orissa Review*, *10*, 42–45.

Nandwani, D. (Ed.). (2016). *Organic Farming for Sustainable Agriculture*. Springer. doi:10.1007/978-3-319-26803-3

Oliveira, T. H. M., Painho, M., Santos, V., Sian, O., & Barriguinha, A. (2014). Development of an agricultural management information system based on open-source solutions. *Procedia Technology*, *16*, 342–354. doi:10.1016/j.protcy.2014.10.100

Prasad, B. R., & Agarwal, S. (2016). Comparative study of big data computing and storage tools: A review. *International Journal of Database Theory and Application*, *9*(1), 45–66. doi:10.14257/ijdta.2016.9.1.05

Sabarinaand & Priya. (2015). Lowering data dimensionality in big data for the benefit of precision agriculture. *International Conference on Intelligent Computing, Communication & Convergence*.

Tian, L., Meng, Q., Wang, L., & Dong, J. (2014). A study on crop growth environment control system. *International Journal of Control and Automation*, *7*(9), 357–374. doi:10.14257/ijca.2014.7.9.31

van de Kerkhof, van Persiea, Noorbergena, Schoutenb, & Ghauharalic. (2015). Spatio-temporal analysis of remote sensing and field measurements for smart farming. *Spatial Statistics 2015: Emerging Patterns*.

van Evert, Fountas, Jakovetic, Crnojevic, Travlos, & Kempenaar. (n.d.). Big Data for weed control and crop protection. *Weed Research*. Doi:10.1111/wre.12255

Varian, H. (2014). Big Data: New Trick for Econometrics. *The Journal of Economic Perspectives*, *28*(2), 3–28. doi:10.1257/jep.28.2.3

Wimmer, H., & Powell, L. M. (2015). A comparison of open source tools for data science. *Proceedings of the Conference on Information Systems Applied Research*, 8, 4–12.

Woodard, J. D. (2016). Data Science and Management for Large Scale Empirical Applications in Agricultural and Applied Economics Research. *Applied Economic Perspectives and Policy*, *38*(3), 373–388. doi:10.1093/aepp/ppw009

Chapter 7
Automated Soil Residue Levels Detecting Device With IoT Interface

Adiraju Prasanth Rao
https://orcid.org/0000-0002-5119-3987
Anurag Group of Institutions, India

K. Sudheer Reddy
Anurag Group of Institutions, India

Sathiyamoorthi V.
https://orcid.org/0000-0002-7012-3941
Sona College of Technology, Salem, India

ABSTRACT

Cloud computing and internet of things (IoT) are playing a crucial role in the present era of technological, social, and economic development. The novel models where cloud and IoT are integrated together are foreseen as disruptive and enable a number of application scenarios. The e-smart is an application system designed by leveraging cloud, IoT, and several other technology frameworks that are deployed on the agricultural farm to collect the data from the farm fields. The application extracts and collects the information about the residue levels of soil and crop details and the same data will be hosted in the cloud environment. The proposed e-smart application system is to analyze, integrate, and correlate datasets and produce decision-oriented reports to the farmer by using several machine learning techniques.

INTRODUCTION

The historical backdrop of Horticulture in India goes back to Hindu Valley in development time and even before that in certain pieces of south-India. India reaches 2nd worldwide in farm outputs. In 2008, Agriculture employed 50% of India work force and contributed 17%-18% of national's GDP. However,

DOI: 10.4018/978-1-7998-2566-1.ch007

in India still farmers are facing scrupulous problems by not getting minimal price for their crop. Agriculture Sector in India is diminishing day after day resulting in not only lesser farm outputs but also fast disappearance of the traditional knowledge base of thousands of years of practical experience of farming. There is need to resolve this problem and guide the farmers in effective way by proposing smart agricultural system. The smart agriculture system should include making use of latest technology for better productivity in the agriculture field for different activities. These activities such as loosening the soil, seeding, special watering, moving plants when they grow bigger and lead to abundant growth of a crop. Pesticide buildup alludes to the pesticides that may stay on or in the food after they are applied to the food crops or to the dirt. The most extreme permitted levels of these buildups in food or soil are frequently endorsed by administrative bodies in numerous nations. By their tendency, pesticides are destructive to certain types of life. It is in this way to be expected that, at a specific degree of presentation, they might be unsafe to people. The amount of poisons in wheat can be incredibly high, and may represent a danger to human wellbeing. To the extent medical issues because of pesticide deposits in staples are concerned, a few nations have begun food tainting checking programs which assess information of pesticide buildups as per models and rules suggested by the Codex Committee on Pesticide Residues, just as by the European Union. The main steps for agricultural practices include preparation of soil, sowing, adding manure and fertilizers, irrigation, harvesting and storage. In village, farmers need information throughout the entire farming cycle for taking effective decision in time. The proposed Automated Soil Residue Levels Detecting Device (ASRLDD) with IoT interface need modern tools and technologies that can improve production efficiency, product quality, schedule and monitoring the crops, fertilizer, spraying, planting…etc and monitoring geospace time which helps the farmers choosing their best suitable crop. The ASRLDD with IoT interface model uses an IoT technology and a few kinds of sensors which are deployed in the crop field area, helps us in collecting the data from agriculture sector. The smart Agriculture System receives data from IoT devices which are configured with the system and same data will be uploaded into a cloud server. Cloud computing and Internet of Things (IoT) are two different advancement that are already part of our life. Their adoption and use are expected to be more and more pervasive, making them important components of the Future Internet. The smart Agriculture System uses different devices or smart things and these are interconnected for communication purpose. These devices collect the data and stores in cloud for analysis. The main objective of this proposal is to develop an automated embedded device for finding the pesticides residue levels in the soil or food in a given agriculture land. The proposed system integrates, analyzes, and correlates different data sets of information collected from agriculture sector and generates analysis report to the farmer using machine learning techniques. The purpose of this chapter is to introduce the various technologies as a frame of reference for effective way of analyzing agriculture data.

The main objective of this chapter is to describe crop and soil management for agriculture using low cost automated detecting device with IoT interface. This System is also useful to the farmers to know which type of crop should be cultivated and to estimate the productivity of that crop for particular season. The cropping details and data generated from the system are stored in cloud and proper machine learning technique is used for analyzing this data. It is also useful to the farmers to know which type of crop should be cultivated and to estimate the productivity of that crop for particular season. It makes a multidisciplinary research circumstance for exploring and tentatively approving profoundly inventive and progressive thoughts in the Agriculture area.

ASRLDD Objectives:

1. Developed an automated soil residue levels detecting device with IoT applications through cloud of resources.
2. Development of Application Software for effective Cropping, to know the Pesticide Residual level in the Soil and Maximize Agricultural Business Performance.
3. Crop Production Rate increases
4. Monitoring agriculture is much easier.
5. Creates research facility in the field of Agriculture Domain.
6. Quality food produced without any side effects

In the following paragraphs gives detailed description about the organization of the rest of the chapter. The section 2 presents the back ground of problem, section 3 presents ASRLDD architecture diagram, Section 4 gives implementation methodology and results. The conclusions and future enhancement presents in section 5.

BACKGROUND

The intention of this chapter is to implement a highly enabled crop field monitoring system without human interactions. In agricultural applications, for precision Sensors are used and they are very much essential nowadays. This Chapter presents details about how to utilize sensors in crop field area and their applications in real time environment. The fundamental concept of this Chapter is to provide a highly enabled monitoring of crop field. The system consists of a large number of low cost sensors which are deployed in the sensing area. These low cost sensors will sense the parameters of soil, moisture content etc., at that particular area where the sensor is placed, and transmit the information gathered to the observer for further analyzing and processing. These kinds of sensors will eliminate the physical connectivity between devices and hence installation cost and maintenance will be reduced. Potential benefits from these would be avoiding catastrophic failures, improvement in production and yield, conservation of natural resources, and respond to natural disasters and emergency immediately.

The system mainly consists of microcontroller system, solar PV module; backup power unit for power the circuitry, wireless sensors, and ADC unit etc. The microcontroller unit processes the data received from wireless sensors (ADC unit present in sensor converts analog signal into digital form) and sends through another network to either central server or cloud. It also performs various tasks provided in the program, and controls the various components present in the system. The Critical Review of latest Status of the Technology in the Agriculture to improve productivity with complete references as presented below.

The authors Peter O. Onuwa, Ishaq S. Eneji, Adams U. Itodo and Rufus Sha'Ato(2017) aim to mine pesticide residues in few edible crops and soils from farm lands so as to determine their concentration in order to assess their safety status. They used Phase extraction technique to extract pesticides content mainly of organ chlorine class from some edible crop plants and soils as well as determining some main physicochemical parameters of the soils.

A Review proposed by Narmilan a (2017) on E-Agricultural Concepts for Improving Productivity. Agriculture plays important role in the economy of any developing country, so it is important to develop the field of agriculture through ICTs. The best way to enhance the agriculture production is by E-Agriculture method. The field of agriculture itself is very vast field, through ICTs the complete data of agriculture can be utilized for instant, important, necessary decisions and even to analyze and forecast the agriculture yield. So, ICTs role and usage is very important and its growing day by day and impact can be seen in the present farming owners. It has certainly high impact on the production of agriculture by transferring the necessary information when it is required through the rural communities and also its applications depends on the need of the agriculture stakeholders who depend on agriculture either directly or indirectly. Based on these principals, the application of emerging trends in ICT may be applied to almost all the processes involved in Agriculture as well as related to it. Thus, it will always be helpful in both the product efficiency and process efficiency by means of reducing the cost and time in the functionalities involved in Agriculture. Mohammad AbdurRazzaque, Andrei Palade, and Siobhán Clarke Middleware (2016) have proposed the Internet of Things (IoT) which envisaged a future in which digital and physical things or objects (e.g., Smartphone's, TVs, cars..etc) can be connected by means of suitable information and communication technologies, to enable range of applications and services. Marcel Fafchamps et.al., 2012 have proposed a method to help the Farmers to know about the market and weather information which will come to the Farmer's mobile phone as a SMS, so that any kind of decisions on crop can be taken.

The authors Sharma Meenakshi and Singh Ranveer (2008) have focused on "Post-Harvest Losses in Fruits and Vegetables in Himachal Pradesh." As the name suggests, the authors concluded that post harvest losses occurred at wholesaler or retailer level with 18.31 to 24.85% with respect to total production and production level with 18.98 to 28.25% with respect to total production for selected fruits and vegetables. Nalini Ranjan Kumar, Pandey N. K. and Rana R. K.(2008) authors studied production rate and Marketing of Potato in Banaskantha District of Gujarata. The authors emphasized on the recent decrease in production of potatoes and the main reason behind the same is the Farmers are lagging in know how to produce the potatoes. Singh L. P. (1992), has emphasized the "Economics of Tobacco Cultivation, Production and Exchange". In this work, the authors discussed elaborately about tobacco and production of tobacco with respect to other cash crops.

Many farmers in India cannot perform soil assessment with enough attention due to lack of awareness and technological advancement. The advancement and accomplishment in micro/nano electronics and IoT systems performs an effective smart forming and diagnostics. These systems effectively assess the health of the soil and management to achieve high production with excessive use of fertilizers and pesticides. The authors Md. Azahar Ali, Liang Dong, Jaspreet Dhau, Ajit Khosla, and Ajeet Kaushik presented detailed report on electrochemical sensor-based soil quality assessment (2020).

The main objective of smart irrigation and monitoring system is to provide an effective cropping, reduce water wastage and high production rate. This system mainly evaluates the water required for a plant by the parameters such as soil moisture, air humidity and temperature. The authors Raju Anitha, D Suresh, P Gnaneswar, M M Puneeth(2019) developed a product called the smart irrigation and monitoring system for the farmers so that they can choose the specific type of plant that is being cultivated and it can be calibrated for different types of plants too. Machine learning is used by the proposed system which compares actual values obtained from sensors with threshold values already fed to machine learning algorithm for analysis purpose.

The authors Mustapha F. A. Jallow, Dawood G. Awadh, Mohammed S. Albaho, Vimala Y. Devi and Nisar Ahmad investigated the levels of pesticides residues in fruits and vegetables samples were contaminated with pesticide residues, with concentration above the MRL. The observed pesticides in fruits and vegetables leads to health risk for customers and pesticides monitoring highly recommended (2017).

The authors M Lavanya and Sujatha Srinivasan(2018) has done extensive research for publishing papers in various journals in domain agriculture and green house using IoT and WSN.These researchers mainly contributed for predicting and controlling the parameter like weather, soil, pest,CO2,water level, crop yield using machine learning algorithms and cloud computing in their work for system is more intelligent.

The literature review and issues and challenges identified are presented above and summary of this survey is the problem statement of Automated Soil Residue Level Detecting Device (ASRLDD).

ASRLDD ARCHITECTURE DIAGRAM

An Agriculture IoT system consists of multiple monitoring nodes and these are controlled by centralized controller. A microcontroller based embedded device within the node capture data from sensors and sends the same data to the cloud for further processing. Data stored in the cloud and different applications of software are configured with the system for analyzing the data. The centralized controller is aware of the status of all end nodes and sends control commands to the nodes. The end nodes are equipped with various sensors placed at different locations for monitoring and managing agriculture data. Data analysis is the process of evaluating data using analytical and statistical tools to discover useful information and aid in business decision making. There are a several data analysis methods including data mining, text analytics, business intelligence and data visualization. There are many software tools such as Image processing (IM toolki, VTK toolkit, OpenCV library), Machine Learning tools (Google TensorFlow, R, weka..etc), Cloud –based platforms for large-scale information storing, analysis and computation such as Cloud era, EMC corporation, IBM Info Sphere BigInsights,IBMPureData system for analytics, Aster SQLMapReduce,Pivotal GemFire,Pivotal Green plum, MapR Coverage data platform, Horton works and Apache Pig Cloudera, EMC corporation, IBM Info Sphere BigInsights,IBMPureData system for analytics, Aster SQLMapReduce,Pivotal GemFire,Pivotal Green plum, MapR Coveraged data platform, Horton works and Apache Pig. The Agriculture managing and monitoring Architecture Diagram as shown Figure 1.

Figure 1. ASRLDD Architecture Diagram

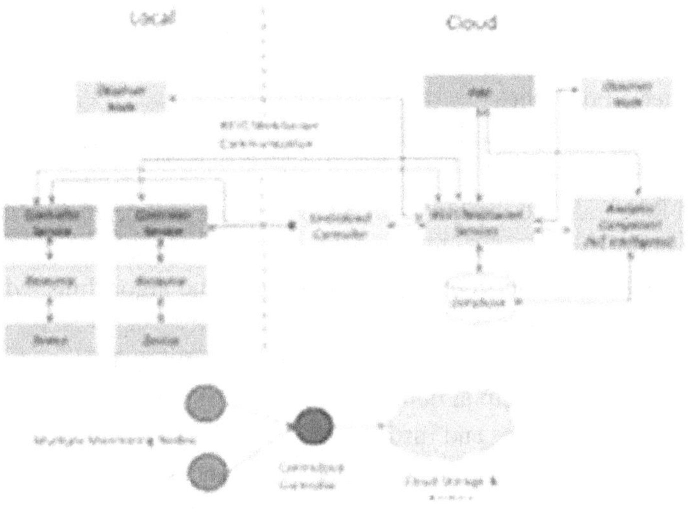

The ASRLDD Architecture Diagram is Comprises the three major computing components as shown in the figure 1.

Local Nodes

The field consists of observer nodes, controller Service for given agriculture sector and these nodes capture the data from site and sends to cloud using communication channels.

Observer Nodes

The agriculture system consists of multiple independent nodes are placed at different locations for collecting data, communicating to other parts of the system and receiving analyzed data. This node are equipped with various sensors such as Temperature, Humidity, water level and IR sensor and sends the data to cloud server using controller service and communication protocols.

Controller Service

Each agriculture node at particular area runs its own controller service that sends the data to the cloud. The interconnection of different devices and resources are interfaced to the controller that uses sensors to collect data. This type interconnecting embedded system uses a communication protocols such WiFi, Bluetooth, 802.11.4 or custom communication system. The type communication protocol is selected based on the distribution of nodes and amount of data to be collected.

Communication Channels

The data which is collected from the local nodes can communicated to centralized server through rest/ web socket protocol for further processing.

Centralized Controller

The centralized controller monitors and manages the multiple independent nodes in the agriculture field. The main challenge of the centralized controller in Agriculture Technology provides identifying the right business model for better productivity.

The Functions of Centralized Controller helps the farmers as given below.

1. Crop Production Rate increases and monitoring agriculture is much easier.
2. Plan harvesting; optimize labor scheduling, track food provenance and food safety.
3. A data service to help researchers create new knowledge and algorithms, which in turn feed back into our data sets.
4. Develop research facility in the field of Agriculture Sector using IoT platform technology which is enabling us to rapidly pivot into agriculture.
5. Invite partnerships from Industry and Institutions.
6. Publish research outcome in reputed journals and conferences.

Communication Service

The Sensor measurement can change across the farm due to water input, seeds, soil nutrients, soil moisture…etc from different nodes in Agriculture Area. All such type data can indicate useful practice in farms and make better decision for effective cropping. So there is need effective communication for collecting sensor data requires to establish network connection across agriculture field. Sensors, Cameras, IoT devices and Drones can connect to the base station over a Wi-Fi front end. This ensures high bandwidth connectivity within the farm. The first step requires connectivity between data generated units such as various kinds of embedded devices or from sensors in agriculture and global storage unit (Cloud).The device configuration in the agriculture field is important due the following reasons:

1. Establish connectivity between sensor or IoT device and software system which allows retrieving data from sensor or device.
2. Data communication major task in IoT environment
3. Designing effective communication, scheduling strategies and configuring IoT device under heterogeneity environment are challenging issue.

The management of IoT becomes very difficult in a large distributed environment and without a careful management design, agriculture system results in significant performance degradation. These embedded devices need to be configured before assigning a task and also need to define a protocol stack to address all devices and plan to achieve the proposed tasks.

CLOUD STORAGE AND ANALYTICS

Cloud computing is a transformative computing patterning that involves delivering applications and services over internet. The smart Agriculture System receives data from IoT devices which are configured with the system and same data will be uploaded into a cloud server. The smart agriculture system uses different devices or smart things and these are interconnected for communication purpose. These devices collect the data and stores in cloud for analysis.

The analytics module is responsible for analyzing the data and generates reports area wise. The analysis IoT data can be performed in the cloud for all nodes for given agriculture area but reports are generated node wise. These IoT applications provide an interface to farmers for monitoring and managing their agriculture land in effective way of cultivation. The cloud enables three functions data accesses from agriculture sector, applications resides in cloud to make crop suggestions and crop farm analytics and generate the reports for farmers. The farmers would able to improve crop yields and make effective use of water, pesticides and in turn wastage of any sort would be reduced to remarkable level to increase productivity.

The major components required implementing our projects are Resistive and Capacitive Sensor for soil analysis, Microcontroller, Wi Fi Camera for image capturing cloud server for data analytics purpose. The different applications in table 1 are developed and uploaded in cloud for analysis purpose.

Table 1. Agriculture Management System

S. No	Application Name	Description
1.	Soil Management	Soil Analysis: Fertilizer identification for various crops a. Environmental Condition b. Residual Fertilizers or Pesticides content in the Soil c. Moisture Content GPS Location
2.	Sensor Management	Different Sensors are placed each node in agriculture area need manage. a. Resistive and Capacitive Sensor b. Temperature Sensor c. Humidity Sensor d. Water Level Sensor e. IR Sensor
3.	Precision Agriculture	An Agriculture IoT application is required accuracy to ensures timely delivery of real time data about weather forecasting, quality of soil, cost of labor and crop reports to farmers
4.	Pest Management	An environmental data monitoring of temperature, moisture, plant growth and levels of pests using Agriculture IoT system to increase production rate.
5	Crop Management	The crop management involves different agriculture activities such as water level, crop cultivation using Agriculture IoT system.
6	Data Analytics	a. Crop Analytics based on the past data b. Soil Analytics (Crop Management and time to spray fertilizer) Pest Analytics based on crop selection and soil analysis

METHODOLOGY

The primary and secondary data are used to critically evaluate the chapter objectives. Beforehand, researcher or cultivator investigations for better crop yield will be always use the major source of data. Regulatory authorities has directed certain norms with regard to the maximum residue levels of the pesticide as they are very much harmful in some or other form to human life with certain level of pesticide exposure, residue here implies the left over pesticide which may be there on or in the food crops when pesticides applied to the food crops. Here, in this project, it is proposed to implement an automated embedded device with IoT enabled system which dig into the soil and compute the residue levels of soil at that particular place and this is carried out for the various slots in that agricultural land and the data accumulated is stored onto the cloud for further processing. The following procedure is adopted in this project:

For given agriculture land in a village, the land is divided into n number of sample space and each space area comprises of certain m slots. The number m, n are integer values and these values changes depending upon the area of agriculture land, flat area and slope area. At least one sampling space for each area for computing residue levels of the soil.

Procedure for residue levels or NPK values in the soil

1. Select Specific location for given agriculture Area.
2. Identify different slots(n) for (a)
3. Identify slopes for each slot(i)
4. Identify flat areas for each slope(i)

5. For each flat area, compute the residue levels using ASRLDD device.
6. Residue levels data can be stored in cloud for further processing.
7. Repeat step (c) to (e) for all slopes.
8. Repeat step (b) to (f) for all n slots
9. Repeat the step (a) but different location for same agriculture land.
10. Repeat steps (b) to (f).
11. Repeat above process for considerable samples.

The distance between each sampling space and the depth of sampling will be determined by the past pesticide usage and the purpose of the testing. The number of sampling space (n) and slots (m) can be determined by identify the slopes in the agriculture land. The numbers of flat area are identified for given slope and the residue levels for each flat are can computed. The above procedure can be repeated by taking different samples for different levels of the agriculture fields.

In this chapter, a novel automated embedded device with IoT enabled system is proposed to know the pesticide residue levels present in the soil, which can be analyzed by taking samples at different locations of the agriculture field, so that usage of the pesticide for the next crop is reduced and also the over concentration of pesticide can be avoided and it would be at allowable levels as per the regulatory bodies.

The primary and secondary data are used to critically evaluate the presented chapter objectives. Off course, the research scholar or farmer investigations for better crop yield will be always the main source of data. Here, in this project, it is proposed to implement an automated embedded device with IoT enabled system which dig into the soil and compute the residue levels of soil at that particular place and this is carried out for the various slots in that agricultural land and the data accumulated is stored onto the cloud for further processing.

FIELD TEST

In Agriculture, a porch is a bit of inclined plane that has been cut into a progression of increasingly collapse level surfaces or stages, which takes after paces, for motivation behind more successful cultivating. Each Agriculture Sector is divided into n number of sample space and m slots which depends upon number of sloped planes. Each slopped plane is known to be one sample space and it further divides into m slots. Each slot is known to be testing area to measure residual levels of the soil using an ASRLDD device which is dipped into that area. The Ph. sensor is interfaced with device to known the quantity of nutrients present in the soil. The above procedure can be repeated by taking different samples for different levels of the agriculture fields.

Similar as a Mobile phone, the specialized types of modems which are wireless networks and works on subscription basis (acknowledging the Subscriber Identity Module (SIM) card embedded in computer) are called as operate Global System for Mobile Communications (GSM) modems. So these kinds of modems will be acting as dedicated mobile phone for computer compared to the traditional which will be used for dialing up the other computer systems. By using GSM module, system can be sends the data to cloud for analysis purpose and generated reports sent to farmers to their mobiles in text format. This device uses different sensors for testing soils which shows the NPK values, temperature, humidity, residues levels of the soil. The sample Ph values as shown in the figure2.

Figure 2. Screen Shot for Ph sensor Value Using Device

The mixtures of three primary mineral nutrients are Nitrogen, Phosphorus and Potassium is required for healthy plant growth. This composition is known to be NPK in which potassium nutrient is essential for any plant growth. German Scientist Von Liebig was responsible for the theory that NPK levels are the basis for determining healthy plant growth. However this theory does not into account of other nutrients such as sulfur, oxygen, carbon, magnesium, etc. Many of researchers talk about the importance of three beneficial soil there different components such Nitrogen, Phosphorous and Potash (Potassium) and can be described with N-P-K. The agriculture industry relies heavily on the use of NPK fertilizer to meet global food supply and ensure health crops.

The calculation process involves NPK (Nitrogen, Phosphorus, and Potassium) value generation and sms alert to end user as shown Figure 3 and Figure 4.

Figure 3. Calculation Process for NPK values using ASRLDD Device

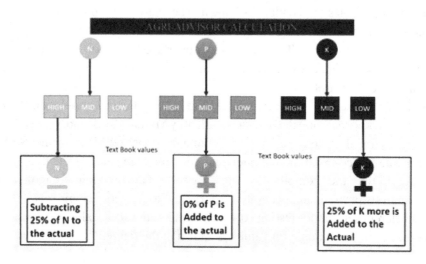

Figure 4. SMS alerts to END user using ASRLDD Device

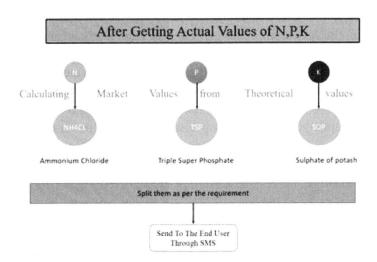

The above Figure 3 and Figure 4 calculate the NPK values and sends message to concerned formers. In similar way an ASRLDD device detects to residue levels of soil which is communicated to farmers for good agriculture practice. Pesticide usage has to be limited, as presently there are certain customs as directed by regulatory authorities in the highest residue levels of the pesticide as they are very much harmful in few or other form to human life with certain level of pesticide exposure, residue here implies the left over pesticide which may be there on or in the food crops when pesticides applied to the food crops.

This chapter presents a novel automated ASRLDD embedded device with IoT enabled system is proposed to know the pesticide residue levels present in the soil, crop and cultivations management system which can be analyzed by taking samples at different locations of the agriculture field. This methodology also helps that usage of the pesticide for the next crop is reduced and also the over concentration of pesticide can be avoided and it would be at allowable levels as per the regulatory bodies.

The primary and secondary data are used to critically evaluate the presented chapter objectives. Off course, the research scholar or farmer investigations for better crop yield will be always the main source of data. Pesticide usage has to be limited, as presently there are certain norms as directed by regulatory authorities in the maximum residue levels of the pesticide as they are very much harmful in some or other form to human life with certain level of pesticide exposure, residue here implies the left over pesticide which may be there on or in the food crops when pesticides applied to the food crops. Here, in this chapter, it is proposed to implement an automated embedded device with IoT enabled system which dig into the soil and compute the residue levels of soil or pesticides at that particular place and this is carried out for the various slots in that agricultural land and the data accumulated is stored onto the cloud for further processing.

CONCLUSION AND FUTURE ENHANCEMENTS

This main inspiration of this chapter is to guide the farmers in efficient way by proposing e-smart village application. These applications are incorporate data-driven, actionable insights into the farmer's experience. Insights are delivered in context as features in agriculture sector that enable farmers to more efficiently complete a desired task or action. The E-smart village can be making use of latest technology for better productivity in the agriculture field. In all the cultivation related augmentation processes the E-Agriculture plays an important role which is considered to be an industry with exhaustive information and fast in nature. Due negative impact of the globalization, the Indian farmers need contend with farmers of developed nations. In light of this impact, the Indian farmers need to create great quality agriculture products with reasonable cost to compete world market. Hence, Training preparation is required for dealing with the E-agriculture system for better quality products.Pesticide usage has to be limited, as presently there are certain norms as directed by regulatory authorities in the highest residue levels of the pesticide as they are very much harmful in some or other form to human life with certain level of pesticide exposure. For example, the residue level of pesticide in the wheat crop can be very much high and this may lead to threat to life of humans.

The following enhancements can be integrated in the village and also farmers should educate for betterment of agriculture sector. The Usefulness of Developed System to farmer is:

1. Effective crop cultivation and estimate the productivity of that crop for particular season using most modern technology.
2. Study of feasibility of different crops for different soils depending on water availabilities.
3. Quality food produced without any side effects.
4. Create an situation in multidisciplinary research explore, authenticate and experiment the ideas which are highly innovative in the field of Agriculture Sector.
5. Creates employability

REFERENCES

Ali, Dong, Dhau, Khosla, & Kaushik. (2020). Perspective—Electrochemical Sensors for Soil Quality Assessment. *Journal of The Electrochemical Society*.

Anitha, Suresh, Gnaneswar, & Puneeth. (2019). IoT Based Automatic Soil Moisture Monitoring System using Raspberry PI. *International Journal of Innovative Technology and Exploring Engineering, 9*(2).

E-Agricultural Concepts for Improving Productivity: A Review proposed by Narmilan A. (2017). *Scholars Journal of Engineering and Technology, 5*(1), 1-17.

Pradhan & Mohapa. (2015). E-agriculture: A Golden Opportunity for Indian Farmers. *An International Journal Research and Development, A Management Review, 4*(1).

Fafchamps & Minten. (2012). Impact of SMS-Based Agricultural Information on Indian Farmers. Oxford Journals, 26(3), 383–414.

Kumar, Pandey, & Rana. (2008). Production and Marketing of Potato in Banaskanthao District of Gujarat. *Indian Journal of Agriculture Marketing, 22*(1).

Lavanya & Srinivasan. (2018). A survey on agriculture and greenhouse monitoring using IoT and WSN. *International Journal of Engineering & Technology, 7*(2.33), 673-677.

Meenakshi & Singh. (2008). Post Harvest Losses in Fruits and vegetables in Himachal Pradesh. *Indian Journal of Agriculture Marketing, 22*(1).

AbdurRazzaque, Palade, & Clarke. (2016). Middleware for Internet of Things: A Survey. *IEEE Internet of Things Journal, 3*(1).

Mustapha, F. A. (2017). Monitoring of Pesticide Residues in Commonly Used Fruits and Vegetables in Kuwait. *International Journal of Environmental Research and Public Health, 2017*(14), 833. doi:10.3390/ijerph14080833

Namisiko, P., & Aballo, M. (2013). Current Status of e-Agriculture and Global Trends: A Survey Conducted in TransNzoia County, Kenya. *International Journal of Scientific Research (Ahmedabad, India), 2*(7).

Onuwa, Eneji, Itodo, & Sha'Ato. (2017). Determination of Pesticide Residues in Edible Crops and Soil from University of Agriculture Makurdi Farm Nigeria Department of Chemistry. *Asian Journal of Physical and Chemical Sciences, 3*(3), 1-17.

Singh, L. P. (1992). *Economics of Tobacco Cultivation, Production and Exchange.* Deep and Deep Publications.

Chapter 8
Biofeedback–Based Mental Health Software and Its Statistical Analysis

Rohit Rastogi

https://orcid.org/0000-0002-6402-7638

Dayalbagh Educational Institute, India & ABES Engineering College, Ghaziabad, India

Devendra Kumar Chaturvedi

https://orcid.org/0000-0002-4837-2570

Dayalbagh Educational Institute, India

Sathiyamoorthi V.

https://orcid.org/0000-0002-7012-3941

Sona College of Technology, Salem, India

ABSTRACT

Many apps and analyzers based on machine learning have been designed already to help and cure the stress issue, which is increasing. The project is based on an experimental research work that the authors have performed at Research Labs and Scientific Spirituality Centers of Dev Sanskriti VishwaVidyalaya, Haridwar and Patanjali Research Foundations, Uttarakhand. In the research work, the correctness and accuracy have been studied and compared for two biofeedback devices named as electromyography (EMG) and galvanic skin response (GSR), which can operate in three modes, audio, visual and audio-visual, with the help of data set of tension type headache (TTH) patients. The authors have realized by their research work that these days people have lot of stress in their life so they planned to make an effort for reducing the stress level of people by their technical knowledge of computer science. In the project they have a website that contains a closed set of questionnaires from SF-36, which have some weight associated with each question.

DOI: 10.4018/978-1-7998-2566-1.ch008

INTRODUCTION

As we can see that almost everyone is suffering from many kind of stress and we all get some indicators which shows that we are suffering from stress rather it be physical, emotional, personal, sleep or behavioral. But manually the level of stress is difficult to calculate and also the people are much more reliable on medication for getting relief. Many times, the individual is lost in physical pleasure, accumulation of facilities and due to lack of right understanding about the self, one bears the ignorance about one's own being. Due to which they suffer from stress most of the time. These consist of pharmacological treatment, physical therapy, acupuncture, relaxation therapy or alternative medicine. So main focus of our project is to check the stress level of a person and give remedies to them accordingly. We are more focused on giving remedies to people which do not include any kind of medications.(PyCharm, n.d.; Rastogi, Chaturvedi, Satya, Arora, & Chauhan, 2018)

Motivation

The experimental research work done by us has motivated us to use our knowledge and make an effort to reduce the stress level of people. Automation and mechanization is rapidly increasing with intelligent machines. Science has done miracles and almost in all walks of life, most works are being done by scientific gadgets and it has no doubt made the human life simpler. It has helped to handle complex issues but contrary to this, there is a dark side of the picture that it has created some negative aspects and challenging situations too. The present crisis of science to human life is that the stress, tension, depression, anxiety, hatred, headache, frustration, suicidal tendency and violence is increasing in our world day by day. The happiness index has been reduced rapidly everywhere. The Human personality is degraded in terms of value system.(Arora et al., 2017; Chaturvedi et al., 2018; Rastogi, Chaturvedi, Satya, Arora, Yadav et al, 2018)

Objective of Research

1. To study and compare the correctness and accuracy of Electromyography(EMG) and Galvanic Skin Response(GSR) biofeedback in three modes: audio, visual and audio-visual.
2. Our project is to check the stress level of a person and give remedies to them accordingly, by classifying them into one of the three categories: low, medium & high stress level.
3. Comparing the efficiency of different algorithms used for classification.

SCOPE OF THE RESEARCH WORK

Measuring the effect of various indicators like physical, sleep, behavioral, personal and emotional parameters are indicators of stress on different levels of stress. The purpose is to reduce the use of medication to lower the level of stress. Measuring the accuracy of the range decided to track the level of stress of a person. A runnable system which checks the stress level of a person. The main objective is to develop a system which gives the remedies which do not involve any kind of medication to a person according to their stress level.(Chaturvedi et al., 2017; Satya et al., 2019)

RELATED PREVIOUS WORK

1. MoodKit a popular app based on IOS which uses the foundation of Cognitive Behavioral Therapy (CBT) and provides different mood improvement activities to different users which are more than 200 in number. Developed by two clinical psychologists, MoodKit helps one to change the thinking pattern and method, to develop self confidence, awareness, creativity, situation handling and problem solving and wise healthy attitude(List of best 25 mobile apps used for mental and physical health., n.d.).

2. Another very good mental health helping app is Mind Shift which has been developed to facilitate teen agers and adults to face the challenges of depression and frustration along with anxiety. The app Mind Shift focuses the sight of users about their thought process for(List of best 25 mobile apps used for mental and physical health., n.d.).

3. Khanna A, Paul M, Sandhu JS. exhibited a detailed research work and in depth study to check accuracy and comparison of efficiency of GSR and EMG biofeedback training process and consequently progressive muscle relaxation process for decreasing the blood pressure and respiratory rate for those subjects who were suffering heavily from acute level of headache(What is biofeedback?, 2008).

4. Biofeedback is getting popular now as an alternate therapy and informs the subject and experimenter both about the current status of headache. It also helps to avoid the excessive use of medications and anti-oxidants for muscle relaxation. It helps the subjects from shifting the dependency on costly medications and consecutive side effects(Chauhan et al., 2018).

5. Chronic TTH was found as the most common problem in all subjects of every type of gender, age, rural-urban sector of any demographical regions. Since most of the problems are psycho somatic so psycho and psychosocial factors are in consideration to study it (Kikuchi et al., 2012).

REQUIREMENT SPECIFICATION EXPERIMENTAL PERSPECTIVE

The Proposed experimentation and analysis is totally based on our earlier research work named "Chronic TTH analysis by EMG and GSR biofeedback on various modes and various medical symptoms"(Arora et al., 2019) and on "Analytical Comparison of Efficacy for Electromyography and Galvanic Skin Resistance Biofeedback on Audio-Visual Mode for Chronic TTH on Various Attributes"(Chauhan et al., 2018). These work have been well published and cited by many in the same domain of research.

In this work, we created a website which comprises Short Form of Health Survey popularly known as SF-36 as the initial survey for the mental status of the subject. Each participants was required to answer the questions and based on their reponses, their individual different scores on various parameters were calculated. Some set of questions were giving one kind of score and other set of questions were giving other kind of responses. The scores were clear indicators for the current status of mental, social, physical and inner health of an individual and high score alays indicate that one posses good health and he/she should maintain it. Average score is indicator of precautions and related guidelines and advisory are issued to him/ her. The low score is alarming bell and immediately subject is warned to visit psychiatrist and nearby mental hospital. Since the extreme situation can be panic and worst to be as suicidal tendency. This app is analyzer, a guide for those who want immediate and online relaxation in some critical circumstances.(Rastogi, Chaturvedi, Satya, Arora, Singhal et al, 2018; Satya et al., 2018; Sharma et al., 2018)

SYSTEM INTERFACES

1. Anguler6, CSS, JavaScript and Bootstrap are used for front end of web portal.
2. Node Js and Express Js are widely used in web platform as back end.
3. Mongo Db is applied for data storage and database creation purposes.
4. Jupyter is used to implement Machine Learning Algorithm in Python.
5. Visual Studio Code platform is used to develop the website.(Rastogi, Chaturvedi, Satya, Arora, Sirohi et al, 2018; Vyas et al., 2018)

HARDWARE INTERFACES

The project occurred in different configurations of system as below:

1. **Operating System**: Linux, Unix, Windows
2. x86 - 64 processor
3. 8 GB RAM
4. **Web Server:** local host provided by Angular CLI and NPM server
5. For Mongo Db version 4.0 installed in OS
6. NPM packages should be installed. (Rastogi, Chaturvedi, Satya, Arora, Sirohi et al, 2018; Vyas et al., 2018)

SOFTWARE INTERFACES

1. Python 3.6
2. Angular 6
3. Node 10.0.0
4. Mongo db 4.0
5. **PyCharm Platform:** Very popular now a days as an Integrated Development Environment (IDE). Python specially uses it for computer programming. Designed by the Czech company Jet Brains. Provides end users the code analysis, a graphical debugger, an integrated unit tester, integration with version control systems (VCSes), and supports web development with Django[PyCharm, n.d.].
6. **Machine Learning with Python language:** Machine Learning uses Data Mining techniques and other learning algorithms to build models of what is happening behind some data so that it can predict future outcomes. It's a particular approach to AI.
7. **Deep Learning**: It is one type of Machine Learning that achieves great power and flexibility by learning to represent the world as nested hierarchy of concepts, with each concept defined in relation to simpler concepts, and more abstract representations computed in terms of less abstract ones.
8. **Artificial Intelligence:** It uses models built by Machine Learning and other ways to reason about the world and give rise to intelligent behavior whether this is playing a game or driving a robot/car. Artificial Intelligence has some goal to achieve by predicting how actions will affect the model of the world and chooses the actions that will best achieve that goal. It is very much programming based.(Saini et al., 2018) Machine Learning is the name given to generalizable algorithms that en-

able a computer to carry out a task by examining data rather than hard programming. It's a subfield of computer science and Artificial intelligence that focuses on developing systems that learn from data and help in making decisions and predictions based on that learning. ML enables computers to make data-driven decisions rather than being explicitly programmed to carry out a certain task. Math provides models; understand their relationships and apply them to real-world objects.(Bansal et al., 2018)

9. **Supervised Learning:** These are "predictive" in nature. The purpose is to predict the value of a particular variable (target variable) based on values of some other variables or explanatory variables). Classification and Regression are examples of predictive tasks. Classification is used to predict the value of a discrete target variable while regression is used to predict the value of a continuous target variable. To predict whether an email is spam or not is a Classification task while to predict the future price of a stock is a regression task. They are called supervised because we are telling the algorithm what to predict. Methods are Linear Regression, Logistic Regression, Decision Trees, Random Forests, Naïve Bayes Classifier, Bayesian Statistics and Inference, K-Nearest Neighbor. (Yadav et al., 2018)

10. **Unsupervised Learning:** These are "descriptive" in nature. The purpose is to derive patterns that summarize the underlying relationships in data. Association Analysis, Cluster Analysis and Anomaly detection are examples of Unsupervised Learning. They are called unsupervised because in such cases, the final outcome is not known beforehand. With unsupervised learning there is no feedback based on the prediction results. Methods are K-Means Clustering, Hierarchal Clustering, Clustering using DBSCAN, Feature Selection and Transformation, Principal Components Analysis (PCA).(Gupta et al., 2019)

MEMORY CONSTRAINTS

To run data on python programs, 2 GB memory space will be required and for both to run the node local host server and angular frontend local host, 1 GB space will be used.

OPERATIONS

Operations that will be done by user on our product are:

1. An user can do registration if they are new user.
2. After successful registration, user will be able to login to our site any time.
3. All those registered users, if don't have given any test then they will be redirected to test page as soon as they will login.
4. All those users who have successfully registered, if they have responded to questionnaire earlier they will be redirected to their dashboard.
5. On their dashboard they will find displayed stress level along with three options: given a re-questionnaire responses, remedies and statics.
6. He can go to any of the options.
7. All the users will get some remedies to follow and practice in their daily life.

8. After few days they can go through the retest.

The time duration for whole experiment was 6 months which included stress recognition through biofeedback devices and providing its remedy through app. For stress level measurements, Short form of health Survey SF-36 questionnaire was used questionnaire and Biofeedback therapy to know current intensity, duration and frequency of headache of subject and for remedy, we applied meditative techniques and alternate therapies. For backup, we stored the data in Google Drive or Hard Disk to avoid any data loss.(Saini et al., 2019; Singhal et al., 2019)

FUNCTIONS OF EXPERIMENTAL APP

1. Our product measured the subject stress level in specified time and helped them to handle it as per their scores and stress intensity. 2. We are using dataset of SF-36(Dataset for SF-36, n.d.) and we have clustered it into three clusters using k-means algorithm and after clustering we have modified and added the dataset with their respective clusters and used it as new dataset for training and testing of classification algorithms
2. We have used 70% data to train four classification algorithms Naïve Baye's, Logistic Regression, SVM and Decision tree and 30% for testing purpose.
3. Out of which Decision tree has most high accuracy in our case.
4. Now in Decision tree we have used various test cases given as the input to the trained model and by the help of outputs of these test cases we were able to find the range in which the new weight will be classified: low, medium or high.
5. We have used the same range limit in website for decided the stress level of the person depending upon the weights of the questions he has answered.

USER CHARACTERISTICS

Subject under considerations were users of all ages (18-65), genders, locality and is mainly focused on adolescents.

CONSTRAINTS

1. The system complied with all local regulatory policies and ethical committee.
2. The users had to answer all the questions honestly otherwise they may be classified into wrong stress level.
3. Our research work was based on EMG and GSR machines with are very costly and very hard to find and do analysis.
4. This product will be windows-based. So all the users must have windows operatingsystem running on their pc's.
5. Our product will use client server architecture and therefore be able to handle multiple participants at onetime.

6. Our product will use cookies to help identify the registered users attempting to use the product via the internet.

7. Our product will provide a backup capability to protect the data.

ASSUMPTIONS AND DEPENDENCIES

It is assumed that every user who will use our product will have windowsoperating system or Linux and all will satisfy the software and hardware requirements mentioned above.

APPORTIONING OF REQUIREMENTS

We may not be able to do thermal imaging. We only used questionnaires to measure the participant stress level. The different diagrams of Mental Health Analyzer(MHA) App are as below.

Figure 1. Use Case Model of MHA App

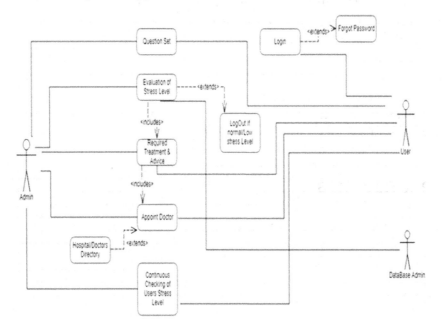

UML SPECIFICATIONS

Use case model was used to exhibit the functions and activities of all users and participants of the study. It also demonstrates the functioning of the app shows the functions that can be done by a particular user according to their position.

In the figure 1, we can see that a particular participant can login, register on site, can take test, can get a result. An administrator can manage the whole database and login on website. The user will get the question set and the evaluation of stress level will be done which will be saved in the database. If the stress level is too high, then he will be advised to go to doctor or psychiatrist.

SYSTEM DESIGN AND METHODOLOGY

System Design

System Architecture

In figure 2, Flowchart shows the flow in which the whole work of site will go on. In this flowchart we can see that when the user will login into the site then they will counter a questionnaire. They will attempt that on basis of given answer their result will be calculated and remedies will be given to them, according to where they lie whether low, medium or high.

Figure 2. Flowchart of MHA App

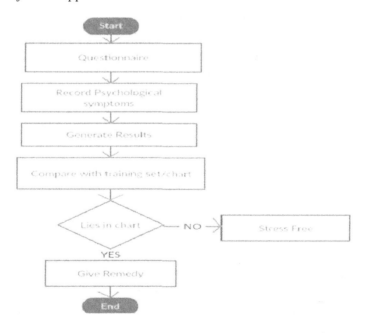

Figure 3, the activity diagram shows all the activities performed in the project are shown.
In the figure 4, data flow diagram level 0 is shown.
In the figure 5, data flow diagram level 1 is shown.
In the figure 6, data flow diagram level 2 is shown.
In the figure 7, Entity relationship diagram is shown with entities, attributes and relationship that are used in the project.

Figure 3. Activity Diagram of MHA App

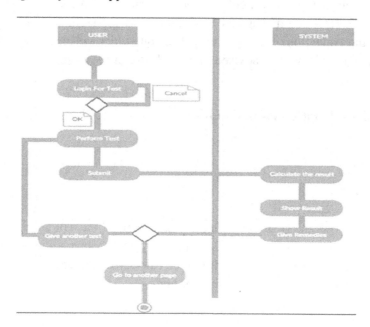

IMPLEMENTATION AND RESULTS

Software and Hardware Requirements

Software Requirements

1. Python 3.6
2. Angular 6
3. Node js 10.0.0
4. Express js
5. Mongo db 4.0
6. PyCharm
7. Angular CLI
8. Mongo shell
9. Visual Studio Code
10. Tablue (Data visualization)

Hardware Requirements

1. Operating System: Linux, Unix or Windows
2. Web Server: Node js and Express js provided by NPM package
3. Ram size: 8 GB
4. x86 - 64 processor
5. EMG (only used for research not for website)
6. GSR (only used for research not for website)

Figure 4. DFD level 0 of MHA app

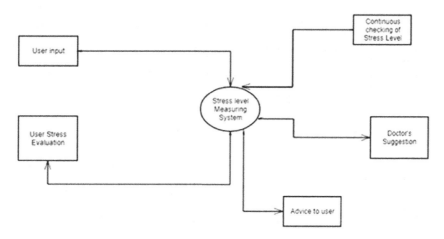

Figure 5. DFD level 1 of MHA app

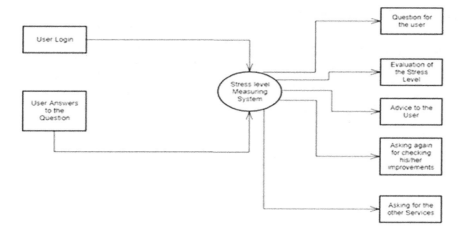

Figure 6. DFD level 2 of MHA app

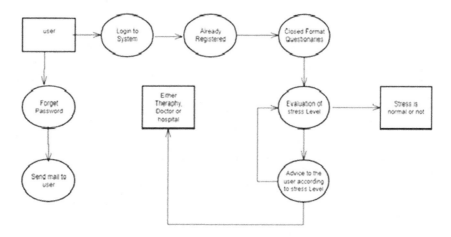

Figure 7. ER Diagram of MHA app

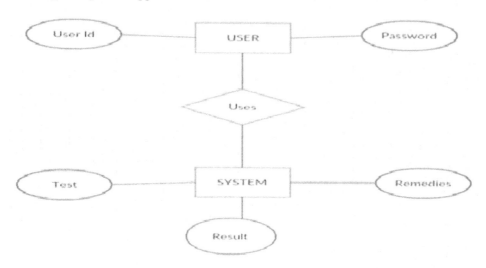

ASSUMPTIONS AND DEPENDENCIES

It is assumed that every user who will use our product will have windows operating system and will satisfy all the software and hardware requirements mentioned above.

IMPLEMENTATION DETAILS

Snapshots of Interfaces

In the figure 8, Home page which will be loaded on the screen of user

Figure 8. Home Page of the MHA app

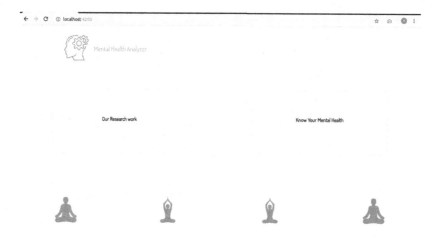

In the figure 9, Login screen will be shown after clicking on Know your mental health option the user will have to login or register if he is new to our website.

Figure 9. Login Page of MHA app

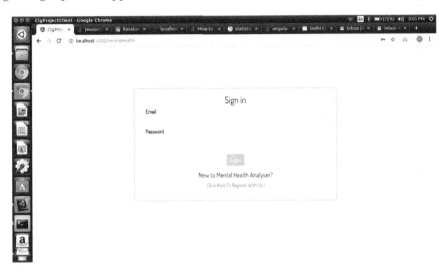

In the figure 10, Test page is shown in which the user will answer the questions and submit.

Figure 10. Test Page of MHA app

In the figure 11, figure 12, figure 13 and figure 14, dashboard is shown which will be opened after the user has given first time his test. This page will contain the result along with three other options to go with i.e. Retest, Remedy and Statics. He can again give retest or go to the remedy page.

Figure 11. Dashboard of MHA app with Medium level of Stress

Figure 12. Dashboard of MHA app with Low level of Stress

In figure 15 remedies depending upon the stress level of the user is shown. It is expected from the user that they will follow the steps sincerely.

TEST CASES

1. If stress level lies in range of S >= 25 and S <=57.
2. If stress level lies in range of S >= 58 and S <=68.
3. If stress level lies in range of S >= 68 and S<=125.

Figure 13. Dashboard of MHA app with High level of Stress

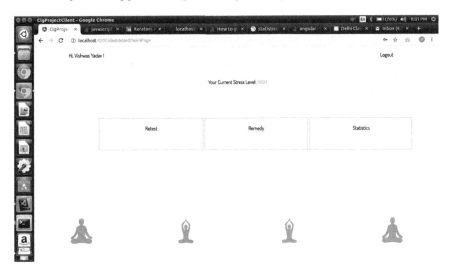

Figure 14. Log of Different responses by an user of MHA app

Figure 15. Remedies proposed of MHA app

RESULT OF OUR RESEARCH WORK

We have find the result that EMG in Audio mode is best among all the other modesof EMG as well as it is also better than GSR in all modes i.e. Audio, Visual andAudio-visual. We have published this results in a book chapter (Arora et al., 2019).

Figure 16. Mean of all questions

q1	2.967419
q2	2.716792
q3	3.022556
q4	2.832080
q5	2.350877
q6	2.852130
q7	3.225564
q8	2.451128
q9	2.238095
q10	2.832080
q11	2.694236
q12	2.471178
q13	2.696742
q14	2.057644
q15	2.558897
q16	1.822055
q17	2.203008
q18	1.944862
q19	2.203008
q20	2.859649
q21	2.498747
q22	1.794486
q23	2.263158
q24	2.403509
q25	3.035088
Total	62.994987

RESULTS OF EXPERIMENTS

In the figure 16, mean calculated by the python code is shown. It is the mean of all the questions answered by 399 people as present in the dataset.

1. We have successfully clustered responses from dataset into three clusters i.e. low, medium & high stress level by the help of K-means algorithms and now we classify new user into one of these three classes.

Figure 17. Clusters of the analyzed datasets

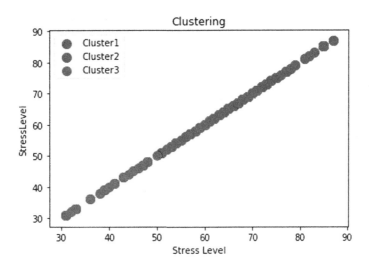

The Figure 17 shows the clusters that we have got using k-means algorithm on the dataset of 399 peoples response of SF-36 questionnaires (Dataset for SF-36, n.d.).

Cluster 1 represents Low Stress Level
Cluster 2 represents Medium Stress Level
Cluster 3 represents High Stress Level

2. After making three clusters we have modified the dataset and added the respective clusters in each row and used the new dataset to train various classification algorithms that we have used: Logistic Regression, Naïve Bayes, SVM, Decision Tree algorithm.
3. For training the machines, we used 70% data and for testing and accuracy, 30% data was used for the purposes.
4. Out of all the algorithms Decision tree gives the best accuracy so we have find out the range of each class i.e. low, medium and high using various test cases onDecision tree algorithm and we have got range limits from it that we are using in ourwebsite for giving results.

The Figure 18 shows the accuracy of various classification algorithms that are used for classification.

CONCLUSION

Performance Evaluation

We have used 70% data for training and 30% for testing purposes. (Saini et al., 2019; Singh et al., 2019) Out of all the algorithms Decision tree gives the best accuracy as shown in table 1, so we have find out the range of each class i.e. low, medium and high using various test cases on Decision tree algorithm and we have got range limits from it that we are using in our website for giving results.

Figure 18. Accuracy of various algorithms applied

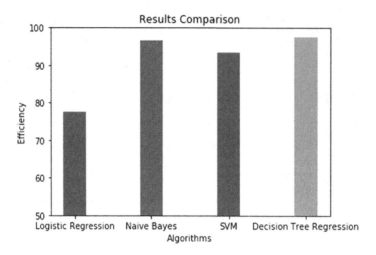

Table 1. Accuracy of various Algorithms applied

S.NO	Algorithm Name	Accuracy(%)
1.	Logistic Regression	77.5
2.	Naïve Bayes Classifier	96.667
3.	SVM	93.333
4.	Decision Tree Regression	97.5

EXPERIMENTAL RESEARCH BASED LEARNING

1. Different technologies like: Angular 6, Mongo db, Node js, Express js, Python, Tableu, k-mean clustering, logistic regression algorithm.
2. Practical implementation of tools like: Visual Studio, Tableu and Mongo Shell
3. Team Work.
4. Dividing and Managing the work.

FUTURE DIRECTIONS

1. Give suggestion of nearby hospitals or psychiatrists by tacking GPS location of the user's device.
2. Send the result with the remedies to the user through email.
3. Make a team for doing survey among people in our college and offices for getting
4. larger dataset so that we may increase the accuracy.
5. Conducting awareness camps for telling people to use this type of application for
6. getting better stress-free lifestyle.

ACKNOWLEDGMENT

Author is a research scholar on domain of scientific spirituality and thankful with gratitude for his guide and co-guides of various prestigious academic institutions to understand the concept well and for showing the path ahead. The Scientific spirituality is the emerging field of future and all spiritual organizations working for betterment of society and humanity in large are acknowledged for their great deeds. The acknowledgement to all those forces which choose us to make this world a better place to live in.

REFERENCES

Arora, N., Rastogi, R., Chaturvedi, D. K., Satya, S., Gupta, M., Yadav, V., Chauhan, S., & Sharma, P. (2019). Chronic TTH Analysis by EMG & GSR Biofeedback on Various Modes and Various Medical Symptoms Using IoT. In Big Data Analytics for Intelligent Healthcare Management. doi:10.1016/B978-0-12-818146-1.00005-2

Arora, N., Trivedi, P., Chauhan, S., Rastogi, R., & Chaturvedi, D. K. (2017). Framework for Use of Machine Intelligence on Clinical Psychology to study the effects of Spiritual tools on Human Behavior and Psychic Challenges. *Proceedings of NSC-2017.*

Bansal, I., Rastogi, R., Chaturvedi, D. K., Satya, S., Arora, N., & Yadav, V. (2018). Intelligent Analysis for Detection of Complex Human Personality by Clinical Reliable Psychological Surveys on Various Indicators. *The National Conference on 3rd MDNCPDR-2018 at DEI.*

Chaturvedi, D. K., Rastogi, R., Arora, N., Trivedi, P., & Mishra, V. (2017). Swarm Intelligent Optimized Method of Development of Noble Life in the perspective of Indian Scientific Philosophy and Psychology. *Proceedings of NSC-2017.*

Chaturvedi, D.K., Rastogi, R., Satya, S., Arora, N., Saini, H., Verma, H., Mehlyan, K., & Varshney, Y. (2018). Statistical Analysis of EMG and GSR Therapy on Visual Mode and SF-36 Scores for Chronic TTH. *Proceedings of UPCON-2018.*

Chauhan, S., Rastogi, R., Chaturvedi, D. K., Satya, S., Arora, N., Yadav, V., & Sharma, P. (2018). Analytical Comparison of Efficacy for Electromyography and Galvanic Skin Resistance Biofeedback on Audio-Visual Mode for Chronic TTH on Various Attributes. In Proceedings of the ICCIDA-2018. Springer.

Dataset for SF-36. (n.d.). https://www.kaggle.com/janiferroborts/sf-36-dataset

Gupta, M., Rastogi, R., Chaturvedi, D. K., Satya, S., Verma, H., Singhal, P., & Singh, A. (2019). Comparative Study of Trends Observed During Different Medications by Subjects under EMG & GSR Biofeedback. *ICSMSIC-2019*, 748-756. https://www.ijitee.org/download/volume-8-issue-6S/

Kikuchi, H., Yoshiuchi, K., Yamamoto, Y., Komaki, G., & Akabayashi, A. (2012). Diurnal variation of tension-type headache intensity and exacerbation: An investigation using computerized ecological momentary assessment. *Biopsychosoc Med, 6*(18). doi: . doi:10.1186/1751-0759-6-18.Page-11,12

List of best 25 mobile apps used for mental and physical health. (n.d.). https://www.psycom.net/25-best-mental-health-apps

PyCharm. (n.d.). https://en.wikipedia.org/wiki/PyCharm

Rastogi, R., Chaturvedi, D. K., Satya, S., Arora, N., & Chauhan, S. (2018). An Optimized Biofeedback Therapy for Chronic TTH between Electromyography and Galvanic Skin Resistance Biofeedback on Audio, Visual and Audio Visual Modes on Various Medical Symptoms. *National Conference on 3rd MDNCPDR-2018 at DEI.*

Rastogi, R., Chaturvedi, D. K., Satya, S., Arora, N., Singhal, P., & Gulati, M. (2018). Statistical Resultant Analysis of Spiritual & Psychosomatic Stress Survey on Various Human Personality Indicators. *The International Conference Proceedings of ICCI 2018.* 10.1007/978-981-13-8222-2_25

Rastogi, R., Chaturvedi, D. K., Satya, S., Arora, N., Sirohi, H., Singh, M., Verma, P., & Singh, V. (2018). *Which One is Best: Electromyography Biofeedback Efficacy Analysis on Audio, Visual and Audio-Visual Modes for Chronic TTH on Different Characteristics. In Proceedings of ICCIIoT-2018, 14-15 December 2018 at NIT Agartala.* Elsevier. https://ssrn.com/abstract=3354375

Rastogi, R., Chaturvedi, D. K., Satya, S., Arora, N., Yadav, V., Chauhan, S., & Sharma, P. (2018). SF-36 Scores Analysis for EMG and GSR Therapy on Audio, Visual and Audio Visual Modes for Chronic TTH. Proceedings of the ICCIDA-2018.

Saini, H., Rastogi, R., Chaturvedi, D. K., Satya, S., Arora, N., Gupta, M., & Verma, H. (2019). An Optimized Biofeedback EMG and GSR Biofeedback Therapy for Chronic TTH on SF-36 Scores of Different MMBD Modes on Various Medical Symptoms. In Hybrid Machine Intelligence for Medical Image Analysis. Springer Nature Singapore Pte Ltd. doi:10.1007/978-981-13-8930-6_8

Saini, H., Rastogi, R., Chaturvedi, D. K., Satya, S., Arora, N., Verma, H., & Mehlyan, K. (2018). *Comparative Efficacy Analysis of Electromyography and Galvanic Skin Resistance Biofeedback on Audio Mode for Chronic TTH on Various Indicators. In Proceedings of ICCIIoT-018.* Elsevier. https://ssrn.com/abstract=3354371

Satya, S., Arora, N., Trivedi, P., Singh, A., Sharma, A., Singh, A., Rastogi, R., & Chaturvedi, D. K. (2019). *Intelligent Analysis for Personality Detection on Various Indicators by Clinical Reliable Psychological TTH and Stress Surveys. In Proceedings of CIPR 2019 at Indian Institute of Engineering Science and Technology.* Springer.

Satya, S., Rastogi, R., Chaturvedi, D. K., Arora, N., Singh, P., & Vyas, P. (2018). Statistical Analysis for Effect of Positive Thinking on Stress Management and Creative Problem Solving for Adolescents. *Proceedings of the 12th INDIA-Com,* 245-251.

Sharma, S., Rastogi, R., Chaturvedi, D. K., Bansal, A., & Agrawal, A. (2018). Audio Visual EMG & GSR Biofeedback Analysis for Effect of Spiritual Techniques on Human Behavior and Psychic Challenges. *Proceedings of the 12th INDIACom,* 252-258.

Singh, A., Rastogi, R., Chaturvedi, D. K., Satya, S., Arora, N., Sharma, A., & Singh, A. (2019). Intelligent Personality Analysis on Indicators in IoT-MMBD Enabled Environment. In *Multimedia Big Data Computing for IoT Applications: Concepts, Paradigms, and Solutions.* Springer. Advance online publication. doi:10.1007/978-981-13-8759-3_7

Singhal, P., Rastogi, R., Chaturvedi, D. K., Satya, S., Arora, N., Gupta, M., Singhal, P., & Gulati, M. (2019). Statistical Analysis of Exponential and Polynomial Models of EMG & GSR Biofeedback for Correlation between Subjects Medications Movement & Medication Scores. *ICSMSIC-2019*, 625-635. https://www.ijitee.org/download/volume-8-issue-6S/

Vyas, P., Rastogi, R., Chaturvedi, D. K., Arora, N., Trivedi, P., & Singh, P. (2018). Study on Efficacy of Electromyography and Electroencephalography Biofeedback with Mindful Meditation on Mental health of Youths. *Proceedings of the 12th INDIA-Com*, 84-89.

What is biofeedback?. (2008). *Association for Applied Psychophysiology and Biofeedback, 12*(5), 12.

Yadav, V., Rastogi, R., Chaturvedi, D. K., Satya, S., Arora, N., Yadav, V., Sharma, P., & Chauhan, S. (2018). Statistical Analysis of EMG & GSR Biofeedback Efficacy on Different Modes for Chronic TTH on Various Indicators. *Int. J. Advanced Intelligence Paradigms, 13*(1), 251–275. doi:10.1504/IJAIP.2019.10021825

Chapter 9
Social Media Content Analysis:
Machine Learning

D. Sudaroli Vijayakumar
 https://orcid.org/0000-0001-8270-6223
PES University, Bangalore, India

Senbagavalli M.
 https://orcid.org/0000-0003-3806-8257
Alliance University, Bangalore, India

Jesudas Thangaraju
Mahendra Engineering College (Autonomous), Namakkal, India

Sathiyamoorthi V.
 https://orcid.org/0000-0002-7012-3941
Sona College of Technology, Salem, India

ABSTRACT

Today's wealth and value are data. Data, used sensibly, are making wonders to make wise decisions for individuals, corporates, etc. The era of spending time with an individual to understand them better is gone. Individual's interests, requirements are identified easily by observing the activities an individual performs in social media. Social media, started as a tool for interaction, has grown as a platform to make and promote business. Social media content is unavoidable as the data that are going to be dealt with is huge in volume, variety, and velocity. The demand for using machine learning in analysing social media content is increasing at a faster pace in identifying influencers, demands of individuals. However, the real complexity lies in making the data from social media suitable for analysis. The type of data from social media content may be audio, video, image. The chapter attempts to give a comprehensive overview of the various pre-processing methods involved in dealing the social media content and the usage of right algorithms at the right time with suitable case examples.

DOI: 10.4018/978-1-7998-2566-1.ch009

INTRODUCTION

The influence of social media in one's life has achieved massive growth. It is very hard to find an individual who does not use Facebook and twitter daily thus contributed a lot in terms of connectivity. It is also been estimated that more than 80% of online users use this social network. Thus, social networks like any network consist of users who are connected to each other through a common web-based application. Nodes here in these social networks are the users and the connectivity is formed through the various commonalties or matches among users through some pattern. This connectivity has improved the way of collecting social data. This drift in technology has eventually replaced the conventional approaches to computational intelligence. The power of social media is so strong, so organizations use this as a tool to identify accurately their competitors, business trends etc (Beier and Wagner, 2016; Senbagavalli and Tholkappia, 2016). This conversion of adopting computational intelligence on social network assist one to do better decision making not only in business but also to spread news faster, take precautions against natural calamities, etc. This social media content analysis gained a lot of popularity due to the closeness results towards the real happenings. This proximity between real and predicted results is made possible because of the huge amount of data that is been used to get insights. The number of users using social networks is increasing at a constant rate so the percentage of accuracy on social media analysis will be incremented.

Despite the numerous benefits, doing a social network analysis involves many complexities as the type of data that has to be handled comes in various forms. Making the data suitable for the analysis itself is a huge task in social networks. It is because most of the data that we obtain through social networks is unstructured. The computational approaches in social networks still in its inception because of the complexities involved in understanding the human language as it varies from person to person.

Another challenge is in the amount of data that must be structured and make it understandable (Chaudhary et al., 2016; TAM, 2016). Assume an organization is having 100 employees. Every employee is having their own set of friends forming around 6 friends' group. In group 1 an employee discusses her resignation to her set of friends on Monday. Tuesday a person from group 2 asks her about her resignation. It was shocking news as the person from group 2 informed her that the whole organization knows about her resignation. This was made possible because of the interrelationship among the six groups. So, to identify who are friends with whom, an analysis process is involved that starts off with the construction of a graph with 100 nodes and edges are drawn as per the friendship node 1 share. This will create a huge number of connections that make a supercomputer unable to analyse this huge data. Another distinctive complexity is in preserving the individual's privacy (Mo & Li, 2015; Bowcott, 2015). With such a huge connectedness, it becomes nearly impossible to maintain an individual's privacy.

Considering the challenges discussed above, it is really a cumbersome activity to make the data suitable for analysis. The type of data can be of various forms. Data collection from multiple sources should necessarily perform data analysis to get some conclusions about the data. What type of analysis should be carried out to what type of data and how to collect and clean different types of data? Answers to these questions come in the form of understanding the different types of data available online. In Section 2 overview the different forms of social data available and the various steps associated with making the data suitable for analysis. Thus, section 2 focuses on the complexities associated with pre-processing social media data. Once the data is collected and cleaned, what type of analysis must be performed? In section 3 discussion on various types of analysis methods and approaches along with specific use cases for the approaches. After getting an insight into the different analysis methods, depending on the problem one must choose the analysis method and relative algorithms. Section 4 gives an idea about the relative algorithms in social network analysis. Once the algorithm is selected knowledge on implementing the algorithm and understanding the output becomes mandatory. Section 5 explores the various tools and frameworks for performing data analysis effectively. Section 6 draws the conclusion and future directions.

TYPES OF SOCIAL DATA

The era of collecting social media data for pursuing any study on the same is no more a jargon. Much of commercial services are available to access the most widely used social networks like Facebook, twitter either through open source, API's or through tools.

The era of collecting social media data for pursuing any study on the same is no more a jargon. Much of commercial services are available to access the most widely used social networks like Facebook, twitter either through open source, API's or through tools(Li and Li,2013)

Classification of Social Media Data Based on Sources

If a user wants to perform a detailed analysis on improving the business strategy or to understand how customers are responding for the new launch, it needs detailed analysis considering the data from multiple sources (Kolog et al., 2018). Considering only the sources of social media, the data comes from multiple sources and they are as follows:

- **Social Networking Sites** These are the data that is certainly obtained from common social networking websites like Facebook, LinkedIn, Twitter, etc. Data about an individual in the form of pictures, text, photos, videos and live discussion. Mainly this type of data allows one to understand an individual's likes and dislikes. This data becomes a great source when it comes to textual analysis to reach a set of audiences for promotions or in identifying potential partners for business etc.
- **Social Review Sites** These are the type of data that is identified from the common review websites discussing a topic. The reviews may be about a product, place etc. This data is useful both from the customer side as well as from the business perspective.
- **Image Sharing and Video Hosting Sites** Another source for getting social media content is the image sharing websites like Instagram. Images and videos are essentially a tool to influence others. These types of medium can help with promotions (Zeng et al., 2010).
- **Discussion Sites and Blogs** This source of information again in collaboration with another type of social media data can help in identifying similar interests' people to connect for personal or in enhancing the businesses.

Formats of Social Media Data From these different sources, the data comes in various formats. Understanding the format of the data holds importance to do the associated pre-processing activity effectively. Social media data can be collected in any of the formats depicted in the figure 1 below:

Generally, these social media real feeds are collected in any of the formats like HTML, XML, JSON and CSV.HTML and XML stands for mark-up language in which the contents of the feeds are contained within an HTML/XML tag.CSV is a comma-separated file and every column is separated by a column and a new line denotes the next row of a table. JSON stands for Javascript object notation in which the

Figure 1. Data formats of social media data

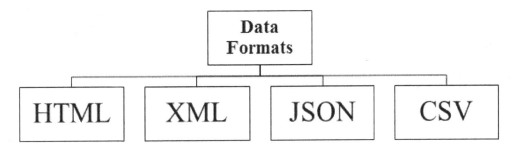

text format adopted is language-independent making it widely used format while handling the social media data (Hanneman and Riddle, 2005).

The raw data collected from the above sources in any one of the above-mentioned formats should be combined with other forms to enjoy the privileges of the analytics. While considering raw data, the data may be data that is collected from news websites and other sources before a period of time and the RSS feeds from the current traffic should be combined appropriately to derive values from it and to find appropriate answers.

Pre-Processing in Social Media Data

The essence of any analytical activity can be utilized to its full extent if the content of considered data is crisp enough and understandable. As we discussed in the previous sections, raw data comes in various forms and formats. Thus, data cleaning is a crucial task before we perform an analysis of the considered data. Irrespective of the forms of data we obtain, data cleaning must be performed to obtain the essential features. The major part of analysis happens in the text obtained in social media in the form of user profiles, verbatims etc. The overall objective in pre-processing considering the textual data is feature extraction that is carried out in various ways (Agreste et al., 2015). In this section, an overview of the various feature extraction methods is discussed.

Basic Data Cleaning/Pre-Processing on Textual Data

The more common way to use the textual data from social media is to identify the positive and negative feelings of customers about a product. This form of data can be in any form if it has HTML tags, removal of tags and the removal of white spaces, punctuation, splitting words, join splitter words and special characters resulting only in the data that must be analyzed. Apart from these regular cleaning, stemming and lemmatization is performed.

Stemming and Lemmatization

Stemming is to find the root word and replacing all the stemmed words with the actual root word. For E.g.: replacing the words like men, troubled, etc with its root word man and troubled. The process of stemming follows a heuristic approach to cut down a few of the end letters in the actual word to identify the actual word. The heuristic is defined by the algorithm chosen.

Lemmatization follows the same process of identifying the root word and replacing all the stemmed words with the root words. Lemmatization usually uses the dictionary to identify more meaningful words. Identification of words happens through specific rule-based thus this method may produce better accuracy in prediction (Prom-on et al., 2016).

Stop Word Removal

Analyses can give better results if low information words are removed. With this context, a set of commonly used words like the, an, a, etc are removed. This process may not provide any betterment in terms of classification and prediction. But this provides feature reduction so that a decent model can be built.

Normalization

A very important pre-processing step through which the actual text gets transformed into its canonical form, as well as mapping of near-identical words, is performed. This is required as most of the population today post their text in short forms. For e.g: OTW gets transferred as on the way. There is no single rule to perform this step and it varies depending on the data we are trying to normalize. This should be carried out for any form of unstructured data.

Noise Removal

Another important domain-specific pre-processing step in text processing is noise removal that includes the removal of unnecessary characters attached to the word. For e.g.: cat <, cat.., ;cat. In these terminologies the word cat comes in conjunction with unwanted characters and this should be removed as this is noise.

Text Augmentation

Another interesting pre-processing step that has a direct impact on the predictive behaviour of the model. In this method, we try to enrich the semantics of the text by introducing new words.

Lowercasing

In this method, the given word is converted completely to lowercase which again has impact on the predictiveness.

Basic data cleaning involves all the above techniques. For a particular use case is it necessary to perform all the above pre-processing technique. To understand the vitality of the pre-processing steps below classification diagram in figure 2 helps:

Frequent words removal, rare words removal and tokenization are also considered as a basic pre-processing activity. The choice of pre-processing and the amount of pre-processing required will varies according to the use cases.

Figure 2. Choosing the necessary pre-processing step

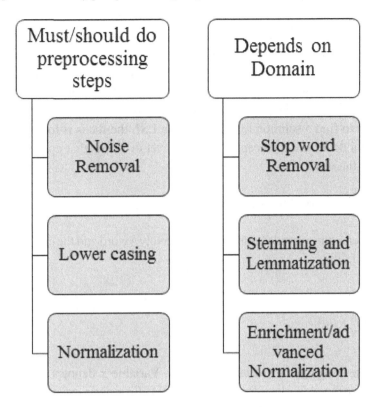

Feature Extraction/Selection

The process of identifying the relevant features from the processed data is referred to as feature extraction. Relevant features are obtained by removing one feature if the values of the two features are correlated. This redundancy removal is completely acceptable as the removal of one does not have any impact on the other (Yu and Liu, 2004). Generally, feature selection is classified into four categories as filter-based selection; Wrapper based selection, embedded selection and hybrid methods (Alelyani et al., 2013). Some of the common basic feature extraction that can be performed on the textual data is counting the number of words, number of characters, average word length, number of uppercase words, etc. Most of the simple extraction techniques help us to identify the feelings about an individual who is posting the information. The general intuition is the number of words expressed reflects the individual's emotion on the product, process, etc.

Statistical approaches for feature selection are the most widely accepted form of selection methods as it is completely automatic. The statistical approach considers the whole document as either Bag of Words or as a string. We have discussed in the previous section about the various selection methodologies associated with Bag of words. So, in the next subsection, we are discussing the statistical methods in feature selection.

Latent Semantic Indexing (LSI)

With the aid of singular value decomposition, LSI tries to identify relevant documents based on the search word. If the search word is "Apple" it denotes two different meanings. The apple is associated with fruit as well as to a famous mobile brand. LSI tries to relate a concept to the search word. The possibility of associating a single concept for each word in English like language is very difficult as the language itself possesses a lot of ambiguities. Comparing words to find relevant documents is a tedious task and LSI attempts to find a solution for the same. In LSI, the focus is to find the number of times a word is repeated in a document. Concepts denote the set of words that appear together exhibiting a linear combination of the word.

Point-Wise Mutual Information (PMI)

The association between a considered feature more concretely a word and the class. The general formulae to calculate PMI is as follows:

$$PMI(x, y) = \log \frac{P(x, y)}{P(x)P(y)}$$

PMI essentially uses two random variables x and y. Variable x denotes the occurrence of a word and y denotes the occurrence of a class. By calculating PMI for x and y we can decide if the considered feature is informative or not. Through this value, whether the considered feature can be selected or not can be decided. Thus, PMI is a measure that can effectively reduce the features depending on the correlation strength.

Chi-Square

Feature selection based on Chi-square value is no different from PMI, but chi-square behaves better than PMI as the selection happening here yields normalized value (Deerwester et al., 1990). This technique attempts to identify the association between two categorical values. The association is measured in terms of dependency. If the categorical variable is independent, the value of the independent variable does not affect the probability distribution of the other variable and if the variables are dependent the probability distribution of one affects the other. The general formulae for calculating the chi-square is as follows:

$$x^2 = \varepsilon \frac{(f_0 - f_c)}{f_c}$$

Where f_0 and f_c denotes the observed counts and expected values. Thus, Chi-square tries to select features based on dependency.

Gini Value

Gini index or Gini coefficient is another form of statistical calculation that can be adopted for effective feature selection. Gini index denotes a value ranging between 0 and 1. Calculation of Gini index value over a sample the value of 0 denotes the feature that must be selected. If all the samples of a class possess uniform distribution, then the Gini value reaches maximum denoting the features that holds lesser value. The usage of Gini value for feature selection is not commonly adopted, however this can be helpful in social media analytics as there is always a possibility of features that hold lesser value in social media content. The Gini value is calculated using the below formulae:

$$g\left(s\right) = 1 - \sum_{i=1}^{n} P_i^2$$

Where $g(s)$ denotes the Gini Index value and P_i^2 denotes the probability value.

By adopting any one of the above statistical calculation, the feature selection should be employed to create a better classifiers and fruitful predictions. Accuracy in deriving valuable insights is possible only through a crisp and useful feature.

Different Approaches on Social Media

In the previous sections, we gained knowledge on the different types of social media data, its formats and the cleaning process. At this stage, the type of data available would be structured enough to be used for analysis. What type of analysis must be performed on the structured data purely depends on the type of the problem that we are dealing with? To identify what type of analysis for which problem? a complete knowledge on the varieties of social media analysis would help. Social media analysis is a process followed to identify the hidden valuable business insights in the data. The different types of social media data may be in structured or unstructured form generally gets analysed for identifying the trend/topic related queries, sentiment related queries or in identifying the structural attribute. Based on the use case, one must select the analysis/analytics method and derive value from it. To identify which analysis and analytics have to be performed knowledge on the different methods is essential. In this section, we will explore the different types of analysis and analytics on social media.

Statistical Analysis

The most basic form of analysis that is used for getting some valuable insights on the considered data is statistical analysis. This denotes the quantitative results obtained from the historical data like observational and survey data. For Example: An organization wants to understand the response for their newly launched product. The response for the product is collected through a survey form with aid of social media websites and with all the survey data, organization creates a visualization by adopting any one of the statistical methods. This basic form of analysis which is like the descriptive analytics tries to identify the trends based on historical data. The output of any statistical analysis is limited to graphs and tabular form. "For a sample of data collected previously, applying statistical formulas to represent it in form of table or graph and tries to identify the relationship among it".

Social Network Analysis

Social Network Analysis is another form of analysis coming under the category of structural attribute. This analysis is generally carried out to map and measure relationship. The relationship may be between people, organizations, computers, etc. (Gandomi and Haider, 2016; Newman, 2003) defines the social network analysis as a methodology to identify and track changes in a network and make decisions by examining the link, influence etc. There are different variants of the social network analysis and they are as follows:

Influence Analysis

Social media a greater source for diffusing valuable information do influence the people using it. In the recent days, many of us came across a suicidal game that got spread through a social media influenced people to do many undesirable things. Thus, social media influence analysis is another important social media analysis in which the concentration is to model the influence networks. With the aid of these influence networks, one tries to identify the most influential person, how are they influencing others and the target groups of these influencers etc. This analysis is particularly useful in many areas including recommendations, rumour spreading, etc. The influence analysis tries to value for maximum influence, minimum influence and individual influence (Wu et al., 2013).

This influential analysis is generally carried out through the centrality metrics in graph. Centrality helps one to uncover the position of a node in a network that contributes in measuring how dominant that node in a network. More commonly, as much as influence analysis is concerned, the objective is to find the experienced users who can set trends for the entire network.

Link Analysis

Another commonly used data analysis technique in social media is to find an individual's association with other contents in a social media. Link analysis tries to identify the relationship between nodes. A user tries to access multiple shopping websites for a product, or a user want to find a group of friends possessing the similar interests. A system can give recommendations to these users adopting a collaborative recommendation strategy. This is the idea behind link analysis, and this is generally carried out through a page ranking mechanism. Through link analysis one can identify patterns, anomalies and new patterns of interest.

Community Detection

Another important analysis to identify the communities to associate a node to a community. This detection is carried out through various analysis procedures like static, temporal and predictive analysis. At a particular instant of time, what are the communities existing is through the historical data and that is termed as static analysis followed by identifying the reasons of how this community flourished using temporal analysis and what is the expectation that this community will grow or not through predictive analysis. This community detection again is done with the aid of clique graph.

Sentiment Analysis

The major business tool nowadays is social media. Every piece of information in social media is used by organizations to increase their revenues. Sentiment analysis simply monitoring the various posts and discussions about a brand in social media. With this input, organizations aim to take decisions on their business. The use cases look simple however the real complexity lies in understanding the human language notations. The next step of descriptive analytics is predicting the future trends is predictive analytics. Sentiment analysis is one form of predictive analytics in which the text is studied and attempts to identify if the content of the text gives positive or negative response. With this, businesses can be optimized by understanding what users are feeling about the product, etc.

Content Analysis

Content analysis comes under the category of trend/topic analysis in which the entire analysis is done after choosing a topic. Content analysis provides a summarized quantitative value in terms of numbers and percentages by analysing various aspects of the content. After choosing the topic, sample size and units to be counted are decided. Categories are constructed on which the analysis is performed on collected data.

Trend Analysis

Most commonly used use case is predicting the stock price. This trend analysis is one step ahead of the predictive analytics. Based on the current value, future value is predicted often termed as prescriptive analytics. Trend is simply a curve that denotes the direction of a business. To identify this pattern of growth in the curve is going to change or not trend analysis is done through which a comparative analysis is carried out (Bakshy et al., 2012).

In short, the approaches followed in social media analysis can take any one of the above-mentioned analysis methods. An example under each analysis is discussed that aids anyone to decide on the type of analysis that must be performed for the considered use case.

RELATIVE MACHINE LEARNING ALGORITHMS IN SOCIAL NETWORK ANALYSIS

Through section 2 and 3 detailed explanation on the different types of social media data and the various forms of social media analysis is discussed. One after choosing the type of cleaning process and the analysis method, the next step would be to identify the type of machine learning algorithm that goes well with the selected features and the selected analysis method. In this section, we are going to give a comprehensive idea on the different type of machine learning algorithms that can be used along with the selected methodology.

Machine learning is a general terminology associated with any system that will know what to do next based on its previous experience. It's basically a model building mechanism in which a model is constructed using the available input and output dataset and if new data is been fed on to the built model, the model knows how to behave as it has already learned how to behave with the given dataset. Through various approaches and statistical methods different machine learning models are built. The general classification of machine learning is supervised and unsupervised learning.

The classic difference between the supervised and unsupervised machine learning model is in terms of the data given as input as well as the data that we wish to see as output. In supervised learning, both the input as well as output data is fed as input to the model and the output is in the form of numeric values or categorical value. In unsupervised learning, the model is built only on the input data and the output is in category. A thorough analysis on the social media data and analysis methodologies narrowed down us to a single terminology "text analytics". Any form of unstructured data is considered and that must be analysed to answer various forms of questions. Through social media data, the first exercise we want to try is grouping the similar words. To carry out any type of analysis in social media data, the input is "Bag of Words". These bag of words after it goes through the process of cleaning and selection, algorithm to create a model again depends on the use case.

Use Case 1

Consider the case of a student's academic performance. We want to identify how the various occurrences in student's life affect their academic performance. For this use case, data from students comes in the form of text. Basically, text that shares their bitter experiences which had direct impact on their academic performance [16]. To solve this problem, we need to identify the sentiment associated with the given text. This form of sentiment analysis can be carried out with the aid of machine learning approach. The text given by every student is "Bag of Words" that must be pre-processed. First any student is associated with parent, peer and teacher. Grouping of words associated with parent, peer and teacher resulted a one-dimensional vector space. After this pre-processing step, clusters are created. This clustering is required to identify the set of all students who possess domestic influence, peer influence or teacher influence. Based on the type of words used in their context, set of all students are grouped into three clusters. This requires the assistance of unsupervised machine learning algorithms.

Unsupervised Clustering Algorithms in Sentiment Analysis

Clustering is a process of grouping objects based on similar attributes. In social media analysis, mostly clustering aims to group similar words as one group or segregating all words that belongs to one specific group. This is achieved with the aid of various machine learning clustering algorithms and they are as follows:

K-Means Clustering

This is one of the simplest methods of clustering in which the algorithm takes K as input. Here K denotes the number of clusters required and these K are kept at random places. These are termed as centroids. Between data point and each centroid, Euclidean distance is calculated and the one with closest value, the data point is allotted in that cluster.

Fuzzy C-Means Algorithm

Another variant of clustering algorithm that aims to fit the datapoint in a cluster based on its strength of membership on that cluster. Instead of relying on Euclidean distance, this algorithm calculates the fuzzy coefficient based on probability distribution result.

Hierarchical Clustering

This is different from K-means as every cluster treat all datapoints in their own cluster after which it starts building the hierarchy based on the Euclidean distance and identify the closest pair of points. Then these closest pair of points are merged in a cluster. And this process continues till all items are clustered into one cluster.

For the considered use case, the data came as text and it is collected from the students. Assume that the same form of data is collected from social media and if it requires analysis, the above-mentioned unsupervised learning algorithms can be used, and evaluation can be done through perplexity or Silhouette index.

Use Case 2

Assume that you have launched a new product and you are exploring the user's feedbacks on social media to forecast the future sales of the product. The use cases for this category is endless and the algorithm adoption purely depends on the use cases

Supervised Machine Learning Algorithms in Social Media Analysis

The supervised learning algorithms can output numerical values as well as categorical values. Based on this, the supervised machine learning can be classified as regression models, decision trees, etc.

Regression Models

Some of the use cases that can use regression strategies are

§ Predicting whether a customer will stay with the bank or not.
§ Optimizing prices, sales, etc.

As much as social media analysis is concerned, based on user reviews organization tries to identify the if the stock prize of a company will increase or decrease. Since this use case requires the output in the form of categories logistic regression algorithm is best. Generally, the logistic regression algorithms try to fit the best hyperplane. The type of regression adoption depends on the relationship between the dependent and independent variables. The simplest form of regression is linear regression in which we are trying to identify the relationship between an input and output variables and use this relationship for forecasting by framing a hypothesis in the form of linear equation. Various forms of regression include LASSO, polynomial, ridge etc.

Support Vector Machines

Another form of supervised learning algorithm that can be used in conjunction with classification and regression models. This differs from regression as this includes transformation of linear data to non-linear data through a kernel function. Typical use case that requires SVM is to predict how likely someone is to click on an online ad.

Decision Trees

Typical use case for decision trees is to group the words for a class. This grouping is done based on various parameters starting from root. (Hsu et al., 2017). Typical use case that requires decision tree for making decisions is considering the post and social information, predicting the view count of the post. By adopting random forest, CART or ID3 algorithms, generally a tree is constructed starting from root node. Every root node includes a leaf and internal node in which internal nodes are explored further till it reaches the target variable. In the form of conditions, the prediction is done.

Naives Bayes

In social media analysis, one classifier that is often been tested to identify the sentiment associated with a product based on reviews. This classifier works effectively to classify the text based on category. This review is positive review denoting one category another one denoting another category. The naive Bayes classifier is a set of algorithms aiming for effective classification.

Neural Network

Handwriting Analysis is a typical use case for supervised learning algorithm that requires neural network-based algorithms. Classification focusing on non-linear boundaries adopt neural network-based algorithms. Artificial Neural networks are built based on genetic, gradient based or evolutionary algorithms.

The various analysis approaches that can be used along with the social media data is explored with suitable use cases in this section and given in figure 3.

Frameworks for Performing Social Media Analytics

Through this chapter, we are attempting to give guidelines on all the methodologies required to perform the social media content analysis. Social media content analysis requires huge processing as the data we are relying on is big data. Traditional methodologies will not be a suitable method for carrying out big data processing as it largely demands on distributed processing. This section gives an overview about the various tools that are helpful for performing social media analytics:

Programming Tools

When we think of machine learning implementation, everyone remembers Python the first. Scikit-learn package in python provides numerous functionalities for performing various types of content analysis and built in classifiers like Naïve. As much as the influence analysis is concerned, NetworkX is the package

Figure 3. Overall machine learning approach in social media

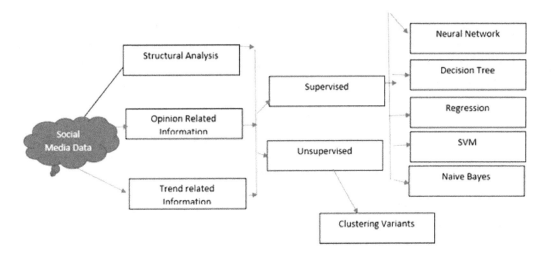

in python that allows one to create symmetric, asymmetric networks and provides various functions to identify the influencers based on centrality measures choosing various parameters. Another commonly used programming language to gain insights on the social media data is MATLAB. MATLAB is equipped with array-based statistics and time series analysis. Irrespective of its easy GUI and faster results, this is still viewed as a complex toolkit due to its built-in plotting functions restricting one to create powerful computational algorithm. Another powerful programming language for statistical analysis is R. Computational tool Mathematica is generally used for carrying out various processing apart from the text data. Some of the tools Listed below:

Sprout Social

It is one of the most widely used tool in Industry. It uses advanced analytics to make great reports on social content and keyword research. It is conveniently track performance of your content published on different platforms and work on new approaches based on these reports.

Features:

- Features In-built Customer Relationship Management (CRM) system
- 24/7 content monitoring
- Compatible with iOS and Android
- Supports teams, multiple profiles, departments and companies
- Security and ability to set specific levels for roles and permission
- Comprehensive analytics and reports
- Helpdesk facility on premium plans

HootSuite

Hootsuite includes everything that you'd need to publish, monitor and strategies your content across platforms. The analytics are accurate enough to guide you on better content distribution, which eventually leads to an increased conversion rate. Hootsuite is an affordable option catering to business of all sizes. It serves all four purposes:

1. Publishing, monitoring, analytics and team collaboration.
2. It is a user-friendly platform that can be mastered without any training.

Features:

- Easy-to-understand user interface
- Compatible with all leading social networks
- UberUV monitoring solution allows integration of free apps
- API facility to connect with existing market and other business systems and Nexgate, Safeguard and Global Relay features offer impressive compliance.

Adobe Social

Adobe Social is a feature-rich social media management and content integration tool that enables social listening, publishing, content moderation, monitoring and analytics. It is best suited for small and mid-sized businesses. This tool helps us to create and manage deep relationships with customers likes and comments.

Features:

- Covers multiple international languages
- Create, edit and share content within the tool
- Integrated social insights and automatically attach tracking codes to social accounts
- Integrates with Omniture SiteCatalyst data and photo editing tools

NUVi

NUVi is an insightful and data-driven app designed for businesses to track, manage and plan their social media content in a structured manner. It is more like a co-driver, who guides you through right directions, especially when you find yourself lost in the woods. Here, you will see how your content is performing on the move. You can also interact with influencers as soon someone mentions your brand's name.

Features:

- Real-time data visualisation and Reports customisation.
- Track keyword, hashtags, Uniform Resource Identifier (URI) or combination of search terms.
- Accurate and real-time social content reports.

- Publish and schedule content on all accounts from one platform.
- Access to in-depth competitor analysis.

Simply Measured

It provides in-depth analysis of social networks, including tracking Facebook, Twitter etc., and the performance of paid campaigns. Offering a wide range of product variations, it is a handy tool for businesses of any size (small, medium and large). It is quite useful for defining and adding context under possible crisis.

Features:

- Pulls data from multiple social channels
- Easy to export dashboard
- Stellar customer service
- Social traffic and traffic source analysis
- Competitive and Content performance analysis

Text Analytics Tools

To identify the sentiment hidden inside the text, the text must undergo the various stages that we discussed in the previous sections. So, if we are going to use a tool to get this insight, the considered tool is expected to possess these capabilities of importing any format of data, Natural language processing and multiple language support, user friendly interface with visualization capability (Kossinets and Watts, 2006)

Text analysis works by breaking sentences and phrases into number of components, and then evaluating each part's role and meaning by using machine learning algorithms and complex software rules. Text analytics forms the foundation of numerous natural language processing (NLP) features, including named entity recognition, categorization, and sentiment analysis.

Data analysts and other professionals use text mining tools to originate useful information and context-rich insights from large volumes of raw text information, such as social media comments, online reviews etc. In this way, text analytics software forms the backbone of business intelligence programs, including voice of customer/customer experience management, social listening and media monitoring, and voice of employee/workforce analytics.

How does text analytics work?

Text analytics starts by breaking down each sentence and phrase into its basic parts. Each of these components, including parts of speech, tokens, and chunks, serve a vital role in accomplishing deeper natural language processing and contextual analysis is shown in figure 4.

There are seven computational steps involved in preparing an unstructured text document for deeper analysis:

1. Language Identification
2. Tokenization

3. Sentence breaking
4. Part of Speech tagging
5. Chunking
6. Syntax parsing
7. Sentence chaining

Some text analytics functions are accomplished exclusively through rules-based software systems. Other functions require machine learning models (including deep learning algorithms) to achieve.

Figure 4. Lexalytics' text analytics technology and NLP feature stack

CONCLUSION

Social media is taking its twist and turns every second and the research in this domain is still vibrant. Pursuing research in this domain is still more easy because of the availability of API's. Through this chapter, some of the relevant steps necessary to get valuable insights on the data is discussed. A comprehensive overview on the various types of analysis with relevant use cases are discussed. Furthermore, we focused on the different machine learning algorithms that are generally used in social media analysis. This chapter overall can serve as a guideline for anyone who wants to start with social media analysis in the form of network and content.

REFERENCES

Agreste, S., De Meo, P., Ferrara, E., Piccolo, S., & Provetti, A. (2015). De, Ferrara, Piccolo, Provetti, (2015), Trust networks: Topology, dynamics, and measurements. *IEEE Internet Computing, 19*(6), 26–35. doi:10.1109/MIC.2015.93

Alelyani, S., Tang, J., & Liu, H. (2013). Feature selection for clustering: a review. In Data clustering: algorithms and applications. Chapman & Hall/CRC.

Bakshy, E., Rosenn, I., & Marlow, A. (2012). The role of social networks in information diffusion. *Proceedings of the 21st International Conference on World Wide Web, 519.*

Beier, M., & Wagner, K. (2016). Social media adoption: barriers to the strategic use of social media in SMEs. *Proceedings of the European conference on information systems.*

Bowcott, O. (2015). UK-US surveillance regime was unlawful 'for seven years'. *The Guardian.* Available: https://www.theguardian.com/uk-news/2015/feb/06/gchq-mass-internetsurveillance-unlawful-court-nsa

Chaudhary, P., Gupta, S., Gupta, B. B., Chandra, V. S., Selvakumar, S., Fire, M., Goldschmidt, R., Elovici, Y., Gupta, B. B., Gupta, S., & Gangwar, S.(2016). Auditing defence against XSS worms in online social network-based web applications. In Handbook of Research on Modern Cryptographic Solutions for Computer and Cyber Security. IGI Global.

Deerwester, S., Dumais, S. T., Furnas, G. W., Landauer, T. K., & Harshman, R. (1990). Deerwester, Dumais, Landauer, Furnas & Harshman.(1990).,Indexing by latent semantic analysis. *JASIS, 41*(6), 391–407. doi:10.1002/(SICI)1097-4571(199009)41:6<391::AID-ASI1>3.0.CO;2-9

Gandomi, A., & Haider, M. (2015). Beyond the hype: Big data concepts, methods, and analytics. *International Journal of Information Management, 35*(2), 137–144. doi:10.1016/j.ijinfomgt.2014.10.007

Hanneman, R. A., & Riddle, M. (2005). *Introduction to Social Network Methods.* Academic Press.

Hsu, C.-C., Lee, Y.-C., Lu, P.-E., Lu, S.-S., Lai, H.-T., Huang, C.-C., … Su, W.-T. (2017). Social Media Prediction Based on Residual Learning and Random Forest. *Proceedings of the 2017 ACM on Multimedia Conference - MM '17.* doi:10.1145/3123266.3127894

Kolog, E. A., Montero, C. S., & Toivonen, T. (2018). Using Machine Learning for Sentiment and Social Influence Analysis in Text. *Advances in Intelligent Systems and Computing,* 453–463. doi:10.1007/978-3-319-73450-7_43

Kossinets, G. & Watts. (2006). Empirical analysis of an evolving social network. *Science, 311*(5757), 88–90.

Li, Y. M., & Li, T. Y. (2013). Deriving market intelligence from microblogs. *Decision Support Systems, 55*(1), 206–217. doi:10.1016/j.dss.2013.01.023

Mo, Z., & Li, Y. (2015). Research of big data based on the views of technology and application. *Am. J. Ind. Bus. Management., 05*(04), 192–197. doi:10.4236/ajibm.2015.54021

Newman, M. E. J. (2003). The structure and function of complex networks. *SIAM Review*, *45*(2), 167–256. doi:10.1137/S003614450342480

Prom-on, S., & Ranong, S. N. (2016). DOM: A big data analytics framework for mining Thai public opinions. In R. Buyya (Ed.), Big Data: Principles and Paradigms. Morgan Kaufmann.

Senbagavalli, T., & Arasu, G. T. (2016, August). Opinion Mining for Cardiovascular Disease using Decision Tree based Feature Selection. *Asian Journal of Research in Social Sciences and Humanities*, *6*(8), 891–897. doi:10.5958/2249-7315.2016.00658.4

Tam, P.W. (2016). The government answers apple in the iPhonecase. *The New York Times*. Available: https://www.nytimes.com/2016/03/12/technology/the-government-answers-apple-in-the-iphone-case. html?ribbon-ad-idx=4&rref=technology&module=Ribbon&version=origin&region=Header&action =click&contentCollection=Technology&pgtype=articleover&_r=0

Wu, D., Schaefer, D., & Rosen, D. W. (2013). Cloud-based design and manufacturing systems: A social network analysis. *ICED13: 19th International Conference on Engineering Design*.

Yu, L., & Liu, H. (2004). Efficient feature selection via analysis of relevance and redundancy. *Journal of Machine Learning Research*, *5*, 1205–1224.

Zeng, D., Chen, H., Lusch, R., & Li, S. H. (2010). Social media analytics and intelligence. *IEEE Intelligent Systems*, *25*(6), 13–16. doi:10.1109/MIS.2010.151

Chapter 10
Challenges and Applications of Recommender Systems in E-Commerce

Taushif Anwar

https://orcid.org/0000-0002-6937-7258
Pondicherry University, Pondicherry, India

V. Uma

https://orcid.org/0000-0002-7257-7920
Pondicherry University, Pondicherry, India

Md Imran Hussain

Pondicherry University, Pondicherry, India

ABSTRACT

E-commerce and online business are getting too much attention and popularity in this era. A significant challenge is helping a customer through the recommendation of a big list of items to find the one they will like the most efficiently. The most important task of a recommendation system is to improve user experience through the most relevant recommendation of items based on their past behaviour. In e-commerce, the main idea behind the recommender system is to establish the relationship between users and items to recommend the most relevant items to the particular user. Most of the e-commerce websites such as Amazon, Flipkart, E-Bay, etc. are already applying the recommender system to assist their users in finding appropriate items. The main objective of this chapter is to illustrate and examine the issues, attacks, and research applications related to the recommender system.

DOI: 10.4018/978-1-7998-2566-1.ch010

INTRODUCTION

Recommender system (RS) plays a remarkable role in recommending appropriate items, services to users in fields such as e-commerce, e-learning, e-banking etc. A considerable number of applications and web sites, including Netflix, Amazon, e-bay, Flipkart and many others, adopted RS to offer their users more appropriate items according to his/her interests. Nowadays, the rapid increase in the number of internet users and exponential growth of online data create an information overhead problem. They are finding the appropriate information in the proper time has emerged as a problematic and time-ingesting problem because of overhead information problems. Recommender system has been a significant factor in tackling the information overhead problem. RS plays a central role in a broadway of e-commercial services, online shopping, and social networking applications. Numerous big organizations have successfully applied recommendation approach in recommending relevant items or products to the user and evaluate the potential preferences of customers.

Figure 1. Block diagram of a recommender system

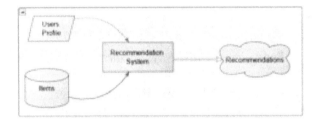

According to the knowledge source and way of recommending items, RS can be broadly classified as Collaborative filtering (CF), Content-based filtering (CBF) and Hybrid filtering (HF). Collaborative filtering is a widely implemented and most popular approach, considering its easy implementation in other domains. CF operates based on the user rating and by finding users having a rating history similar to that of the current user. Especially in cross-domain, CF provides a better recommendation than other approaches such as content-based filtering (CBF). CF has the significant limitation of not having the capability of suggesting new items for which ratings are absent (also known as a cold-start problem) ensuing in low customer satisfaction (Kumar, & Thakur, 2018).

The simple idea behind collaborative filtering is to provide item recommendations based on opinions of other related users. The primary assumption of CF is that if the user had a relevant sense of taste in the past, they will have a similar sense of taste in the future (Anwar & Uma, 2019a; Kumar, Kumar, & Thakur, 2019). To similarity in the feeling of two similar users is evaluated on the basis of the similarity of users rating history.

Content-based recommender system also known as cognitive filtering, suggests items on the basis of a comparison between the user profile and content of items. It can suggest items once information about items is available. The content-based recommender system can alleviate the cold-start problem in case of new items. The Content-based recommender system suffer from problems namely overspecialization, Data sparsity, privacy and limited content analysis.

Figure 2. Types of recommender system

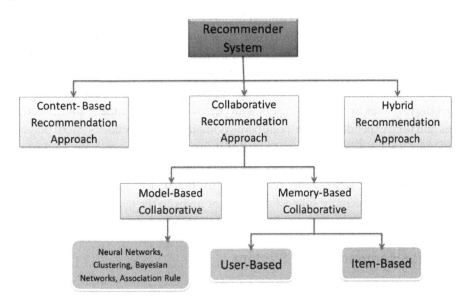

Figure 3. Collaborative filtering recommendation model

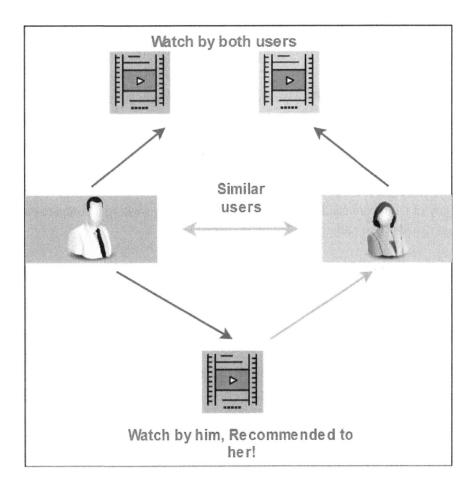

A hybrid recommender system merges two or more recommendation approaches. The main goal of the Hybrid recommender system is to overwhelm the limitation of the traditional recommender system as well as enhance the performance of the individual recommender system. There are various approaches of hybridization namely mixed, weighted, cascade, switching, meta-level, feature augmentation and feature combination. Limitations of traditional recommender systems such as data sparsity, cold-start and overspecialization can be easily overcome with hybridization of recommendation.

RS enhances the revenues by providing users with personalized recommendation, decrease the transaction expenses and time expended in an e-commerce domain. Recommender system plays a remarkable role in recommending appropriate items and is helpful for both service provider and user. Nowadays, a huge amount of data is generated day by day and users experience difficulties in selecting items and services that are relevant and useful due to information overhead. The main work of RS is it overcomes the information overload problem by suggesting relevant items to the users based on their personalized interest and preference.

Simple Model for Recommender System

RS recommends items to users based on their behaviors and interest (Ricci, Rokach, & Shapira, 2015). In Figure. 2 a simple model of a conventional recommender system is shown. The vital role of users and items in the recommendation process is highlighted. The figure illustrates that item features and user's profile are obtained by profile and item manipulation. CF recommend on the basis of the user's profile and rating given by the users.

Metrics for Recommendation

Making decent decisions for the user using recommendation system is necessary while selecting the items. Recommendation system play an important role in providing a good choice for their users. The recommendation system is implemented based on the rating and ranking of the product or items. To evaluate a recommendation system, some metrics are used in literature.

Recommendation can be provided by performing classification task. The metrics used are recall, precision, and F1-score (Li et al., 2017).

The efficiency of the recommender system can be analyzed by making a comparison between the predicted rating(x_i) and actual rating provided by the user(x).

(i)   **Mean Absolute Error (MAE)**

$$\text{MAE} = \frac{1}{n} \sum_{i=1}^{n} |x_i - x|$$

where n is the number of items, |xi-x| represents absolute error and

(ii)   **Root Mean Error (RME).**

$$RME = \sqrt{\frac{(MAE)^2}{N}}$$

where N is the total number of ratings in the test set.

Ranking Metrics

The primary purpose of ranking the items in the recommender system is to make users convenient by recommending items of their interest. The ranking performs on the previously ordered items by the user. The order can be built with less interesting items at the bottom and the essential and interesting items at the top. Two most popular ranking metrics are used namely Mean average precision (MAP) and Normalized Discounted Cumulative Gain (NDCG).

Figure 4. Simple model of recommender process

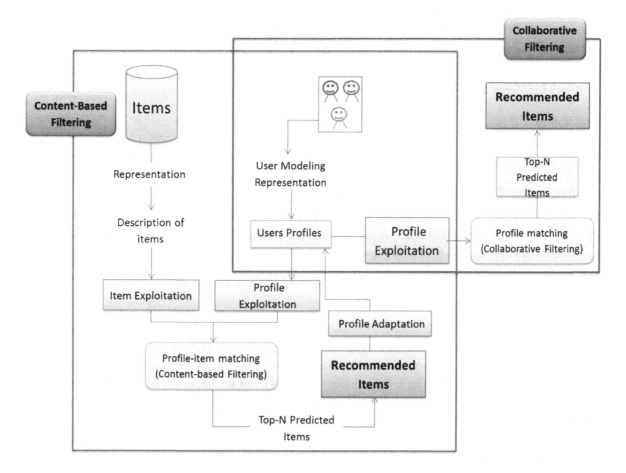

ISSUES IN RECOMMENDER SYSTEM

Types of Issues in Collaborative Filtering

Data Sparsity Problems

The issue emerges when the very lesser number of users which may bring about extremely lesser choice and numerous unrated items, which is the reason of data sparsity problems. In this case, searching users with interesting items is quite difficult (Al-Bashiri, Abdulgabber, Awanis, and Norazuwa, 2018). The data sparsity problem can be handled using the missing rating prediction, singular value decomposition and cross-domain recommendation.

Cold Start Problem

It is also called as a start-up or ramp-up problems. This problem can be classified into two similar problems: new user or and new items (things) problem. This problem happens when the new item and new user enters the system and sufficient information is not collected previously (earlier) about them (Zhu et al., 2019). For providing better recommendation, the systems required a vast amount of data representing the users or items. After the user's rate, the system can suggest new items. There are some ways to deal with the cold start problem such as applying demographic information, knowing the user's interest, Cross-domain, etc (Anwar & Uma, 2020).

Scalability

Scalability problems occur when the number of the customer, products and evaluation is vast for the system, in that case, time taken for real-time processing is very high in some cases resource is unavailable. This issue is present in both CBF and CF approaches. To handle scalability issue and provide accurate recommendations clustering, dimensionality reduction, matrix factorization and Bayesian networks are used. Clustering increases the recommendation's performance but decreases accuracy. The matrix factorization method cannot deal with big datasets and so it is not preferable in the e-commerce recommendations with large datasets.

Gray Sheep

If the users have an unusual interest, the gray sheep problem occurs. Because of this reason, there are no convenient neighbours and so the recommendation may be imprecise (inaccurate). This issue can be solved by fully CBF (Ghazanfar & Prügel-Bennett, 2014). For instance, if the system recognizes the users are interested in some of the particular area or file, then the system can directly recommend the items to the user, even if items are not popular.

Early Rater Problem

For the newly added items, the collaborative filtering is not able to provide a recommendation because, at that time of the recently added items, the previous rating is not available. When the users begin to provide the rating, it is still difficult to provide precise recommendations even if sufficient ratings have been collected for the items. Also, for those users who have rated only a few items, the recommendations provided may not be precise (Rashid, Karypis, & Riedl, 2008).

Synonymy

Synonymy problem arises when similar items have several names and the RS fails to predict accurate items (Isinkaye, Folajimi, & Ojokoh, 2015). In these conditions, the recommendation system face difficulty in detecting the details (terms) of the given items in terms of identifying the similarity between items.

For instance, the term "Bollywood film" and "Bollywood movie" are treated differently in memory-based Collaborative filtering systems. To overcome with synonymy problem, numerous ways including Ontologies, Single Value Decomposition and Latent Semantic Indexing are used.

Shilling Attack

Shilling attackers are also known as Malicious users. The shilling attack occurs mainly when unauthorized users enter the system and give biased ratings to manipulate the recommendation ranking. e.g., provides a lower rating for their competitors and a lot of higher ratings for their items. Its main motive is to manage the user's decision and increase or decrease the item's popularity (Chen, Chan, Zhang, & Li, 2019). This type of attacks reduces the trust and accuracy of the RS.

Privacy

RS generally perform on the massive data which is gathered from user interest (Cheng et al., 2016). As the recommender system requires huge user rated data, it may lead to data security and privacy concern issues. They also bring concern about privacy as this data includes demographic records, product-related data, impressions that users leave, web browsing data (buying and search nature) which can reveal the particular user identity (social security number, email).

The user data may be in misuse because the information of users is generally stored in the consolidate storage in collaborative filtering. So, for dealing with this problem and avoid the misuse of user's information some methodologies i.e. Natural Language Processing and cryptographic techniques are used (Heupel, Fischer, Bourimi, & Scerri, 2015).

TYPES OF ISSUES IN CONTENT-BASED FILTERING

Limited Content Analysis

When two distinct types of items are represented by using the same set of attributes, it creates ambiguity for that product resulting in limited content analysis problem. Because of this reason identifying the product has become quite challenging. The content availability is limited and hence it leads to the over-specialization problem (Flores-Parra, Castanon-Puga, Martinez, Rosales-Cisneros, & Gaxiola-Pacheco, 2017). The selection and representation of items are on the basis of the attributes of the subject. The attributes of the subject should be select manually, or content is to be automatically parsed for getting the suitable attributes of the subject. Automatization of parsing is quite simple for text features; however, it is difficult for videos and images.

Overspecialization

Overspecialization occurs when the recommendation system recommends only those items which are having more assessment against the user's profile. The previous user activities proof and evidence are required for the content-based filtering approach to select or recommend the items. For example, if the user does not have experience with flight travel, the user will never get a recommendation though the Airline is available in the city or country. Sometimes, when the user wants to try something new and novel items related to their interest, but the system is not providing the details of those items. And then used work to know from the other options and they found new things so it may decrease the diversity of recommender system. Diversity is playing a vital role in the recommendation approach. To deal with the overspecialization problem some methodologies like similarity measuring, sampling, and dimensionality reduction are used in collaborative filtering.

Learning Algorithm Problem

The efficiency of learning techniques plays a significant role in decision making. Because of this, selecting an efficient learning algorithm is also a problem. In managing the user profiles, which may be in large amount, storage space and computational complexity of the algorithm are primary issues. Genetic algorithms and neural networks require several iterations to resolve the document appropriateness and for that reason, it is quite slower than the other learning methods. In increasing the speed and performance of the learning algorithm, Relevance feedback and Bayesian classifier are used.

RELATED WORK REGARDING RECOMMENDER SYSTEM ISSUES

The origin of the recommender system started with the research article on collaborative filtering by W.Hill et al. (Hill, Stead, Rosenstein, & Furnas, 1995) and Resnick et al. (Resnick, Iacovou, Suchak, Bergstrom, & Riedl, 1994). After that various techniques namely neural network, k-NN, clustering, decision tree, regression are used in implementing recommender system. There are some challenges and problems i.e. cold-start, shilling attack, gray sheep, latency, privacy, data sparsity problems that are encountered by RS.

Khalil Damak et al. [Damak, K., & Nasraoui, O. (2019)] presented a hybrid song recommender system on the basis of song content and ratings. The presented model is a combination of CF and deep learning sequence models to deliver more personalized recommendations and overcome cold start problems. For experimental evaluation, Million Song Dataset and MIDI dataset were used.

Taushif Anwar et al. [Anwar, T., & Uma, V. (2019, March)] proposed an MRec-CRM movie recommendation based on CF and rule mining approach. In this proposed method, five different types of similarity techniques namely Euclidean, Correlation, Cosine, Jaccard and Manhattan were used for finding the similarity between user and items. Using the TopSeq rule mining algorithm the frequent sequential pattern is generated. The proposed approach overcomes new user and sparsity problems.

Sujoy Bag et al. [Bag, S., Ghadge, A., & Tiwari, M. K. (2019)] presented an integrated RS model for online companies, with the capability of producing personalized recommendations to their users. Significant Nearest Neighbors (SNN) is used for finding similarity matrices for performing the RS. MovieLens 100K datasets is used for experimental evaluation. The presented recommender system model helps to enhance the revenue of online companies by recommending preferred portfolio and diverse items to their users.

Yulong Gu et. al [Gu, Y., Ding, Z., Wang, S., & Yin, D. (2020, January)] proposed a Hierarchical User Profiling (HUP) model to solve the hierarchical user profiling problem in E-commerce based recommender systems. In this proposed model, Pyramid Recurrent Neural Networks is implemented with Behavior-LSTM to express users hierarchical real-time interests at various scales. For experimental evaluation, JD Micro Behaviors Datasets obtained from the JD.com e-commerce site is used. The experimental result shows the flexibility and effectiveness of the model, in recommending category and item.

Comparative Analysis of Collaborative and Content-Based Filtering Approaches

Table 1. Comparative analysis of issues for collaborative filtering and content-based filtering approaches

S.No.	Types of Issues	Collaborative Filtering	Content-based Filtering
1	Data Sparsity	Issues Present	Issues Present
2	New Item (Cold Start) Problem	Issues Present	Issues Solved
3	New user (Cold Start) Problem	Issues Present	Issues Present
4	Scalability	Issues Present	Issues Present
5	Gray Sheep	Issues Present	Issues Solved
6	Early Rater Problem	Issues Present	Issues Solved
7	Synonymy	Issues Present	Issues Present
8	Shilling Attack	Issues Present	Issues Solved
9	Privacy	Issues Present	Issues Present
10	Limited content analysis	Issues Present	Issues Present
11	Overspecialization	Issues Present	Issues Present
12	Learning Algorithm Problem	Issues Present	Issues Present

Common Attacks Related to Recommender System

Initially, we should find out the main purpose of the attacks to evaluate the recommender system accountability. Basically, we should find the attacker's financial or commercial advantages because of the attacks as it might result in more recommendations for attackers' items and less recommendations for their competitors' items. It is in the form of (i) Push attack: which is providing bogus rating to attacker's product by the attackers. and (ii) Nuke attack: which is providing unfair rating to competitor's product by the attackers. Following are the push attack discussed below:

Random Attack

The main reason for random attack is low knowledge and low information (Karthikeyan et al., 2017).

The random attack is also called a low knowledge attack in which profiles are first created. A profile is chosen randomly by the attackers and items are rated. This attack is easy to implement but it has lesser efficiency.

Average Attack

The average attack is more complex compare to other attacks because it is required details information of the system, datasets for practical implementation and recommendation algorithm (Zhou, Wen, Xiong, Gao, & Zeng, 2016). It is performed by selecting random items and uses the statistical method i.e. standard deviation and normal distribution with mean. This attack can be effective if the attackers have previously maintained real data with a complete hidden information index in the recommender system.

Bandwagon

Bandwagon attack is also known as a popular attack. In the Bandwagon attack, attackers only focus on popular items which are already rated by different users to make the items popular in the recommender system. In another hand, Attackers take the help of Zipf's law distribution of popularity and make the items popular in an unfair manner to get the highest rating of the items. So, the attacker need not use the statistical method to find the items rating from an average attack.

Reverse Bandwagon Attack

Reverse Bandwagon Attack is also called a less popular attack. In the reverse bandwagon attack, attackers focus on only less rated items that are previously rated by the different users. The main goal of this attack to give less rating to the target items and make it less popular, expanding the probability that the system will produce low anticipated evaluations for those items.

Segment Attack

In the segment attack, attackers mainly focus on certain users. A segment attack first boosts the recommendation of interesting items for the precise customers and raise the recommendation of that particular product to the users. In this attack, the system does not require more information.

Probe Attack

The probe attack in the recommendation system occurs when an attacker develops attack profiles similar to the marketing profile that has been rated by the authentic user of the recommender system. Therefore, there exists a high chance of correlation between the items in the attacker profile and an authentic profile.

Love-Hate Attack

In the love/hate attack, the attacker gets along with the attack profiles and provides less rating to the target items and high rating to other items. The profile creation technique is as impressive as a nuke attack. Particularly, this profile generation method is much influential in a nuke attack (Burke, Mobasher, Williams, & Bhaumik, 2006).

ATTACKS DETECTIONS STRATEGIES RELATED TO RECOMMENDER SYSTEM

The reason for Collaborative-recommender systems must be available to the user's input. It isn't easy to make a new framework that cannot be under any attack. It is essential to detect malicious users and identify items that have been under attack.

Profile Classification

This technique involves identifying suspected profiles that do not have authentication and deduction of their activity on the items. For the suspicious profile, we need to set some parameters that can help to classify the profiles, such as extensive profiles, fixed types profiles, and intra-profiles.

Anomaly Detection

In this technique, we need to focus on the items which have some suspicious manners. For the detection of an anomaly, the technique is performed with the statistical methods we need to perform a distribution, including mean, median, mode, and quantiles on to the user's data. Global outliers, contextual outliers, and collective outliers are the main types of time series anomalies to detect.

APPLICATIONS OF RECOMMENDER SYSTEMS

In the past few years, several popular e-commerce RS has been developed and designed to present a guideline to online individual users. In e-commerce systems, rating is considered a general method for any item. For example, in Amazon, users can give feedback for the purchase items and the rating between 1 and 5 for the items. This rating data can consequently be applied to provide an appropriate recommendation. Various e-commerce websites namely eBay, Amazon, Flipkart apply RS to assist their users in finding items easily. In e-commerce websites, items can be suggested based on user demographics information, previous buying behavior, rating pattern and the top sellers (Jiang et al., 2019; Zhang, Abbas, & Sun, 2019). Nowadays e-commerce RS are web and smart devices based, which are generally used in online purchasing for physical goods such as mobile, books, etc. and digital products such as movies, web services, music, etc.

In general, RSs are designed to complement "buyer-side" systems. So, earlier RSs were considered only on the user side. But, in the modern scenario, RS not only improves the utility of users but at the same time it improves the utility of business. One challenging issue in developing RS is to determine how to get more money from the user using their information.

Challenges and Applications of Recommender Systems in E-Commerce

E-learning based RS has become more successful in the educational websites since early 2000. The main aim of this type of RS is to assist the learner to choose the subject, courses, learning activities and learning materials (Tarus et al., 2017). Nowadays, E-learning also treated as e-commerce. As we know the current situation of COVID-19 many of the institutions selling their lectures, notes and materials online.

E-tourism based RS is developed to provide tourist information easily. Mobile and internet devices provide tourist with more details about tourism. But, the exponential rise in the number of availability of tourism-choices make it difficult task for tourists to decide which choice is better (Logesh & Subramaniyaswamy, 2019). E-tourism based RS is developed to give appropriate suggestions for tourists.

RESEARCH AREA ASSOCIATED WITH RECOMMENDER SYSTEM

Sentiment Analysis (SA) is a modern research topic in the field of text mining. SA provides relevant information for decision making in several domains. In the recommender system field, the sentiment is used for improving the performance of recommendation. The sentiment or opinions of the user expressed as emotions, ratings and reviews are considered to represent negative, positive and neutral sentiments. The items which have received positive feedback from the past/previous users are suggested for the current users. Amel ZIANI et. al (Ziani et al., 2017) proposed RS through Sentiment Analysis. In this proposed approach, RS and SA were combined for generating the most appropriate recommendations. Semi-supervised SVM was applied for detecting the opinions polarity score.

In terms of RS, an analysis technique of Data Mining (DM) is used to build the recommendation model or infer recommendation rule from large datasets. DM approaches are frequently being applied in both stand-alone RS and hybrid systems to generate an accurate recommendation. RS that includes DM approach provides a recommendation based on attributes of the user and knowledge gathered from the action. The data mining algorithms applied in RS are clustering, classification and association rule mining.

The clustering approach works by recognizing a group of users who appear to have similar preferences and interests. Classification is the comprehensive computational model for assigning a category to the input (Kumar, & Thakur, 2020). The input may be data about the relationship among the items or vector of attributes of the items being classified. For building an RS, the classifier information about the product and customer is taken as input and the output shows how strongly the product can be suggested to the user.

Text Mining also referred to as Text Analytics is the exponentially emerging area that can be described as a statistical machine learning technique for converting the unstructured information into structured information. It can be mined, classified, trained for better and high-quality information. Information extraction, data mining, pattern recognition are perfomred in Text Mining and are referred to as Natural Language Processing (NLP) (Liu, Vernica, Hassan, & Damera Venkata, 2019). RS is one application of TM which can assist e-commerce. RS based on TM can examine user attributes and behavior; can discover user profile on the basis of long-term user behavior analysis.

CONCLUSION

In the past few decades, recommender systems have been applied, with the various possible solutions for online business and e-commerce, to reduce information overhead problems by recommending relevant items to the users. In this consideration, various advancements have been made to fine tune and develop high-quality RS. Nevertheless, developer faces numerous leading challenges and issues. In this book chapter, we study and illustrate the recommender system approaches namely collaborative filtering, content-based filtering and hybrid filtering. The main motive of this study is to highlight the issues and attacks related to collaborative filtering and content-based filtering. We hope that this chapter will give an inspiring direction and can be beneficial to lead the research related to the recommender system and provide support to researchers and new practitioners.

REFERENCES

Al-Bashiri, H., Abdulgabber, M. A., Awanis, R., & Norazuwa, S. (2018). A Developed Collaborative Filtering Similarity Method to Improve the Accuracy of Recommendations under Data Sparsity. *International Journal of Advanced Computer Science and Applications*, *9*(4), 135–142. doi:10.14569/IJACSA.2018.090423

Anwar, T., & Uma, V. (2019, March). MRec-CRM: Movie Recommendation based on Collaborative Filtering and Rule Mining Approach. In *2019 International Conference on Smart Structures and Systems (ICSSS)* (pp. 1-5). IEEE. 10.1109/ICSSS.2019.8882864

Anwar, T., & Uma, V. (2019a). CD-SPM: Cross-domain book recommendation using sequential pattern mining and rule mining. *Journal of King Saud University-Computer and Information Sciences*.

Anwar, T., & Uma, V. (2019b). *A Review of Recommender System and Related Dimensions Data, Engineering and Applications*. Springer.

Anwar, T., & Uma, V. (2020). A Study and Analysis of Issues and Attacks Related to Recommender System. In *Convergence of ICT and Smart Devices for Emerging Applications* (pp. 137–157). Springer. doi:10.1007/978-3-030-41368-2_7

Badsha, S., Yi, X., Khalil, I., & Bertino, E. (2017). *Privacy preserving user-based recommender system.* Paper presented at the 2017 IEEE 37th International Conference on Distributed Computing Systems (ICDCS).

Bag, S., Ghadge, A., & Tiwari, M. K. (2019). An integrated recommender system for improved accuracy and aggregate diversity. *Computers & Industrial Engineering*, *130*, 187–197. doi:10.1016/j.cie.2019.02.028

Burke, R., Mobasher, B., Williams, C., & Bhaumik, R. (2006). Classification features for attack detection in collaborative recommender systems. *Proceedings of the 12th ACM SIGKDD international conference on Knowledge discovery and data mining.* 10.1145/1150402.1150465

Jiang, L., Cheng, Y., Yang, L., Li, J., Yan, H., & Wang, X. (2019). A trust-based collaborative filtering algorithm for E-commerce recommendation system. *Journal of Ambient Intelligence and Humanized Computing*, *10*(8), 3023–3034. doi:10.100712652-018-0928-7

Karthikeyan, P., Selvi, S. T., Neeraja, G., Deepika, R., Vincent, A., & Abinaya, V. (2017). *Prevention of shilling attack in recommender systems using discrete wavelet transform and support vector machine.* Paper presented at the 2016 Eighth International Conference on Advanced Computing (ICoAC). 10.1109/ICoAC.2017.7951753

Kumar, P., Kumar, V., & Thakur, R. S. (2019). A new approach for rating prediction system using collaborative filtering. *Iran Journal of Computer Science*, 2(2), 81–87.

Kumar, P., & Thakur, R. S. (2018). Recommendation system techniques and related issues: A survey. *International Journal of Information Technology*, 10(4), 495–501.

Kumar, P., & Thakur, R. S. (2020). Liver disorder detection using variable-neighbor weighted fuzzy K nearest neighbor approach. *Multimedia Tools and Applications*, ●●●, 1–21.

Li, C., Ma, X., Jiang, B., Li, X., Zhang, X., Liu, X., . . . Zhu, Z. (2017). *Deep speaker: an end-to-end neural speaker embedding system.* arXiv preprint arXiv:1705.02304

Liu, L., Vernica, R., Hassan, T., & Damera Venkata, N. (2019). Using text mining for personalization and recommendation for an enriched hybrid learning experience. *Computational Intelligence*, 35(2), 336–370. doi:10.1111/coin.12201

Logesh, R., & Subramaniyaswamy, V. (2019). *Exploring hybrid recommender systems for personalized travel applications. In Cognitive informatics and soft computing.* Springer.

Ricci, F., Rokach, L., & Shapira, B. (2015). *Recommender systems: introduction and challenges. In Recommender systems handbook.* Springer. doi:10.1007/978-1-4899-7637-6

Zhang, Y., Abbas, H., & Sun, Y. (2019). Smart e-commerce integration with recommender systems. *Electronic Markets*, 29(2), 219–220. doi:10.100712525-019-00346-x

Zhou, W., Wen, J., Xiong, Q., Gao, M., & Zeng, J. (2016). SVM-TIA a shilling attack detection method based on SVM and target item analysis in recommender systems. *Neurocomputing*, 210, 197–205. doi:10.1016/j.neucom.2015.12.137

Ziani, A., Azizi, N., Schwab, D., Aldwairi, M., Chekkai, N., Zenakhra, D., & Cheriguene, S. (2017). *Recommender system through sentiment analysis.* Academic Press.

Chapter 11
Language Classification and Recognition From Audio Using Deep Belief Network

Santhi Selvaraj
https://orcid.org/0000-0002-3252-4728
Mepco Schlenk Engineering College, India

Raja Sekar J.
Mepco Schlenk Engineering College, India

Amutha S.
Mepco Schlenk Engineering College, India

ABSTRACT

The main objective is to recognize the chat from social media as spoken language by using deep belief network (DBN). Currently, language classification is one of the main applications of natural language processing, artificial intelligence, and deep learning. Language classification is the process of ascertaining the information being presented in which natural language and recognizing a language from the audio sound. Presently, most language recognition systems are based on hidden Markov models and Gaussian mixture models that support both acoustic and sequential modeling. This chapter presents a DBN-based recognition system in three different languages, namely English, Hindi, and Tamil. The evaluation of languages is performed on the self built recorded database, which extracts the mel-frequency cepstral coefficients features from the speeches. These features are fed into the DBN with a back propagation learning algorithm for the recognition process. Accuracy of the recognition is efficient for the chosen languages and the system performance is assessed on three different languages.

DOI: 10.4018/978-1-7998-2566-1.ch011

INTRODUCTION

An automatic Language Classification and Recognition is the task of automatically recognizing a language from the given spoken utterance. It is the process of classifying an utterance as belonging to formerly encountered languages. "Automatic", means the decision is performed by machine, it means the process is independent of content, context, task, vocabulary, sex, age as well as noise by the communication channel. Language Recognition is one of the most basic steps in natural language processing tasks like summarization, question answering and machine translation need to know the language of a given text in order to process it. Language classification is one of the most important applications of Data Analytics with Deep Learning.

OVERVIEW OF LANGUAGE RECOGNITION AND CLASSIFICATION

Language classification is the method of categorizing the languages from its audio speeches and take out the information presented in the speeches. It is used to recognize the language of the particular audio and to reduce the complexity of the audio sample. It plays a very important role and responsibilities for audio, speech and language processing applications.

Types of Language Recognition

The language recognition can be divided into two main types, namely

- Audio language recognition
- Visual language recognition

Audio Language Recognition

Audio language recognition is a mature technology, able to discriminate quite reliably between tens of spoken languages spoken by speakers that are unknown to the system, using just a few seconds of representative speech.

Visual Language Recognition

In this method information derived from the visual appearance and movement of the mouth to recognize the spoken language, without the use of audio information.

CHARACTERISTICS OF LANGUAGES

The characteristics of languages are known as Language Identification cues. The following characteristics differ from one language to another language.

- Phonology
- Morphology
- Syntax
- Prosody

Phonology

A phoneme is a basic representation of a phonological unit in a language. A "phone" is a realization of an acoustic-phonetic unit or segment. A "phonotactics" is the rules governing the sequences of allowable phones and phonemes can also be different.

Example
    Word - celebrate
    Phoneme - /s eh l ix b r ey t/
    Phone - [s eh l ax bcl b r ey q]

Morphology

The word roots and lexicons are usually different from language to language. Each language has its own vocabulary and own formation of words.

Example
    "Pigs like mud" is a sentence containing three words - pigs, like, mud

Syntax

The sentence patterns are different among languages, (i.e) more than one languages share a word and the sets of words that may precede and follow the word will be different.

Example
    The word "bin" in English and German

Prosody

Prosody is concerned with the "music" as opposed to the "lyrics" of speech. Languages have characteristic sound patterns which can be analyzed in terms of duration of phonemes, speech rate, pitch contour and stress.

Example
    Rhyme sentences

LANGUAGE RECOGNITION TECHNIQUES

Language recognition is a mature field of research, with many successful techniques developed to achieve high levels of language discrimination in only a few seconds of test data.

There are many techniques in language identification, namely

1. Phone-based tokenization
2. Gaussian Mixture Model tokenization
3. Artificial Neural Network

Phone-Based Tokenization

There are several approaches to recognition, which exploit the difference in phonetic content between languages to achieve language discrimination. Such techniques require the training of a phone recognizer, usually comprising a set of Hidden Markov Models (HMM), which are used to segment input speech into a sequence of phones. The phone based tokenization consist of three methods, namely

1. Phone Recognition Language Modeling (PRLM)
2. Parallel Phone Recognition Language Modeling (PPRLM)
3. Parallel Phone Recognition (PPR)

Phone Recognition Language Modeling (PRLM)

In this method, phonotactics is the feature of language used for discrimination. Phonotactics govern the allowable sequence of phonemes in a given language. The contention here is that different languages have different rules regarding the syntax of phones, and this can be captured in a language model. PRLM learns discriminatory information such as this form language specific training data.

PRLM system in Figure 1 presents the three subsystems. The first subsystem is the extraction of features from the speech input using Mel-frequency Cepstral coefficients (MFCC). The second subsystem is a method of tokenizing the incoming features, typically into frames, phones, or syllabic units using Vector Quantization. Next, statistical language models are built for each language, from phone sequences belonging to language specific training data. Here three languages are described such as English, Hindi and Tamil. Finally, likelihoods can be calculated from each language model for a given phone sequence, and these can be processed in some way that classifies the utterance.

- Front-end - Single-Language Phone Recognition
- Back-end - N-gram Language Modeling

Parallel Phone Recognition Language Modeling (PPRLM)

Although PRLM is an effective means of recognizing the language of speech messages, know that the sounds in the languages to be identified do not always occur in the one language used to train the front-end phone recognizer. Thus, it seems natural to look for a way to incorporate phones from more than one language into a PRLM-like system. On the other hand, PPRLM is simply to run multiple PRLM

Figure 1. Block Diagram of Phone Recognition Language Modeling

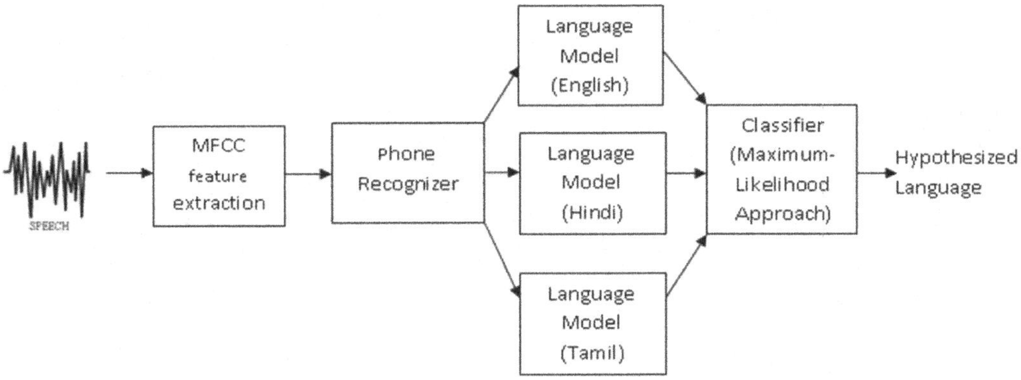

systems in parallel with the single language front-end recognizers each trained in a different language. This approach requires that labeled training speech be available in more than one language, although the labeled training speech does not need to be available for all, or even any, of the languages to be recognized.

The PPRLM system in Figure 2 presents language specific phone tokenizer is built effectively and several language recognition systems are running in parallel. All data are processed by all tokenizers and language models, and this produces n^2 language model likelihoods per utterance, where n is the number of tokenizers. This gives a higher dimensional vector of likelihoods, which lends itself to use a discriminatory backend classifier such as Support Vector Machine (SVM).

Figure 2. Block Diagram of parallel phone recognition language modeling

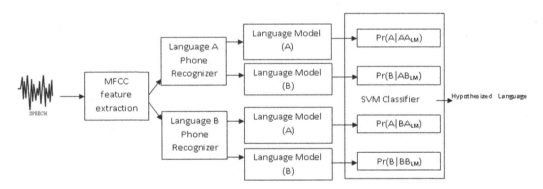

Parallel Phone Recognition (PPR)

The PPR system in Figure 3 presents the use of the phonological differences between languages. In the PPR language recognition system the language dependent phone recognizers are implemented using Hidden Markov Model tool kit (HTK), have the same configuration as the single-language phone recognizer used in PRLM.

Figure 3. Block Diagram of Parallel Phone Recognition

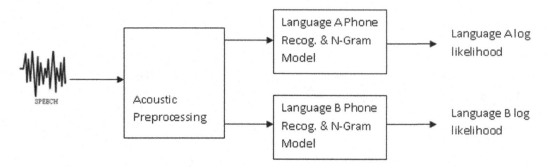

PPR language recognition is performed by Viterbi decoding the test utterance once for each language dependent phone recognizer. Each phone recognizer finds the most likely path of the test utterance through the recognizer and calculates the log likelihood score for that best path.

Gaussian Mixture Model tokenization

Gaussian Mixture Model (GMM) is trained for each language from language specific acoustic data. Each GMM can be considered to be an acoustic dictionary of sounds, with each mixture component modeling a distinct sound from the training data. The decoded sequence is used to train the language models and Gaussian classifier can be used to combine the language model scores. Given a Mel-frequency Cepstral coefficient (MFCC) frame, the mixture component is found which produces the highest likelihood score, and the index of that component becomes the token for that frame. Finally, the language models are constructed in order to identify the particular language. Gaussian Mixture Model tokenization in Figure 4 presents the model constructions of language recognition.

Figure 4. Block diagram of gaussian mixture model language recognition

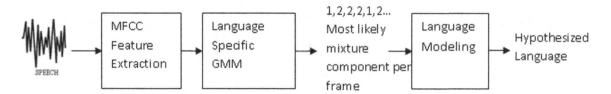

Artificial Neural Network

Artificial Neural Network contains several nodes that can be used to find the estimated functions or classify the data into similar classes such as phonemes, syllables and words.

Properties of Neural Network

- Trainability
- Generalization
- Nonlinearity
- Robustness
- Uniformity
- Parallelism

Types of Neural Networks

Neural Networks are divided into three main categories:

1. Feed Forward Neural Network
2. Radial Basis Neural Network
3. Recurrent Neural Network

Feed Forward Neural Network

It means nodes are connected only forward in time and connections between the nodes do not form a directed cycle. It has three types:

1. Time delay neural network
2. Single-layer perceptron
3. Multi-layer perceptron

Radial Basis Neural Network

It means the output of the network is linearly combined with inputs of the radial basis functions and parameters of the neuron. It has four types:

1. Gaussian neural network
2. Multi quadric neural network
3. Inverse quadric neural network
4. Inverse multi quadric neural network

Recurrent Neural Network

It means the output of a neuron is multiplied by a weight and fed back to the inputs of the neuron itself with a delay. Directed cycles are formed between the nodes. It has four types:

1. Fully recurrent neural network
2. Simple recurrent neural network
3. Bi-directional recurrent neural network

4.   Hierarchical recurrent neural network

Deep Belief Networks

Deep belief networks (DBNs) are one of the probabilistic models which will be composed of multiple layers of latent variables. The latent or stochastic variables have binary values and it is known as hidden units or feature detectors. The top two layers are undirected and creating the symmetric connections between layers to form an associative memory. The lower layers are directed and it receives the information from top two layers. DBN is one of the feed forward neural network type and powerful machine learning technique. Figure 5 presents the Neural Network based Language Recognition using Deep Belief Network Construction.

Figure 5. Block diagram of neural network based language recognition

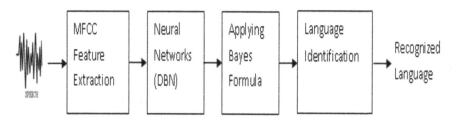

BACKGROUND AND LITERATURE REVIEW

This section focuses on reviewing the various approaches to language classification and recognition which have used to recognize and discriminate the languages. In Hidden Markov Models (K. F. Lee et al, 1989), training data are divided into two ways, such as context dependent and context independent. Additionally, smoothing algorithm is applied for training and recognition process and also achieves higher accuracy in terms of context and continuous parameters. Segment-based language recognition (Timothy J. Hazen et al, 1993) is used to extract the different components and properties such as phonotactic, prosodic and acoustic features. This approach includes the various steps like determination of segments and classes, language, prosodic and acoustic modeling. Gaussian Mixture Model tokenization (P.A. Torres-Carrasquillo et al., 2002) is used for recognition of more than one language spoken around the world. Here speech is given as input to the system, then MFCC features are extracted from the speech and the languages are classified by using GMM classification. Parallel sub-word recognition (Jayaram et al., 2003) is an automatic segmentation followed by the segment clustering and HMM modeling which is an alternative to the Parallel Phone Recognition system. Researchers (Haizhou Li et al., 2007) dealt with the design of Vector Space Modeling (VSM) language recognition where each and every spoken language can be categorized by the Acoustic Segment Models (ASMs) and then decoded into a sequence of ASM units. VSM framework is based on unsupervised learning algorithm and it was evaluated by using NIST-LRE databases.

MAIN FOCUS OF THE CHAPTER

This chapter presents deep learning techniques like Deep Belief Network for language classification and recognition finally compares the accuracy of this method with conventional data mining and machine learning algorithm. This language classification and recognition are one of the main applications for Natural Language Processing, Machine Learning and Deep Learning.

Data Collection

In corpus collection, training and testing samples are collected using sound recorder. For preparation of this database, mono channel recording is done for fifteen speakers in English, Hindi and Tamil language, in a closed and quiet noise free room. For digitization, 16 kHz of sampling frequency and 16-bit quantization are used. All speakers are female speakers in the age group of 20-24. Each sample in the database is approximately 2-3 seconds long in duration. The sentence considered for training and testing is indicated in Table 1.

Table 1. Sentence considered for training and testing

Language	Sentence considered
English	"Let this day be a blessed day for you"
Hindi	इस दनि को आपके लिए एक धन्य दनि होने दें
Tamil	இந்த நாள் உங்களுக்கு ஒரு ஆசீர்வதிக்கப்பட்ட நாளாக இருக்கட்டும்

To train the system properly, each speaker is instructed to utter the same sentence 5 times from which 3 utterances are used for training and the remaining 2 utterances are used for testing. Thus the training phase has a total of 135 samples and testing phase has 90 samples is indicated in Table 2.

Table 2. Database description

Lang.	No. of Speaker (N)	No. of times word repeated by each speaker (t)	Total training sample (N*3)	Total testing sample taken (N*2)	Sampling frequency	Characteristics of the speaker
English	15	5	45	30		
Hindi	15	5	45	30	16 kHz	Age group of 20-24 years
Tamil	15	5	45	30		
Total	**45**	**15**	**135**	**90**		

Methodology

The Language Recognition system comprises of three phases: feature extraction phase, deep belief network construction and applying Bayes formula phase, recognition phase. Feature extraction phase is used to extract the Mel Frequency Cepstral Coefficients features from the audio. A Deep belief network construction phase is used to find the state posteriors value for audio and then state likelihoods values are calculated using Bayes formula phase. Recognition phase is used to identify the particular languages from the audio sample. Methodology in Figure 6 presents the overall system design for language identification.

Figure 6. System diagram for language identification model

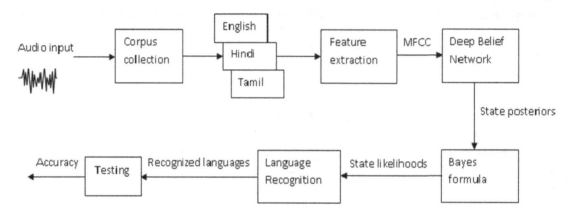

Feature Extraction Phase

Feature extraction is a special form of dimensionality reduction. The main aim of the feature extraction is to extract the formants or an MFCC feature which is the most commonly used features in speech recognition. Feature extraction module in Figure 7 presents the following steps.

1. Pre-emphasis
2. Frame blocking
3. Hamming windowing
4. Fast Fourier Transform
5. Triangular band-pass filter
6. Discrete Cosine Transform
7. Log energy
8. Delta cepstrum

The overall flow of Feature Extraction can be given as,

Algorithm Feature Extraction (wav file, sampling frequency)

```
// Input                    : Speech Signal
// Output                   : MFCC Features
{
        For every speech do
                For every frame in speech do
                Apply pre-emphasis and hamming window for continuity
of          the frame
                Apply Fast Fourier Transform for finding the magni-
tude        and phase of the signal
                Convert the linear frequency into mel frequency
                Apply Discrete Cosine Transform to compute MFCC
                        Append to Bag of Features
                        Set Label such as x₁,x₂,…xₜ
                end for
        end for
}
```

Figure 7. Various modules of Feature extraction Phase

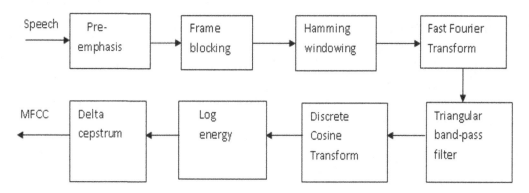

Pre-Emphasis

It is used to reduce the dynamic range of Fourier spectrum by increasing the magnitude of high frequency components. The speech signal s (n) is sent to a high-pass filter:

$$s_1(n) = s(n) - a * s(n-1)$$ (1)

where $s_1(n)$ is the output signal and the value of a is usually between 0.9 and 1.0. The z-transform of the filter H (Z) is

$$H(Z) = 1 - a * Z^{-1}$$ (2)

Frame Blocking

The speech signal characteristics staying stationary in a sufficiently short period of time interval is called as quasi-stationary. For this reason, speech signals are processed in short time intervals. It is divided into frames with sizes generally between 30 and 100 milliseconds. Each frame overlaps its previous frame by a predefined size. The goal of the overlapping scheme is to smooth the transition from frame to frame.

Hamming Windowing

The windowing technique applies to all frames. This is done in order to eliminate discontinuities at the edges of the frames. In this method the speech signal is blocked into overlapped frames with minimized discontinuity effect. Typically, window length may be 20-30 ms to tradeoff the temporal and spectral resolution. The windowing function is defined as $w(n)$, $0 \leq n \leq N-1$ where N is the number of samples in each frame.

$$w(n, a) = (1 - a) - a\cos(2\pi n / (N - 1)), 0 \leq n \leq N - 1 \tag{3}$$

where the value of a is set to 0.46.

Fast Fourier Transform

It is used to transform the speech signal into the frequency domain, where the most important speech/speaker information has resided. FFT is a fast way of Discrete Fourier Transform and it changes the domain from time to frequency. FFT is usually performed to obtain the magnitude, frequency response of each frame.

Triangular Band-Pass Filter

The human ear perceives the frequencies, non-linearly. So scaling is performed because it produces the linear frequency up to 1 kHz and logarithmic the above frequency. The Mel-Scale filter bank is characterized by human ear perceiveness of frequency. It is used as a band pass filtering for this stage of identification. The signals for each frame is passed through Mel-Scale band pass filter to mimic the human ear.

$$mel(f) = 1125 * ln(1 + f / 700) \tag{4}$$

The reasons for using triangular band-pass filters are twofold:

- Smoothen the magnitude spectrum such that the harmonics are flattened in order to obtain the envelope of the spectrum with harmonics.
- Reduce the size of the features involved.

Discrete Cosine Transform

Discrete Cosine Transform is used to transform the spectral information to the cepstral domain in which the energy is dominated by fewer coefficients. The cepstral coefficients are less cross-correlated so thus leading to the diagonal covariance matrix modeling in Figure 8 presents the spectrum to cepstrum conversion.

Figure 8. Spectrum to cepstrum conversion

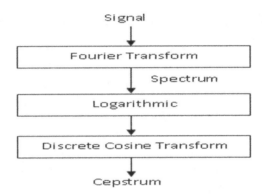

The formula for Discrete Cosine Transformation is

$$C_m = \sum_{k=1}^{N} \cos\left[m * (k - 0.5) * \lambda / N\right] * E_k, m = 1, 2, \dots L \tag{5}$$

where N is the number of triangular band-pass filters, L is the number of mel-scale cepstral coefficients. Usually set N = 20 and L = 12.

Log Energy

The energy within a frame is also an important feature that can be easily obtained. Hence the log energy is usually added as the 13th feature of MFCC. Some other features are added at this step including pitch, zero cross rate, high order spectrum momentum and so on.

Delta Cepstrum

In this step the dynamic coefficients are derived, i.e. time derivative of MFCC is calculated. It is very useful in automatic speech recognition system, especially in improving the noise robustness. The first order dynamic coefficients are represented as ΔMFCC and the second order dynamic coefficients are represented as $\Delta\Delta$MFCC which can be calculated with the same procedure.

It is also advantageous to have the time derivatives of energy and MFCC as new features, which shows the velocity and acceleration of energy and MFCC.

$$\Delta C_m\left(t\right) = \left[\sum_{\ddot{A}=-M}^{M} C_m\left(t+\ddot{A}\right)\ddot{A}\right] / \left[\sum_{\ddot{A}=-M}^{M} \ddot{A}^2\right] \tag{6}$$

The value of m is usually set to 2. If add the velocity (τ), the feature dimension is 26.

Deep Belief Network Construction Phase

A Deep Belief Network is a feed forward, artificial neural network that has more than one layer of hidden units between its inputs and its outputs. The idea is to train each layer independently and greedily using the hidden variables. Training Deep Belief Networks contain the following steps:

- Generative pre-training
- Learning procedure for RBMs
- Modeling real-valued data
- Stacking RBMs to make a deep belief network

Deep Belief Network (DBN) is created as a stack of its main building blocks which are undirected graphical models called Restricted Boltzmann Machines (RBMs). An RBM is a particular type of Markov random field that has a two layer architecture, in which the visible stochastic units v (typically Bernoulli or Gaussian) is connected to the hidden stochastic units h (typically Bernoulli). Normally, all visible units are connected to all hidden units and there is no visible to visible or hidden to hidden unit connection.

Figure 9. Deep belief network training

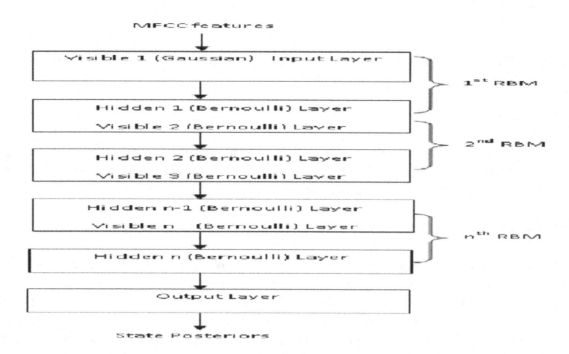

The Deep Belief Network is used to produce the state posterior values. Normally, DBNs were built by stacking Restricted Boltzmann Machines (RBMs) with binary units. However, features used in language identification (e.g. MFCC) are continuous value. In first RBM Gaussian visible units are used to represent the continuous speech features, and Bernoulli has hidden units, whereas all upper RBMs are Bernoulli-Bernoulli.

Deep belief network model in Figure 9 presents the four basic steps in training for language identification. After unsupervised training the first RBM, the activation probabilities of its hidden units are used as the visible data for the second RBM, and so on. When applying DBN for language identification, the final layer of variables is added to represent the desired outputs. Next, a discriminative learning fine-tunes all of the network weights using labeled training data.

The weights of the connections and biases of the individual units form a joint probability distribution P (v, h|Θ) over the visible unit's v and hidden units h given the model parameters Θ. The distribution is computed based on an energy function E (v, h|Θ):

$$P\left(v, h|\theta\right) = exp\left(-E\left(v, h|\theta\right)\right) / Z\left(\theta\right) \tag{7}$$

where $Z\left(\Theta\right)$ is known as the normalizing constant and its defined as:

$$Z\left(\theta\right) = \sum_{v}\sum_{h} exp\left(-E\left(v, h|\theta\right)\right) \tag{8}$$

With different types of visible and hidden units, different energy functions are defined. In the case of the visible and hidden units which are Bernoulli, the energy function is defined as

$$E\left(v, h|\theta\right) = -\sum_{i=1}^{V}\sum_{j=1}^{H} w_{ij} v_i h_j - \sum_{i=1}^{V} b_i v_i - \sum_{j=1}^{H} a_j h_j \tag{9}$$

Similarly, in the case of the visible and hidden units which are Gaussian and Bernoulli respectively, the energy function is defined as,

$$E\left(v, h|\theta\right) = -\sum_{i=1}^{V}\sum_{j=1}^{H} w_{ij} v_i h_j - 1/2\sum_{i=1}^{V}\left(v_i - b_i\right)^2 - \sum_{j=1}^{H} a_j h_j \tag{10}$$

where, model parameters Θ= { w, b, a }, w_{ij} is the weight between visible unit i and hidden unit j, b_i and a_j are biases for visible unit i and hidden unit j. V, H are the number of visible and hidden units, v_i is a Gaussian distribution respectively.

The overall flow of Deep Belief Network Construction algorithm can be given as,

Algorithm Deep Belief Network (wav file, features)

```
// Input                    : Speech Features
// Output                   : State Posteriors
{
      For every Speech Feature do
          Initialize RBM with 100 hidden units
              For each hidden units do
                      Initialize the weights and learning rate
                      Train RBM for classification
              end for
              Initialize DBN with two layers and 100 hidden units
              For each hidden units do
                      Initialize the weights and learning rate
                      Train DBN for classification and finding the
state                         posteriors
                      Set Label such as S1,S2,...Si
              end for
      end for
}
```

Apply Bayes Formula

It is used to convert the state posteriors value into state likelihood values. Likelihood values are estimated within the range of 0 to 1. Identifying the languages of the audio file based on this likelihood values.

Given a feature vector f_t, DBNs estimate the state posteriors $P(s_i \mid f_t)$ of state s_i. The likelihood value is calculated using following formula:

$$P(f_t \mid s_i) = P(s_i \mid f_t) P(f_t) / P(s_i) \qquad (11)$$

Where $P(s_i|f_t)/P(s_i)$ is the scaled likelihood since $P(f_t)$ the scaling factor is a constant for all states and does not affect the classification decision.

The Bayes algorithm can be given as,

Algorithm Bayes Formula (state posterior, feature vector)

```
// Input                    : State Posteriors
// Output                   : State Likelihoods
{
      For every states do
              Speech feature vector is labeled as x_t
              State is labeled as s_i
              Initialize the scaling factor
              Convert the posteriors into the scaled likelihoods
              Assign and Classify the likelihood values
```

```
                    if the likelihood values are matched then
                            Phones are identified
                    else
                            Phones are not recognized
                    end if
            end for
}
```

Language Recognition and Testing Phase

It is the pre-final and most important step of this work. This step has been done from using the previous state posteriors and state likelihoods value. This process the language is identified based on the likelihood values. Language recognition in Figure 10 presents the following steps.

- Obtain the state posteriors from DBN construction.
- Convert the state posteriors into state likelihoods.
- Choose the state likelihoods value as zero to one.
- Compare the likelihoods value after that recognize the language.
- If state likelihood value is 0.65 to 0.75 then the recognized language is Tamil, else if the value is 0.76 to 0.85 then the recognized language is English, and the value is 0.86 to 0.95 the recognized language is Hindi, otherwise the language is not recognized.

Figure 10. Language recognition and testing

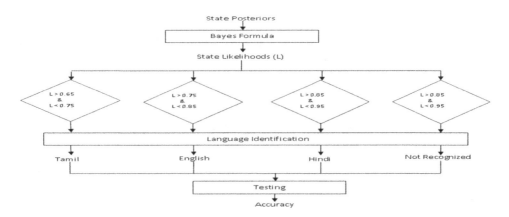

Finally, the accuracy of the identified language is calculated at the testing phase. Accuracy is intended in two ways:

- DBN state posteriors for training and testing samples
- Increasing the number of speakers

DBN State Posteriors

In this way the state posteriors are evaluated as speaker dependent model. State posteriors probability for each training and testing samples are compared and achieved the high accuracy.

Number of Speakers

In this way increasing the number of speakers in step of 3, 6, 9, 12 and 15 for three different languages and attained the high accuracy.

Accuracy is calculated by using the following formula:

```
Accuracy = (correct samples / total samples)     (12)
where, correct  -    Number of samples correctly modeled or classified.
          total    -     Total number of samples given for testing
```

Implementation Results

The language recognition system has been implemented and tested on 15 speaker speech sample database. This speech acquisition result consists of training and testing audio sample that specify the three languages such as English, Hindi and Tamil. Figure 11 presents the signal waveform of each audio sample and it's plotting points.

Figure 11. Results of speech acquisition for three languages like (a) English (b) Hindi (c) Tamil

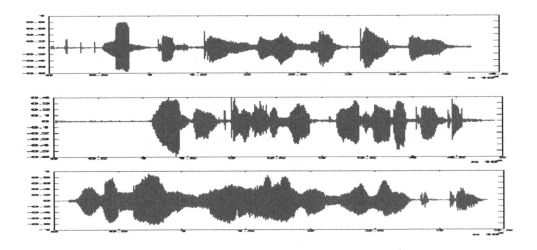

Feature extraction process is used to extract the 12-dimensional MFCC features. Pre-emphasis is used to reduce the dynamic range of Fourier spectrum by increasing the magnitude of high frequency components. Results in Figure 12 presents the Pre-emphasis output.

Hamming windowing is used to keep the continuity of the first and last points in the frame. Figure 13 presents the Hamming windowing output.

Figure 12. Pre-emphasis output

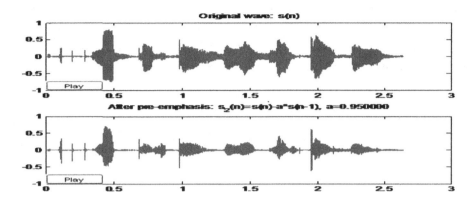

Figure 13. Hamming windowing output

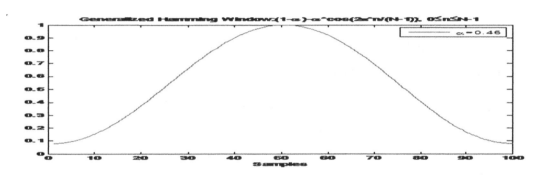

Results in Figure 14 presents the Fast Fourier Transform for obtaining the magnitude frequency of each frame.

Figure 14. Output of Fast Fourier Transform

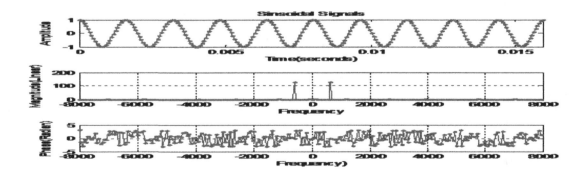

Triangular band-pass filter is used to convert the linear frequency into mel frequency wave and smooth the magnitude spectrum. Outputs in Figure 15 presents the conversion wave signal and results in Figure 16 presents the triangular band-pass filter output.

Discrete Cosine Transform is used to produce the MFCC wave, and transforms the frequency domain into a time-like domain. Results in Figure 17 presents the output of MFCC wave.

Figure 15. Linear frequency to mel frequency wave output

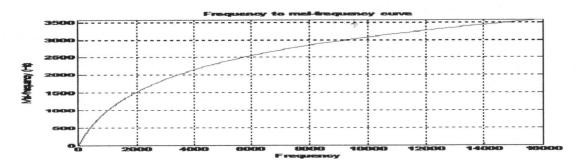

Figure 16. Output of Triangular band-pass filter

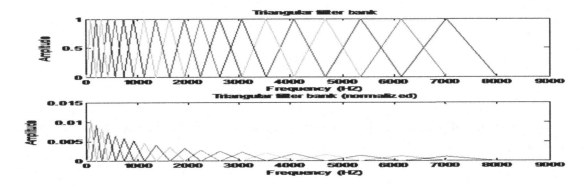

Figure 17. MFCC wave output

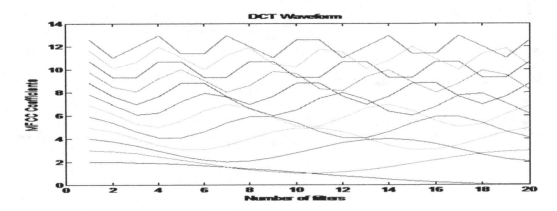

Deep Belief Network construction and training is used to produce the state posteriors value, Bayes formula is used to convert the state posteriors value into state likelihoods value finally recognize the languages. DBN state posteriors is indicated in Table 3, state likelihoods is indicated in Table 4.

Table 3. State Posteriors

Training Data	Tamil	English	Hindi
Data 1,2,3	0.8676	0.9576	1.0749
Data 4,5,6	0.8506	0.9549	1.0622
Data 7,8,9	0.8334	0.9263	1.0937
Data 10,11,12	0.8736	0.9125	1.0666
Data 13,14,15	0.8046	0.9134	1.0727
Data 16	**1.2820 (Sowrastra)**		

Table 4. State Likelihoods

Training Data	Tamil	English	Hindi
Data 1,2,3	0.7230	0.7980	0.8958
Data 4,5,6	0.7088	0.7957	0.8852
Data 7,8,9	0.6945	0.7719	0.9114
Data 10,11,12	0.7280	0.7604	0.8888
Data 13,14,15	0.6705	0.7612	0.8939
Data 16	**1.0683 (Sowrastra)**		

Figure 18 presents the Language classification and recognition module is done by using matlab.

Figure 18. Language Recognition using matlab

```
TotalLikelihood =

  Columns 1 through 10

    0.7980    0.8958    0.7230    0.7957    0.8852    0.7088    0.7719    0.9114    0.6945    0.7604

  Columns 11 through 16

    0.8888    0.7280    0.7612    0.8939    0.6705    1.0683

Likelihood value = 0.798    ---> The Recognized Phone of the Language is English
Likelihood value = 0.89575  ---> The Recognized Phone of the Language is Hindi
Likelihood value = 0.723    ---> The Recognized Phone of the Language is Tamil
Likelihood value = 0.79575  ---> The Recognized Phone of the Language is English
Likelihood value = 0.88517  ---> The Recognized Phone of the Language is Hindi
Likelihood value = 0.70883  ---> The Recognized Phone of the Language is Tamil
Likelihood value = 0.77192  ---> The Recognized Phone of the Language is English
Likelihood value = 0.91142  ---> The Recognized Phone of the Language is Hindi
Likelihood value = 0.6945   ---> The Recognized Phone of the Language is Tamil
Likelihood value = 0.76042  ---> The Recognized Phone of the Language is English
Likelihood value = 0.88883  ---> The Recognized Phone of the Language is Hindi
Likelihood value = 0.728    ---> The Recognized Phone of the Language is Tamil
Likelihood value = 0.76117  ---> The Recognized Phone of the Language is English
Likelihood value = 0.89392  ---> The Recognized Phone of the Language is Hindi
Likelihood value = 0.6705   ---> The Recognized Phone of the Language is Tamil
Likelihood value = 1.0683   ---> The Phone is not recognized (Sowrastra)
```

Performance Evaluation

Performance of the deep belief network system is evaluated based on the accuracy calculation. Accuracy is defined as the ratio between the number of correct samples and total number of samples. Here, the DBN system performance is evaluated by two taxonomies:

- DBN state posteriors for training and testing samples
- Increasing the number of speakers

Performance Evaluation Based on State Posteriors

This evaluation has performed based on state posteriors probability for training and testing samples are compared and achieved high accuracy at speaker dependent model. The audio samples and DBN state posteriors are listed in table 5. These values are plotted in bar chart as shown in figure 19.

Table 5. DBN State Posteriors for training and testing Samples

Audio Samples	Training	Testing	Audio Samples	Training	Testing
S1	0.9576	0.9876	S8	1.0937	1.1356
S2	1.0749	1.0749	S9	0.8334	0.8334
S3	0.8676	0.8885	S10	0.9125	0.9252
S4	0.9549	1.0328	S11	1.0666	1.0243
S5	1.0622	0.9665	S12	0.8736	0.8736
S6	0.8506	0.8506	S13	0.9134	0.9200
S7	0.9263	0.9536	S14	1.0727	1.0066
			S15	0.8046	0.8018

Figure 19. Performance for audio samples Vs state posteriors

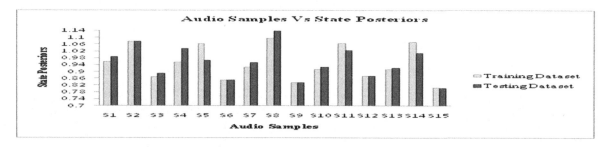

Performance Evaluation Based on Speakers

In this way increasing the number of speakers in steps of 3, 6, 9, 12, 15 for three different languages and attained high accuracy for English and Hindi language. The speaker's values and respective accuracy values for English, Hindi and Tamil is indicated in Table 6. The graph in Figure 20 presents the plotting of increasing the number of speakers.

Table 6. Accuracy of three languages for different number of speakers

No. of Speakers	3	6	9	12	15
English	33	50	78	83	**100**
Hindi	33	67	78	92	**100**
Tamil	67	67	75	83	94

Figure 20. Performance for Speakers Vs Accuracy

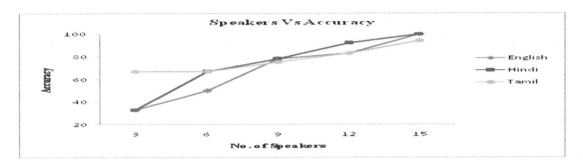

FUTURE RESEARCH DIRECTIONS

This work can be extended to more number of speakers by increasing the accuracy of the language recognition system. This system can be trained and tested with any other languages except English, Hindi and Tamil. Future work into language classification and recognition could focus on testing the system on a large speech corpus, combining the three languages into single audio file and recognizing the languages using optimized DBN parameters.

CONCLUSION

A technique for language recognition with Deep Belief Network is proposed with the objective of improving the classification and recognition performance for speaker dependent model and minimizing the computational complexity. The results presented in this work represent a step towards more flexible and adaptable systems. The proposed algorithm is tested with fifteen speakers of 135 training samples and 90 testing samples having 16 kHz frequency. MFCC extraction technique is applied on the enhanced audio samples to extract the audio features and reduce the noise and error of the audio signal. MFCC features such as pitch, spectrum, sharpness, etc. are extracted and combined with classification system in order to improve the accuracy. DBNs are trained as using the Restricted Boltzmann Machine (RBM) construction and that significant gains could be achieved by initial stage of training. DBNs could be trained much faster than multi layer perceptrons with same architecture. When the network size is large, DBNs outperformed MLPs consistently. From the experimental results it is observed that DBN runs faster because it does not require any detailed hypothesis and combine both discrete and continuous features. From the evaluation results obtained it is clear that higher identification rate can be achieved and the performance is evaluated by computing the performance metrics including accuracy. The error rates are minimized and accuracy is increased in this work. To conclude, Deep Belief Network is efficient for three languages at speaker dependent mode. The system can be tested in better way if the author can increase the number of speakers in the database. DBN gives best results when size of the database is large and different languages.

REFERENCES

Abdel-rahman, M., Sainath, T. N., Dahl, G., Ramabhadran, B., Hinton, G. E., & Picheny, M. A. (2011). Deep Belief Networks Using Discriminative Features for Phone Recognition. *Proc. ICASSP 2011.*

Bou Nassif, A., Shahin, I., Attili, I., & Azzeh, M. (2019). Speech Recognition Using Deep Neural Networks: A Systematic Review. *IEEE Access: Practical Innovations, Open Solutions, 7,* 19143–19165. doi:10.1109/ACCESS.2019.2896880

Cheng, S.-S., Wang, H.-M., & Fu, H.-C. (2004). A Model-Selection-based Self Splitting Gaussian Mixture Learning with Application to Speaker Identification. *EURASIP Journal on Applied Signal Processing, 17,* 2626–2639.

Dahl, G. E., Ranzato, M., Mohamed, A., & Hinton, G. E. (2010). Phone Recognition with the mean-covariance restricted Boltzmann machine. *Advances in Neural Information Processing Systems, 23,* 469–477.

Hinton, G. E., Osindero, S., & Teh, Y. W. (2006). A fast learning algorithm for deep belief nets. *Neural Computation, 18*(7), 1527–1554. doi:10.1162/neco.2006.18.7.1527 PMID:16764513

Le, H.-S., Oparin, I., Allauzen, A., Gauvain, J.-L., & Yvon, F. (2013). Structured Output Layer Neural Network Language Models for Speech Recognition. *IEEE Transactions on Audio, Speech, and Language Processing, 21*(1), 195–204.

Lee, K. F., & Hon, H. W. (1989). Speaker-independent phone recognition using hidden Markov models. *IEEE Transactions on Audio, Speech, and Language Processing, 37*(11), 1641–1648.

Li, H., Ma, B., & Lee, C.-H. (2007). A Vector Space Modeling Approach to Spoken Language Identification. *IEEE Transactions on Audio, Speech, and Language Processing, 15*(1), 271–284. doi:10.1109/TASL.2006.876860

Mohamed, A., Dahl, G. E., & Hinton, G. E. (2009). Deep belief networks for phone recognition. *NIPS Workshop on Deep Learning for Speech Recognition and Related Applications.*

Mohamed, A., Dahl, G. E., & Hinton, G. E. (2012). Acoustic Modeling Using Deep Belief Networks. *Transactions on Audio, Speech, and Language Processing, 20*(1), 14–22. doi:10.1109/TASL.2011.2109382

A. Mohamed, D. Yu, L. Deng (2010). Investigation of full-sequence training of deep belief networks for speech recognition. *Proc. Interspeech'10.*

Newman, J., & Cox, S. (2012). Language Identification Using Visual Features. *IEEE Transactions on Audio, Speech, and Language Processing, 20*(7), 1936–1947. doi:10.1109/TASL.2012.2191956

Roy, P., & Das, P. K. (2011). Language Identification of Indian Languages Based on Gaussian Mixture Models. *International Journal on Wisdom Based Computing, 1*(3), 54–59.

Sai Jayaram, A. K. V., Ramasubramanian, V., & Sreenivas, T. V. (2003). Language identification using parallel sub-word recognition. *IEEE Int. Conf. on Acoustics, Speech, and Signal Proc, 1,* 32-37.

Santhi, S., & Raja Sekar, J. (2013). An Automatic Language Identification Using Audio Features. *International Journal of Emerging Technology and Advanced Engineering, 3*(1), 358–364.

Torres-Carrasquillo, P. A., Reynolds, D. A., Deller, J. R. Jr, Singer, E., Greene, R. J., & Kohler, M. A. (2002). Language identification using Gaussian Mixture Model Tokenization. *IEEE Int. Conf. on Acoustics, Speech, and Signal Proc.* 10.1109/ICASSP.2002.1005850

Ueda, N., Nakano, R., Ghahramani, Z., & Hinton, G. (2000). SMEM Algorithm for Mixture Models. *Neural Computation, 12*(9), 2109–2128. doi:10.1162/089976600300015088 PMID:10976141

Witt. (2005). *Data Analysis in Speech Applications* (Vol. 1). AVIOS.

Wong & Sridharan. (2001). Fusion of Output Scores on Language identification System. *Workshop on Multilingual Speech and Language Processing.*

Zissman, M. (1996). Comparison of four approaches to automatic language identification of telephone speech. *IEEE Transactions on Audio, Speech, and Language Processing, 4*(1), 31–34. doi:10.1109/TSA.1996.481450

Zissman, M. A., & Berkling, K. M. (2001). Automatic language identification. *Speech Communication, 35*(1), 115–124. doi:10.1016/S0167-6393(00)00099-6

Zue, V. W., & Hazen, T. J. (1997). *Automatic Language Identification Using a Segment-Based Approach.* Proceeding Eurospeech. doi:10.1121/1.418211

ADDITIONAL READING

Tanprasert, C., Wutiwiwatchai, C., & Sae-tang, S. (2000). Text-dependent Speaker Identification Using Neural Network on Distinctive Thai Tone Marks. *Technical Journal, 1*(6), 249–253.

KEY TERMS AND DEFINITIONS

DBN: Deep belief networks are one of the probabilistic models which will be composed of multiple layers of latent or hidden variables. Deep belief network is a set of restricted Boltzmann machines stacked on top of one another.

GMM: Gaussian mixture model is one of the probabilistic models which states that all data points are derived from a mixture of Gaussian distributions.

HMM: Hidden Markov model is a statistical language model which can be modeled by a markov process with hidden states.

Language Recognition: Language recognition is the method of categorizing the languages from its audio speeches and take out the information presented in the speeches.

MFCC: Mel-frequency cepstral coefficients (MFCCs) are derived from a cepstral representation of the speeches from audio.

Chapter 12
Machine Learning Approach:
Enriching the Knowledge of Ayurveda From Indian Medicinal Herbs

Roopashree S.

https://orcid.org/0000-0003-1327-1267

Dayananda Sagar University, India & Visvesvaraya Technological University, India

Anitha J.

RV Institute of Technology and Management, India

Madhumathy P.

Dayananda Sagar Academy of Technology and Management, India

ABSTRACT

Ayurveda medicines uses herbs for curing many ailments without side effects. The biggest concern related to Ayurveda medicine is extinction of many important medicinal herbs, which may be due to insufficient knowledge, weather conditions, and urbanization. Another reason consists of lack of online facts on Indian herbs because it is dependent on books and experts. This concern has motivated in utilizing the machine learning techniques to identify and reveal few details of Indian medicinal herbs because, until now, it is identified manually, which is cumbersome and may lead to errors. Many researchers have shown decent results in identifying and classifying plants with good accuracy and robustness. But no complete framework and strong evidence is projected on Indian medicinal herbs. Accordingly, the chapter aims to provide an outline on how machine learning techniques can be adopted to enrich the knowledge of Indian herbs, which advantages both common man and the domain experts with wide information on traditional herbs.

DOI: 10.4018/978-1-7998-2566-1.ch012

INTRODUCTION

Ayurveda – "Science of Life" active from 5000 years ago is a traditional Indian Vedic culture. Ayurveda knowledge is already well incorporated in Tibetan and Chinese traditional medicines. It being an Indian Traditional System, even today it focusses on personalizing the health care system. Ayurveda therapeutics incorporates the concept of individual nature. The herbs (Ayurveda leaves) being the key component of Ayurveda Medicines is generally used for body cleansing, boosting immunity against diseases and keep a balanced mind, body and soul. Usage of herbs is the key component of Ayurveda medicine. Most of the herb species are best classified by recognizing their leaves.

Many plants are used for both medicine as well as for ornamental purpose. Numerous plants can be used to soothe inflammations and wounds. It has to be noted that plants needed for medicinal purpose do not need a large area to grow, they can even be grown easily in kitchen garden. This motivates in constant growth of herbs which benefits in treating many ailments naturally. Some of the herbs that can be grown effortlessly are:

- **Tulsi / Basil:** In Ayurveda, it is called as 'Elixir of life'. A well-known and found in almost all south Indian home. Tulsi is even listed in NASA list as air purifier, has anti-cancer properties, treats digestive problems, flu and common cold.
- **Coriander / Cilantro:** Used as garnishing in almost all of the south Indian dishes as it is well known for refreshing and treating digestive issues.
- **Mint:** A most common home-grown medicine herb. Its unique fragrance refreshes mind and well treats insomnia, diarrhea, cold and cough.
- **Lemon grass:** Lemon grass through tea relieves sore throat, menstrual pain, treats stress and insomniac. It has anti-pyretic properties.
- **Carom / Ajwain:** An edible plant with ridged leaves. It is believed as good luck by ancient Chinese. Treats stomach disorders and digestive problems.

Many developing countries consider using medicinal plants as a living tradition (WHO, 2013). It is estimated that majority of the primary needs of developing countries are met by the traditional medicine which depends on plants as the main source. The author Karunamoorthi, K. (2013) has given overview on how the traditional knowledge plays a major role in developing countries helping the poor for a healthier life. It is saddened that many medicinal plants are at extinction in big number because of many reasons and those reasons will be listed in the next section. Also, efforts to be taken care by every individual to reintroduce the species which are vulnerable and extinct. Few of the endangered medicinal plants found in India are:

- **Elephant's Foot**
  - Scientific Name: Dioscorea deltoidea
  - Native place: India, China, Afghanistan, Bhutan, Cambodia, Nepal, Pakistan, Thailand and Vietnam,
  - Used parts: The dried rhizomes are used both as traditional medicine
  - Benefits: Gastric problems, and as steroidal drugs designed for western medicine.
- **Jatamansi**
  - Scientific Name: Nardostachys grandiflora

- ○ Native Place: India, China Bhutan and Nepal
- ○ Used Parts: Roots and rhizomes
- ○ Benefits: fits, heart palpitations, constipation, regulate urination, digestion and menstruation.
- **Kutki**
  - ○ Scientific Name: Picrorhiza kurrooa
  - ○ Native place: India and Pakistan
  - ○ Used parts: Rhizomes
  - ○ Benefits: Antibiotic and liver ailments
- **Red Sanders**
  - ○ Scientific Name: Pterocarpus santalinus
  - ○ Native place: India
  - ○ Used parts: Heartwood and timber
  - ○ Benefits: Diabetes and soothing inflammation and timber to make furniture and source of red dye.
- **Snakeroot**
  - ○ Scientific Name: Rauvolfia serpentine
  - ○ Native place: India, Bangladesh, Bhutan, China, Indonesia, Malaysia, Myanmar, Nepal, Sri Lanka, Thailand and Vietnam
  - ○ Used parts: Roots
  - ○ Benefits: Central nervous disorders, anxiety, maniacal behaviour related with psychosis, intestinal disorders, schizophrenia, insomnia, insanity and epilepsy.
- **Himalayan Yew**
  - ○ Scientific Name: Taxus wallichiana
  - ○ Native place: India, China, Afghanistan, Bhutan, Indonesia, Malaysia, Myanmar, Pakistan, Nepal, Philippines and Vietnam
  - ○ Used parts: bark and leaves
  - ○ Benefits: sedative, aphrodisiac, respiratory diseases, scorpion stings, snake bites, headache, diarrhea and taxanes.

Plants Identification and Dataset Building Methods

Plants are identified manually by botanists, researchers and domain experts. Manual identification is cumbersome, consumes time and may be prone to errors. Also, the knowledge of medicinal herb should be widely spread to public and not be inherent to experts. Plants can be categorized by several methods by its leaves. Few procedures are: chemical identification, spectroscopy and optical identification. Classical and instrumental methods are the two types under chemical identification. The classical method consists of flame and chemical tests. Under spectroscopy, auger spectroscopy and hyper-spectra are the two variations. Optical identification consists of processing the digital images. It is considered to be at much higher-level when compared to analog processing as it has wide range of techniques that can be applied to the images and noise can be removed before processing.

For all the above reasons, rather than manual vision, vision of machine can be implemented for better accuracy of look-alike herbs. To increase in the usage and growth of herbs it is of vital importance to study and classify them appropriately. Hence, there is much need for an intelligent sub-system to categorize the ayurvedic herb by their leaf image. This in turn helps in maintaining the credibility and quality of medicines.

Today computers and smart phones play a vital role in everyone's daily routine. This is because of easy availability of internet, inexpensive storage devices, digital cameras and smart phones. The data from every device is huge and led researchers and domain experts to build systems useful for society including government and local public. Several noteworthy developments have been observed in many real-world researches such as recognition of digital signatures, finger-print identification, automatic diagnosis and treatments, video processing, optical character recognition, plant/object recognition system and many more. Awareness and accessibility on medicinal herb and thus about Ayurveda can be built easily by using web-based and smart phone-based applications.

The chapter highlights on many computer vision and machine learning techniques like feature extraction and classification algorithms used for categorizing the Indian Medicinal Herbs. Why machine learning? Machine learning is known to be a critical component of Artificial Intelligence (AI). It is used for predicting, optimizing, extracting and summarizing. To implement an automatic recognition system using AI approach, digital images of the herbal leaves are essential. As there is no publicly available dataset on herbal leaves, a new database has to be created. Haralick, R. M., & Shapiro, L. G. (1992) described that images for the dataset can be captured using a common computer-based system consisting of digital camera / scanner and analyzed using particularly developed software. Certain standards are to be followed to build the database. They are:

- Still images of the herbs to be collected after removing its petiole
- The herb to be placed on the white background on a completely flat surface
- Using the DSLR camera the pictures are clicked
- Clicked image background is removed and placed on a white canvas of same size for all images and few others to be followed

Different Approaches on Images

The images in the dataset are to be further processed. Image processing is part of computer vision and machine learning. The images are to be pre-processed before forwarding to the machine learning algorithms. There are many image processing procedures to enhance the image which is also known as image enhancement. Image analysis is also another significant step in image processing domain.

The techniques in machine learning helps to build an authentic system for herbal leaf classification. They consist of many feature extraction and classification algorithms. It has to be known that the pre-processed digital image fed to feature extraction would be in the form of matrix. Feature extraction algorithms consists of extracting local features, global features or combination of local and global features of the leaf which results in feature vector/set. The extracted features from the feature vector can be classified into its respective species by many supervised, semi-supervised or unsupervised algorithms.

Recognizing and categorizing using the automatic system (Gaston, K. J 2004) benefits the society. In relation to Ayurveda it assists in maintaining the health and wellness in natural way with better satisfaction. The taxonomists, botanists, drug designers and many stakeholders also would benefit to a great extent. The endangered medicinal plants checklist (Sharma S and Thokchom 2014), the Red List from IUCN (Singh, N. R., & Singh, M. S. 2009) shows many herbs which are vulnerable and extinct. Care to be taken by all towards the protection and growth of Traditional Indian herbs which indeed benefits the Indian society in abundance.

The main objective of the chapter is on the review of various computer vision and machine learning approaches that can be applied on the pre-processed digital images of the Indian herbs. Discussion on features, its extraction, identification and finally revealing the associated information of the herbs. Highlighting many of the techniques used so far on classification of herbs would attract interest of many readers. Porting the machine learning application onto web and mobile phone (Android / iPhone) would widen the sharing of Ayurveda knowledge in every common man. Brief study on the endangered species of medicinal plants would benefit the society at large.

The chapter begins by outlining the advantages of using the machine learning techniques on recognition of Indian herbs, framework and discussion of its components. The components involve the medicinal herb list including few extinct herbs, feature extraction and classification technique.

BACKGROUND

Being in the fast-moving world, it is evident that the society is moving far from nature world. This affects enormously on the life style. A change to be incorporated in the day-today life would benefit in healthy and energetic lifestyle. The change would be the knowledge of Ayurveda.

Ayurveda relies on nature's natural powers and ingredients in curing many ailments without side effects. It is truly a worthy alternative to synthetic drugs which has perilous effect on overall health. The principle behind it is that every plant in nature has some quality in treating multitude of diseases. The herbs used in Ayurveda are rich source of anti-bacterial, anti-toxic, anti-oxidant and nutritional properties. These herbs are well known to cure the diseases from its roots to help in staying fit and healthy for long duration. Many Indian medicinal herbs are used in formulating perfumes, natural dyes, pest control and many more. People are slowly realizing the contrast between the chemically treated products and herbal ones. Many are moving towards herbal in various disciplines. This can be more successful in spurting the essence of Ayurveda in every common man. The knowledge of Indian medicinal herbs has many stake holders like botanists, researchers, physicians, trekkers, taxonomists, firms monitoring the vulnerable and endangered species and local public. Patwardhan, B. et. al. (2005) has given a wide view on how China has successfully authorized its traditional treatments with agreeable scientific research and a strong evidence proof in Traditional Chinese Medicine. China has confidently supported its therapies over the world with science-based methodology. Ayurveda – Indian Traditional Medicine yet lacks a strong evidence based and a systematic approach.

To build the awareness on Ayurveda, initial step would be in recognizing the medicinal herbs available locally and nationally and also about its medicinal properties. Every species on earth has unique features is the remarkable diversity. Assigning a label to an unknown type is known as identification. To conserve the medicinal species requires skills on identification, experience and intensive training. Some of the manual identification method includes expert determination, recognition, comparison and use of keys (taxonomic literature) and devices. This type of recognition is an extended procedure. With new emerging techniques in computer vision and machine learning the identification of Ayurveda herb can be an automated process with better accuracy and robustness in reality.

In the book Mohammed M. et. al. (2017) defined machine learning as a set of rules developed by a computer on its own to solve common problems. Basic principle would lie in predicting the outcome based on the derived patterns. The most important factors which has led in flourishing of machine learning, computer vision and AI are advent of parallel processors, inexpensive storage devices and big data. It consists of different types of learning such as supervised learning, reinforcement learning and deep learning. In brief, supervised learning feeds in with few samples of any type and allow the system to calculate the similarities between them for exact recognition. Reinforcement learning outputs the right or wrong decision by carrying out sufficient iterations to predict the result. In deep learning, the calculations are performed by the system iteratively to determine the patterns by itself. The chapter focusses on the identification of the plants based on the resemblance of morphological features and discriminatory characters of the leaf and finally concluding with respective plant species name. The features can be qualitative or quantitative. Quantitative features can be counted and measured such as width and height of the leaf. Qualitative features such as shape, color etc. Gaston, K. J. and O'Neill (2004) had given a thought of automatic identification based on digital images captured by digital camera and scanners. But had concluded that the process is overpriced as digital cameras and other sources to build images were expensive. Wäldchen J and Mäder P (2018) has briefed on multiple techniques in machine learning exclusively for plant identification.

Images are made up of pixels. Each pixel carries various information about the image. This pixel information cannot be directly fed to machine learning algorithm as they are jumbled and extensive. Hence, the quality information has to be derived as feature vectors from the image which can be used to classify the species. Features determine the dataset quality and the amount of insights drawn from it. Feature extraction is also known as dimensionality reduction. It is a method where variables of the dataset are combined into features by reducing the dimension and thus ensuring the accurateness and description of the original dataset. The quality of the features extracted can be improved by a method known as feature selection. The choice of the feature extraction has impacts on classification time, classification cost, classification accuracy and number of examples to be learned.

Features that can be extracted are categorized broadly as

- General features (Independent Features):
    - Pixel-level feature: Identified at pixel level. E.g. Location and color
    - Local features: Calculated at the portion of edge detection / image segmentation. They extract the interesting points from the image. E.g. SIFT, SURF, ORB and BRIEF
    - Global features: Calculated over the whole image or part of the image
- Domain-specific features (Application dependent features): They combine low-level features for a specific domain

ISSUES: AYURVEDA – MACHINE LEARNING

Leaf Features and its Extraction Techniques for Automated Identification

Plants can be identified by various characters such as shape, texture, pattern, vein structure and color. These leaf features are used in depth for normal identification and few benefits the automated process.

Shape of Leaf

It is the most preferred feature for the classification. General leaf shape can be easily recognized by many people. There are few sub-classes in leaf shape such as oblique, ovate and oblanceolate. In machine leaning, basic geometric descriptions such as rectangularity, aspect ratio, eccentricity are used. Sophisticated descriptors like fourier descriptor, invariant moment and contour distance are extracted. Shape features are divided mainly into region-based – where complete leaf area is of interest and another one is contour-based- uses local features such as boundary segments. Derivation of the shape features consists of two step process. 1. Feature extraction and 2. Similarity measurement between the extracted features.

Leaf Texture

Texture of the leaf has high discriminative ability when compared to leaf shape. Leaf structure includes leaf directional properties, venation information and in detail the micro-texture at the surface of the leaf. Texture can be analyzed by only a small part of the leaf without depending on complete leaf shape. Few texture features are

- Statistical measures – entropy, homogeneity and contrast
- Wavelets
- Fractals

The most known texture analysis method is Gray Level Co-occurrence Matrix (GLCM). This method is carried out by gray-level value that occurs in a spatial relationship to a pixel with value.

Vein Structure

Extraction of venation property is not very significant because of low contrast between the leaf blade structure and venation. Special equipment is needed to recognize the veins. Hence, not a good choice of feature for automatic identification for the dataset with images captured from an ordinary digital camera.

Leaf Color

The leaf color feature has very low discriminative property as most of the leaves are in shades of green slightly varying due to different illumination condition. Leaves of same plant may have mixed colors as it purely depends on maturity, water and nutrients. A lot more study is necessary for considering the color feature for automatic identification.

Classification Techniques

It is a categorization or classification technique to assign a unique and desired label for the given data. The applications of classification include: speech recognition, image identification, classification of documents etc. There are mainly two types of classifiers – binary classifier and multi-class classifier. Binary classifier has two unique outputs whereas multi-class classifier categorizes into two or more distinct class labels. Some of the best-known classifiers commonly used for plant classification are:

Naive Bayes

The classifier is based on Bayes theorem assuming independent assumptions among predictors. It is widely used and suitable for large datasets. In simple, this classifier presumes that the existence (non-existence) of specific feature of class is independent to the existence (non-existence) of any other feature depending on the nature of the Naive Bayes model. It utilizes the extracted features by combining them into the classifier for categorization. It computes the posterior probability for every class and the result would be the class with highest probability. Gaussian Naive Bayes are also used for classifying the normal distribution data. It shows better performance on categorical data.

K – Nearest Neighbor (kNN)

It is the simplest and lazy learning algorithm. It classifies on the basis of distant function (similarity measure). The term k defines the neighbors to be considered around the data to be categorized. Few standards to be maintained are the term k should always be odd to avoid ties and scaling is very important. More the closer neighbors the easier the voting.

Support Vector Machine (SVM)

SVM is used for both classification and regression. It can be vigorous even when bias is observed in training examples. Has an excellent generalization ability. It is a supervised algorithm which develops a hyperplane or decision plane to mark the decision boundary for the training points for categorization. It also uses kernels function for given points and transforms to high dimensional space. SVM approach uses the highest margin hyperplane, which is the greatest separation between two linearly separable classes.

Controversies

Wu, S. G et. al. (2007) proposed automated recognition of leaf images using 12 digitals. Combining the five basic leaf features and morphological features for generating the feature vector and as classifier used probabilistic neural network on 20 plants species with an accuracy of 90%. Sathwik, T. et al (2013) used analysing texture feature using statistical method known as Gray Level Co-occurrence Matrix (GLCM) of leaf images to classify the nine types of medicinal plants. The accuracy attained is 94% considering eleven of its features. Gopal, A. et. al. (2012) achieved 92% of accuracy by extracting moment features, boundary-based features & colour features from 100 medicinal leaves with ten species and used the dissimilarity measure for matching the query image. Kadir, A. et. al. (2013) extracted color, shape, vein and texture features along with Probabilistic Neural Network as a classifier with an accuracy of 93.75% on publicly available Flavia dataset. Janani R & Gopal A (2013) distinguished the medicinal plants such as Thulasi, Curry, Neem, Henna Hibiscus and Thuduvalai using shape, color and texture features by Aritificial Neural Network with an accuracy of 94.4%. Rahmani, M. E., et. al. (2016) used leaves dataset from UCI archives. They combined three leaf features shape, margin and texture together and proved that combination of features gives the best results with all different type of supervised classifiers such as Naive Bayes, Decision Tree, kNN and Neural network.

C. H. Arun (2013) accomplished using texture analyses which includes grey textures, Local Binary Pattern (LBP) and Grey Tone Spatial Dependency Matrices (GTSDM) combinations of texture. Classifiers used were Stochastic Gradient Descent, kNN classifier and Decision Tree on Flavia dataset. Kumar, E. S., & Talasila, V (2014) attempted to prove that the leaf features are gaussian distributed on few medicinal plants such as Hibiscus, Betle, Ocimum, Leucas, Vinca, Murraya, Centella, Ruta and Mentha extracting features like area, color histogram and edge histogram with decent results. Begue, A. et. al. (2017) built a medicinal plant recognition system using smartphone to build the dataset. Extracted leaf features such as width, length, area, perimeter, color, hull area and number of vertices using random forest as classifier with an accuracy of 90.1%. The author proved that random forest outperformed SVM, kNN, neural network and Naive Bayes classifier. The medicinal plants dataset built for the leaves found in island of Mauritius.

Manojkumar P. et al. (2017) used Weka tool to extract geometric, texture, HU invariant moments, zernike moments and color features from 40 different Ayurvedic herbs. The author showed Multilayer perceptron (MLP) classifier outperformed Support Vector Machine (SVM) with an accuracy of 94.5%. Nithiyanandhan, K., & Reddy, T. B. (2017) examined Artificial Neural Network (ANN) on peepal, betel and hibiscus medicinal leaves by extracting its edges. Kan, H. X. et. al. (2017) proposed work for Traditional Chinese Medicine (TCM) by extracting ten shape features and five texture characters to classify the 12 different medicinal leaves using support vector machine classifier with recognition rate of 93.3%. Venkataraman, D., & Mangayarkarasi, N. (2016) have shown a brief review on medicinal plant using Support Vector Machine, Probabilistic Neural Network, and Principal Component Analysis. Extracted centroid, area, aspect ratio and vein features of 5 different neem leaves for identification purpose. They proved that aspect ratio of the leaf does not vary as size of the leaf varies but the leaf roundness does vary.

Pushpa BR et. al. (2016) mined ayurvedic leaves for different morphologic features such as standard deviation, mean, isoperimetric quotient, convex hull ratio, entropy and eccentricity and classified by a novel method by considering the leaf factor from the extracted features and achieved an accuracy of 93.75%. Sana O M, and R. Jaya (2015) implemented an android mobile application for identification of Ayurvedic herbal plants using Gray-Level Co-occurrence Matrices (GLCM). This type of system is needed for cosmetic and medical industries as well as for gardening. Anami, B. S.et. al. (2012) worked on images of medicinal plants such as tulsi, papaya, aloevera and neem to segregate into shrubs, herbs and trees. Color histograms like RGB, YCbCr and HSV along with edge direction histograms are deployed using mean square error, euclidean distance and similarity distance measures with an average accuracy of 94%.

Anami, B. S. et. al. (2010) worked on classifying Indian medicinal plants as trees, shrubs and herbs using color and edge histogram together with SVM and ANN with an accuracy of 94% and 90% respectively. Zaidah Ibrahim et. al. (2018) have conducted recognition of Malaysian herbal plants using Speeded-Up Robust Features (SURF), Histogram of Oriented Gradients (HOG) and Local Binary Pattern (LBP) with SVM. Authors constructed a new dataset for herbal leaves and showed the comparison with online dataset i.e. Flavia proving HOG and LBP performed better than SURF. Ananthi, C (2014) et. al. developed a system using neural network as classifier extracting texture and shape features of betel, castor, hibiscus and manathakali proving an accuracy of 70.87%. Mulyana Iyan et. al. (2013) developed an automatic system for Indonesian medicinal plants extracting texture and fractal dimension of the leaves. They clustered the features using Fuzzy C-means with an average accuracy of 83%.

Internet assets comprising of recognition and revealing of relevant information on Indian medicinal plants cannot be found as they are all within particular bounds. For e.g. Tota, K. et. al. (2013) provides details of plants for treating diabetes disease, D K Ved et. al. (2016) lacks showcasing the additional associated details of recognised plants and (NMPB & FRLHT) medicinal Plants lacks in the structure of leaves. The role of traditional medicine in health care systems, current challenges and opportunities and WHO's role (WHO, 2002) in strategies for traditional medicine states very clearly that traditional medicine is a significance for health care in few regions/states, but in other regions/states the role of traditional medicine is treated as complementary or a substitute medicine. One of the positive pearls in the treasure of Chinese cultural inheritance is Traditional Chinese Medicine (TCM) given by author Tang, J. L et. al. (2008). Hesketh T. and Zhu W. TCM (1997) show the widely used herbs for many herbal product developments and the result of thousand years of observation. With TCM, China has been fruitful in endorsing its traditional therapies using science-based methodology with acceptable scientific research and evidence, but Ayurveda needs more systematic research and evidence base.

Chainapaporn, P., & Netisopakul, P (2012) proposed a work on extracting Thai herb information from websites using HTML parser which is one of the methods to extract the information from various websites. Mahdikhanlou, K., & Ebrahimnezhad, H. (2014) showed a good performance results by building a leaf classification system using Swedish leaf dataset and Flavia dataset on PNN Classifier using centroid distance and axis of least inertia as feature extractors. Pundkar, S.V (2014) has concluded that multiple approaches has to be considered towards recognition of the medicinal plants. Hence, combining multiple areas such as image processing, machine learning and computer vision can classify the medicinal herbs with accuracy.

From the survey assessment, it settled on, that heaps of work have been accomplished for foreign country's plant recognition but for Indian country medicinal leaves very minor quantity of work has been through. Internet assets comprising all of the relevant information on Indian medicinal plants cannot be publicly found for till date. So, in forthcoming, work for Indian medicinal leaf recognition system using computer vision is very necessary for both robustness and efficiency and finally revealing the associated information of the identified plants that can be useful to experts and common man.

Also, development of plant database would be efficient in drug designing in having a common database since all the related properties of the plant would be stemmed from the medicinal reputed botanies.

If the above survey yields the need for an automatic recognition model using machine learning for the Indian medicinal plants then the other side of consideration is to conserve the vulnerable / endangered list of Indian medicinal plants using the benefits of the database.

Reasons for extinction of plants with medicinal properties Emily Roberson. (2008):

- Due to increase in research facility
- Interest of western world in medicinal plants and its parts has led to commercialization and hence over exploitation
- Destruction of the habitat: Many medicinal plants grow in protected areas hence disappears unknowingly
- Due to lack of conservation many plants are in depletion
- The rise of urbanization and attraction towards urban jobs
- The wide spread of allopathy health care to rural areas has eroded the traditional system
- The ideal growth of few plants is well known only to native communities

Hence, efforts in planning big scale cultivation, avoiding exploitation due to commercialization, long-term conservation strategies and public awareness on medicinal properties and usage of the plants will surely improve the Indian Traditional Medicine system. Along with this, developing a machine learning automated tool for easy and robust recognition of the herbs collaborating with an Ayurveda expert is

Figure 1. List of few endangered and economically significant medicinal plants of India

Sl. No.	Scientific Name	Common Name	Explants	Few Medicinal Uses	Reference
1	Aegle marmelos	Bael	Shoot tip & nodal segments	Diarrhea, dysentery, and peptic ulcers and laxative	Yadav and Singh (2011)
2	Acorus calamus	Calamus	Rhizome	Ulcers, diarrhea and intestinal gas	Yadav et. al. (2011)
3	Celastrus paniculatus	Black oil plant / Intellect plant	Seeds, nodal sections & shoot tip	Memory booster, brain tonic & memory disorders	Lal, D., & Singh, N. (2010)
4	Commiphora mukul	Guggul / Gugul	Nodal and leaf parts	Arthritis, lowering cholesterol and acne	Singh et. al. (1997)
5	Bacopa monnieri	Waterhyssop, brahmi	Nodal and leaf parts	Alzheimer's disease, improving memory, anxiety & attention deficit-hyperactivity disorder (ADHD)	Mohapatra, H. P., & Rath, S. P. (2005)

very essential. This combination would overcome major of the persisting problems. Figure 1 briefs on the few endangered herbs and its medicinal uses.

From all the above facts, it is clear that in the branch of therapeutic, plants play a vital role in health care system and has been considered as the potential source for maintaining the good health and treating many diseases. Some medicinal plants are under the threat of depletion and exploitation. Strategies on managing the afforestation and exhaustion is necessary. The recent advances in artificial intelligence domain has motivated in building automatic system for medicinal plant species. This enables the public and the experts in identifying the unknown species with much more accuracy by saving ample time. Enhancing knowledge on the traditional Indian medicine is truly a worth alternative way when compared to consuming synthetic medicines. It is a known fact that allopathy is expensive and has side effects though can cure at faster rate. A web-based or a mobile platform would be ideal to build the medicinal herb knowledge in everyone. There is a very much need of a model using latest machine learning techniques which consist of novel combination of feature extraction and classification technique. The model needs to be robust with good accuracy.

Problems in Recognizing Medicinal Herbs

The existing research on Indian herb identification using the machine learning proves a decent accuracy with a very few datasets of medicinal plants of their respective region. Issues pertaining to medicinal herb dataset are:

- A dataset consisting of Indian Herbs has to be built freshly as it is not available online. Constructing dataset of Ayurveda leaf images and extracting the medicinal properties, origin and many more from different sources

- It is only the botanists or the Ayurveda experts who are well aware of the Indian herb species to a great extent
- Common man has no easy and user-friendly means for the same.
- Number of species to be discriminated are in big number
- Considering individual leaves of the same plant that vary in their morphology characteristics: The features of the leaf vary enormously from tender to mature phase. Hence attempts to be taken to collect all types of varieties in large scale.
- Different plants which are enormously similar to each other
- Rare Species has to be concentrated and
- Diverse image acquisition methods have to be considered to build the herb dataset

The machine learning techniques consisting of feature extraction like color, shape, edge, corners, SIFT, ORB and many low-level and high-level features can be fed as an input to the classifiers for the classification. Issues with reference to machine learning techniques are:

- Building model with faster accuracy rate and few induced human error
- Design of a complete data-driven system with an ability to examine large amount of data in small interval of time
- A sensible chance of belief to public that the benefits of medicinal plant persists for longer years.
- Building dataset with digital images either by scan, pseudo-scan or clicking pictures of leaf on white background using digital cameras

Problems relating to the concern of the endangered species is its reintroduction of identified vulnerable or endangered species, regular monitoring and field survey, control of overharvesting.

SOLUTIONS AND RECOMMENDATIONS

Enriching the Knowledge of Ayurveda From Indian Medicinal Herbs Using ML Techniques

In this chapter, an integrative framework is proposed as a common communication platform which is drawn from previous research, a dataset for identifying the herbs to build an effective evidence of Ayurveda Medicinal herbs and ensuring its availability to every common man. This platform would be a systematized and unified for enriching Ayurveda. It can be argued as timely, because until now many are unaware of the Ayurveda, its benefits, the medicinal herbs behind Ayurveda and its importance in daily life for a better living. The current inflation and side effects would strongly recommend all to strive for an alternative – The Ayurveda.

The studies also prove that the machine learning techniques are booming with good accuracy in recognizing and classifying the still images to their respective species. Adopting these techniques would ease the framework. Thus, emphasize on different algorithms for extracting the features, removing noise before extraction and classification to their respective species.

Some of the recommendations are:

- Porting the machine learning system onto mobile platform (Android and iOS), web platform and desktop application – This would ensure spreading the awareness of Ayurveda and its medicinal uses to public and all other end-users.
- Construction of new dataset for Indian medicinal herbs – Motivates many computer scientists and researchers to work on robust model for classification of medicinal plants.
- Inspire the taxonomists to evolve more efficient technique for distinguishing
- Use of deep learning concepts and IOT devices for building the cost-effective machine learning model
- Considering the IUCN list as an alarm and act against the vulnerability of the natural world
- Implementation of Real-Time identification system combining machine learning and Internet of Things for Indian Medicinal Herbs
- A real-time automatic system which reveals minimum of five closest species as its classification outcome.

Machine Leaning Based Analytics for Ayurveda Plants

The analysis of the traditional knowledge on herbs consists of collecting data by capturing the images of various herbs, consulting Ayurveda doctors and books, websites and CD's available on medicinal herbs. It has been proved by many countries that various techniques under Artificial Intelligence can be used in recognizing the herbs. Hence, to build a model for Ayurveda herbs requires a huge amount of data for predicting and analyzing. Different analytics techniques can be incorporated to provide data for the AI model.

Advanced analytics refers to many techniques and tools from fields such as pattern recognition, data mining and machine learning. The analytics tool and AI models require clean and normalized data. Machine Learning requires a large amount of data to generate insight from it. Hence analytics tools and techniques are essential for any accurate predictions of the ML model. The traditional analysis of data thus might not yield good variables in predicting using the ML model.

Hall P et. al. showed that the main pitfall in machine learning in plants consist of very low size of leaf samples. As leaves in plants consists of numerous attributes with very few specimens for training the model. Hence, the ML model fits the training dataset well but showcases poor performance on testing samples. Many cases consist of weaker or redundant features and as a consequence the model built might have poor classification accuracy. Some of the techniques such as dimensionality reduction is efficient to overcome the above cases. There are scenarios, where data might be incomplete or missing. Removing the incomplete data may not be appropriate. Little, R. J., & Rubin, D. B. disclosed that instead a method of imputation, where missing data are substituted with certain values. A common method in ML is Multiple Imputation.

Challenges in analytics of Ayurveda herbs include (1) Building the herb dataset (2) Analysis of the recognized herb (3) Construction of herb database with complete information for most attributes. Application of analytical tools on Ayurveda Herbs is necessary to enhance the knowledge of medicinal herbs in every common man motivating for a healthy and natural lifestyle. Hence leaving behind the synthetic drugs for any ailments.

FUTURE RESEARCH DIRECTIONS

The proposed chapter provides new features which benefits to the society. It recommends on the conservation and sustainable use of Indian herbs. Awareness on Ayurveda through medicinal herbs present in India to every common man and experts of many areas. Indian red listed herb information showed will provide better understanding on the extinct leaves. The result of this chapter would be of great advantage to trekkers, researcher community on Indian herbs and also practitioners. Thus, the framework consequences as a common communication platform for the society.

It can be concluded that, technique of assigning every discrete leaf image to its relevant plant species known as classification is tedious and may be prone to errors if carried out manually. Hence, with the advent of machine learning, computer-aided recognition of medicinal plants is still in testing errand mainly because of insufficient recognition of model and public availability of herb dataset. A concrete system with systematic feature extraction in par with tough classifier with a good recognition rate should be evident.

Analysis of different combination of legitimate features such as morphological features, shape, text, contour, scale invariant feature transform (SIFT), speeded up robust features (SURF), oriented FAST and rotated BRIEF (ORB) and many more. The best extractor to be figured out after numerous tests on the newly built dataset. It has been demonstrated by many investigators / analysts that SIFT creates good set of descriptors ideal for accurate image classification. Texture features in combination with shape and edge produces decent feature list. Thus, combining local and global features produces good set of features crucial for classification.

Numerous common supervised classification methods such as Principal Component Analysis, k-Nearest Neighbor (kNN), Naive Bayes, Support Vector Machine (SVM), Genetic Algorithm and many more.

- kNN: Effortless but consumes more time for larger dataset.
- Probability Neural Network (PNN): Robust, swift and uncomplicated but complexity is the draw back.
- Support Vector Machine (SVM): High dimensional data classification is straightforward and computing complexity is much tapered.
- Principal Component Analysis (PCA): Though dimensionality reduction is an upper hand; classification into classes is not well supported.

CONCLUSION

Preferably, a model with novel combination of feature extraction and classification technique is demanded for Indian medicinal plants. Approach towards implementation of a desktop, mobile or web application for building interaction between computer scientists, ecologist, botanists, general public and many other end-users.

Kumar, N. et. al. (2012) implemented an iOS application on general leaves of North America known an "Leaf Snap Application". Similar one by Goëau, H., Bonnet (2013) devoted to general leaves of Europe is known Pl@ntNet – an android, iOS and web-based application. On the same grounds, an application on Indian Medicinal herbs would be a promising solution in motivating people to use and grow herbs, enhancing the Ayurveda skills and in turn a small rise to Indian revenue. Indeed, a small contribution to Indian horticulture.

REFERENCES

Anami, B. S., Nandyal, S. S., & Govardhan, A. (2010). A combined color, texture and edge features based approach for identification and classification of Indian medicinal plants. *International Journal of Computers and Applications*, *6*(12), 45–51. doi:10.5120/1122-1471

Anami, B. S., Nandyal, S. S., & Govardhan, A. (2012). Color and Edge Histograms Based Medicinal Plants' Image Retrieval. International Journal of Image, Graphics &. *Signal Processing*, *4*(8).

Ananthi, C., Periasamy, A., & Muruganand, S. (2014). Pattern recognition of medicinal leaves using image processing techniques. *Journal of Nanoscience and Nanotechnology*, *2*(2), 214–218.

Arun, C. H., Emmanuel, W. S., & Durairaj, D. C. (2013). Texture feature extraction for identification of medicinal plants and comparison of different classifiers. *International Journal of Computers and Applications*, *62*(12), 1–9. doi:10.5120/10129-4920

Begue, A., Kowlessur, V., Mahomoodally, F., Singh, U., & Pudaruth, S. (2017). Automatic recognition of medicinal plants using machine learning techniques. *International Journal of Advanced Computer Science and Applications*, *8*(4), 166–175. doi:10.14569/IJACSA.2017.080424

Chainapaporn, P., & Netisopakul, P. (2012, July). Thai herb information extraction from multiple websites. In Knowledge and Smart Technology (KST) (pp. 16-23). IEEE. doi:10.1109/KST.2012.6287734

Gaston, K. J., & O'Neill, M. A. (2004). Automated species identification: Why not? *Philosophical Transactions of the Royal Society of London. Series B, Biological Sciences*, *359*(1444), 655–667. doi:10.1098/rstb.2003.1442 PMID:15253351

Goëau, H., Bonnet, P., Joly, A., Bakić, V., Barbe, J., Yahiaoui, I., ... Molino, J. F. (2013, October). Pl@ntnet mobile app. In *Proceedings of the 21st ACM international conference on Multimedia* (pp. 423-424). ACM. 10.1145/2502081.2502251

Gopal, A., Reddy, S. P., & Gayatri, V. (2012, December). Classification of selected medicinal plants leaf using image processing. In *2012 International Conference on Machine Vision and Image Processing (MVIP)* (pp. 5-8). IEEE. 10.1109/MVIP.2012.6428747

Hall, P., Marron, J. S., & Neeman, A. (2005). Geometric representation of high dimension, low sample size data. *Journal of the Royal Statistical Society. Series B, Statistical Methodology*, *67*(3), 427–444. doi:10.1111/j.1467-9868.2005.00510.x

Haralick, R. M., & Shapiro, L. G. (1992). *Computer and robot vision* (Vol. 1). Addison-wesley.

Hesketh, T., & Zhu, W. X. (1997). Health in China: traditional Chinese medicine: one country, two systems. *BMJ (Clinical Research Ed.)*, *315*(7100), 115–117. doi:10.1136/bmj.315.7100.115 PMID:9240055

Ibrahim, Sabri, & Mangshor. (2018). Leaf Recognition using Texture Features for Herbal Plant Identification. *Indonesian Journal of Electrical Engineering and Computer Science, 9*(1).

Iyan, M., Yeni, H., & Hartono, W. S. (2013). *The Identification of Medicinal Plants based on Fractal using Fuzzy C-Means Clustering.* Central Library of Bogor Agricultural University. https://repository. ipb.ac.id/handle/123456789/57517

Janani, R., & Gopal, A. (2013, September). Identification of selected medicinal plant leaves using image features and ANN. In *2013 international conference on advanced electronic systems (ICAES)* (pp. 238-242). IEEE.

Kadir, A., Nugroho, L. E., Susanto, A., & Santosa, P. I. (2013). *Leaf classification using shape, color, and texture features.* arXiv preprint arXiv:1401.4447

Kan, H. X., Jin, L., & Zhou, F. L. (2017). Classification of medicinal plant leaf image based on multi-feature extraction. *Pattern Recognition and Image Analysis, 27*(3), 581–587. doi:10.1134/S105466181703018X

Karunamoorthi, K., Jegajeevanram, K., Vijayalakshmi, J., & Mengistie, E. (2013). Traditional Medicinal Plants: A Source of Phytotherapeutic Modality in Resource-Constrained Health Care Settings. *Journal of Evidence-Based Complementary & Alternative Medicine, 18*(1), 67–74. doi:10.1177/2156587212460241

Kumar, E. S., & Talasila, V. (2014, April). Leaf features based approach for automated identification of medicinal plants. In *2014 International Conference on Communication and Signal Processing* (pp. 210-214). IEEE. 10.1109/ICCSP.2014.6949830

Kumar, N., Belhumeur, P. N., Biswas, A., Jacobs, D. W., Kress, W. J., Lopez, I. C., & Soares, J. V. (2012, October). Leafsnap: A computer vision system for automatic plant species identification. In *European Conference on Computer Vision* (pp. 502-516). Springer. 10.1007/978-3-642-33709-3_36

Lal, D., & Singh, N. (2010). Mass multiplication of Celastrus paniculatus Willd: An important medicinal plant under in vitro conditions via nodal segments. *International Journal of Biodeversity and Conservation, 2*(6), 140–145.

Little, R. J., & Rubin, D. B. (2002). *Statistical analysis with missing data.* John Wiley & Sons. doi:10.1002/9781119013563

Mahdikhanlou, K., & Ebrahimnezhad, H. (2014, May). Plant leaf classification using centroid distance and axis of least inertia method. In *2014 22nd Iranian conference on electrical engineering (ICEE)* (pp. 1690-1694). IEEE. 10.1109/IranianCEE.2014.6999810

Manojkumar, P., Surya, C. M., & Varun, P. Gopi. (2017). Identification of Ayurvedic Medicinal Plants by Image Processing of Leaf Samples. *Third International Conference on Research in Computational Intelligence and Communication Networks (ICRCICN).*

Mohammed, M., Badruddin, M., & Mohammed, B. (2017). *Machine learning: algorithms and applications.* CRC.

Mohapatra, H. P., & Rath, S. P. (2005). *In vitro studies of Bacopa monnieri—an important medicinal plant with reference to its biochemical variations.* Academic Press.

Nithiyanandhan, K., & Reddy, T. B. (2017). Analysis of the Medicinal Leaves by using Image Processing Techniques and ANN. *International Journal of Advanced Research in Computer Science, 8*(5).

NMPB & FRLHT. (n.d.). http://www.medicinalplants.in/aboutfrlhtdb

Patwardhan, B., Warude, D., Pushpangadan, P., & Bhatt, N. (2005). Ayurveda and traditional Chinese medicine: A comparative overview. *Evidence-Based Complementary and Alternative Medicine, 2*(4), 465–473. doi:10.1093/ecam/neh140 PMID:16322803

Pundkar, S.V. (2014). *Study of Various Techniques for Medicinal Plant Identification.* Academic Press.

Pushpa, B. R., Anand, C., & Nambiar, P. M. (2016). Ayurvedic plant species recognition using statistical parameters on leaf images. *International Journal of Applied Engineering Research, 11*(7), 5142–5147.

Rahmani, M. E., Amine, A., & Hamou, R. M. (2016). Supervised Machine Learning for Plants Identification Based on Images of Their Leaves. *International Journal of Agricultural and Environmental Information Systems, 7*(4), 17–31. doi:10.4018/IJAEIS.2016100102

Roberson. (2008). *Nature's Pharmacy, Our Treasure Chest: Why We Must Conserve Our Natural Heritage. A Native Plant Conservation Campaign Report.* Academic Press.

Sana & Jaya. (2015). Ayurvedic Herb Detection Using Image Processing. *International Journal of Computer Science and Information Technology Research, 3*(4).

Sathwik, T., Yasaswini, R., Venkatesh, R., & Gopal, A. (2013, July). Classification of selected medicinal plant leaves using texture analysis. In *2013 Fourth International Conference on Computing, Communications and Networking Technologies (ICCCNT)* (pp. 1-6). IEEE. 10.1109/ICCCNT.2013.6726793

Sharma, S., & Thokchom, R. (2014). A review on endangered medicinal plants of India and their conservation. *Journal of Crop and Weed, 10*(2), 205–218.

Singh, K., Chander, R., & Kapoor, N. K. (1997). Guggulsterone, a potent hypolipidaemic, prevents oxidation of low density lipoprotein. *Phytotherapy Research: An International Journal Devoted to Medical and Scientific Research on Plants and Plant Products, 11*(4), 291–294. doi:10.1002/(SICI)1099-1573(199706)11:4<291::AID-PTR96>3.0.CO;2-R

Singh, N. R., & Singh, M. S. (2009). Wild medicinal plants of Manipur included in the red list. *Asian Agri-History, 13*(3), 221–225.

Tang, J. L., Liu, B. Y., & Ma, K. W. (2008). Traditional chinese medicine. *Lancet, 372*(9654), 1938–1940. doi:10.1016/S0140-6736(08)61354-9 PMID:18930523

Tota, K., Rayabarapu, N., Moosa, S., Talla, V., Bhyravbhatla, B., & Rao, S. (2013). InDiaMed: A comprehensive database of Indian medicinal plants for diabetes. *Bioinformation, 9*(7), 378–380. doi:10.6026/97320630009378 PMID:23750084

Ved, Sureshchandra, Barve, Srinivas, Sangeetha, Ravikumar, Kartikeyan, Kulkarni, Kumar, Venugopal, Somashekhar, Sumanth, Begum, Rani, Surekha, & Desale. (2016). *FRLHT's ENVIS Centre on Medicinal Plants.* Academic Press.

Venkataraman, D., & Mangayarkarasi, N. (2016, December). Computer vision based feature extraction of leaves for identification of medicinal values of plants. In *2016 IEEE International Conference on Computational Intelligence and Computing Research (ICCIC)* (pp. 1-5). IEEE. 10.1109/ICCIC.2016.7919637

Wäldchen, J., & Mäder, P. (2018). Plant species identification using computer vision techniques: A systematic literature review. *Archives of Computational Methods in Engineering*, *25*(2), 507–543. doi:10.100711831-016-9206-z PMID:29962832

World Health Organization. (2002). *WHO traditional medicine strategy 2002-2005*. Geneva: World Health Organization. https://www.who.int/medicines/library/trm/trm_strat_eng.pdf

World Health Organization. (2008, December). W*HO Traditional Medicine, Fact Sheet No 134, Technical report*. WHO.

World Health Organization. (2013). *The WHO Traditional Medicine (TM) Strategy 2014–2023*. WHO. https://www.who.int/iris/bitstream/10665/92455/1/9789241506090_eng.pdf?ua=1

Wu, S. G., Bao, F. S., Xu, E. Y., Wang, Y. X., Chang, Y. F., & Xiang, Q. L. (2007, December). A leaf recognition algorithm for plant classification using probabilistic neural network. In *2007 IEEE international symposium on signal processing and information technology* (pp. 11-16). IEEE.

Yadav, K., & Singh, N. (2011). In vitro propagation and biochemical analysis of field established wood apple (Aegle marmelos L.). *Analele Universitatii din Oradea. Fascicula Biologie*, *18*(1).

Yadav, K., Singh, N., & Aggarwal, A. (2011). Influence of arbuscular mycorrhizal (AM) fungi on survival and development of micropropagated Acorus calamus L. during acclimatization. *Agricultural Technology (Thailand)*, *7*(3), 775–781.

Chapter 13
Machine Learning for Business Analytics

Kağan Okatan

https://orcid.org/0000-0002-0517-665X

İstanbul Kültür University, Turkey

ABSTRACT

All these types of analytics have been answering business questions for a long time about the principal methods of investigating data warehouses. Especially data mining and business intelligence systems support decision makers to reach the information they want. Many existing systems are trying to keep up with a phenomenon that has changed the rules of the game in recent years. This is undoubtedly the undeniable attraction of 'big data'. In particular, the issue of evaluating the big data generated especially by social media is among the most up-to-date issues of business analytics, and this issue demonstrates the importance of integrating machine learning into business analytics. This section introduces the prominent machine learning algorithms that are increasingly used for business analytics and emphasizes their application areas.

INTRODUCTION

Big data, machine learning and business analytics concepts are trending topics in today's businesses. There have been much discussions going on these topics but there is also a need to explain these concepts. The large data volume does not classify it as just the big data age, because there have always been larger volumes of data than we can effectively work with. What separates the present as the big data age is the change in the behavior of companies, governments and non-profit organizations. During this period, they want to start using all the data they can collect to improve their business for an unknown purpose, present or future (Dean, 2014).

Big Data sources which make big data 'big' are sensors, digitizers, scanners, digital modeling, mobile phones, the Internet, videos, emails and social networks (Yang, Huang, Li, Liu, & Hu, 2017). Data types flowing from these sources in a very large and diverse range include text, geometries, images, videos, sounds and a combination of each. such data can be directly or indirectly converted into purpose-oriented business information.

DOI: 10.4018/978-1-7998-2566-1.ch013

Both academics and practitioners attach great importance to the value that institutions can create through big data and business analytics. This is mainly due to the fact that information technologies, business analytics and related technologies enable organizations to better understand workload and markets" and increase the opportunities offered by abundant data and domain-specific analytics". Top-performing organizations make decisions based on rigorous analysis more than twice the rate of underperforming organizations and state that analytical insight is used 'to guide both future strategies and day-to-day operations' (Sharma, Mithas, & Kankanhalli, 2014).

The irresistible charm of processing big data requires understanding and application in other very important concepts, which is where the real competitive advantage goes. 'Machine learning' is a key concept to use the big data in order to boost your enterprise's marketing and other business operations' performance. The term 'machine learning' is often, incorrectly, interchanged with Artificial Intelligence, but machine learning is a sub field/type of Artificial intelligence. Machine learning is also often referred to as predictive analytics, or predictive modelling.

Mostly the term 'machine learning' seems to be intertwined with 'Artificial Intelligence', but machine learning is a subspace / type of artificial intelligence. Machine Learning is not a new concept. Machine learning is closely related to Artificial Intelligence. Artificial intelligence becomes possible with machine learning. The term 'machine learning' is coined by American computer scientist Arthur Samuel in 1959, is defined yet the 'computer's ability to learn without explicit programming' (Wakefield, 2019). Through machine circulation, computer systems can be classified, clustered, predicted, pattern recognition, and so on. Learn to perform such tasks. To archive the learning process, systems are trained using various algorithms and statistical models to analyze sample data. Sample data is generally characterized by measurable properties called properties, and a machine learning algorithm attempts to find a relationship between properties and some output values called labels. The information obtained during the training phase is then used to identify patterns or make decisions based on new data. Ideal for problems such as machine learning, regression, classification, clustering, and setting association rules. Machine learning is also often called predictive analytical or predictive modeling (Zantalis, Koulouras, Karabetsos, & Kandris, 2019).

Machine learning is an activity that allows the computer machine to learn data from data to make data-driven decisions. The machine learning algorithm is used to learn the data to form the decision model. Decision models are then used to decide (Singh, Leavline, Muthukrishnan, & Yuvaraj, 2018). This is the point where machine learning meets business analytics.

A McKinsey global report described Big Data as "Data whose scale, distribution, diversity, and/or timeliness require the use of new technical architectures and analytics to enable insights that unlock the new sources of business value" (Elshawi, Sakr, Talia, & Trunfio, 2018).

Learning algorithms are increasingly used due to their values that make a difference in solving the problems we face in our daily business world. The most prominent features of these algorithms are that they provide solutions or statistical reality to our business problems from experience, especially big data. This explains why machine learning and the use of deep learning are rapidly shifting from laboratory interest to business applications (Al-Garadi, Mohamed, Al-Ali, Du, & Guizani, 2018). The motivation behind this section is to raise awareness of leading machine learning algorithms, which contribute greatly to business analytics.

BUSINESS ANALYTICS

"Information is the oil of the 21st century, and analytics is the combustion engine." Peter Sondergaard

Business interest in data has continued and will continue to increase over the years. The biggest motivation in the information technology investments of the enterprises was to understand the data in the best way and more importantly, to have the data that could not be captured yet. It hasn't been enough to see data and produce reports for quite some time. The available data should strongly support any business decision. This is where business analytics come into play.

Business analytics can be defined as the use of data and related views developed through applied analytical disciplines such as statistical, quantitative and cognitive methods to guide factual planning, decision-making, measurement and learning (Holsapple, Lee-Post, & Pakath, 2014). Business analytics conduct all these quantitative analyzes on data from one or more incoming sources. Speaking of this point, it is necessary to define data analytics, which is an integral part of business analytics.

Data analytics is the science of integrating heterogeneous data from different sources, making inferences and making innovation possible, gaining competitive business advantage, and making predictions to help strategic decision making. The field of data analytics has evolved under various names, including online constitutional processing, data mining, visual analytics, big data analytics and cognitive analytics. Furthermore, the term analytical is used to refer to any data-based decision-making. In fact, analytics is a very common term and is used in many different problem areas (Gudivada, 2017).

Figure 1 shows us the types of data analytics and what questions they answer. All these types of analytics derive from the business needs. Among all these analytics types, 'predictive analytics' comes to the fore. Our desire to 'know the future' is not very different in business. Especially if this information will bring us more income.

Figure 1. Types of data analytics

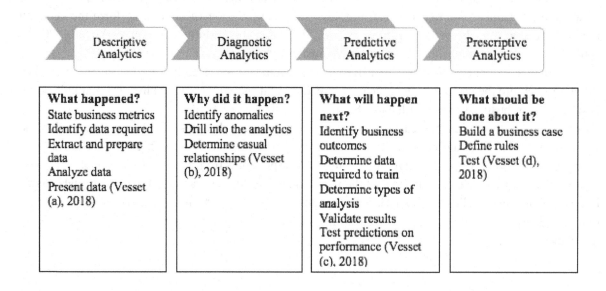

Nowadays, there is data everywhere that our eyes see, ears hear and our hands touch, and this data is now beyond simple databases. Social media is constantly producing data, and it is an invaluable treasure to understand consumer habits and trends. Big Data Analytics is now considered a game changer that increases business efficiency and intelligence. High operational and strategic potential plays a major role in this. The current big data analytics literature has demonstrated a positive relationship between customer analytics diffusion and firm performance. Big data analysis enables companies to analyze and manage the strategy through a data lens (Wamba, et al., 2017). The availability of data with large volume, speed and diversity resulted in the Big Data revolution, which has the potential to improve the firms' associated competitive advantages and decision-making performance.

Big data analytics, including those based on predicted analytics, statistics, data mining, artificial intelligence, and natural language processing, often involve processes and tools, including those applied to large and possibly dispersed datasets, to gain invaluable insights to improve decision-making. Over the past two decades, data analytics has become a critical enterprise Information Technology expertise due to increasing volumes, rate of change and business types of data. Firms need to develop their data analytics capabilities to make better, more informed, and faster decisions. (Ghasemaghaei, Ebrahimi, & Hassanein, 2018) At this point, Big Data analytics has become an important component of business decision-making and will go even further.

Big Data Analytics is now considered to be an important differentiator between high performing and low performing organizations as it enables companies to be proactive and forward-looking, reducing customer acquisition costs by approximately 47% and increasing firm earnings by 8% (Wamba, et al., 2017).

The desire to provide products and services in the fastest way according to behaviors and trends and to be competitive with personalized content according to potential customers causes the companies to demand more capabilities from business analytics systems more than ever. This point led machine learning to take big place in business analytics.

MACHINE LEARNING

Machine learning is the study of computational methods to automate the process of obtaining information from samples. This discipline developed to eliminate the laborious and expensive knowledge engineering process involved in the development of knowledge-based systems (Bose & Mahapatra, 2001).

Supervised Learning

In supervised learning, the method is teaching the machine with examples. It is provided with a known dataset containing the desired inputs and outputs. At this point, the algorithm should find a method that determines how these inputs and outputs can be reached. While the correct answers are known, the algorithm identifies patterns in the data learns from observations and makes predictions. The algorithm makes predictions and they are corrected by the supervisor, and this process continues until the algorithm achieves a high level of accuracy (Wakefield, 2019).

Supervised machine learning can be described as one of the most widely used and successful types of machine learning. Here we create a machine learning model from the input - output pairs that make up our training set and our goal is to make accurate predictions for data that has never been seen before.

Figure 2. Machine Learning Algorithms

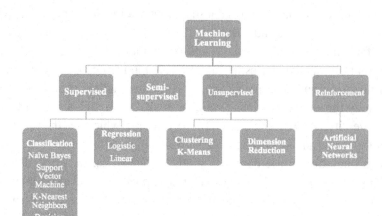

Human involvement is required to build a supervised learning training set. It is an inconvenience, but it will significantly automate and accelerate a hard or impossible task in the future (Abellera & Bulusu, 2018).

There are three major supervised machine learning problems, called classification, regression and forecasting.

Classification

In classification tasks, the machine learning program should draw a conclusion from the observed values and determine which category the new observations fall into. This is the process of predicting classes based on observations. This is achieved using supervised learning only. Thus, the classification categories are already in place and well defined. The data classified in this way can be in normal text format or even in images, can be of any type (Wakefield, 2019).

This is the process of predicting classes based on observations. This is achieved using supervised learning only. Therefore, classification categories are already in place and well defined. The data classified in this way can be in normal text format or even in images, can be of any type. The training of the model is done to further classify any data according to the correct categories. The context of each word is calculated as a probability by the classification program, and with this probabilistic weight all linked content is moved or tagged below a predefined classification. The most common applications in this class are spam detectors. In addition, these applications can be trained by the user to identify more types of spam. The user manually identifies some mail as spam, and the system further educates himself to use this criterion. Google search and Google news also fall into this category (Kumar, 2017).

Classification is sometimes separated into *binary classification* and *multiclass classification*. Binary classification can be described as a distinguish between two classes and multiclass classification is the classification between more than two classes which can be understood from its name. We can think of binary classification as trying to answer 'yes' or 'no' question (Muller & Guido, 2017).

Figure 3. The process of supervised machine learning (Kotsiantis, Zaharakis, & Pintelas, 2007)

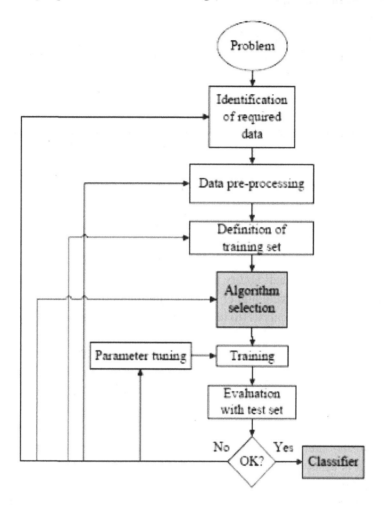

Figure 4. Classification

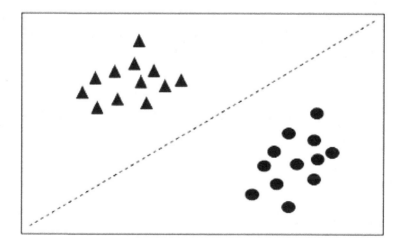

Naïve Bayes Classifier Algorithm

The Naive Bayes classifier is based on the Bayes theorem and classifies each value independent of the other values. It allows us to estimate a class or category based on a set of properties using its probability (Wakefield, 2019). The assumption here is that the value of any property is independent of the value of any other property. This is called the assumption of independence, which is the naive part of the Naive Bayes classifier (Joshi, 2017). Despite its simplicity, the classifier is often used because it performs surprisingly well and outperforms more sophisticated classification methods (Wakefield, 2019).

The four common applications of Naïve Bayes algorithm can be highlighted as:

1. Real-time Prediction: Naive Bayes can be used for making predictions based on the given data in real time according to its fast processing.
2. Multi-class Prediction: This algorithm can predict the background probability of multiple classes of the target variable.
3. Text Classification / Spam Filtering / Emotion Analysis: Naive Bayes classifiers are used mostly in text classifications due to their ability to achieve better results in multi-class problems and independence rule, and they have a higher success rate than other algorithms. It is widely used in spam filtering and Emotion Analysis (to identify positive and negative customer emotions in social media analysis).
4. Recommendation System: Along with algorithms such as Collaborative Filtering, Naive Bayes Classifier makes a Recommendation System that uses machine learning and data mining techniques to filter out invisible information and predict whether a user wants a specific resource (Kumar A., 2018).

Naive Bayes classifiers are popular applications for classifying text documents as we mentioned above. The fact that it is easily usable and that it can be run efficiently even if data is not known in advance plays an important role in this. Spam filtering is a classic use of text classification, and Naive Bayes classification has become particularly popular in spam filtering. Many modern mail clients use Bayesian spam filtering variants.

Naive Bayes classifiers are also used for fraud detection. For example, in the field of automobile insurance, based on a training set with characteristics such as driver rating, vehicle age, vehicle price, historical claims made by the policyholder, police report, status and demand reality, Naive Bayes can provide probability-based classification of whether a new claim is real or not (EMC Education Services, 2015).

Naïve Bayes Algorithm is very popular in 'fraud detection'. This algorithm can distinguish whether an input is fraudulent or not. Bayes Classifiers are very effective even for classifying complex documents. A study on the sensitivity of Tweets at Stanford found that a Naive Bayes Classifier ("naive" comes from the classifier that assumes that the appearance of each word is independent of the appearance of each other word) provides 85% accuracy in the analysis. Again, another study at the Massachusetts Institute of Technology found that the Naïve Bayes Classifier was able to classify articles in the institute's student newspaper with 77% accuracy. Other potential applications include the task of identifying the authors as well as predicting whether a brain tumor will recur after treatment or its likelihood of progression (Narula, 2019).

Advantages of Naïve Bayes Classifier Algorithm:

- It is generally easy to implement as well as much more sophisticated algorithms. This makes a good first line machine learning algorithm for Bayesian Classifiers.
- It is easy to interpret. Each feature has a possibility, so you can see which one is strongly related to certain classifications.
- It is an online technique, meaning it supports incremental education. After a Bayesian Classifier is trained, each feature has a certain conditional probability depending on it. You update the possibilities to add a new data sample - you don't need to reconsider the original data set.
- It is very fast. Bayesian classifiers combine pre-computed probabilities so that new classifications can be made very quickly, even in large and complex data sets. (Narula, 2019).

Disadvantages of Naïve Bayes Classifier Algorithm:

- It cannot work with results associated with a combination of features. The assumption of this algorithm is that each will be independent of each other and sometimes h can reduce accuracy. To give an example of this, normally the words "online" and "pharmacy" may not be a strong spam indicator in an email unless they are used together. A Bayes Classifier cannot remove the interdependence of these two features (Narula, 2019).

Support Vector Machine Algorithm

Support Vector Machine algorithms are supervised learning models which categorize the data obtained by providing a set of training examples, each marked as belonging to one or two categories, and typically analyze the data used for classification and regression analysis. Support Vector Machine algorithms work to create a model that assigns new values to one category or another.

Figure 5. Support vector machine classification

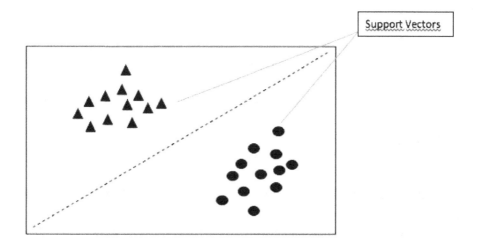

For example; Three of the four items shown get the same one different. Usually the difference is the size or color of the item, depending on what is taught in the relevant scope. Support The basic concept in the classification of vector algorithms is divided into two groups. This concept is particularly useful when the differences between the elements are not clearly understood and there are hundreds or thousands of qualities to consider.

Support Vector Machines' main inconveniences can be specified as;

- **Binary Classification:** Support Vector Machine models are naturally only binary classifiers. This makes it possible to use the algorithm only when a binary response is required. For nominal targets, the problem must be repeated in binary. This technique works but requires a lot of extra processing.
- **Limited Interpretability:** Unlike the regression models, which have a special meaning for decision trees or coefficients that are easy to interpret, it is very difficult to interpret what the numbers from a Support vector machine actually mean. Therefore, the use of a support vector machine for predictive modeling requires that the predictive power be balanced with a lack of interpretation (Dean, 2014).

Support vector machines are good at 'face recognition'. They classify where parts of the image are faces and where they are not faces, and then create a new square boundary around the class designated as face. This machine learning algorithm can be used as an alternative or joint contact verification method to password-entered operations and thus can create value.

Support Vector Machine algorithms contribute to business analytics especially below business issues;

- **Credit or Loan Decision Analysis:** It can be predicted that a customer will default to a debt or not from a given list of customer transaction attributes.
- **Fraud Analysis:** The organization can estimate the likelihood of its employees sending fraudulent charges or not based on the various invoices sent for reimbursement for employees, food, travel, medical expenses and so on.

The Support Vector machine solution matches what the intelligent human agent would naturally choose as the limit of decision, that is, the farthest from both clusters. This makes the decision of the Support Vector Machine stronger against errors (both random and systematic).

For example, it can be better used for some financial ratios, such as the debt / equity ratio, are based on accountable subjective valuation of accountants' intangible assets which tend to cause errors (Vishwakarma & Solanki, 2018).

Advantages of Support Vector Machine Algorithms:

- Classifying new data is very fast. Reviewing training data for new classifications is not necessary.
- They can work for a mixture of categorical and numerical data.
- SVMs are robust up to high dimensional, which means that they can work even with many features.
- They are highly accurate (Narula, 2019).

Disadvantages of Support Vector Machine Algorithms:

- It is a "black box" technique. SVMs cannot easily present the data that Bayesian Classifiers and Decision Trees provide "under the header". Although an SVM is a highly effective classifier, you may have a hard time figuring out why it makes these classifications.
- One of the biggest drawbacks is that a very large data set is often required. Working with small datasets can provide interesting output in other methods, such as Decision Trees, but this may not be available with a Support Vector Machine
- SVMs are not an online method and will need to be updated each time you add new training data. (Narula, 2019).

K-Nearest Neighbors Algorithm

The K-Nearest Neighbors algorithm is can be easily defined as the simplest machine learning algorithm. The creation of the model consists only of storing the training data set. To predict a new data point, the algorithm finds the nearest data points in the training data set, and these are the so-called nearest neighbors.

k-Neighbors Classification

In its simplest version, the k-NN algorithm only considers exactly the nearest one; this is the training data closest to the point we want to estimate. The prediction is then a known result for this training point.

Instead of just thinking about the closest neighbor, we can think of an arbitrary number of neighbors (k). The name of the k-nearest neighbor algorithm also comes from here. When multiple neighbors are considered, we vote to assign a label. This means that for each test point, we count how many neighbors belong to class 0 and how many neighbors belong to class 1. Then we discard the more frequent class, in other words, the k-majority class among the nearest neighbors. k-NN is often used in search applications where you look for "similar" items; it is called 'k-NN search' (Muller & Guido, 2017).

Figure 6. K-NN classification

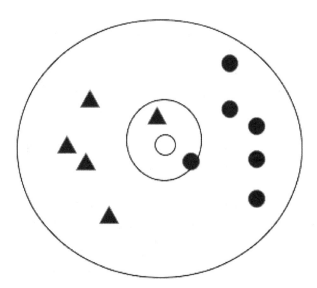

This machine learning algorithm is widely used to detect patterns in the use of credit cards. It is used for the analysis of recording data and for identifying unusual patterns that may be suspicious.

K-The "K" in the nearest neighbors is a placeholder value for the number of closest values averaged, and this is for us to make predictions. In this algorithm, weighted averages can also be used where values are more weighted in determining the mean. Variables may need to be scaled - for example, when estimating home prices using the number of bedrooms and square meters, we could choose to multiply the number of square meters and bedrooms by 1000 to keep the two variables on the same scale. We can use K-nearest neighbors to predict home prices (as demonstrated in the simplified example above), the prices of goods in the market and also use to make product recommendations (Narula, 2019).

Advantages of K-Nearest Neighbors Algorithm

- It is an online technique. K-nearest Neighbors can support incremental training like Naïve Bayes classifiers.
- They are easy to interpret and can handle complex numeric functions. You also have the opportunity to see exactly which neighbors are used for the final estimates.
- It is very useful when collecting data will be difficult or costly. The unimportant variables to make predictions can reveal during the scaling process and therefore they can be thrown out (Narula, 2019).

Disadvantages of K-Nearest Neighbors Algorithm

- In this algorithm, you will need all the training data to make predictions. As a result, large data sets will require a very slow work and a lot of space.
- It will be very tedious to find the right scaling factors, especially if you have millions of variables. In addition, the cost of this calculation will be high (Narula, 2019).

Decision Trees

A decision tree uses a tree structure to determine the order of decisions and results. Given the input X = {x1, x1, •• xn), the target is to predict a response or output variable Y. Estimation can be achieved by creating a decision tree with test points and branches. it is decided to select a specific branch and move the tree down at each test point. Finally, a final point is reached, and an estimate can be made. Each test point in a decision tree involves testing a specific input variable (or attribute), and each branch represents the decision taken.

Decision trees are often used in data mining applications for classification purposes. Its flexibility and easy visualization have a major impact on this. The input values of a decision tree can be categorical or continuous.

A decision tree employs a structure of test points (called nodes) and branches, which represent the decision being made. A node without further branches is called a leaf node. The leaf nodes return class labels, and, in some implementations, they return the probability scores. A decision tree can be converted into a set of decision rules (EMC Education Services, 2015).

Figure 7. Decision trees

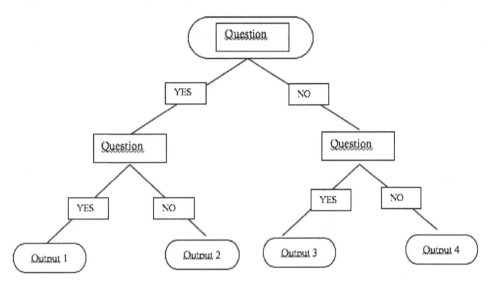

The branching structure of decision trees offers a structured and systematic structure to reach a logical conclusion in business decisions. It is a preferred algorithm in a wide range from investment decisions to solving problems.

BP used a decision tree to separate oil and gas and "replace a hand-designed rules system… [the decision tree] outperformed human experts and saved BP millions." A study in MIT examined how decision trees could be used to predict whether an applicant would receive a loan, and whether that applicant would default (Narula, 2019).

Advantages of Decision Trees Algorithm:

- Decision trees are easy to interpret and explain. Decision Trees simulate data as if it were a human decision-making process through an "if-then" flowchart until they categorize the data.
- It can be viewed graphically. The decision tree is essentially a branched flowchart (an algorithmically tuned tree for optimal splits only), and even non-technical people can interpret smaller decision trees displayed graphically.
- Both categorical and numerical data can be easily used; For example, this car red "Is the diameter of the car tire between six and eight inches?" does it work as well? In other classifiers to deal with such a problem, you must create a "dummy" variable.
- Decision trees can deal with interactions of variables. In the example of the "online pharmacy" that confuses the Bayes Classifier, we mentioned above, a decision tree divides the dataset whether it contains the world "online" and the result includes "online pharmacy" = spam while "online" and "pharmacy" = not spam (Narula, 2019).

Disadvantages of Decision Trees Algorithm:

- The tendency of Decision Trees to "overfit" data may cause them not to be as accurate as other classification algorithms (ie, they make perfect predictions within the dataset used to train them but make weaker predictions for new data coming). However, there are several methods of "pruning" the tree to increase accuracy.

- Decision Trees are not an online technique, meaning that the entire tree needs to be rebuilt from scratch to incorporate new data, because the variables that divide the data best can vary.
- The number of nodes in a decision tree can become extremely large and complex with larger data sets, often resulting in slow classifications (Narula, 2019).

Random Forests

The random forest, as the name implies, consists of many individual decision trees working as a community. Each decision tree in the random forest predicts a class, and the class we encounter most often becomes the prediction of our model.

In fact, the basic concept behind the random forest is 'the wisdom of the majority'. In the opinion of data science, the reason why random forest model works so well is:

Many relatively unrelated models (trees) operating as a committee will surpass any one of the individual constituent models.

Figure 8. Random forest algorithm (Jha, 2017)

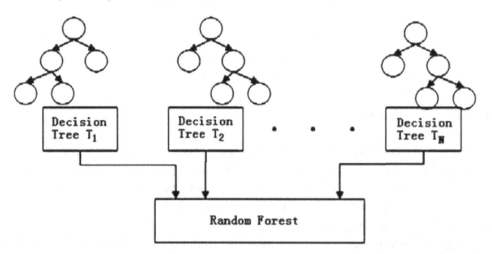

The low correlation between the models is the key. Unrelated models can produce combined estimates that are more accurate than any of the individual estimates. The reason for this wonderful effect is to protect each other from individual faults (unless they are constantly in the same direction). While some trees are wrong, many others will be right, so as a group the trees can move in the right direction.

Random forest ensures that the behavior of each tree is not related to the behavior of other trees in the model in two ways:

- **Bagging (Bootstrap Aggregation):** Decisions trees are very sensitive to the data they are trained on — small changes to the training set can result in significantly different tree structures. Random forest takes advantage of this by allowing each individual tree to randomly sample from the dataset with replacement, resulting in different trees. This process is known as bagging.

- **Feature Randomness:** In a normal decision tree, when it is time to split a node, every possible feature is considered and the one that produces the most distinction between observations on the left node vs. those in the right node is selected. In contrast, each tree in a random forest can only select from a random subset of properties. This forces more diversity among the trees in the model, resulting in less correlation and greater diversity among the trees (Yiu, 2019).

In the case of random forest models, the technology learns to form more sophisticated predictive results using those individual decision trees to build its random forest consensus. One way that this could be applied to business is to take various product property variables and use a random forest to indicate potential customer interest.

For example, if there are known customer interest factors such as color, size, durability, portability or anything else that customers have indicated interest in, those attributes can be fed into the data sets and analyzed on the basis of their own unique impact for multifactor analysis (Stoltzfus, 2020).

Advantages of Random Forests Algorithm:

- The predictive performance can compete with the best supervised learning algorithms.
- They provide a reliable feature importance estimate.
- They offer efficient estimates of the test error without incurring the cost of repeated model training associated with cross-validation (Jansen, 2018).

Disadvantages of Random Forests Algorithm:

- An ensemble model is inherently less interpretable than an individual decision tree.
- Training many deep trees can have high computational costs (but can be parallelized) and use a lot of memory.
- Predictions are slower, which may create challenges for applications (Jansen, 2018).

Regression

In general, regression analysis attempts to explain the effect of a group of variables on the outcome of another variable of interest. Usually, the result variable is called a dependent variable because the result depends on other variables. These additional variables are sometimes called input variables or independent variables. Regression analysis is a useful explanatory tool that can identify input variables that have the greatest statistical impact on the outcome. With this knowledge and insight, it may be possible to try to produce more favorable values of the input variables of environmental changes (EMC Education Services, 2015). There are basically two types of regression analysis which are 'logistic' and 'linear'.

Logistic Regression

Logistic regression is a predictive analysis method used to solve classification problems. In logistic regression, the aim is to find the model that best fits the regression curve $y = f(x)$. Here, y represents the dependent categorical variable and x represents the independent variable which can be both continuous

Figure 9. Regression

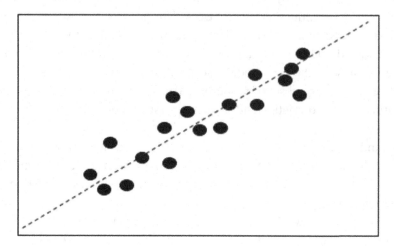

and categorical at the same time (Juozenaite, 2018). Logistic regression is used to estimate a discrete result based on variables that can be discrete, continuous, or mixed. Therefore, logistic regression is a widely used technique when the dependent variable has two or more discrete results (Sukhadeve, 2017).

Since logistic regression is an easy-to-understand classification technique, it is frequently used to solve various business problems. It is widely used in 'customer churn forecasting', 'customer segmentation', 'direct marketing' and 'finance'. Logistic regression can achieve good results with appropriate data conversion (Juozenaite, 2018).

Advantages of Logistic Regression Algorithm:

- It is easy to interpret. Logistic regression outputs a number between 0 and 1, which can loosely be interpreted as a probability (0.312 could be interpreted as 31.2% chance of a credit card transaction being fraudulent). Feature weights easily show which features are more important than others in determining classifications (Narula, 2019).

Disadvantages of Logistic Regression Algorithm:

- It tends to overfitting. Often it may require a large training set to make accurate predictions outside of the training set.
- It is not an online technique, so it requires running gradient descent again to include new data.
- Has tradeoffs with gradient descent. The faster gradient descent determines the final feature weights, the more likely it is to miss the optimal weights. Finding the optimum trade-off of speed versus accuracy can be difficult at times, and trial-and-error can be time consuming.
- It is necessary to use dummy variables for categorical data. Since logistic regression produces only real-value output, categorical data must be transformed into real values via a dummy variable. (as an example, transforming "red or not red" to "1 or 0" where red = 1, not red = 0) (Narula, 2019).

Linear Regression

We can say that linear regression is the most basic type of regression. Simple linear regression allows us to understand the relationship between two continuous variables. Simple linear regression is a type of regression analysis where the number of independent variables is one and there is a linear relationship between independent (x) and dependent (y) variables. More specifically, (y) can be calculated from a linear combination of input variables (x) (Brownlee, 2016).

Linear models have been greatly developed in the pre-computer era of statistics, but even in today's computer age, we still have reasons to study and use them. They are simple and often provide a sufficient and interpretable explanation of how inputs affect output. For forecasting purposes, they can perform better than nonlinear models, especially in situations with few training situations, low signal-to-noise ratio, or sparse data (Hastie, Tibshirani, & Friedman, 2016).

Advantages of Linear Regression:

- Linear Regression performs well when the dataset is linearly separable. We can use it to find the nature of the relationship among the variables.
- Linear Regression is easier to implement, interpret and very efficient to train.
- Linear Regression is prone to over-fitting, but it can be easily avoided using some dimensionality reduction techniques, regularization (L1 and L2) techniques and cross-validation.

Disadvantages of Linear Regression

- Main limitation of Linear Regression is the assumption of linearity between the dependent variable and the independent variables. In the real world, the data is rarely linearly separable. It assumes that there is a straight-line relationship between the dependent and independent variables which is incorrect many times.
- Prone to noise and overfitting: If the number of observations is lesser than the number of features, Linear Regression should not be used, otherwise it may lead to overfit because is starts considering noise in this scenario while building the model.
- Prone to outliers: Linear regression is very sensitive to outliers (anomalies). So, outliers should be analyzed and removed before applying Linear Regression to the dataset.
- Prone to multicollinearity: Before applying Linear regression, multicollinearity should be removed (using dimensionality reduction techniques) because it assumes that there is no relationship among independent variables (Kumar N., 2019).

Forecasting

Machine Learning is a powerful tool that can be used to predict future nature of historical data. Machine Learning algorithms work by creating a model from input samples to make future data-driven predictions or decisions. The growing concept of Big Data has been very successful in the field of data science; provides data scalability in a variety of ways that empowers data science. Machine Learning can also be used with Big Data to create effective predictive systems or solve complex data analytics problems (Rahman, Esmailpour, & Zhao, 2016).

All the machine learning algorithms mentioned in this section can be used for estimation. Support Vector Machines are promising for predicting financial time series because they use a regular risk function derived from the empirical error and structural risk mitigation principle (Kyoung, 2003).

Semi Supervised Learning

Semi-supervised learning is like supervised learning, but it uses both labeled and unlabeled data instead. Labeled data is essentially information with meaningful labels, so unlabeled data lacks this information and the algorithm can understand the data. Using this combination, machine learning algorithms can learn to label unlabeled data. Typically, large amounts of unlabeled data and small amounts of labeled data are used. Because of this feature, semi-supervised learning falls between unsupervised learning and supervised learning.

Unsupervised Learning

In unsupervised learning, the machine learning algorithm examines the data to identify patterns. There is no answer key or human operator to give instructions. Instead, the machine analyzes existing data to determine correlations and relationships. In an unsupervised learning process, the machine learning algorithm is left to interpret large data sets and handle these data accordingly. The algorithm tries to organize this data in a way to define its structure. This may mean that the data is grouped into clusters or arranged to appear more organized (Wakefield, 2019).

Figure 10. Unsupervised learning process

Unsupervised learning can also be defined as 'without teacher learning' . The aim is to directly understand the characteristics of this probability density without the help of a supervisor or teacher who provides the correct answers or degree of error for each observation (Hastie, Tibshirani, & Friedman, 2016). As you evaluate more data, the ability to make decisions about these data is increasing and refining (Wakefield, 2019).

Unsupervised learning covers two main tasks as 'clustering' and 'dimension reduction'.

Clustering

Clustering involves grouping similar data groups according to defined criteria. It is useful to analyze data on each set of data to divide the data into several groups and find patterns. The purpose of unsupervised clustering is to maximize intra-cluster similarity and to minimize inter-cluster similarity when a similarity / difference criterion is given. It uses a distinct objective function. It uses a dataset that does not have a target variable (Wakefield, 2019).

Because clustering is often used in an unsupervised manner, a measure must be taken to assess the quality of clusters provided by a particular algorithm. These evaluation criteria are mainly used to determine the variability or noise in clusters and the number of clusters best suited to the data, to compare clustering algorithms with the quality of their solutions, and to compare the two result sets obtained from the results. The first of these criteria is an 'internal evaluation criterion', which is part of the cluster analysis and is method specific. This criterion is calculated for the data used for cluster analysis. Second is the 'external evaluation criterion' derived from a separate data set not used for cluster analysis. This criterion is used to measure how representative the clusters are when they are given class labels, or how coherent they are to different clusters when obtained using different parameters or methods (Dean, 2014).

K-Means Clustering Algorithm

The K-Means clustering algorithm is an unsupervised type of learning used to categorize unlabeled data, that is, data that does not contain defined categories or groups. It is one of the most widely used clustering techniques. The algorithm works by finding the groups in the data with the number of groups represented by the variable K. It is then repeated to assign each data point to one of the K groups based on the given properties.

The number of desired cluster centers is selected, for example the R and K-mediator procedure moves the centers recursively to minimize the sum within the cluster variability.

K-means clustering algorithm has two main steps:

- For each center, a subset of training points closer to other centers is identified;
- For each set of data points, the means of each property are calculated, and this average vector becomes the new center for this set.

These two steps are repeated until convergence. Typically, the first centers are randomly selected R observations from training data. Details of the K-mediator procedure are also given in generalizations that allow different types of variables and more general distance criteria (Hastie, Tibshirani, & Friedman, 2016).

There are some interesting uses cases for K-Means Clustering in business;

Consumer Segmentation

After completing the cluster analysis, you can define consumer segments. To do this, you can use demographic, psychographic and behavioral data and performance data to cluster your consumers according to a product category.

Then, you can then profile your clusters to better understand your consumers and define them based on the variables used for cluster analysis. You can use this information to tailor your marketing messages, product types and overall shopping experience to meet your customers' needs and increase your return on investment (Hodgson, 2020).

Delivery Optimization

Retailers and suppliers have sought to optimize delivery processes using k-means clustering. Delivery routes and models of trucks and drones were tracked to find the most suitable departure locations, routes and destinations for the company (Hodgson, 2020).

Document Sorting and Grouping

You can group electronic files by category, tags, content or frequency of use using k-means clustering. The algorithm displays each document as a vector and the frequency of specific terms to classify and group documents. (Hodgson, 2020).

Advantages of K-Means Clustering Algorithm:

- Quite effective as an unsupervised method.
- Works well for large-scale data.
- No distributional assumption about the data.
- Easy to implement as compared other complex clustering approaches.
- K-means clustering algorithm is good in capturing structure of the data if clusters have a spherical-like shape (Sengupta, 2019).

Disadvantages of K-Means Clustering Algorithm:

- K-means clustering algorithm doesn't let the data points that are far away from each other share the same cluster even though they obviously belong to the same cluster.
- If the clusters have a complex geometric shape, k means does a poor job in clustering the data (Sengupta, 2019).

Dimensionality Reduction

The main purpose of dimensionality reduction techniques is to find an intensified presentation of the information provided in a time series for further analysis. Sometimes the original data contains too many columns and unnecessary records. This creates noise for the analysis. Instead of looking directly at the original data, a new and concise data set with fewer observations but the most important features of the original data are created. The purpose of dimensionality reduction is to extract the most necessary parts for analysis from the original data (Dean, 2014).

Advantages of Dimensionality Reduction:

- Dimensionality reduction aids in data compression and therefore reduces storage space.
- Dimensionallity reduction shortens the time spent on calculation.
- It also helps to remove unnecessary features if they are present.
- In particular, it speeds up the time required to do the same calculations.
- If there are fewer dimensions, it will lead to less calculations. In addition, dimensions may allow the use of algorithms that are not suitable for many dimensions.
- It deals with multicollinearity, which improves model performance. It removes unnecessary features. For example, it makes no sense to store a value in two different units (meters and inches).

- Reducing the dimensions of the data to 2D or 3D can enable us to draw and visualize it precisely. This allows us to observe patterns more clearly (Dataflair, 2018).

  Disadvantages of Dimensionality Reduction

- Basically, it may cause some data loss.
- Although Principal Component Analysis tends to find linear correlations between variables, this can sometimes be seen as undesirable.
- Also, Principal Component Analysis fails in cases where mean and covariance are not enough to define datasets.
- Moreover, we may not know how many key components to keep in practice, some basic rules apply (Dataflair, 2018).

Reinforcement Learning

Let's go further than supervised learning and express the concept of how output will change as input changes. That is the basis of reinforcement learning. To put it differently, if an agent interacts with any environment, it will continue to adjust its output to varying inputs in that environment. The agent is not an integral part of this environment but interacts with it.

Empowerment learning tries to apply biological behavioral learning. We don't learn everything through guidance in our lives. We learn many things by experiencing ourselves. That's exactly how empowerment learning works. There are many cases of business use in the fields of finance, insurance, medical research and so on (Kumar, 2017).

Artificial Neural Networks

Working on artificial neural networks, commonly referred to as "neural networks' began with the acceptance of the human brain's working in a completely different way from a conventional digital computer. The brain is a highly complex, nonlinear and parallel computer. It is capable of editing structural components known as neurons to make some calculations many times faster than the fastest digital computer available today (Haykin, 2009).

An artificial neural network comprises "units" arranged in a series of layers, each of which is connected to the layers on both sides. Artificial neural networks are inspired by biological systems such as the brain and how information is processed. Artificial neural networks are basically several interconnected processing elements that work together to solve specific problems.

Artificial neural networks also learn by example and experience, which are extremely useful for modeling nonlinear relationships in high-dimensional data or when it is difficult to understand the relationship between input variables (Wakefield, 2019).

Companies are using neural networks in various ways, depending on their business model. For instance, social media companies use neural networks along with linear text classifiers to detect spam or abusive content in the feeds when it is created (Morphy, 2018). While Amazon uses Neural Networks to create product recommendations; Massachusetts General Hospital uses deep learning to improve patient diagnosis and treatment; Facebook uses deep Neural Networks for facial recognition; Google is strengthening Google Translate with Neural Networks (Narula, 2019).

Figure 11. Artificial neural networks

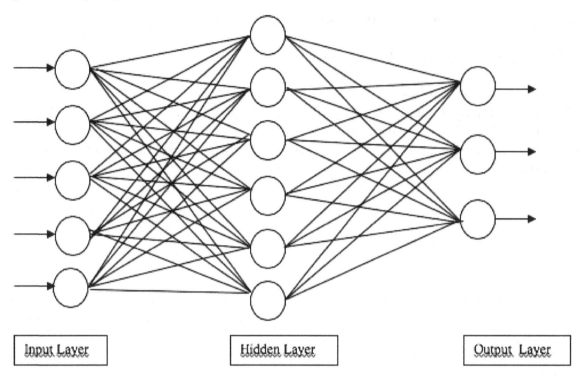

Advantages of Neural Networks:

- It is extremely scalable. With large data sets, Neural Network performance can continue to improve while other algorithms may (eventually) flatten out in performance.
- It is an online method, so Neural Networks can train incrementally using new data.
- They are space efficient. They are represented by a list of numbers like Bayesian Classifiers, (while this list represents feature probabilities for Bayesian Classifiers, they represent synapse weights for Neural Networks) (Narula, 2019).

Disadvantages of Neural Networks:

- It can be thought of as the black box method. In large Neural Networks containing thousands of nodes and one row more synapses, it is difficult, if not impossible, to understand how the algorithm determines its output.
- As demonstrated by even this highly simplified description of Neural Networks, the level of complexity means that highly skilled Artificial Intelligence researchers and practitioners are needed to properly implement them. (Narula, 2019).

So far, we have seen various machine learning algorithms. Of course, we did not explain all machine learning methods in detail. The algorithms we process in this book section are the algorithms we use mostly in our daily business life. The examples we give while describing the algorithms give an idea about the reflection of these algorithms on our business life.

In order to decide which of these algorithms to use in the face of a business problem, it will always be useful to follow up-to-date applications from world experience. In general, our problem is experienced in any part of the world and internet resources (websites, blogs, etc.) in the field of machine learning are very useful for us. But what is especially important to us is to make the first decision. For this, we can easily decide which of the basic machine learning methods we should choose according to their features below and then select our algorithm under the field we select.

Supervised Learning:
• Good for problems where each input data point is labelled or belongs to a category.

Unsupervised Learning:
• Good for problems where each data is not labelled or does not belong to a category. These algorithms are good for clustering/ grouping complex data into classes.

Reinforcement Learning:
• Good for problems where future actions are based on the outcome of existing responses and subsequent actions need to be anticipated (Malik, 2018).

CONCLUSION

Initiatives, businesses and organizations from all sectors began to gain a critical understanding of structured data collected through various corporate systems and analyzed by commercial relational database management systems. Over the past few years, web intelligence, web analytics, and mostly 'social media analytics' and the ability to adopt unstructured user-generated content, have entered a new and exciting era, offering many opportunities to recognize consumer insights, customer needs and new business opportunities. Now, in this era of Big Data, we have met with all the decisive uncertainties brought about by new and potentially revolutionary technologies (Chen, Chiang, & Storey, 2012).

Machine learning is now inextricably integrated into business analytics and even business models itself. The importance of big data and reproduction of data channels is of great importance. Machine learning makes a difference in business analytics thanks to its ability on deciding based on processing many complex statistical models. It should be noted that the place of machine learning in our lives will increase every day. Open source software such as Python and R are developing machine learning libraries that they use day by day, and companies are now looking for data scientists, especially those who use them. Businesses' understanding of the invaluable value of data has led to a significant expansion of data science departments. More and more data scientist jobs are being advertised.

The large data volume does not classify it as just the big data age, because there have always been larger volumes of data than we can effectively work with. What separates the present from the big data age is the change in the behavior of companies, governments and non-profit organizations. During this period, they want to start using all the data they can collect to improve their business for an unknown purpose, present or future (Dean, 2014).

This section aims to raise awareness of the contribution of machine learning to business analytics. There is a large area in this field, especially for future studies on the role of artificial intelligence in business applications.

REFERENCES

Abellera, R., & Bulusu, L. (2018). *Oracle Business Intelligence with Machine Learning: Artificial Intelligence Techniques in OBIEE for Actionable BI*. Apress. doi:10.1007/978-1-4842-3255-2

Al-Garadi, M. A., Mohamed, A., Al-Ali, A., Du, X., & Guizani, M. (2018, August 12). *A survey of machine and deep learning methods for internet of things (IoT) security*. Retrieved from arXiv.orgLogin Search... Help | Advanced Search: https://arxiv.org/

Bose, I., & Mahapatra, R. K. (2001). Business data mining—A machine learning perspective. *Information & Management*, *39*(3), 211–225. doi:10.1016/S0378-7206(01)00091-X

Brownlee, J. (2016). *Linear Regression for Machine Learning*. Retrieved 8 21, 2019, from machinelearningmastery.com: https://machinelearningmastery.com/linear-regression-for-machine-learning/

Chen, H., Chiang, R. H., & Storey, V. C. (2012). Business Intelligence and Analytics: From Big Data to Big Impact. *Management Information Systems Quarterly*, *36*(4), 1165–1188. doi:10.2307/41703503

Dataflair. (2018). *What is Dimensionality Reduction – Techniques, Methods, Components*. Retrieved 07 12, 2020, from Dimensionality Reduction Tutorials: https://data-flair.training/blogs/dimensionality-reduction-tutorial

Dean, J. (2014). *Big Data, Data Mining, and Machine Learning: Value Creation for Business Leaders and practitioners*. John Wiley & Sons. doi:10.1002/9781118691786

Elshawi, R., Sakr, S., Talia, D., & Trunfio, P. (2018). Big Data Systems Meet Machine Learning Challenges: Towards Big Data Science as a Service. *Big Data Research*, (14), 1-11.

EMC Education Services. (2015). *Data science & big data analytics: discovering, analyzing, visualizing and presenting data*. Wiley.

Ghasemaghaei, M., Ebrahimi, S., & Hassanein, K. (2018). Data analytics competency for improving firm decision making performance. *The Journal of Strategic Information Systems*, *27*(1), 101–113. doi:10.1016/j.jsis.2017.10.001

Gudivada, V. N. (2017). Data Analytics: Fundamentals. In M. Chowdhury, A. Apon, & K. Dey (Eds.), Data Analytics for Intelligent Transportation Systems (pp. 33-45). Elsevier.

Hastie, T., Tibshirani, R., & Friedman, J. (2016). *The Elements of Statistical Learning Data Mining,Inference,and Prediction*. Springer.

Haykin, S. (2009). *Neural Networks and Learning Machines* (3rd ed.). Prentice Hall.

Hodgson, E. (2020). *K-Means Clustering And Why It's Good For Business*. Retrieved 07 12, 2020, from dotactiv.com: https://www.dotactiv.com/blog/why-k-means-clustering-is-good-for-business

Holsapple, C., Lee-Post, A., & Pakath, R. (2014). A unified foundation for business analytics. *Decision Support Systems*, *64*, 130–141. doi:10.1016/j.dss.2014.05.013

Jansen, S. (2018). *Hands-On Machine Learning for Algorithmic Trading: Design and implement investment strategies based on smart algorithms that learn from data using Python*. Packt Publishing.

Jha, V. (2017). *Random Forest – Supervised classification machine learning algorithm*. Retrieved 8 24, 2019, from https://www.techleer.com: https://www.techleer.com/articles/107-random-forest-supervised-classification-machine-learning-algorithm/

Joshi, P. (2017). *Artificial intelligence with python*. Packt Publishing Ltd.

Juozenaite, I. (2018). *Application of machine learning techniques for solving real world business problems: the case study-target marketing of insurance policies (Project Work presented as partial requirement for obtaining the Master's degree in Information Management)*. Academic Press.

Kotsiantis, S. B., Zaharakis, I., & Pintelas, P. (2007). Supervised machine learning: A review of classification techniques. *Emerging Artificial Intelligence Applications in Computer Engineering*, 3-24.

Kumar, A. (2018). *Naive Bayesian Model*. Retrieved 8 24, 2019, from www.acadgild.com: https://acadgild.com/blog/naive-bayesian-model

Kumar, N. (2019, May 9). *Advantages and Disadvantages of Linear Regression in Machine Learning*. Retrieved July 9, 2020, from The Professionals Point: http://theprofessionalspoint.blogspot.com/2019/05/advantages-and-disadvantages-of-linear.html

Kumar, R. (2017). *Machine Learning and Cognition in Enterprises: Business Intelligence Transformed*. Apress. doi:10.1007/978-1-4842-3069-5

Kyoung, J. K. (2003). Financial time series forecasting using support vector machines. *Neurocomputing*, *55*(1-2), 307–319. doi:10.1016/S0925-2312(03)00372-2

Malik, F. (2018). *Machine Learning Algorithms Comparison*. Retrieved 7 12, 2020, from FinTechExplained: https://medium.com/fintechexplained/machine-learning-algorithm-comparison-f14ce372b855

Morphy, E. (2018). *What Is a Neural Network and How Are Businesses Using Them?* Retrieved 8 24, 2019, from CMSWire: https://www.cmswire.com/digital-experience/what-is-a-neural-network-and-how-are-businesses-using-it/

Muller, A. C., & Guido, S. (2017). *Introduction to machine learning with Python: a guide for data scientists*. O'Reilly Media.

Narula, G. (2019, May 19). *Machine Learning Algorithms for Business Applications – Complete Guide*. Retrieved July 7, 2020, from https://emerj.com/: https://emerj.com/ai-sector-overviews/machine-learning-algorithms-for-business-applications-complete-guide/

Rahman, M. N., Esmailpour, A., & Zhao, J. (2016). Machine learning with big data an efficient electricity generation forecasting system. *Big Data Research*, 9-15.

Sengupta, S. (2019). Machine Learning. Packt Publishing.

Sharma, R., Mithas, S., & Kankanhalli, A. (2014). Transforming decision-making processes: A research agenda for understanding the impact of business analytics on organisations. *European Journal of Information Systems*, *23*(4), 433–441. doi:10.1057/ejis.2014.17

Singh, D., Leavline, E., Muthukrishnan, S., & Yuvaraj, R. (2018). Machine Learning based Business Forecasting. *I.J. Information Engineering and Electronic Business*, 40-51.

Stoltzfus, J. (2020). *How might companies use random forest models for predictions.* Retrieved July 7, 2020, from https://www.techopedia.com/: https://www.techopedia.com/how-might-companies-use-random-forest-models-for-predictions/7/32995

Sukhadeve, A. (2017). *Introduction to Logistic Regression.* Retrieved 8 20, 2019, from www.analyticsinsight.net: https://www.analyticsinsight.net/introduction-to-logistic-regression/

Vesset, D. (2018a). *Descriptive analytics 101: What happened?* Retrieved 5 24, 2019, from Analytics for all: https://www.ibm.com/blogs/business-analytics/descriptive-analytics-101-what-happened/

Vesset, D. (2018b). *Diagnostic analytics 101: Why did it happen?* Retrieved 8 24, 2019, from Analytics for all: https://www.ibm.com/blogs/business-analytics/diagnostic-analytics-101-why-did-it-happen/

Vesset, D. (2018c). *Predictive analytics 101: What will happen next?* Retrieved 8 24, 2019, from Analytics for all: https://www.ibm.com/blogs/business-analytics/predictive-analytics-101-will-happen-next/

Vesset, D. (2018d). *Prescriptive analytics 101: What should be done about it?* Retrieved 8 24, 2019, from Analytics for all: https://www.ibm.com/blogs/business-analytics/prescriptive-analytics-done/

Vishwakarma, A. C., & Solanki, R. (2018). Analysing Credit Risk using Statistical and Machine Learning Techniques. *International Journal of Engineering Science and Computing*, *8*(6), 18397–18404.

Wakefield, K. (2019). *A guide to machine learning algorithms and their applications.* Retrieved from https://www.sas.com/en_gb/insights/articles/analytics/machine-learning-algorithms.html

Wamba, S. F., Gunasekaran, A., Akter, S., Ren, S. J., Dubey, R., & Childe, S. J. (2017). Big data analytics and firm performance: Effects of dynamic capabilities. *Journal of Business Research*, *70*, 356–365. doi:10.1016/j.jbusres.2016.08.009

Yang, C., Huang, Q., Li, Z., Liu, K., & Hu, F. (2017). Big Data and cloud computing: Innovation opportunities and challenges. *International Journal of Digital Earth*, *10*(1), 13–53. doi:10.1080/17538947.2016.1239771

Yiu, T. (2019). *Understanding Random Forest.* Retrieved 8 2019, from https://towardsdatascience.com/understanding-random-forest-58381e0602d2>

Zantalis, F., Koulouras, G., Karabetsos, S., & Kandris, D. (2019). *A Review of Machine Learning and IoT in Smart Transportation.* Future Internet. doi:10.3390/fi11040094

Chapter 14
A Comprehensive Study of Data Analytics in Social Perspectives

Arram Sriram
https://orcid.org/0000-0002-8250-5437
Anurag Group of Institutions, India

Prasanth Rao Adhiraju
https://orcid.org/0000-0002-5119-3987
Anurag Group of Institutions, India

Praveen Kumar Kalangi
Anurag Group of Institutions, India

Sathiyamoorthi V.
https://orcid.org/0000-0002-7012-3941
Sona College of Technology, Salem, India

ABSTRACT

Social media websites enable users to create and share content or to participate in social networking. The main advantage of social media is the ability to communicate with different people to share their knowledge and discuss social events. The impact of social media on people and their behavior is enormous and also solves many problems if it works fine. But there may be negative aspects as well when they are exchange their ideas between people of very different cultures, religions, different age group, and misbehavior of a few users. These problems are addressed using data analytics, which takes people context into account, learns from it, and takes proactive steps according to their situation and expectations, avoiding user intervention as much as possible. This chapter presents all possible problems in social media and enabling those scenarios with effective solutions.

DOI: 10.4018/978-1-7998-2566-1.ch014

INTRODUCTION

Social media has evolved over the last decade to become an crucial driver for acquiring and spreading facts in different domains, consisting of business (Beier & Wagner, 2016), entertainment (Shen, Hock Chuan, & Cheng, 2016), science (Chen & Zhang,2016), disaster management (Hiltz, Diaz, & Mark, 2011; Stieglitz, Bunker, Mirbabaie, & Ehnis, 2017a) and politics (Stieglitz & Dang-Xuan, 2013). One purpose for the recognition of social media is the possibility to receive or create and percentage public messages at low charges and ubiquitously. The enormous boom of social media utilization has brought about an growing accumulation of information, which has been termed Social Media Big Data. Social media systems offer many opportunities of information formats, consisting of textual information, pictures, videos, sounds, and geolocations. Generally, this information may be divided into unstructured information and established information (Baars & Kemper, 2008). In social networks, the text is an instance of unstructured information, even as the friend/follower dating is an instance of established information.

The boom of social media utilization opens up new possibilities for analyzing numerous elements of, and styles in communication. For instance, social media information may be analyzed to benefit insights into issues, trends, influential actors and different types of facts. Golder and Macy (2011) analyzed Twitter information to have a look at how people's temper modifications with time of day, weekday and season. In the field of Information Systems (IS), social media information is used to have a look at questions consisting of the influence of community function on facts diffusion (Susarla, Oh, & Tan, 2012).

Many current studies papers are remoted case studies (Kim, Choi, & Natali, 2016; Li &Huang, 2014; Oh, Hu, & Yang, 2016) that gather a big information set for the duration of a specific time body on a specific problem and examine it quantitatively. Despite the type of disciplines such initiatives may be determined in, they've a good deal in common. The steps essential to benefit beneficial facts or maybe understanding out of social media are frequently similar. Therefore, the field of "Social Media Analytics" objectives to combine, extend, and adapt techniques for the evaluation of social media information (Stieglitz, Dang-Xuan, Bruns, & Neuberger, 2014). It has received considerable interest and sooner or later every day in instructional studies, however there may be nonetheless a loss of complete discussions of social media analytics, and of general fashions and approaches. Aral, Dellarocas, and Godes (2013) provided a framework to prepare social media studies, and van Osch and Coursaris (2013) proposed a framework and studies schedule explicitly confined to organizational social media. Both frameworks are geared closer to classifying regions of studies and, by extension, studies questions, now no longer techniques to cope with those questions. While such frameworks are beneficial to determine what to studies, and to find individual initiatives inside a bigger context, they do now no longer offer steering on a way to convey out the studies, and which demanding situations may arise. Of course, there may be also studies that discusses demanding situations researchers face whilst using specific techniques for reading social media information, consisting of social community evaluation (Kane, Alavi, Labianca, & Borgatti, 2014) or opinion mining (Maynard, Bontcheva,& Rout, 2012), and there are literature opinions centered on specific goals consisting of the identification of customers who're influential offline (Cossu, Labatut,& Dugué, 2016) or on specific subjects consisting of social bots (Stieglitz, Brachten, Ross, & Jung, 2017b). Yet social media analytics is composed of numerous steps, of which information evaluation is simplest one. Before the information may be analyzed, they ought to be discovered, collected, and prepared. An evaluate of the demanding situations of social media analytics is wanted as a way to manipulate the complexity of carrying out social media analytics.

We consequently accomplished a systematic literature review, arguing that the complexity of those equally crucial steps has now no longer but been accurately included in studies, and there are no extensively everyday requirements on a way to continue inside every of the steps. We explicitly centered on papers that address the demanding situations researchers face whilst coming across subjects, and whilst gathering and getting ready social media information for evaluation, no matter the approach they later use for the duration of the evaluation.

THEORETICAL BACKGROUND

The interdisciplinary research field of Social Media Analytics (SMA) deals with methods of analyzing social media data. Researchers have divided the analytics process into several steps. We use the steps of discovery, collection, preparation, and analysis, which we adapted from Stieglitz et al. (2014). The particular challenges of social media data, however, have not been addressed comprehensively in the SMA literature. To be able to classify these challenges, we draw on theory from the big data literature instead. In particular, we use the four V's: volume, velocity, variety, and veracity.

SOCIAL MEDIA ANALYTICS

Since the upward push of social media utilization with inside the ultimate decade, human beings had been searching for to benefit records from the group as a further supply to standard media. We use the time period social media to refer to "Internet-primarily based totally programs that construct at the ideological and techno- logical foundations of Web 2. zero", wherein Web2.zero method that "content material and programs are not created and posted via way of means of individuals, however rather are constantly modified via way of means of all customers in a participatory and collaborative fashion" (Kaplan & Haenlein, 2010). Because of the large definition of social media, its software functions are manifold.

The time period "Social Media Analytics" defined as "an rising interdisciplinary studies field that objectives on combining, extending, and adapting techniques for evaluation of social media records" (Zeng, Chen, Lusch, & Li, 2010). Whilst the attitude at the device is one essential component, every other component is the attitude at the customers who create the content material. Research that adopts this attitude explores different roles with inside the conversation and the effects a respective position can have at the conversation and the diffusion of records (Stieglitz et al., 2017c).Influencers or opinion leaders, for instance, may be identified thru a social community evaluation, and via way of means of analyzing their follower community, you can still monitor the attain of such an individual (Mirbabaie, Ehnis, Stieglitz, & Bunker, 2014;Mirbabaie & Zapatka, 2017). Furthermore, the behavior of the jobs is tested so one can apprehend the reasons of a key position with inside the community and the effects it has on the general community (Bhattacharya, Phan, & Airoldi, 2015;Kefi, Mlaiki, & Kalika, 2015; Mirbabaie et al., 2014; Zhang, Zhao, Lu, &Yang, 2016).Companies which includes media businesses have diagnosed the significance of influencers and use them e.g. for product placement. Furthermore, the evaluation of social media content material developed with inside the previous couple of years to one of the essential studies functions in Information Systems. One studies purpose is probably to pick out and examine the records diffusion (Liu, 2015; Zhang & Zhang,2016).

Among others, 3 domain names wherein social media is essential and generates visible benefits are 1) in corporations, in 2) disaster conversation, specially in disaster management, and in 3) journalism and political conversation.

In one of the essential regions of social media analytics, corporations employ social media records, for numerous functions (Kleindienst, Pfleger, & Schoch, 2015).Social media records may be beneficial for detecting new developments with inside the conversation or troubles which can contain uncontrollable terrible publicity (Bi, Zheng, &Liu, 2014). Social media is likewise used as a channel to talk with customers (Griffiths & McLean, 2015; Pletikosa Cvijikj et al., 2013). For supporting decision-making processes, agencies employ social media reports, created ex put up and primarily based totally on predefined key overall performance indicators, or they employ a dashboard for purchasing on-going evaluation primarily based totally on real-time social media records(Tsou et al., 2015). Social Media is likewise used for product placement (Liu,Chou, & Liao, 2015) within side the social web.

Crisis conversation studies is an instance of a field wherein social media records has had an impact. Social media is frequently used as a channel for emergency management businesses to tell human beings in an affected vicinity at the modern-day fame of the respective disaster or the way to behave (Liu, 2015). Social media records with inside the context of disaster conversation also can be analyzed to benefit additional, formerly unknown records, if volunteers e.g. take pix or films and unfold the records into the group. Collected social media records may be additionally analyzed for detecting a specific region or vicinity wherein the disaster occurs. By analyzing GPS records if it's far blanketed with inside the records or via way of means of making use of the technique of Named Entity Recognition the region might be additionally derived from the text (Alsudais& Corso, 2015; Bendler, Ratku, & Neumann, 2014; Mirbabaie, Tschampel,& Stieglitz, 2016). The unfold of a disorder may be monitored via way of means of mining emotional tweets (Ji, Chun, Wei, & Geller, 2015). Especially for Emergency Management Agencies, it's far essential to apprehend the conversation conduct and the modern-day fame thru social media, if you want to react quicker and extra efficiently. Furthermore, such businesses also are capin a position to utilize the benefits of attaining a crowd thru social media and diffuse applicable and life-saving records of their channels (Gill, Alam, & Eustace, 2014; vanGorp, Pogrebnyakov, & Maldonado, 2015).

Finally, social media structures have been hooked up in current years as re assets of records on political conversation and for journalism. People debate on modern-day troubles and in addition moves of politicians and talk the consequences. Social media analytics examines, for instance, elements that influence political participation (Johannessen &Følstad, 2014; Meth, Lee, & Yang, 2015). Political events and govern-ments use social media as a channel to talk with customers, to attain a broader audience, so one can benefit extra fans on their political opinions(Blegind & Dyrby, 2013; Hofmann, 2014; Jungherr, Schoen, & Jürgens,2016). People specific their scepticism, fury, standard delight or propose adjustments in social media. Through accomplishing social media analytics, governments and political events are aiming to benefit insights from the conversation for deriving beneficial techniques for the subsequent length of elections (Nulty, Theocharis,Popa, Parnet, & Benoit, 2016; Vaccari et al., 2013).

However, social media records also can have poor facet effects (Wendling, Radisch, & Jacobzone, 2013). This has been currently categorized as "the darkish facet of social media" (Jalonen & Jussila,2016; Kalhour & Ng, 2016; Payton & Conley, 2014). Rumours and fake record sought to have a poor influence at the conduct of different social media customers. Therefore it will become vital to pick out misinformation (Li, Sakamoto, &Chen, 2014; Wang, Ding, & Yang, 2014), rumors and pretend news (Qin, Cai, & Wangchen, 2015), and the general credibility of a user (Yu & Zou,2015). Therefore, mechanisms are wanted for detecting those classes of content material. Another component is using junk mail in social media records, that is not associated with the subject and represents e.g. advertisement. Spam will increase the quantity of records and makes the evaluation extra difficult.

Overall, it could be said that social media analytics is a tremendously complicated system with different factors concerning the respective software area and the usage of different techniques. It is therefore beneficial and vital to standardize this phenomenon to a system model, thinking about every step.

STEPS OF SOCIAL MEDIA ANALYTICS

However, few studies articles don't forget the stairs of social media analytics. Such frameworks take the shape of manner models. Fan and Gordon (2014) recommend a manner for social media analytics together with 3 steps "seize", "understand", and "present". The authors country that the step of seize includes collecting the records and preprocessing it, while pertinent records is extracted from the records in this step. Afterwards, noisy records, if current with inside the records, must be removed. However, the center of this step includes making use of a key technique, along with a sentiment evaluation or social community evaluation, for understanding the records. In the remaining step the findings must be summarized and presented (Fan& Gordon, 2014).

We adapt their framework, including a discovery segment that comes earlier than the monitoring segment, for the subsequent reasons. The framework become initially advanced with inside the context of political communication. In principle, it could effortlessly be tailored for other studies domains. The desires and evaluation techniques is probably different, however the manner is basically the same. The researchers nonetheless want to take the same selections concerning records sources, approaches, software program structure and records storage. In politics, it's miles frequently regarded in advance which subjects must be tracked, e.g. the triumphing sentiment surrounding a political party. In a extra general context the subjects may not be regarded a priori, and need to be observed first. Even while the subject on which records might be collected, along with a crisis situation, is already regarded, those techniques can assist pick out the key phrases and hashtags regularly used to speak approximately this subject matter. When hired as ainitial step, this may assist re- searchers attain higher insurance of a subject matter than could were viable with phrases defined a priori. Additionally, current studies has identified demanding situations usually encountered in subject matter discovery (Chinnov, Kerschke, Meske, Stieglitz, & Trautmann, 2015). This suggests that the addition of this step and its express inclusion in a literature evaluate effects in a extra complete insurance of demanding situations.

THIS RESULTS IN THE FOLLOWING FOUR-STEP FRAMEWORK

Discovery: The "uncovering of latent structures and patterns" (Chinnov et al., 2015)
Tracking: This step involves decisions on the data source (e.g. Twitter, Facebook), approach, method and output. A detailed sub- division of this step can be found in Stieglitz et al. (2014). In several studies the completeness of different Twitter sources was compared (Driscoll & Walker, 2014; Morstatter, Pfeffer, & Liu, 2014; Morstatter, Pfeffer, Liu, & Carley, 2013).
Preparation: Beyond this, the original framework does not elaborate on the preparation steps necessary.
Analysis: Depending on the purpose there are several methods available, including social network analysis and opinion mining.

APPLICATIONS OF SOCIAL NETWORKS

Our networked world, with the ever present information creation, famous that community ideas are widely determined for the duration of a number disciplines. Online Social Network (OSN) is a modern kind of community whose records is particularly brief however turbulent. The creation of mass adoption of on-line Social Networking Sites (SNS) has caused a shift on how humans talk and percentage know-how, how groups operate and compete and the way politicians contest and influence. In the studies location, OSN evaluation has nearly changed any traditional social technological know-how device (surveys, interviews, questionnaires) pronouncing thus, the computational social technological know-how. In the groups field, social community evaluation is carried out to benefit perception into markets and communities, with the "social enterprise" being the brand new necessity with a purpose to control know-how, improvement, change, cooperation and risk. For information connections like how humans are related collectively via way of means of the machines and the way, as a whole, they devise a monetary market, a government, a enterprise and different social systems Alex Pentland and Asu Ozdaglar have these days created the MIT Center for Connection Science and Engineering. To illustrate the effect of the manner that social large information has converted our everyday lives, appearance no similarly than how the film condominium enjoy has modified which is now a provider that makes use of a sizable array of information factors to generate recommendations.

The outstanding growth of SNS may be taken into consideration as a spark that burst the Big Data era. It makes to be had an remarkable scale of private information, information approximately occasions and social relationships, public sentiments and behaviors that after are mined and interpreted are of an extensive value. New varieties of utility are arisen with the smart use of OSN information, therefore introducing a brand new wave of effective growth. OSN is a wealthy supply of opinionated textual content and multimedia content material that has these days received massive popularity, specifically with inside the location of tracking political or advertising and marketing campaigns. The diffusion of breaking news, specifically in Twitter, is taken into consideration to be disseminating an awful lot quicker than in any traditional news media. Therefore, early occasion detection and social community evaluation play a unfavorable function with inside the control of herbal disasters, epidemics and terrorism breakouts. Social community data additionally has recently integrated inadvice systems. The latter are able to managing the troubles of data overload and data filtering.

The time period Social Network is used to explain web-primarily based totally offerings that permit people to create a public/semi-public profile inside a website such that they could communicatively hook up with different customers in the community. In community theory, a social community is typically modeled via way of means of a graph which includes customers or businesses referred to as nodes related via way of means of styles of contacts or interactions referred to as edges or links. The particular detail of social networked information is that they create new possibilities to apprehend people and society, furnished the acceptance and trust, people have proven in the direction of them. Figure 1 highlights the records of Internet customers amongst on-line communities.

However, social community information are voluminous, even from a unmarried social community site, mainly unstructured and their dynamic nature is evolving at a really speedy tempo that avoid the information evaluation and extraction of know-how. Having shifted far from the evaluation of unmarried small graphs and the residences of character nodes to attention of large-scale residences of graphs, the want for brand new information evaluation equipment and strategies is inevitable. Although many medical endeavors had been carried out and made development towards precise social community ana-

Figure 1. Popularity of OSN among online users

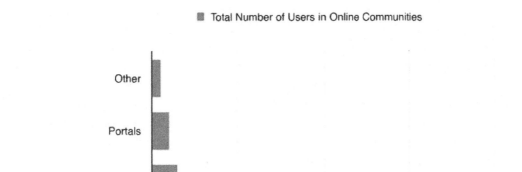

lyticssubtasks, deriving know-how from social community-sourced information stays a great mission, basically due to reasons.

Firstly, the social nature of nodes in social networks makes information subjective to many privateness concerns. A wonderful instance is that customers' touchy data can be used via way of means of the OSN admin and via way of means of business corporations to recognise the customers possibilities andto become aware of the target target market for his or her commercial consequences in violation of customers' privateness and security. Actually, the most important mission of Big Data is indeed privateness and lots of researches approximately the relied on float of private information are taken into consideration; and as social networks incorporate private information and are greatly embedded into the everyday living, many researches approximately the privateness retaining in OSN are conducted. An unique undertaking in privateness retaining is an up-to-dateand innovative recommender machine device that advanced with a purpose to assist customers to shield their information in OSNs.

Secondly, technological know-how is nonetheless some distance from routinely reading unstructured human communique information due to the fact machines aren't but capable of apprehend human language; and therefore social large information technological know-how continues to be developing. Additionally, the rubbish inputrubbish output adage of yore is alive and well. Due to the casual language information trade over OSN and the medium's noisy nature, traditional technologies of preprocessing are inadequate. To this extent, deficit to mention that, whilst the information supply is social networks all demanding situations associated with Big information end up even extra salient and making sure excellent of the information along with privateness retaining are nonetheless open studies problems.

In reaction to this chaotic rising technological know-how of social information and predictive know-how, this studies is guided in the direction of the second one mission and analyzes the social community information phenomenon from a technical perspective. In particular, we surveyed up-to-date information evaluation frameworks of the field, thinking about the distinct varieties ofevaluation, the range of techniques and the functionalities supplied via way of means of these. The relaxation of the paper is established as follows. In Section 2, we talk approximately the functions of information in OSNs and in brief introduce the kinds of information evaluation techniques and approaches. The survey's motivations and studies goals also are given here. Section three affords an outline of social community evaluation equipment and a correlation among equipment' inherent metrics and graph-evaluation techniques. Section four affords the diverse subject matter detection and tracking approaches, strategies and the corresponding equipment. Sentiment evaluation and collaborative advice frameworks, along with their associated algorithms and strategies, are investigated in Section five and 6, respectively. In phase 7 wegift evaluation problems and the capability of Computing Intelligence paradigm.

DATA ANALYTICS METHODS IN OSN

Given a totally massive records set, a chief task is to determine out what records one has and the way to research it. Social networks generally incorporate a high-quality quantity of content material and linkage records which may be leveraged for evaluation. These sorts may be in addition divided into unstructured and based records respectively, relying on whether or not they are prepared in a pre-described manner (based records) or not (unstructured records). To illustrate this with an example, time-primarily based totally activities are based, while occasion records primarily based totally on tweets and "likes" are unstructured. Structured records in OSN are typically graph-based. In the maximum fundamental framework, they are modeled with a social community that's represented as a graph $G = (V, E)$ in which V is a hard and fast of nodes or entities (e.g., humans, organizations, and products) and E is a hard and fast of edges or relationships that connects the nodes via styles of interactions. This sort of records is measured through social community evaluation, an utility of graph analytics that makes a specialty of extracting intelligence from such interconnected records. On the alternative hand, unstructured records are the content material records shared in OSN, additionally called User Generated Content (UGC). They are taken into consideration the lifeblood of SNS and encompass textual content, pix, videos, tweets,product evaluations and different multimedia records which can be generally studied with content material-primarily based totally evaluation whose strategies contain amongst others algorithms for structuring records.

Social community analytics and content material mining processes comply with the interdisciplinary principles of Artificial Intelligence (AI), Statistics and associated areas. Decades before the appearance of OSN AI researches tried to embed the arguable belief of 'intelligence' in machines that allows you to comprehend, motive and study how the global works and for this reason accumulate in addition talents from mere logical computations. OSN may be used as an surroundings of endowing machines with the capability of this not un usual place-experience expertise. The previous couple of years have visible rapid development on long- standing, tough issues in AI and it's far now rapidly reinventing so among the Internet's maximum famous services. Statistics at the different hand contain much less complicated tactics that emphasize to statisticalfashions toward the higher knowledge of records producing system.

Content-primarily based totally evaluation in OSN is studied via huge records analytics, and its attention is on extracting intelligence from the content material created and shared with inside the community. Audio or speech evaluation comply with the Large-Vocabulary Continuous Speech Recognition or the phonetic-primarily based totally technique to extract records from unstructured audio records; video content material evaluation entails a number of strategies to monitor, analyze, and extract significant records from video streams; picture evaluation techniques varies from easy to state-of-the-art relying at the evaluation assignment even as techniques for face reputation and for sentiment extraction in social media records are attacking excellent attention.

Figure 2. Data types and analysis

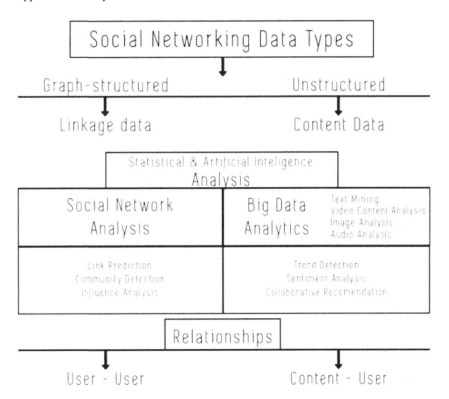

Text mining extracts styles from textual records through way of records retrieval, textual content summarization and Natural Language Processing (NLP). It is frequently included with the alternative strategies. Image evaluation and textual content mining have diagnosed huge packages in OSN for the reason that customers frequently put up pix both by myself or in addition to textual content of their messages. Also video content material evaluation is included with textual content mining. For instance, it could installation a bag-of-phrases illustration of the video transcripts to extract a few hidden styles. In general, evaluation practices together with occasion detection and sentiment evaluation are usually employed in video and picture evaluation. Provided that maximum of the frameworks are oriented toward the textual content material, we on the whole attention on textual content mining strategies, although, some frameworks that extract records from video, audio and picture are additionally analyzed.

Content mining and SNA aren't together distinct processes, a long way from it, need to co-exist in an evaluation. Content records in distinctive elements of the community is frequently closely associated with its shape and consequently combining each reassets of records is being taken into consideration to carry out higher in an evaluation. For instance, sentiment evaluation can use each linkage records and textual content. Previous sentiment evaluation methodologies frequently assumed that texts are independent; however withinside the context of Social Networks, records are networked and this option shouldn't be overlooked. In addition to that, social relationships amongst customers are recently taken into consideration as similarly precious records in recommender structures as content material styles which can be shared amongst customers. The precise detail of social networked records is after all, that they monitor records approximately interactions between customers- communities-content material.

It is obvious that analytics is a complicated system that needs humans with know-how in cleaningup records, knowledge and choosing right techniques and strategies anddecoding the evaluation results. Tools are essential to assist humans carry out those tasks. However, the expertise discovery system has come to be even more tangled with the advent of the huge records era; in which new gear are constantlyrising to update the traditional non powerful ones and a hybrid of strategies is now a demand to get cost of the records. Regarding the place of social networking, there may be a great deal confusion amongst records scientists because of the lack of (i) a clean definition-categorization of the plethora of strategies and gear, (ii) a standardization of methods and (iii) evaluation frameworks that hold records quality. Contributing to the above expertise hole is the goal studies of this survey. A huge records analytics technique into social networks via the angle of gear, techniques and strategies is given. In particular, all frameworks are divided in phrases of the maximum not unusual place evaluation practices in OSN, specifically social community evaluation, subject matter detection, sentiment evaluation and collaborative recommendation. These practices are frequently approachedvia each huge records analytics together with textual content and multimedia mining and social community analytics together with hyperlink prediction, have an impact on evaluation and community detection. This survey is huge for lots reasons. First, it provides state-of-the-art categorization of a massive variety of latest articles in accordance to the records evaluation practices, gear and frameworks toward social networking records. This perspective ought to advantage researchers with inside the area to pick a specific valuation exercise and examine its sort of gear and strategies that may be used for an evaluation purpose. We additionally divide the strategies worried in each evaluation framework and their corresponding obstacles if any; consequently,practitioners operating in business packages in addition to researchers who are acquainted with sure techniques could be capable of select, make use of and beautify a variety of strategies that maximum in shape a sure utility. This survey may be beneficial additionally for brand new comer researchers to increase a wide ranging view at the entire area of social networking records evaluation because it covers records evaluation processes, techniques, strategies, algorithms, gear and practices.

SOCIAL NETWORK ANALYSIS

SNA is a time period that encompasses descriptive and shape-primarily based totally evaluation, just like structural evaluation. It is vital if one desires to recognize the shape of the community which will benefit insights approximately how the community "works" and make selections upon it via way of means of both analyzing node/hyperlink characteristics (e.g. centrality) or via way of means of searching metrics on the complete community cohesion (e.g. density).Comparing networks, monitoring adjustments in a community over the years, revealing groups and vital nodes, and figuring out the relative function of people and clusters inside a community are a number of its not unusual place procedures. These contain both a static or dynamic evaluation. The former presumes that asocial community adjustments progressively over the years and evaluation at the complete community may be finished in batch mode. Conversely, dynamic evaluation, that's more intricate, encompasses streaming information which are evolving in time at excessive rate. Dynamic evaluation is regularly with inside the place of interactions among entities where as static evaluation offers with homes like connectivity, density, degree, diameter and geodesic distance.

In a vast sense, social media refers to a conversational, disbursed mode of content material generation, dissemination, and verbal exchange amongst groups. Different from the broadcast-primarily based totally conventional and business media, social media has torn down the bounds among authorship and readership, while the facts intake and dissemination manner is turning into intrinsically intertwined with the manner of producing and sharing facts.

Application and Impact

The Internet and cell technology had been the number one pressure at the back of the upward thrust of social media, offering technological systems for statistics dissemination,content material era, and interactive communications. In fact, important components of social media inclusive of user-generated content material or purchaser-generated media have been regarded because the defining traits of Web 2.0. From a tool perspective, an array of Web-primarily based totally packages outline the manner social media functions. Examples consist of weblogs, microblogs, on-line forums, wikis, podcasts, lifestyles streams, social bookmarks, Web communities, social networking, and avatar-primarily based totally digital reality.

From an software perspective, many web sites committed to social media are among the maximum popular—Wikipedia (collective expertise era), My Space and Facebook (social networking), YouTube (social networking and multimedia content material sharing), Digg and Delicious (social browsing, information ranking, and bookmarking),Second Life (digital reality), and Twitter (social networking and microblogging), to call only a few.

Because social media is already a essential a part of the statistics atmosphere and as social media systems and packages advantage tremendous adoption with unheard of attain to users, consumers, voters, corporations, governments, and nonprofit businesses alike, hobby in social media from all walks of life styles has been skyrocketing from each software and studies perspectives.For-income corporations are tapping into social media as each a wealthy supply of statistics and a business-execution platform for product layout and innovation, purchaser and stakeholder members of the family management, and marketing. For them, social media is an crucial thing of the next-era business intelligence platform. For politicians, political parties, and governments, social media represents the right car and statistics base to gauge public opinion on guidelines and political positions in addition to to construct community assist for applicants going for walks for public offices. Public-fitness official sought to doubtlessly use social media as precious, early clues approximately disease outbreaks and to offer remarks on public-fitness guidelines and response measures. For native land safety and intelligence evaluation communities, social media affords vast possibilities to look at terrorist institution behavior, consisting of their recruiting and public relation schemes and the grounding social and cultural contexts. Even assume tanks and social technology and business researchers are conceptually the usage of social media as an independent sensor community and a laboratory for herbal experimentation, offering precious signs andassisting check hypotheses approximately social manufacturing and interactions in addition to their economic, political, and societal implications.

For many individuals, social media has grow to be a completely unique statistics supply to deal with statistics- and cognitive-overload problems, locate solutions to specific questions, and find out greater precious possibilities for social and economic exchange. In addition, it has grow to be a platform for them to community and make contributions to all forms of dynamic dialogues via way of means of sharing their understanding and opinions. It is secure to assert that social media has already penetrated a spectrum of packages with splendid impact. Given the continuing hobby and the ever-developing statistics and meta-statistics generated via social media, it's far predicted to maintain permitting new thrilling packages andrevolutionizing many present ones.

SOCIAL MEDIA ANALYTICS AND INTELLIGENCE RESEARCH

Research on social media has substantially intensified with inside the beyond few years given thee normous hobby from the utility's attitude and the associated specific technical and social technology demanding situations and opportunities. This studiesschedule is multidisciplinary in nature and has drawn interest from studiesgroups in all foremost disciplines. From an statistics technology standpoint, social media studies has mostly targeted on social media analytics and, extra recently, social media intelligence.

Social media analytics is worried with growing and evaluating informatics gear and frameworks to collect, monitor, analyze, summarize, and visualize social media statistics, typically pushed with the aid of using precise necessities from a goal utility. Social media analytics studies serves numerous purposes: facilitating conversations and interplay among on-line groups and extracting beneficial styles and intelligence to serve entities that consist of, however aren't restricted to, lively individuals in ongoing dialogues.

From a technical attitude, social media analytics studies faces numerous specific demanding situations. First, social media consists of an enriched set of statistics or meta data, that have now no longer been dealt with systematically in statistics- and text-mining literature. Examples consist of tags (annotations or labels the usage of free-shape keywords);person-expressed subjective opinions, insights, evaluation, and perspectives; ratings; person profiles; and each express and implicit social networks. Second, social media packages are a outstanding instance of human-focused computing with their very own specific emphasis on social interactions amongst users. Hence, troubles including context-structured person profiling and wishes elicitation as well as diverse styles of human-laptop interplay issues have to be reexamined. Third, even though social media guarantees a brand new method to tackling the noise and statistics-overload hassle with Web-primarily based totally statistics processing, troubles including semantic inconsistency, conflicting evidence, lack of structure, inaccuracies, and issue in integrating special styles of indicators abound in social media. Fourth, social media statistics are dynamic streams, with their quantity swiftly increasing. The dynamic nature of such statistics and their sheer length pose enormous demanding situations to computing in trendy and to semantic computing in particular.

Second, social media intelligence studies calls for well-articulated and clearly described overall performance measures due to the fact a great deal of it have to be carried out inutility settings with an purpose to help decisions. However, in a broad spectrum of packages wherein social medial intelligence can be relevant, it's far difficult to quantify those measures. This dimension hassle makes it particularly tough to choose social media intelligence's go back on investment(ROI), and it results in modeling difficulties.

Third, from a natural modeling and choice-making attitude, social media intelligence represents a completely unique elegance of troubles with the want for green statistics-pushed, dynamic choice making; uncertainty and subjective threat analysis; and modeling and optimization over huge dynamic networks. As social media intelligence studies matures and unearths real-time packages, researchers will possibly want to expand new analytical and computational frameworks and methods.

Figure 3. The social media analytics framework

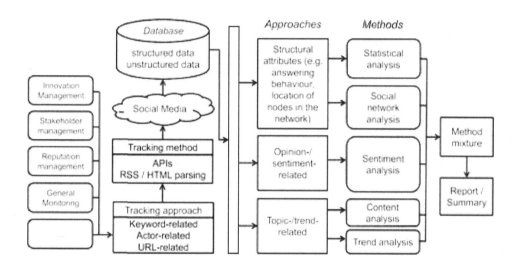

CONCLUSION

Social media analytics remains a rather new studies area, however it's miles of great hobby to the Information Systems network and lots of re- searchers are embarking on SMA tasks in our field. This article contributes to the Information Systems literature through offering a precis of the principle demanding situations and difficulties researchers face with inside the steps of the social media analytics studies method that come earlier than the information is analyzed: discovery, collection and preparation. As a 2nd contribution to the literature, we additionally point researchers to feasible answers for those demanding situations. These findings are similarly applicable to practitioners, as groups are more and more more searching to extract significant statistics from social media information, and are going through many of the identical demanding situations researchers do.

Conceptualizing the hassle the usage of the three-step social media analytics framework through Stieglitz et al. (2014) and the four "massive information" V's affords a framework wherein to reflect on consideration on feasible difficulties earlier than they arise. Which extent of information can we expect? How can we find out the components that are applicable to our studies? Do we have good enough infrastructure to deal with that extent whilst gathering and getting ready the information? Which layout will the information be in? If the information is unstructured, how are we able to extract the applicable dependent statistics from it? This article is intended to assist researchers ask and find solutions to questions along with those. If the demanding situations highlighted above are ad- dressed successfully, the social media analytics task can be more likely to be a success.

REFERENCES

Abbasi, A., Fu, T., Zeng, D., & Adjeroh, D. (2013). Crawling credible online medical sentiments for social intelligence. *Proceedings – SocialCom/PASSAT/Bigdata/EconCom/BioMedCom2013*, 254–263. . doi:10.1109/SocialCom.2013.43

Adedoyin-Olowe, Gaber, & Stahl. (2014). A Survey of Data Mining Techniques for Social Network Analysis. *J. Data Min. Digit. Humanit.*

Aggarwal, C. (Ed.). (2015, April). Social Network Data Analytics. *International Journal of Information Management*, *35*(2), 137–144.

Agreste, S., De Meo, P., Ferrara, E., Piccolo, S., & Provetti, A. (2015, November). Trust Networks: Topology, Dynamics, and Measurements. *IEEE Internet Computing*, *19*(6), 26–35. doi:10.1109/MIC.2015.93

Al-Qurishi, M., Al-Rakhami, M., Alrubaian, M., Alarifi, A., Rahman, S. M. M., & Alamri, A. (2015). Selecting the best open source tools for collecting and visualizing social media content. *2015 2nd world symposium on web applications and networking (WSWAN)*, 1–6. 10.1109/WSWAN.2015.7210346

Alhajj, R., & Rokne, J. (Eds.). (2014). *Encyclopedia of Social Network Analysis and Mining*. Springer New York. doi:10.1007/978-1-4614-6170-8

Alsubaiee, S., Carey, M. J., & Li, C. (2015). LSM-Based storage and indexing: an old idea with timely benefits. In *Second international ACM workshop on managing and mining enriched geo-spatial data*. New York, NY: ACM. .278600710.1145/2786006

Alsudais, K., & Corso, A. (2015). GIS, big data, and a tweet corpus operationalized via natural language processing. *AMCIS 2015 Proceedings*.

Anderson, K. M., Aydin, A. A., Barrenechea, M., Cardenas, A., Hakeem, M., & Jambi, S. (2015). Design Challenges/Solutions for environments supporting the analysis of social media data in crisis informatics research. *Proceedings of the annual Hawaii in- ternational conference on system sciences*, 163–172. .2015.2910.1109/HICSS

Aral, S., Dellarocas, C., & Godes, D. (2013). Introduction to the special Issue—Social media and business transformation: A framework for research. *Information Systems Research*, *24*(1), 3–13. doi:10.1287/isre.1120.0470

Artikis, A., Etzion, O., Feldman, Z., & Fournier, F. (2012). Event processing under un- certainty. *Proceedings of the 6th ACM international conference on distributed event-based systems (DEBS '12)*, 32–43. 10.1145/2335484.2335488

Baars, H., & Kemper, H.-G. (2008). Management support with structured and un- structured data – An integrated business intelligence framework. *Information Systems Management, 25*(2), 132–148. doi:10.1080/10580530801941058

Bakshy, E., Rosenn, I., Marlow, C., & Adamic, L. (2012). The role of social networks in information diffusion. *Proceedings of the 21st international conference on World Wide Web - WWW '12*, 519. 10.1145/2187836.2187907

Beier, M., & Wagner, K. (2016). Social media adoption: barriers to the strategic use of social media in SMEs. *Proceedings of the European conference on information systems.*

Bem, D. J. (1995). Writing a review article for Psychological Bulletin. *Psychological Bulletin, 118*(2), 172–177. doi:10.1037/0033-2909.118.2.172

Bendler, J., Ratku, A., & Neumann, D. (2014). Crime mapping through geo-spatial social media activity. *Proceedings of the international conference on information systems.*

Bhattacharya, P., Phan, T., & Airoldi, E. (2015). *Investigating the impact of network effects on content generation: Evidence from a large online student network.* Academic Press.

Bi, G., Zheng, B., & Liu, H. (2014). Secondary crisis communication on social media: The role of corporate response and social influence in product-harm crisis. *PACIS 2014 Proceedings.*

Bindra, G. S., Kandwal, K. K., Singh, P. K., & Khanna, S. (2012). Tracing information flow and analyzing the effects of incomplete data in social media. *2012 Fourth international conference on computational intelligence, communication systems and networks*, 235–240. 10.1109/CICSyN.2012.51

Blegind, T., & Dyrby, S. (2013). Exploring affordance of facebook as a social media platform in political campaigning. *Proceedings of the European conference on information systems.*

Blei, D. M., Ng, A. Y., & Jordan, M. I. (2003). Latent dirichlet allocation. *Journal of Machine Learning Research, 3*, 993–1022. . 993. doi:10.1162/jmlr.2003.3.4-5

Bonchi, F., Castillo, C., Gionis, A., & Jaimes, A. (2011). Social Network Analysis and Mining for Business Applications. ACM Trans. Intell. Syst. Technol. Artic., 2(22). doi:10.1145/1961189.1961194

Bowcott, O. (2015). UK-US surveillance regime was unlawful 'for seven years'. *The Guardian.* Available: http://www.theguardian.com/uk- news/2015/feb/06/gchq-mass-internet-surveillance-unlawful-court-nsa

boyd, d., & Crawford, K. (2012). Critical questions for big data: Provocations for a cultural, technological, and scholarly phenomenon. *Information Communication and Society, 15*(5), 662–679. doi:10.108 0/1369118X.2012.678878

Bruns, A. (2013). Faster than the speed of print: Reconciling 'data' social media analysis and academic scholarship. *First Monday, 18*(10), s1. .v18i10.4879 doi:10.5210/fm

Cagliero & Fiori. (2013). *TweCoM: Topic and Context Mining from Twitter.* Springer.

Cambria, E., & Hussain, A. (2015). *Introduction. In Sentic Computing.* Springer International Publishing. doi:10.1007/978-3-319-23654-4

Cao, G., Wang, S., Hwang, M., Padmanabhan, A., Zhang, Z., & Soltani, K. (2015). A scalable framework for spatiotemporal analysis of location-based social media data. *Computers, Environment and Urban Systems, 51*, 70–82. .compenvurbsys.2015.01.002 doi:10.1016/j

Cao, J., Basoglu, K. A., Sheng, H., & Lowry, P. B. (2015). A systematic review of social networks research in information systems: Building a foundation for exciting future research. *Communications of the Association for Information Systems, 36*(January), 727–758. doi:10.17705/1CAIS.03637

Carr, J., Decreton, L., Qin, W., Rojas, B., Rossochacki, T., & Yang, Y. (2015). Social media in product development. *Food Quality and Preference, 40*(Part B), 354–364. . doi:10.1016/j.foodqual.2014.04.001

Chang, Wu, Aiello, Barrat, Schifanella, Cattuto, Markines, Menczer, Blum, Ligett, Roth, Dwork, Kisilevich, Rokach, Elovici, Shapira, Li, Chen, Li, Zhang, Lin, Machanavajjhala, Kifer, Gehrke, Venkitasubramaniam, Samarati, Sweeney, & Sweeney. (n.d.). A New View of Privacy in Social Networks. In *Handbook of Research on Modern Cryptographic Solutions for Computer and Cyber Security*. IGI Global.

Chaudhary, Gupta, Gupta, Chandra, Selvakumar, Fire, Goldschmidt, Elovici, Gupta, Gupta, Gangwar, Kumar, Meena, Gupta, Gupta, Gupta, & Sharma. (n.d.). Auditing Defense against XSS Worms in Online Social Network- Based Web Applications. In *Handbook of Research on Modern Cryptographic Solutions for Computer and Cyber Security*. IGI Global.

Chen, X. C., & Jin, H. (2016). Top-k followee recommendation over microblogging systems by exploiting diverse information sources. *Future Generation Computer Systems, 55*, 534–543. doi:10.1016/j.future.2014.05.002

Clark, J. (2016). Google Sprints Ahead in AI Building Blocks, Leaving Rivals Wary. *Bloomberg*. Available: https://www.bloomberg.com/news/articles/2016-07-21/google-sprints-ahead-in-ai-building-blocks-leaving-rivals-wary

David & Jon. (2010). *Networks, Crowds, and Markets: Reasoning About a Highly Connected World*. Academic Press.

Davis, E., & Marcus, G. (2015, August). Commonsense reasoning and commonsense knowledge in artificial intelligence. *Communications of the ACM, 58*(9), 92–103. doi:10.1145/2701413

EY. (2014). *Big data-Changing the way businesses compete and operate*. Author.

Fire, M., Tenenboim-Chekina, L., Puzis, R., Lesser, O., Rokach, L., & Elovici, Y. (2013, December). Computationally efficient link prediction in a variety of social networks. *ACM Transactions on Intelligent Systems and Technology, 5*(1), 1–25. doi:10.1145/2542182.2542192

Ghazinour, Matwin, & Sokolova. (2016). Yourprivacyprotector, A recommender system for privacy settings in social networks. *Int. J. Secur. Priv. Trust Manag., 2*(4).

Hanneman & Riddle. (2005). *Introduction to Social Network Methods*. Academic Press.

Hansen, D., Shneiderman, B., & Smith, M. A. (2010). *Analyzing Social Media Networks with NodeXL: Insights from a Connected World*. Morgan Kaufmann.

He & Chu. (2010). *A Social Network-Based Recommender System*. SNRS.

Hu, X., Tang, L., Tang, J., & Liu, H. (2013). Exploiting social relations for sentiment analysis in microblogging. *Proceedings of the sixth ACM international conference on Web search and data mining - WSDM '13*, 537. 10.1145/2433396.2433465

Jiang, S., Rho, S., Chen, B.-W., Du, X., & Zhao, D. (2015, June). Face hallucination and recognition in social network services. *The Journal of Supercomputing, 71*(6), 2035–2049. doi:10.100711227-014-1257-z

Kaisler, S., Armour, F., Espinosa, J. A., & Money, W. (2013). Big Data: Issues and Challenges Moving Forward. *2013 46th Hawaii International Conference on System Sciences*, 995–1004. 10.1109/HICSS.2013.645

Kaushik, R., Apoorva Chandra, S., Mallya, D., Chaitanya, J. N. V. K., & Kamath, S. S. (2016). *Sociopedia: An Interactive System for Event Detection and Trend Analysis for Twitter Data*. Springer India.

Khalid, O., Khan, M. U. S., Khan, S. U., & Zomaya, A. Y. (2014). OmniSuggest: A Ubiquitous Cloud-Based Context-Aware Recommendation System for Mobile Social Networks. *IEEE Transactions on Services Computing, 7*(3), 401–414. doi:10.1109/TSC.2013.53

Kolaczyk, E. D., & Csárdi, G. (2014). *Statistical Analysis of Network Data with R*. Springer. doi:10.1007/978-1-4939-0983-4

Kossinets, G., & Watts, D. J. (2006). Empirical Analysis of an Evolving Social Network. Science, 311(5757), 88–90. doi:10.1126cience.1116869

Kurka, Godoy, & Von Zuben. (2015). *Online Social Network Analysis: A Survey of Research Applications in Computer Science*. Academic Press.

Li, D., Chen, C., Lv, Q., Shang, L., Zhao, Y., Lu, T., & Gu, N. (2016). An algorithm for efficient privacy-preserving item-based collaborative filtering. *Future Generation Computer Systems, 55*, 311–320. doi:10.1016/j.future.2014.11.003

Li, Y.-M., & Li, T.-Y. (2013). Deriving market intelligence from microblogs. *Decision Support Systems, 55*(1), 206–217. doi:10.1016/j.dss.2013.01.023

Mackay. (2013). Information and the transformation of sociology: Interactivity and social media monitoring. *Commun. Capital Critique (London), 11*(1), 117–126.

McCranie. (2015). *Dyads and Triads, Reciprocity and Transitivity. In Interuniversity Consortium for Political and Social Research (ICPSR)*. University of Michigan.

Mo & Li. (2015). Research of Big Data Based on the Views of Technology and Application. *Am. J. Ind. Bus. Manag., 5*(4), 192–197.

Newman, M. E. J. (2003, January). The Structure and Function of Complex Networks. *SIAM Review, 45*(2), 167–256. doi:10.1137/S003614450342480

Papadopoulos, S., Troncy, R., Mezaris, V., Huet, B., & Kompatsiaris, I. (2011). Social Event Detection at MediaEval 2011: Challenges, Dataset and Evaluation. *MediaEval 2011 Workshop*.

Pentland. (2016). *Reinventing society in the wake of big data*. Available: https://www.edge.org/conversation/alex_sandy_pentland-reinventing-society-in-the-wake-of-big-data

Poria, S., Cambria, E., Howard, N., Huang, G.-B., & Hussain, A. (2016). Fusing audio, visual and textual clues for sentiment analysis from multimodal content. *Neurocomputing, 174*, 50–59. doi:10.1016/j.neucom.2015.01.095

Prom-on, S., Ranong, S. N., Jenviriyakul, P., Wongkaew, T., Saetiew, N., & Achalakul, T. (2016). *DOM: A big data analytics framework for mining Thai public opinions*. In R. Buyya (Ed.), *Big Data: Principles and Paradigms* (pp. 339–355). Morgan Kaufmann.

Saez-Trumper, D., Comarela, G., Almeida, V., Baeza-Yates, R., & Benevenuto, F. (2012). Finding trendsetters in information networks. *Proceedings of the 18th ACM SIGKDD international conference on Knowledge discovery and data mining - KDD '12*, 1014. 10.1145/2339530.2339691

Siddique, N., & Adeli, H. (2013). *Introduction to Computational Intelligence. In Computational Intelligence: Synergies of Fuzzy Logic, Neural Networks and Evolutionary Computing*. John Wiley & Sons Ltd.

Tam. (2016). The Government Answers Apple in the iPhone Case. *The New York Times*. Available: http://www.nytimes.com/2016/03/12/technology/the- government-answers-apple-in-the-iphone-case.html?ribbon-ad-idx=4&rref=technology&module=Ribbon&version=origin&region=Header&action=click&contentCo llection=Technology&pgtype=articleover&_r=0

Thiel, Kötter, Michael, Silipo, & Winters. (2012). *Creating Usable Customer Intelligence from Social Media Data: Network Analytics meets Text Mining*. Academic Press.

Vavliakis, K. N., Tzima, F. A., & Mitkas, P. A. (2012). Event Detection via LDA for the MediaEval2012 SED Task. *MediaEval 2012 Workshop*.

Yu, Y., Lin, H., Meng, J., & Zhao, Z. (2016, June). Visual and Textual Sentiment Analysis of a Microblog Using Deep Convolutional Neural Networks. *Algorithms, 9*(2), 41. doi:10.3390/a9020041

Zhou, D., Chen, L., & He, Y. (2015). An unsupervised framework of exploring events on twitter: filtering, extraction and categorization. *Proceedings of the Twenty-Ninth AAAI Conference on Artificial Intelligence*.

Zhu, T., Ren, Y., Zhou, W., Rong, J., & Xiong, P. (2014). An effective privacy preserving algorithm for neighborhood-based collaborative filtering. *Future Generation Computer Systems, 36*, 142–155. doi:10.1016/j.future.2013.07.019

Chapter 15
Patient Monitoring System Using Internet of Things

Bollipelly PruthviRaj Goud
https://orcid.org/0000-0003-0540-5798
Anurag Group of Institutions, India

A. Prasanth Rao
https://orcid.org/0000-0002-5119-3987
Anurag Group of Institutions, India

Sravan kumar S.
Anurag Group of Institutions, India

Sathiyamoorthi V.
https://orcid.org/0000-0002-7012-3941
Sona College of Technology, Salem, India

ABSTRACT

IoT comprises billions of devices that can sense, communicate, compute, and potentially actuate. The data generated by the IoTs are valuable and have the potential to drive innovative and novel applications. IoT allows people and things to be connected anytime, anyplace and to anyone with the internet using tiny sensor. One of the best advantages of the IoT is the increasing number of low-cost sensors available along with its functionalities. A few standard sensors include linear accelerator, compass, light sensors, camera, and microphone, moisture, location, heart rate, and heart rate variability. The trend is multi-sensor platforms that incorporate several sensing elements. In such environment, discovering, identifying, connecting, and configuring sensor hardware are critical issues. The cloud-based IoT platforms can retrieve data from sensors IoT is an inter-disciplinary technology, encompassing multiple areas such as RTS, embedded systems. This chapter detailed investigation and presents highly innovative and revolutionary ideas in healthcare application are available.

DOI: 10.4018/978-1-7998-2566-1.ch015

INTRODUCTION

In the very recent to our regular lives, we are habituated and focusing to show some interest in wearable sensors. They are become a part of today's generation. Devices are integrated with human in many aspects to evaluate their health and economic zones. Our main aspect to project the objectives of the Internet of Things and its devices and note the challenges when we are monitoring a patient. The key factors are generated based up on the end user requirements which lead to provide the things as in an enhanced way to achieve the commerciality, availability and flexibilities. Till now there are several devices are ready to provide the services, generating good results and commercially available for personal health care in hospitals, fitness care as gyms, and activity awareness. How they are serving well than a human? The achievements will include lots of complexities to predict the data which is generated with the help of electronic devices. The data which is belongs to health care is accepted as sets of data. The data is individual to person. Production of data is very large due to number of devices are increased in the real world. it is very complex to represent the specific analysis to serve a particular patient. Even it is complex to manage the data with traditional systems or tools. With the help of data Analytics, our job becomes very easy to predict the level of disease, amount of medicine needs to use and able to provide the best friendly services to patient. Now, what is this data analytics? What is the importance for it? Why analysis is required? This Chapter will focus to reveal everything about it.

Importance of Data Analytics in Health Care System

In the software evaluation was started new era in the computer world to make everything as end user centric. The world is more over waiting for features as need of high flexibility, to provide the distributed mechanism, high end availability and user-friendly environments to client. With the help of high-level programming language and developers have start generating 4th generation languages such are helpful to accessing the databases. When we started providing the distributed mechanism to end user, they are expecting high availability of applications. Now industrial Revolution has been (Samir et al.,2016) supporting for even small-scale industries also start providing features in 24*7 manners to fulfill the business requirements as banking, health, finance, commerce and commercial fields. Everything is on finger tips, end user centric applications are grown very fast. Now end user has flexible and high available approaches around in the real world. Usability is also speeded up. It's a good omen for new a business enterprise. While serving an end user when there is a Hugh amount of data is going to be generated. Here, we had resources to store this data like databases. New challenges are produced and questioning new enterprise about speed, gathering exact information, extraction of useful data. This becomes to a new invention which is going to lead the business world. Improvising Data algorithms are introduced to extraction the data from databases. It is providing responsibilities for a Data Analytics to enhancement in the data retrievals, report generation and market analysis or on business requirements. Data Analytics has a key role. It's showing some improvisation and representation for the unstructured data and resolving the real-world problems. The data analytics are going to divide this challenge into two stages. They are Data acquisition and data analysis.

Data Acquisition

The main intention of Data acquisition is a process to gather or collect the data from various resources such as Social media platform, data centers or records and patients. The major challenge for an analyst while collecting the data from manual records or manual entries are producing new challenges to the data analyst. Those are listed below as

- Inappropriate information will be entered which leads to produce the worst results. While serving to end-user, definitely we are into different direction which is not yet all encourage able.
- Collecting the data from manual records is also producing complexity while doing analysis on particular data. To resolve the acquiring data problems, Data required an ability to merge, integrate and access the data across the world. Our challenges are Data Preparation and Data Cleaning.
- **Data Preparation**: Whatever the data acquired from different sites, it will produce in own format. As an analyst, we need to prepare the data before storing into the databases. It is involving multiple steps which are required to prepare data for analysis so that all data is accessible and represented in a single format. This type of Data can be easily analyzing even data represented as data sets, data marts, data warehouses, etc.
- **Data Cleaning**: Data Cleaning focusing on remove duplicates, irrelevant data, old data. Checking and enquiring duty are mandatory for a data record for incorrect entries. The particular fields are going to be corrects the information is known as Data Cleaning.

Data Analysis

Data has gathered from many resources. The risk starts from the second stage i.e. Data analysis. It's nothing but a process of evaluating data using analytical and logical reasoning to expertise data on each aspect. Service will be provided based upon the request. Data from various sources is gathered, viewed, verified and then analyzed. Facts are going to be formed as reports. Researches views will expose a lot from more varieties of specific data analysis method, algorithms of the areas which are included as data mining, text analytics, business intelligence, and data visualizations. In today's advanced analytics environment, self-serve data preparation helps to alleviate many of the issues you will come across in these steps and allows a business user to access, prepare and analyze data without the assistance of a data scientist.

Figure 1. Data acquisition

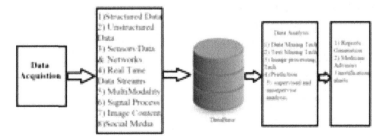

The Major Objectives of Data Analytics

The objectives are going to play major role in the data analytic life. As being as analytics, what we can able to do? What we are able to do? In outs are demonstrated from those objectives. They are constructed based on flow which can be predicted on Figure 1.

1. The main prospective was given to gathering data from multiple spots to project it has a single data. Data analysts may analyze the data based up on the business requirements. This may lead to expose the priority for the actual data which we are peaking up.
2. The second one is generating the selective data based up on the respective request from the teams or individuals can able to deal with the data and it can be exposed as Data Reports, which rise the business opportunity with high rate and further actions are added.
3. The Third Zone is completely defined as client specific. Data analysis allows us to develop the Business which completely concern on customer requirements and experience. This is the key feature, what exactly Industries want?
4. The last priority was given to Perform market analysis. It can be performed to understand the strengths and weakness of competitors and to understand what clients are expecting exactly?, to know this requirements summery we need to work with this data analyst. As well as with these objectives, we are going to construct the IOT objectives.

MONITORING AND MANAGING A PATIENT USING IOT

In this world, the most important Survival objectives for human beings are health, wealth and nature. On those objectives, the most important priority to a human being is represented as on his/her health. Even we are in 20th century, it has biggest issue and challenges. (Fayez,2018) promoted a paper on monitoring and managing a Patient. Those are always provoking the developers or researchers. Specially, in the health care domains are having more relevant and rescue centric issues are existed in the developed and developing countries. There are some industries already started revolutions in the healthcare domain to serve the people where they are in need. There are so many countries are lacking with physicians or doctors to treat them in proper way. From the all complexities, new generations are coming up with new innovative ideas which lead us into a new world. The world needs more advancement in health care domains and it's a good omen to welcoming devices into health care world to serve patient and guide them into a proper way. In the earlier stages, it is imposing lots of complexities to the real human world. They are lacking with believing a system or device. From the so many circumstances and with the help of advancement in computer, computer vision and Artificial intelligence made our lives so easy and protective. Everything can accessible, sharable and advisable for a device from anywhere in the real world. This acceptance can be achieved with the help of Internet of Things.

The authors (Kiran & Mina,2018), gave the wings to devices, where services can made possible for remote monitoring in the healthcare sector, release the potential to keep patients secure and healthy, and empowering physicians to deliver super supportive care. It has also increased patient connectivity, satisfaction and it as usual interactions with doctors have become easier and more efficient. Remote monitoring of patient's health help to save the time reduces his physical efforts, no staying in hospital for long time, less cost effective and improving treatment outcomes. IoT has applications in healthcare that benefits patients, families, physicians, hospitals, doctors and insurance companies.

- **IoT for Patients**: Patient can interact with the help of devices. Those devices are available in the form of wearable just as fitness band which are very easy, comfortable and stylish. Those devices can be connected or wireless to service. Those can be served to check blood pressure and heart rate monitoring, glucometer, calorie count, exercise check, appointments, blood pressure variations.
- **IoT for Physicians**: Now it's a Physician turn. With help of those wearable devices a doctor can keep on track a patient condition. Doctor can advise us about need of medical intention and treatment plans. Keep tracking is helpful for a physician to track the treatment process. Duties of doctor are going to be very easy.
- **IoT for Hospitals:** Aside from observing patients' wellbeing, there are numerous different zones where IoT gadgets are exceptionally helpful in medical clinics while furnishing the therapy with progression. Hardly any gadgets are wheelchairs, defibrillators, nebulizers, oxygen siphons and other checking hardware. Arrangement of clinical staff and make their obligation is simple despite the fact that there are at various areas, can likewise be broke down this present reality.
- **IoT for Health Insurance Companies:** There are parcel of chances for wellbeing safety net providers with IoT-associated insightful gadgets. Insurance agencies can use information caught through wellbeing checking gadgets for their guaranteeing and claims activities. This information will empower them to recognize extortion guarantees and distinguish possibilities for endorsing. IoT gadgets get straightforwardness among back up plans and clients the endorsing, evaluating, claims taking care of, and hazard appraisal measures. In the light of IoT-caught information driven choices in all activity measures, clients will have satisfactory perceive into hidden idea behind each choice made and cycle results. Digitized information in the medical care area is developing enormously with information rolling in from inward just as outer sources, from cell phones, wearable sensor gadgets, Electronic Wellbeing Records (EHR), Radiology pictures, Recordings, clinical notes, online media, sites, distant wellbeing observing gadgets and so on more up to date types of huge information, for example, imaging, sensor perusing is likewise energizing to the need of Large Information answers for deal with these huge and storehouses of information accessible in the medical care industry. The medical services industry needs to chip away at expectation, counteraction and personalization to improve their results. Various measures of information organized, semi-organized and unstructured information are a trademark that makes the medical services information generally testing. A large portion of the information in medical care originates from different sources like X-Beams pictures, X-ray Output reports, Blood test esteem, transcribed remedies, ongoing information, for example, OT room screens for sedation, heart screens, pulse readings and so on.

In modern healthcare systems where every information is stored or updated online there is a need to integrate these huge datasets so as to analyze the healthcare industry to yield better results. By using the above proposed healthcare model healthcare industry data stored in the form of cloud or Big Data can be retrieved and analyzed as per the requirements of various factors such as hospitals, medical actioners, patients, insurance companies and governments. For example, if the doctor wants to analyze the history of a patient before prescribing medication, instead of enquiring the patient about the same which is time consuming in the modern busy life style, he can get the complete history of the patient through this model thoroughly analyzed from various perspectives of healthcare industry. The doctor can then narrow down his search by looking into a particular aspect of the side effects experienced by the patient in his previous treatments due to the type of drugs and doses used in the past. This helps in helping him to come to a conclusion much faster in prescribing medicine for patient with utmost care. Likewise, this model helps insurance companies to understand the overall condition of the patient and suggest the right health policy for their customers. Also, it helps the government officials to pull up the statistics relating to the spreading of a particular disease and the number of patients affected and the prominent symptoms observed in majority of them and also the root causes can be analyzed. Thus, this model helps the actors of the healthcare system to analyze the healthcare data from their perspective and yield the sorted and simplified results making it easy for them to understand the healthcare industry thus contributing to the betterment of healthcare in a much faster pace.

General Approach for IOT Devices In Healthcare

(Vandana et al., 2011) have mentioned many suggested IOT devices. Major intention behind IOT boom is, it has outstanding opportunities, high business scope, and real world really wants a special speed up self-monitoring service system. Moreover, ideas are appearing very complex, it has to be implemented with ease and along with devices and user-defined constraints as to be applied on reliable system which aims to an end user. There are variety of factors are going to affecting on resources. Decision making is going to be very important to reduce the resources spent on. Based upon the general approach and architecture of IOT devices are going to be improving efficiency. There are four layers are available for IOT architecture. We can observe them from Figure 2. Those are

1. Physical Layer.
2. Data Exchange Layer.
3. Data Integration Layer.
4. Application Layer.

Those can be exposed here below:

Figure 2. General approaches for IOT in Health Care

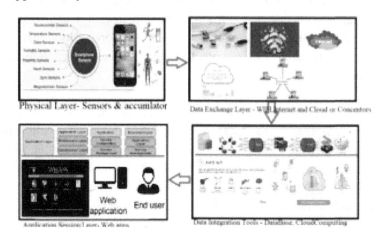

Physical Layer

Physical Layers is consisting of physical devices. It's completely about data generations using wireless and wired sensors or actuators. This is the first step where data is generated and converted into that information. The ability is treated as the biggest task for actuators, the process goes even further, and these devices are able to intervene the physical reality. For example, device can switch off the light and adjust the temperature in a room.

Data Exchange Layer

Still it is working very close to sensors and actuators by keep interacting through networks gates to data acquisition systems while representing the data which is generated from multiple resources or devices. Internet getaways work through Wi-Fi, wired LANs to perform data acquisition process. This is an important stage to collect the vast amount of data which is generated by sensors. Be Responsible to accept the data and passing it through Networks.

Data Integration Layer

Data is generated in the first stage; generated data is transformed to the next level. The challenging tasks are going to happen when you're integrating the data which is generated from multiple resources. Data has to be stored in the database as OLTP, OLAP servers. For an example (Zhe et al., 2016) cloud based approaches, edge IT systems perform enhanced analytics and pre-processing. It refers to machine learning and visualization technologies. The main intention here is to accept the data. Pre-process the data to remove the ambiguities and over heading of data. Data Analytics: There are various data analytics which is used to analyse the data using analytical methods from health care data. There are various algorithms are used to extract patient details and also finding the causes of symptoms. There is a need to apply various algorithms such as data mining techniques and machine learning techniques to interpret the data properly. **Data Interpretation:** Interpreting results of analytics on the healthcare data and also inference drawn from results.

Application Layer

We need the tools to represent the Analysis, management, and storage of data. The major focus on how we can able to interact with application to database. it enables in-depth processing, along with a follow-up revision for feedback., this phase already includes the analytical skills of the highest rank, both in digital and human worlds. Therefore, the data from other sources may be included here to ensure an in-depth analysis

PMOS Using IOT Common Architecture

The Web of Things (IoT) includes billions of gadgets that can detect, impart, register and conceivably activate. The information produced by the Web of Things are important and can possibly drive creative and novel applications. IoT permits individuals and things to be associated whenever, wherever and to anybody, preferably utilizing any way/organization and any assistance. IoT interfaces certifiable items to the web utilizing small sensors or installed gadgets. Probably the greatest favorable position of the IoT is the expanding number of ease sensors accessible for various sorts of functionalities. A couple of standard sensors incorporate accelerometer (for development), direct quickening agent, compass, light sensors, camera, and mouthpiece, dampness, area, pulse and pulse fluctuation. These sensors incorporate an assortment of gadgets and arrangements. The pattern is multi-sensor stages that fuse a few detecting components. In such condition, finding, distinguishing, associating and designing sensor equipment is basic issues. The cloud based IoT stages can recover information from sensors. Along these lines, IoT is an exhaustive between disciplinary innovation, including numerous regions, for examples, Wireless protocols, RTS, installed frameworks, correspondence, microelectronics and software engineering and designing (Pei et al., 2006). It makes a multidisciplinary research condition for examining and tentatively approving exceptionally inventive and progressive thoughts for new systems administration and administration ideal models as appeared in figure 3.

Figure 3. PMS using IOT device architecture

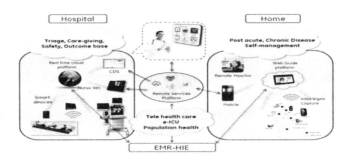

With the help of (Simon et al., 2009) we are able to generated the general approach of PMOS architecture the devices are going to be categorized into different forms. They are represented on bases of use cases.

- **Hearable:** With Apple Air Units' new Live Listen highlight being only one model, hearables are not simply giving constant admittance to remote helpers, however totally changing the path individuals with hearing misfortune can associate with the world. Remote hearables are as of now helping millions around the globe through their cell phones, however the coming expanded ranges and work abilities will just make hearables better and more accommodating.
- **Sweat Sensors:** Till this date, medical care frameworks are having been restricted in the liquids they viably dissect. "Sweat is the fresh blood," Chart Wear is creating wearable that break down your perspiration, a more helpful and savvy approach to gather convoluted wellbeing information than drawing blood.
- **Ingestible:** Any individual who has needed to encounter the option is excited at the new option of gulping a pill-sized sensor. It is anything but a misrepresentation to call ingestible a cutting-edge science wonder. Ingestible sensors aren't just less intrusive yet again less expensive and are discovering use in both diagnosing malady and observing drug's effect on the body.

- **MoodAbles:** Again, seeming like sci-fi, disposition Ables, gadgets used to upgrade patient's prosperity are turning out to be reality. Head mounted, these mind-set changing gadgets send low-power current to our cerebrum to expand and at times even supplant upper drugs.
- **Charting:** It may not sound as showy, yet medical care graphing can diminish a specialist's outstanding task at hand by at least 15 hours every week. IoT-empowered gadgets and dashboards make persistent information more open, computerize excess undertakings, diminish mistakes, and in particular, permit specialists to zero in on what's generally significant, their patients.
- **Smart Distributors:** The quantities of keen prescription containers have detonated. The most recent age allocators are robotized and associated. Associated with the cloud, allocators are associated with patients, their medical services suppliers, their guardians, their insurance agencies, and their different gadgets. Regularly sold pre-filled and pre-modified by the doctor's guidelines, distributors can work naturally for quite a long time, in any event, modifying doses per the specialist's directions dependent on the patient's continuous condition.es per the doctor's instructions based on the patient's real-time condition.

PMOS Using IOT Objectives

Medical care industry has gotten very information concentrated with information coming not the same as different sources. Data integration across heterogeneous data is one the challenging issue. The architecture diagram data generation from heterogeneous sources as the main components is presented below.

- **Information Assortment:** The heterogeneous of medical services information from various sources are gathered and put away in information base. The information designs are unique and coordinating these configurations is one of fundamental testing issues.
- **Data Extraction:** The information which is extricated from various sources is separated and single information sources. Age of Standard Arrangement: Information can be removed in to a standard organization utilizing most recent innovation XML, HL7 and semantic web advances.

The main objectives of proposal of solution of health care system are

1. Analysing the nature of the symptom.
2. Analysing the causes of symptoms.
3. Analysing the human body structure.
4. Analysing proper drug for a given symptom.
5. Analysing side effects of drug for a patient.
6. Reducing emergency waiting time.
7. Following patients, staff, and stock.
8. Improve the medication the board.
9. Guaranteeing accessibility of basic equipment Protection and security.
10. Affordable-cost concern on common man (CCC).
11. Small and portable.
12. Easy to use.
13. Stay-Connected.

PMS USING IOT APPLICATIONS IN HEALTHCARE

The medical care industry has fundamentally underutilized innovation to improve operational proficiency and most frameworks depends on paper clinical records. This outcome in absence of viable correspondence among the partners. Around the world, medical care change possesses commanded that it is energy for medical services data innovation (HIT) to be modernized and distributed computing is at the focal point of this change. The medical services industry is moving toward a data driven consideration conveyance model, empowered partially by open guidelines that help participation, community work processes and data sharing. Distributed computing gives a framework that permits clinics, clinical practices, insurance agencies, and examination offices to tap improved processing assets at lower starting capital expenses. Also, cloud situations will bring down the hindrances for development and modernization of HIT frameworks and applications. Distributed computing obliges the key innovation necessities of the medical services industry.

The majority of partners of medical care framework (Manfred, 2007) utilizes the framework in traditionalist methodology for determination and therapy of patients where specialists rely upon their insight and abilities in diagnosing sickness in patients bringing about a less exact and patient driven. The adaption of Huge Information arrangements will assume a significant function in changing the result of the wellbeing business by advancing proof-based thinking in treatment by empowering a 360-degree perspective on every patient. In this way, the majority of the partners are beginning to grasp the idea of proof dependent on medication a framework where treatment choice dependent on logical proof accessible instead of simply the specialists still and information giving a quantifiable result towards treatment (Simon et al., 2009).

Approaches are clear. Aside from this, there are endless applications are created, accessible and prepared to serve the world. Not many applications are list down in underneath Table 1.

BENEFITS WITH SMART DEVICES

1. Reporting and Monitoring

IoT health care domain-based device is helpful to generating the reports time to time to check the patient condition. Monitoring is going to be very easy for a doctor. Both are working in simultaneously to serve a patient (Sobhan et al., 2017).

2. M2M Connectivity and affordability

It's an easy way to extend feature of IOT domain to automate the devices and there is scope to invent the new devices to monitoring a patient. There are possibilities to build the next generation healthcare facilities. IOT is going to enables interoperability, machine-to-machine communication, information generation and exchange, and data movement that make healthcare service delivery effective. Connectivity protocols are going to be generating bridge between machines. Bridges are like Bluetooth LE, Wi-Fi, Z-wave, ZigBee.

Table 1. Devices in PMS using IOT healthcare

S.no.	Device name	Objective	Specifications	Company
1	Personal EKG	To monitor the heart, need to track of an ECG reports [electrocardiogram]. It is a dedicated app along with the devices which leads produce the ECG. It has a capability to transmit the ECG report to anyone. It will works along with FDA-cleared mobile EKG monitor to track your heart health anytime, anywhere	Kardia Mobile android and IOS App	AliveCor
2	Portable Gluten Tester	a live saver device for those who are having food allergies from glutenor celiac disease. It has six sensors to identify gluten in your food and as well as capsules	NIMA sensors and along with IOS app	NIMA.INC
3	Teeth Whitener:	This product contains everything you need for an efficient, long-lasting teeth whitening procedure with no sensitivity, including mouthpiece and case, lip care balm, and 10 G-Vials of whitening gel. It requires controller and requires four 8-minute application sessions daily to make your teeth up to 5 shades whiter in 5 days	GLO Lit™ Teeth Whitening Tech Kit	GLO SCIENCE
4	Wireless Blood Pressure Monitor:	This is the best suitable device for monitoring a patient when he is not in the hospital also. It is easy and we can utilize it in our regular life without having any difficulties. The device can easily synchronize with Bluetooth automatically. It is very easy and helpful while monitoring ourselves.	NOKIA BPM+ and Android, IOS app.	NOKIA
5	Bio Scarf:	it is the best alternative for the traditional air pollution masks. Bio scarf is the best for comfortable device and it looks like fashion accessory. The device consists several features, it has air filtration and with lower risk rate for health problems like allergens and viral infections and it is useful in any weather conditions.	BIOSCARF- BULIT in 95	BIOSCARF
6	Breath analyzer for smartphone:	if anybody wants to be a smarter drinker. This device or app is very specific to them. A breath analyzer is connecting to your smartphone and it helps to track our BAC levels. Additional features for the device are measure our blood alcohol level quickly and accurately.	Alcohoot device along with android app and IOS app	Alcohoot
7	Stylish Tracker-watch hybrid	A smart watch which is very similar like fit-bit. It will count your number of steps, track your swimming, monitors and sleep. The most important thing rather than others watches, it will also record your calories burned. The main objectives we are getting with it is style, timeless look and most comfortable to wear and extreme battery backup. Additional features as with SMTP to send reports to particular mail-id, POP3 to retrieve the mail we can see the reports. We can also share the reports through BLUETOOTH.	Withings smart watch device	Withings
8	Hearables	This is helpful for those who are suffered from hearing loss. It provides best interaction	Apple IOS along with Beat Electronic Chip	APPLE

continues on following page

Table 1. Continued

S.no.	Device name	Objective	Specifications	Company
9	Moodables (Different categories are available)	Moodables are temperament upgrading gadgets which help in improving our mind-set for the duration of the day. It might seem like sci-fi, however it's not a long way from the real world. Moodables are head-mounted wearable that send low-power current to the cerebrum which raises our temperament.	Halo Neurosciences Head Phones.	Halo Neurosciences
10	Pill identifier	To identifying the pill or medicine based up on capsule or logo. It is also providing the description & limitations of medicine.	Android or IOS applications are available	Drugs.com
11	Ingestible sensors	Ingestible sensors are really a cutting edge science wonder. These are pill-sized sensors which screen the drug in our body and caution us in the event that it recognizes any anomalies in our bodies. These sensors can be a shelter for a diabetic patient as it would help in checking manifestations and furnish with an early notice for sicknesses.	wearable sensor patch and mobile application	Proteus
12	Brain Sensing Headband	Screens your mind movement during contemplation & communicates the data to your PC, Cell phone, or tablet through Bluetooth.	MUSE device and android, IOS app	MUSE
13	Wireless Smart Glucometer	the pack incorporates 10 testing strips, 10 lancets, control arrangement, a spearing gadget, and a convey sack. FDA affirmed glucometer that estimates glucose levels in the blood and afterward shows them on your Cell phone.	iHealth Smart-Gluco kit for android and IOS app	iHealth Lab Inc
14	Groundbreaking Smartphone Ultrasound Device	first Smartphone ultrasound imaging device in the world. It has the flexibility to share the image or video through USB or email only.	Mobius SP1 System along with Windows mobile 6.5	Mobisante, Inc.
15	Remote Cardiac Monitoring System	BIoTricity is handling cardio vascular illness with a constant, high-exactness far off observing innovation. Recently, the organization made sure about FDA510k endorsement for Bioflux, an intended for use by doctors.	3-channel electrocardiogram (ECG) monitoring system	Preventive Solutions in collaboration with Mayo Clinic, BIoTricity
16	Pain Relief Device	Blend of Transcutaneous Electrical Nerve Trigger (TENS) and Controlled Muscle Test system (PMS) which conveys low-voltage heartbeats to the skin to animate nerve filaments, obstructing the agony sign to your cerebrum.	Muscle Stimulator Tens Unit 24 Modes Touch System	TechCare Massager

DATA ACQUISITION AND ANALYSIS IS EASY TO PRODUCE THE DATA

Data has going to be generated with the help of sensors. It is very vast amount of data. The data has been represented in the form of reports and it is exchanging as huge amount between machines with in short time. Working with, the real time applications are going to be hard to store and manage. There are few challenges are exposed in the healthcare devices. Damian et al. (2017) have defined a common methodologies which are implemented based IOT.

1. Primary challenge is for healthcare providers, to acquire data from multiple devices or sources, organizes the data to analyse it in manually.
2. IoT devices can collect the data, able to generate the report and analyses in real-time and store the raw data. High Storage is going to degrade the device performance. Instead of this, data is going to be stored over cloud. Only With the help of providers, we can able to getting access to it and able generated the particular report based up on the doctor requirements.
3. Final challenge is for the healthcare analytics. There is some need to generate high speed data-retrieval policy and speed up policy while decision-making.

Tracking and Alerts

A must and should activity for the tracking applications based on IOT devices in the health care domain (Shubham et al., 2018). Tracking and alerts are generated on-the time when there is a critical event for a patient or life-threatening movement. Health care devices are able to gather the data and transfer that data to a doctor. Now doctor is able to provide the real time tracking assistance to a patient.

Remote Medical Assistance

In the scenario of emergency, patients are able to contact with a doctor. Distance doesn't show any effect on monitoring and services. Through smart mobiles or IOT devices, aim to provide the end user flexibility, instance check-up, immediate problem identification and distributing the drugs based upon patient's prescription. Final achievement is "IOT will improve the patients care".

Research

Adventure and Advancement is always generating the opportunities. In the same way IOT health care domain is used for research purposes. Collecting and analysing the data leads us into statistical world to support the medical research. The IOT research is not about money and time. It's about service and satisfaction.

CHALLENGES AND FUTURE SCOPE IN PMS USING IOT

Data Security and Privacy

IoT devices are facing the most significant issues in the data security and privacy approaches. Devices can capture the data and transfer it on real time (Sufian et al., 2019). IOT devices lacking with data protocols and standards while exchanging the information from one machine to another machine. Even we are comfortable with exchanging the data, next issue with IOT devices is data ownership and ambiguity is another one while differentiating the data. Cybercriminals can modify the content of Personal Health Information (PHI) of both patients as well as doctors. Cybercriminals can misuse patient's data to create fake IDs to buy drugs and medical equipment which they can sell later.

Integration

Basically, data generation is in peaks while using sensor. It is completely proportional to end-user utilization. The biggest challenge for an analyst is data integration when the data is generating from multiple devices. Multiple devices are working together. So, we need focus on communication protocols, standards and its complications and process of data aggregation. The scope of scalability of IoT in healthcare is also considered as a new challenge.

Data Overload and Accuracy

Information collection is giving part of complexities because of the utilization of various correspondence conventions and Norms are utilized here (Sufian et al., 2019). Notwithstanding, IoT gadgets are as yet recording huge amounts of information. The information gathered by IoT gadgets are used to increase crucial experiences. In any case, the measure of information is gigantic to the point that getting experiences from it are getting incredibly hard for specialists which, influences the nature of administration while picking a dynamic way to deal with produce the outcomes. Creation of information is significant however over-burdening will prompt reduction the precision of our application.

Cost

There is a slogan while working IOT devices and its domains i.e. "it's about service not about money". Generation of devices and their approaches are very difficult for developers and making them as artificial human (who can act like a human with affection, service and love) being is big task. Even though, till now, IoT has not made the healthcare facilitates affordable to the common man yet. There is a necessity to make them available for a patient who is being in critical conditions. At least we need to protect one of them who is be need. No place for business, only for service.

CONCLUSION FOR PMS USING IOT

IOT have the scope in healthcare domain. There is need for human being to know about his treatment and prescription. IOT is not yet all provoking the doctors or physician. IOT is about accuracy and advancement in the health care while serving a patient. We can project the content in detailed and as well as digitalized environment with an ease. The challenges and benefits will express and expose the new ideas along with new paths. It's just a beginning. IOT is anywhere, anytime approach for a patient. It's about service, not about money.

REFERENCES

Damian, D., Bartosz, J., & Wlodek, J. K. (2017). IOT-Based Information System For Healthcare Application: Design Methodology Approach. *Applied Sciences (Basel, Switzerland)*, *2017*(7), 596. doi:10.3390/app7060596

Fayez, H.A. (2018). The Application of the Internet of Things in Healthcare. *IJCA*.

Kiran, D. & Mina, M. (2018). Internet of Things for Healthcare: A Review. *International Journal of Advanced in Management, Technology and Engineering Sciences*.

Manfred, B. (2007). Current Developments and Future Chllenges of Coordination in Pervasive Environments. *16th IEEE International workshops on Enabling Technologies: Infrastructure for Collaborative Enterprises,* 51 – 55, doi:10.1109/WIRELESSVITAE.2011.5940920

Pei, L., Zhifeng, T., Zinan, L., Eiza, E., & Shivendra, P. (2006). Cooperative Wireless Communications: A Cross-Layer Approach. *IEEE Wireless Communications*, (August), 84–92. doi:10.1109/WIRELESS-VITAE.2011.5940920

Samir, Zanjala, & Talmaleb. (2016). Medicine Reminder and Monitoring System for Secure Health Using IOT, ICISP2015. *Procedia Computer Science*, 471–476. doi:10.1016/j.procs.2016.02.090

Shubham, B., Isha, M., & Saranya, S. S. (2018), Smart Healthcare Monitoring Using IOT. *International Journal of Applied Engineering Research, 13*(15), 11984-11989. http://www.ripublication.com

Simon, D., Gilles, G., & Jean-Jacques, V. (2009). The Web of Things: Interconnecting Devices with high usability and performance. *ICESS*, 323 – 330. https://hal.inria.fr/inria-00390615

Sobhan, B., Srikanth, K., Ramanjaneyulu, T., & Lakshmi, N. I. (2017). IOT for Healthcare. *International Journal of Scientific Research (Ahmedabad, India)*. Advance online publication. doi:10.3390/app7060596

Sufian, H., Faraz, I. K., & Bilal, H. (2019). Understanding Security Requirements and Challenges in Internet of Things (IoT). *RE:view*. Advance online publication. doi:10.1155/2019/9629381

Vandana, M.R., Neeli, R.P. & Ramjee, P. (2011). *A Cooperative Internet of Things (IoT) for Rural Healthcare Monitoring and Control*. DOI: doi:10.1109/WIRELESSVITAE.2011.5940920

Zhe, Y., Qihao, Z., Lei, L., Kan Z., & Wei, X. (2016). *An IOT-Cloud based wearable ECG monitoring system for smart healthcare*. DOI: doi:10.1007/S10916-016-0644-9

Compilation of References

10 Mizuno, H., Kosaka, M., Yajima, H., & Komoda, N. (1998). Application of neural network to technical analysis of stock market prediction. *Studies in Informatics and Control*, *7*(3), 111–120.

11 Moghaddam, A. H., Moghaddam, M. H., & Esfandyari, M. (2016). Stock market index prediction using artificial neural network. *Journal of Economics, Finance and Administrative Science*, *21*(41), 89–93. doi:10.1016/j.jefas.2016.07.002

12 Rather, A. M., Agarwal, A., & Sastry, V. N. (2015). Recurrent neural network and a hybrid model for prediction of stock returns. *Expert Systems with Applications*, *42*(6), 3234–3241. doi:10.1016/j.eswa.2014.12.003

13 Zhang, G., Patuwo, B. E., & Hu, M. Y. (1998). Forecasting with artificial neural networks: The state of the art. *International Journal of Forecasting*, *14*(1), 35–62. doi:10.1016/S0169-2070(97)00044-7

14 Wang, J. Z., Wang, J. J., Zhang, Z. G., & Guo, S. P. (2011). Forecasting stock indices with back propagation neural network. *Expert Systems with Applications*, *38*(11), 14346–14355. doi:10.1016/j.eswa.2011.04.222

15 Sen, J. (2018). *Stock Price Prediction Using Machine Learning and Deep Learning Frameworks.* . doi:10.13140/RG.2.2.35704.49923

16 Glorot, X., Bordes, A., & Bengio, Y. (2011, June). Deep sparse rectifier neural networks. In *Proceedings of the Fourteenth International Conference on Artificial Intelligence and Statistics* (pp. 315-323). Academic Press.

17 Vatsal, H. S. (2007). *Machine learning techniques for stock prediction.* www.vatsals.com

1 Hamzaebi, C., Akay, D., & Kutay, F. (2009). Comparison of direct and iterative artificial neural network forecast approaches in multi-periodic time series forecasting. *Expert Systems with Applications*, *36*(2), 3839–3844. doi:10.1016/j.eswa.2008.02.042

2 Zhang, G. P. (2003). Time series forecasting using a hybrid ARIMA and neural network model. *Neurocomputing*, *50*, 159–175. doi:10.1016/S0925-2312(01)00702-0

3 Menon, V. K., Vasireddy, N. C., Jami, S. A., Pedamallu, V. T. N., Sureshkumar, V., & Soman, K. P. (2016, June). Bulk Price Forecasting Using Spark over NSE Data Set. *International Conference on Data Mining and Big Data*, 137-146. 10.1007/978-3-319-40973-3_13

4 Heaton, J. B., Polson, N. G., & Witte, J. H. (2017). Deep learning for finance: Deep portfolios. *Applied Stochastic Models in Business and Industry*, *33*(1), 3–12. doi:10.1002/asmb.2209

5 Selvin, S., Vinayakumar, R., Gopalakrishnan, E. A., Menon, V. K., & Soman, K. P. (2017). Stock price prediction using LSTM, RNN and CNN-sliding window model. *International Conference on Advances in Computing, Communications and Informatics*, 1643-1647. 10.1109/ICACCI.2017.8126078

6 Rout, A. K., Dash, P. K., Dash, R., & Bisoi, R. (2015). Forecasting financial time series using a low complexity recurrent neural network and evolutionary learning approach. *Journal of King Saud University-Computer and Information Sciences, 29*(4), 536–552. doi:10.1016/j.jksuci.2015.06.002

7 Yetis, Y., Kaplan, H., & Jamshidi, M. (2014). Stock market prediction by using artificial neural network. *World Automation Congress (WAC)*, 718-722. 10.1109/WAC.2014.6936118

8Roman, J., & Jameel, A. (1996). Backpropagation and recurrent neural networks in financial analysis of multiple stock market returns. *Twenty-Ninth Hawaii International Conference on System Sciences, 2*, 454-460.

9Jia, H. (2016). *Investigation into the effectiveness of long short term memory networks for stock price prediction.* arXiv preprint arXiv:1603.07893

A. Mohamed, D. Yu, L. Deng (2010). Investigation of full-sequence training of deep belief networks for speech recognition. *Proc. Interspeech'10.*

Abbasi, A., Fu, T., Zeng, D., & Adjeroh, D. (2013). Crawling credible online medical sentiments for social intelligence. *Proceedings – SocialCom/PASSAT/Bigdata/EconCom/BioMedCom2013*, 254–263. . doi:10.1109/SocialCom.2013.43

Abdel-rahman, M., Sainath, T. N., Dahl, G., Ramabhadran, B., Hinton, G. E., & Picheny, M. A. (2011). Deep Belief Networks Using Discriminative Features for Phone Recognition. *Proc. ICASSP 2011.*

AbdurRazzaque, Palade, & Clarke. (2016). Middleware for Internet of Things: A Survey. *IEEE Internet of Things Journal, 3*(1).

Abellera, R., & Bulusu, L. (2018). *Oracle Business Intelligence with Machine Learning: Artificial Intelligence Techniques in OBIEE for Actionable BI.* Apress. doi:10.1007/978-1-4842-3255-2

Abouelnaga, Y. (2016). *San Francisco Crime Classification.* Retrieved from https://arxiv.org/abs/1607.03626

Adedoyin-Olowe, Gaber, & Stahl. (2014). A Survey of Data Mining Techniques for Social Network Analysis. *J. Data Min. Digit. Humanit.*

Aggarwal, C. (Ed.). (2015, April). Social Network Data Analytics. *International Journal of Information Management, 35*(2), 137–144.

Agreste, S., De Meo, P., Ferrara, E., Piccolo, S., & Provetti, A. (2015). De, Ferrara, Piccolo, Provetti, (2015), Trust networks: Topology, dynamics, and measurements. *IEEE Internet Computing, 19*(6), 26–35. doi:10.1109/MIC.2015.93

Al-Bashiri, H., Abdulgabber, M. A., Awanis, R., & Norazuwa, S. (2018). A Developed Collaborative Filtering Similarity Method to Improve the Accuracy of Recommendations under Data Sparsity. *International Journal of Advanced Computer Science and Applications, 9*(4), 135–142. doi:10.14569/IJACSA.2018.090423

Alelyani, S., Tang, J., & Liu, H. (2013). Feature selection for clustering: a review. In Data clustering: algorithms and applications. Chapman & Hall/CRC.

Al-Garadi, M. A., Mohamed, A., Al-Ali, A., Du, X., & Guizani, M. (2018, August 12). *A survey of machine and deep learning methods for internet of things (IoT) security.* Retrieved from arXiv.orgLogin Search... Help I Advanced Search: https://arxiv.org/

Alhajj, R., & Rokne, J. (Eds.). (2014). *Encyclopedia of Social Network Analysis and Mining.* Springer New York. doi:10.1007/978-1-4614-6170-8

Ali, Dong, Dhau, Khosla, & Kaushik. (2020). Perspective—Electrochemical Sensors for Soil Quality Assessment. *Journal of The Electrochemical Society.*

Allen, C. (2011, October 19). *LinkedIn Classmates: Explore possibilities by connecting with fellow alumni*. Retrieved from https://blog.linkedin.com/2011/10/19/linkedin-classmates

Allen, C. (2013a, January 30). *Start mapping your career with LinkedIn alumni*. Retrieved from https://blog.linkedin.com/2013/01/30/start-mapping-your-career-with-linkedin-alumni

Allen, C. (2013b, August 19). *Introducing LinkedIn university pages*. Retrieved from https://blog.linkedin.com/2013/08/19/introducing-linkedin-university-pages

Al, N., Bryce, J., Franqueira, V. N. L., Marrington, A., & Read, J. C. (2019). Behavioural Digital Forensics Model : Embedding Behavioural Evidence Analysis into the Investigation of Digital Crimes. *Digital Investigation*, *28*, 70–82. doi:10.1016/j.diin.2018.12.003

Al-Qurishi, M., Al-Rakhami, M., Alrubaian, M., Alarifi, A., Rahman, S. M. M., & Alamri, A. (2015). Selecting the best open source tools for collecting and visualizing social media content. *2015 2nd world symposium on web applications and networking (WSWAN)*, 1–6. 10.1109/WSWAN.2015.7210346

Alsubaiee, S., Carey, M. J., & Li, C. (2015). LSM-Based storage and indexing: an old idea with timely benefits. In *Second international ACM workshop on managing and mining enriched geo-spatial data*. New York, NY: ACM. .278600710.1145/2786006

Alsudais, K., & Corso, A. (2015). GIS, big data, and a tweet corpus operationalized via natural language processing. *AMCIS 2015 Proceedings*.

Alvarez-Rodríguez, J. M., & Colomo-Palacios, R. (2014). Assessing professional skills in a multi-scale environment by means of graph-based algorithms. In *Proceedings of the 2014 European Network Intelligence Conference (ENIC)*, *IEEE* (pp. 106-113). 10.1109/ENIC.2014.12

Anabo, I. F., & Albizuri, I. E. (2017). Linkedin as a tool for higher education programme evaluation. *Revista de Educación a Distancia*, *1*(53), 1–17.

Anami, B. S., Nandyal, S. S., & Govardhan, A. (2010). A combined color, texture and edge features based approach for identification and classification of Indian medicinal plants. *International Journal of Computers and Applications*, *6*(12), 45–51. doi:10.5120/1122-1471

Anami, B. S., Nandyal, S. S., & Govardhan, A. (2012). Color and Edge Histograms Based Medicinal Plants' Image Retrieval. International Journal of Image, Graphics &. *Signal Processing*, *4*(8).

Ananthi, C., Periasamy, A., & Muruganand, S. (2014). Pattern recognition of medicinal leaves using image processing techniques. *Journal of Nanoscience and Nanotechnology*, *2*(2), 214–218.

Anderson, K. M., Aydin, A. A., Barrenechea, M., Cardenas, A., Hakeem, M., & Jambi, S. (2015). Design Challenges/Solutions for environments supporting the analysis of social media data in crisis informatics research. *Proceedings of the annual Hawaii in- ternational conference on system sciences*, 163–172. .2015.2910.1109/HICSS

Anitha, Suresh, Gnaneswar, & Puneeth. (2019). IoT Based Automatic Soil Moisture Monitoring System using Raspberry PI. *International Journal of Innovative Technology and Exploring Engineering*, *9*(2).

Anwar, T., & Uma, V. (2019a). CD-SPM: Cross-domain book recommendation using sequential pattern mining and rule mining. *Journal of King Saud University-Computer and Information Sciences*.

Anwar, T., & Uma, V. (2019, March). MRec-CRM: Movie Recommendation based on Collaborative Filtering and Rule Mining Approach. In *2019 International Conference on Smart Structures and Systems (ICSSS)* (pp. 1-5). IEEE. 10.1109/ICSSS.2019.8882864

Anwar, T., & Uma, V. (2019b). *A Review of Recommender System and Related Dimensions Data, Engineering and Applications*. Springer.

Anwar, T., & Uma, V. (2020). A Study and Analysis of Issues and Attacks Related to Recommender System. In *Convergence of ICT and Smart Devices for Emerging Applications* (pp. 137–157). Springer. doi:10.1007/978-3-030-41368-2_7

Aral, S., Dellarocas, C., & Godes, D. (2013). Introduction to the special Issue—Social media and business transformation: A framework for research. *Information Systems Research*, 24(1), 3–13. doi:10.1287/isre.1120.0470

Arora, N., Rastogi, R., Chaturvedi, D. K., Satya, S., Gupta, M., Yadav, V., Chauhan, S., & Sharma, P. (2019). Chronic TTH Analysis by EMG & GSR Biofeedback on Various Modes and Various Medical Symptoms Using IoT. In Big Data Analytics for Intelligent Healthcare Management. doi:10.1016/B978-0-12-818146-1.00005-2

Arora, N., Trivedi, P., Chauhan, S., Rastogi, R., & Chaturvedi, D. K. (2017). Framework for Use of Machine Intelligence on Clinical Psychology to study the effects of Spiritual tools on Human Behavior and Psychic Challenges. *Proceedings of NSC-2017*.

Artikis, A., Etzion, O., Feldman, Z., & Fournier, F. (2012). Event processing under un- certainty. *Proceedings of the 6th ACM international conference on distributed event-based systems (DEBS '12)*, 32–43. 10.1145/2335484.2335488

Arun, C. H., Emmanuel, W. S., & Durairaj, D. C. (2013). Texture feature extraction for identification of medicinal plants and comparison of different classifiers. *International Journal of Computers and Applications*, 62(12), 1–9. doi:10.5120/10129-4920

Ashok, K. (2018). Big Data in Agriculture: A Challenge for the Future. *Applied Economic Perspectives and Policy*, 40(1), 79–96. doi:10.1093/aepp/ppx056

Austin. (2013). Using methods from the data- mining and machine-learning literature for disease classification and prediction: a case study examining classification of heart failure subtypes. *Journal of Clinical Epidemiology, 66*, 398-407.

Baars, H., & Kemper, H.-G. (2008). Management support with structured and un- structured data – An integrated business intelligence framework. *Information Systems Management*, 25(2), 132–148. doi:10.1080/10580530801941058

Badsha, S., Yi, X., Khalil, I., & Bertino, E. (2017). *Privacy preserving user-based recommender system*. Paper presented at the 2017 IEEE 37th International Conference on Distributed Computing Systems (ICDCS).

Bag, S., Ghadge, A., & Tiwari, M. K. (2019). An integrated recommender system for improved accuracy and aggregate diversity. *Computers & Industrial Engineering*, 130, 187–197. doi:10.1016/j.cie.2019.02.028

Bakshy, E., Rosenn, I., Marlow, C., & Adamic, L. (2012). The role of social networks in information diffusion. In *Proceedings of the 21st International Conference on World Wide Web, ACM* (pp. 519-528). 10.1145/2187836.2187907

Baltrusaitis, T., Ahuja, C., & Morency, L.-P. (2018). Multimodal machine learning: A survey and taxonomy. *IEEE Transactions on Pattern Analysis and Machine Intelligence*, 1–1. PMID:29994351

Bansal, I., Rastogi, R., Chaturvedi, D. K., Satya, S., Arora, N., & Yadav, V. (2018). Intelligent Analysis for Detection of Complex Human Personality by Clinical Reliable Psychological Surveys on Various Indicators. *The National Conference on 3rd MDNCPDR-2018 at DEI*.

Barmpatsalou, K., Cruz, T., & Member, S. (2018). Mobile Forensic Data Analysis : Suspicious Pattern Detection in Mobile Evidence. *IEEE Access: Practical Innovations, Open Solutions*, 6, 59705–59727. doi:10.1109/ACCESS.2018.2875068

Bashir, S., Qamar, U., Khan, F. H., & Naseem, L. (2016). HMV: A Medical Decision Support Framework Using Multi-Layer Classifiers For Disease Prediction. *Journal of Computational Science*, 13, 10–25. doi:10.1016/j.jocs.2016.01.001

Basnet & Bang. (n.d.). The State-of-the-Art of Knowledge-Intensive Agriculture: A Review on Applied Sensing Systems and Data Analytics. *Journal of Sensors*.

Begue, A., Kowlessur, V., Mahomoodally, F., Singh, U., & Pudaruth, S. (2017). Automatic recognition of medicinal plants using machine learning techniques. *International Journal of Advanced Computer Science and Applications, 8*(4), 166–175. doi:10.14569/IJACSA.2017.080424

Beier, M., & Wagner, K. (2016). Social media adoption: barriers to the strategic use of social media in SMEs. *Proceedings of the European conference on information systems.*

Bem, D. J. (1995). Writing a review article for Psychological Bulletin. *Psychological Bulletin, 118*(2), 172–177. doi:10.1037/0033-2909.118.2.172

Bendler, J., Ratku, A., & Neumann, D. (2014). Crime mapping through geo-spatial social media activity. *Proceedings of the international conference on information systems.*

Bent, D., Hughes, D. W., Provine, R. C., Rastall, R., Kilmer, A., Hiley, D., Szendrei, J., Payne, T. B., Bent, M., & Chew, G. (2001). *Notation. In Grove Music Online.* Oxford University Press.

Berger, G. (2016, April 12). *Will this year's college grads job-hop more than previous grads?* Retrieved from https://blog.linkedin.com/2016/04/12/will-this-year_s-college-grads-job-hop-more-than-previous-grads

Bersin, J. (2016). *Predictions for 2016: A bold new world of talent, learning, leadership, and HR technology ahead.* Deloitte Consulting LLP.

Bhattacharya, P., Phan, T., & Airoldi, E. (2015). *Investigating the impact of network effects on content generation: Evidence from a large online student network.* Academic Press.

Bi, G., Zheng, B., & Liu, H. (2014). Secondary crisis communication on social media: The role of corporate response and social influence in product-harm crisis. *PACIS 2014 Proceedings.*

Bindra, G. S., Kandwal, K. K., Singh, P. K., & Khanna, S. (2012). Tracing information flow and analyzing the effects of incomplete data in social media. *2012 Fourth international conference on computational intelligence, communication systems and networks,* 235–240. 10.1109/CICSyN.2012.51

Blegind, T., & Dyrby, S. (2013). Exploring affordance of facebook as a social media platform in political campaigning. *Proceedings of the European conference on information systems.*

Blei, D. M., Ng, A. Y., & Jordan, M. I. (2003). Latent dirichlet allocation. *Journal of Machine Learning Research, 3,* 993–1022. . 993. doi:10.1162/jmlr.2003.3.4-5

Bonchi, F., Castillo, C., Gionis, A., & Jaimes, A. (2011). Social Network Analysis and Mining for Business Applications. ACM Trans. Intell. Syst. Technol. Artic., 2(22). doi:10.1145/1961189.1961194

Bonnici, R. (2018, September 11). *Why I Encourage My Best Employees to Consider Outside Job Offers.* Retrieved from https://hbr.org/2018/09/why-i-encourage-my-best-employees-to-consider-outside-job-offers

Bose, I., & Mahapatra, R. K. (2001). Business data mining—A machine learning perspective. *Information & Management, 39*(3), 211–225. doi:10.1016/S0378-7206(01)00091-X

Bose, L., & Cocke, J. (2003). Visualizing Boolean Construction of Decision Supporting System for Monitoring Function in Sports Training. *Proceedings of PODC.*

Bou Nassif, A., Shahin, I., Attili, I., & Azzeh, M. (2019). Speech Recognition Using Deep Neural Networks: A Systematic Review. *IEEE Access: Practical Innovations, Open Solutions, 7,* 19143–19165. doi:10.1109/ACCESS.2019.2896880

Bowcott, O. (2015). UK-US surveillance regime was unlawful 'for seven years'. *The Guardian*. Available: http://www. theguardian.com/uk- news/2015/feb/06/gchq-mass-internet-surveillance-unlawful-court-nsa

Bowcott, O. (2015). UK-US surveillance regime was unlawful 'for seven years'. *The Guardian*. Available: https://www. theguardian.com/uk-news/2015/feb/06/gchq-mass-internetsurveillance-unlawful-court-nsa

boyd, d., & Crawford, K. (2012). Critical questions for big data: Provocations for a cultural, technological, and scholarly phenomenon. *Information Communication and Society, 15*(5), 662–679. doi:10.1080/1369118X.2012.678878

Bradbury, D. (2011). Data mining with Linkedin. *Computer Fraud & Security, 10*, 5–8.

Britz, M. T. (n.d.). Computer Forensics and Cyber Crime (3rd ed.). Academic Press.

Bronson & Knezevic. (2016). Big Data in food and agriculture. *Big Data & Society*, (January-June). Advance online publication. doi:10.1177/2053951716648174

Brownlee, J. (2016). *Linear Regression for Machine Learning*. Retrieved 8 21, 2019, from machinelearningmastery.com: https://machinelearningmastery.com/linear-regression-for-machine-learning/

Bruns, A. (2013). Faster than the speed of print: Reconciling 'data' social media analysis and academic scholarship. *First Monday, 18*(10), s1. .v18i10.4879 doi:10.5210/fm

Burke, R., Mobasher, B., Williams, C., & Bhaumik, R. (2006). Classification features for attack detection in collaborative recommender systems. *Proceedings of the 12th ACM SIGKDD international conference on Knowledge discovery and data mining*. 10.1145/1150402.1150465

Caers, R., & Castelyns, V. (2011). Linkedin and Facebook in Belgium: The influences and biases of social network sites in recruitment and selection procedures. *Social Science Computer Review, 29*(4), 437–448. doi:10.1177/0894439310386567

Cagliero & Fiori. (2013). *TweCoM: Topic and Context Mining from Twitter*. Springer.

Caldeira, D. C., Correia, R. C., Spadon, G., Eler, D. M., Olivete-Jr, C., & Garcia, R. E. (2017). Data mining on Linkedin data to define professional profile via MineraSkill methodology. In *Proceedings of the 2017 12th Iberian Conference on Information Systems and Technologies (CISTI), IEEE* (pp. 1-6). 10.23919/CISTI.2017.7975730

Cambria, E., & Hussain, A. (2015). *Introduction. In Sentic Computing*. Springer International Publishing. doi:10.1007/978-3-319-23654-4

Cao, G., Wang, S., Hwang, M., Padmanabhan, A., Zhang, Z., & Soltani, K. (2015). A scalable framework for spatio-temporal analysis of location-based social media data. *Computers, Environment and Urban Systems, 51*, 70–82. .compenvurbsys.2015.01.002 doi:10.1016/j

Cao, J., Basoglu, K. A., Sheng, H., & Lowry, P. B. (2015). A systematic review of social networks research in information systems: Building a foundation for exciting future research. *Communications of the Association for Information Systems, 36*(January), 727–758. doi:10.17705/1CAIS.03637

Carcillo, F., Borgne, Y. Le, Caelen, O., & Kessaci, Y. (2019). Combining unsupervised and supervised learning in credit card fraud detection. *Information Sciences*. doi:10.1016/j.ins.2019.05.042

Carcillo, F., Dal, A., Borgne, Y. Le, Caelen, O., Mazzer, Y., & Bontempi, G. (2018). *SCARFF : A scalable framework for streaming credit card fraud detection with spark*. doi:10.1016/j.inffus.2017.09.005

Carr, J., Decreton, L., Qin, W., Rojas, B., Rossochacki, T., & Yang, Y. (2015). Social media in product development. *Food Quality and Preference, 40*(Part B), 354–364. . doi:10.1016/j.foodqual.2014.04.001

Case, T., Gardiner, A., Rutner, P., & Dyer, J. (2013). A Linkedin analysis of career paths of information systems alumni. *Journal of the Southern Association for Information Systems*, *1*(1), 1–13. doi:10.3998/jsais.11880084.0001.102

Catlett, C., Cesario, E., Talia, D., & Vinci, A. (2019). Spatio-temporal crime predictions in smart cities : A data-driven approach and experiments. *Pervasive and Mobile Computing*, *53*, 62–74. doi:10.1016/j.pmcj.2019.01.003

Cetintas, S., Rogati, M., Si, L., & Fang, Y. (2011). Identifying similar people in professional social networks with discriminative probabilistic models. In *Proceedings of the 34th International ACM SIGIR Conference on Research and Development in Information Retrieval* (pp. 1209-1210). 10.1145/2009916.2010123

Chainapaporn, P., & Netisopakul, P. (2012, July). Thai herb information extraction from multiple websites. In Knowledge and Smart Technology (KST) (pp. 16-23). IEEE. doi:10.1109/KST.2012.6287734

Chan, C.-L. (2008). Investigation of Diabetic Microvascular Complication using Data Mining Techniques. *International Joint Conference on Neural Networks (IJCNN 2008)*.

Chandamona, P. (2016). Improved analysis of data mining techniques on medical data. *Int. J. Nano Corr Sci and Eng.*, *3*(3), 85–90.

Chandrashekar, H. M. (2010). Changing, scenario of organic farming in India: An overview. *International NGO Journal*, *5*, 34–39.

Chang, Wu, Aiello, Barrat, Schifanella, Cattuto, Markines, Menczer, Blum, Ligett, Roth, Dwork, Kisilevich, Rokach, Elovici, Shapira, Li, Chen, Li, Zhang, Lin, Machanavajjhala, Kifer, Gehrke, Venkitasubramaniam, Samarati, Sweeney, & Sweeney. (n.d.). A New View of Privacy in Social Networks. In *Handbook of Research on Modern Cryptographic Solutions for Computer and Cyber Security*. IGI Global.

Chaturvedi, D. K., Rastogi, R., Arora, N., Trivedi, P., & Mishra, V. (2017). Swarm Intelligent Optimized Method of Development of Noble Life in the perspective of Indian Scientific Philosophy and Psychology. *Proceedings of NSC-2017*.

Chaturvedi, D.K., Rastogi, R., Satya, S., Arora, N., Saini, H., Verma, H., Mehlyan, K., & Varshney, Y. (2018). Statistical Analysis of EMG and GSR Therapy on Visual Mode and SF-36 Scores for Chronic TTH. *Proceedings of UPCON-2018*.

Chaudhary, Gupta, Gupta, Chandra, Selvakumar, Fire, Goldschmidt, Elovici, Gupta, Gupta, Gangwar, Kumar, Meena, Gupta, Gupta, Gupta, & Sharma. (n.d.). Auditing Defense against XSS Worms in Online Social Network- Based Web Applications. In *Handbook of Research on Modern Cryptographic Solutions for Computer and Cyber Security*. IGI Global.

Chaudhary, P., Gupta, S., Gupta, B. B., Chandra, V. S., Selvakumar, S., Fire, M., Goldschmidt, R., Elovici, Y., Gupta, B. B., Gupta, S., & Gangwar, S.(2016). Auditing defence against XSS worms in online social network-based web applications. In Handbook of Research on Modern Cryptographic Solutions for Computer and Cyber Security. IGI Global.

Chauhan, S., Rastogi, R., Chaturvedi, D. K., Satya, S., Arora, N., Yadav, V., & Sharma, P. (2018). Analytical Comparison of Efficacy for Electromyography and Galvanic Skin Resistance Biofeedback on Audio-Visual Mode for Chronic TTH on Various Attributes. In Proceedings of the ICCIDA-2018. Springer.

Chen, C. (2019, April 11). *Introducing LinkedIn reactions: More ways to express yourself*. Retrieved from https://blog.linkedin.com/2019/april-/11/introducing-linkedin-reactions-more-ways-to-express-yourself

Chen. (2016). An efficient hybrid kernel extreme learning machine approach for early diagnosis of Parkinson's disease. *Neurocomputing*, *184*, 131–144.

Cheng, S.-S., Wang, H.-M., & Fu, H.-C. (2004). A Model-Selection-based Self Splitting Gaussian Mixture Learning with Application to Speaker Identification. *EURASIP Journal on Applied Signal Processing*, *17*, 2626–2639.

Cheng, Y., Xie, Y., Chen, Z., Agrawal, A., Choudhary, A., & Guo, S. (2013). Jobminer: A real-time system for mining job-related patterns from social media. In *Proceedings of the 19th ACM SIGKDD International Conference on Knowledge Discovery and Data Mining* (pp. 1450-1453). 10.1145/2487575.2487704

Chen, H., Chiang, R. H., & Storey, V. C. (2012). Business Intelligence and Analytics: From Big Data to Big Impact. *Management Information Systems Quarterly*, *36*(4), 1165–1188. doi:10.2307/41703503

Chen, X. C., & Jin, H. (2016). Top-k followee recommendation over microblogging systems by exploiting diverse information sources. *Future Generation Computer Systems*, *55*, 534–543. doi:10.1016/j.future.2014.05.002

Cho. (2008). Nonlinear Support Vector Machine Visualization for Risk Factor Analysis Using Nomograms and Localized Radial Basis Function Kernels. *IEEE Transactions on Information Technology in Biomedicine*, *12*(2).

Christopher. (2015). A Swarm Optimization approach for clinical knowledge mining. *Computer Methods and Programs in Biomedicine*, *121*, 137–148.

Clark, J. (2016). Google Sprints Ahead in AI Building Blocks, Leaving Rivals Wary. *Bloomberg*. Available: https://www.bloomberg.com/news/articles/2016-07-21/google-sprints-ahead-in-ai-building-blocks-leaving-rivals-wary

Coble, K., Griffin, T. W., Ahearn, M., Ferrell, S., McFadden, J., Sonka, S., & Fulton, J. (2016). *Advancing U.S. Agricultural Competitiveness with Big Data and Agricultural Economic Market Information, Analysis, and Research (No. 249847)*. Council on Food, Agricultural, and Resource Economics.

Colomo-Palacios, R., Tovar-Caro, E., García-Crespo, Á., & Gómez-Berbís, J. M. (2010). Identifying technical competences of it professionals: The case of software engineers. *International Journal of Human Capital and Information Technology Professionals*, *1*(1), 31–43. doi:10.4018/jhcitp.2010091103

Comput, J. P. D., Kozik, R., Choraś, M., Ficco, M., & Palmieri, F. (2018). A scalable distributed machine learning approach for attack detection in edge computing environments. *Journal of Parallel and Distributed Computing*, *119*, 18–26. doi:10.1016/j.jpdc.2018.03.006

Constantinov, C., Iordache, L., Georgescu, A., Popescu, P.-Ş., & Mocanu, M. (2018). Performing social data analysis with neo4j: Workforce trends & corporate information leakage. In *Proceeding of the 2018 22nd International Conference on System Theory, Control and Computing (ICSTCC), IEEE* (pp. 403-406). 10.1109/ICSTCC.2018.8540645

Constantinov, C., Mocanu, M., Bărbulescu, N., Popescu, E., & Mocanu, A. (2017). Movierate: Considerations on applying a custom social reputation engine for movie reviews. In *Proceedings of the 18th International Carpathian Control Conference (ICCC), IEEE* (pp. 183-188). 10.1109/CarpathianCC.2017.7970394

Constantinov, C., Popescu, P. Ş., Poteraş, C. M., & Mocanu, M. L. (2015). Preliminary results of a curriculum adjuster based on professional network analysis. In *Proceedings of the 2015 19th International Conference on System Theory, Control, and Computing (ICSTCC), IEEE* (pp. 860-865). 10.1109/ICSTCC.2015.7321402

Dahl, G. E., Ranzato, M., Mohamed, A., & Hinton, G. E. (2010). Phone Recognition with the mean-covariance restricted Boltzmann machine. *Advances in Neural Information Processing Systems*, *23*, 469–477.

Damian, D., Bartosz, J., & Wlodek, J. K. (2017). IOT-Based Information System For Healthcare Application: Design Methodology Approach. *Applied Sciences (Basel, Switzerland)*, *2017*(7), 596. doi:10.3390/app7060596

Dasgupta, D., & Dasgupta, R. (2009). *Social networks using Web 2.0*. IBM Corporation.

Das, P., & Das, A. K. (2019). Knowledge-Based Systems Graph-based clustering of extracted paraphrases for labelling crime. *Knowledge-Based Systems*, *179*, 55–76. doi:10.1016/j.knosys.2019.05.004

Dataflair. (2018). *What is Dimensionality Reduction – Techniques, Methods, Components*. Retrieved 07 12, 2020, from Dimensionality Reduction Tutorials: https://data-flair.training/blogs/dimensionality-reduction-tutorial

Dataset for SF-36. (n.d.). https://www.kaggle.com/janiferroborts/sf-36-dataset

David & Jon. (2010). *Networks, Crowds, and Markets: Reasoning About a Highly Connected World*. Academic Press.

Davis, E., & Marcus, G. (2015, August). Commonsense reasoning and commonsense knowledge in artificial intelligence. *Communications of the ACM, 58*(9), 92–103. doi:10.1145/2701413

Dean, J. (2014). *Big Data, Data Mining, and Machine Learning: Value Creation for Business Leaders and practitioners*. John Wiley & Sons. doi:10.1002/9781118691786

Deerwester, S., Dumais, S. T., Furnas, G. W., Landauer, T. K., & Harshman, R. (1990). Deerwester, Dumais, Landauer, Furnas & Harshman.(1990).,Indexing by latent semantic analysis. *JASIS, 41*(6), 391–407. doi:10.1002/(SICI)1097-4571(199009)41:6<391::AID-ASI1>3.0.CO;2-9

Dewani & Yonah. (2017). A novel holistic disease prediction tool using best fit data mining techniques. *Int. J. Com. Dig. Sys., 6*(2).

Diaby, M., & Viennet, E. (2014). Taxonomy-based job recommender systems on Facebook and Linkedin profiles. In *Proceedings of the 2014 IEEE Eighth International Conference on Research Challenges in Information Science (RCIS)* (pp. 1-6). 10.1109/RCIS.2014.6861048

Diaby, M., Viennet, E., & Launay, T. (2013). Toward the next generation of recruitment tools: an online social network-based job recommender system. In *Proceedings of the 2013 IEEE/ACM International Conference on Advances in Social Networks Analysis and Mining, ACM* (pp. 821-828). 10.1145/2492517.2500266

Diciolla, M., Binetti, G., Di Noia, T., Pesce, F., Schena, F. P., Vågane, A. M., Bjørneklett, R., Suzuki, H., Tomino, Y., & Naso, D. (2015). Patient classification and outcome prediction in IgA nephropathy. *Computers in Biology and Medicine, 66*, 278–286. doi:10.1016/j.compbiomed.2015.09.003 PMID:26453758

Diebold, F. X. (2012). *A Personal Perspective on the Origin(s) and Development of "Big Data": The Phenomenon, the Term, and the Discipline, Second Version*. University of Pennsylvania, Penn Institute for Economic Research, Working PaperNo.13-003.

Dogantekin, E., Dogantekin, A., Avci, D., & Avci, L. (2010). An intelligent diagnosis system for diabetes on Linear Discriminant Analysis and Adaptive Network Based Fuzzy Inference System: LDA-ANFIS. *Digital Signal Processing, 20*(4), 1248–1255. doi:10.1016/j.dsp.2009.10.021

Dunn, J. (2016, May 9). *Introducing FBLearner Flow: Facebook's AI backbone*. Retrieved from https://code.facebook.com/posts/1072626246134461/introducing-fblearner-flow-facebook-s-ai-backbone

Dutta, M., & Husain, Z. (2009). *Munich Personal RePEc Archive Determinants of crime rates : Crime Deterrence and Growth*. Academic Press.

Dwi, N., Cahyani, W., Hidayah, N., Rahman, A., Glisson, W. B., & Choo, K. R. (2016). The Role of Mobile Forensics in Terrorism Investigations Involving the Use of Cloud Storage Service and Communication Apps. *Mobile Networks and Applications*. Advance online publication. doi:10.100711036-016-0791-8

Dyer, J. (2016). *The Data Farm: An Investigation of the Implications of Collecting Data on the Farm*. Nuffield Australia Project No 1506.

E-Agricultural Concepts for Improving Productivity: A Review proposed by Narmilan A. (2017). *Scholars Journal of Engineering and Technology, 5*(1), 1-17.

Easley, D., & Kleinberg, J. (2010). *Networks, crowds, and markets: Reasoning about a highly connected world.* Cambridge University Press. doi:10.1017/CBO9780511761942

Elshawi, R., Sakr, S., Talia, D., & Trunfio, P. (2018). Big Data Systems Meet Machine Learning Challenges: Towards Big Data Science as a Service. *Big Data Research,* (14), 1-11.

EMC Education Services. (2015). *Data science & big data analytics: discovering, analyzing, visualizing and presenting data.* Wiley.

EY. (2014). *Big data-Changing the way businesses compete and operate.* Author.

Fafchamps & Minten. (2012). Impact of SMS-Based Agricultural Information on Indian Farmers. Oxford Journals, 26(3), 383–414.

Fan, J., Han, F., & Liu, H. (2014). Challenges of Big Data Analysis. *National Science Review, 1*(2), 293–314. doi:10.1093/nsr/nwt032 PMID:25419469

Fayez, H.A. (2018). The Application of the Internet of Things in Healthcare. *IJCA.*

Fire, M., Tenenboim-Chekina, L., Puzis, R., Lesser, O., Rokach, L., & Elovici, Y. (2013, December). Computationally efficient link prediction in a variety of social networks. *ACM Transactions on Intelligent Systems and Technology, 5*(1), 1–25. doi:10.1145/2542182.2542192

Frommholz, I., Martin, H. M., Zinnar, P., Mitul, G., & Emma, S. (2016). *On Textual Analysis and Machine Learning for Cyberstalking Detection.* doi:10.100713222-016-0221-x

Gandomi, A., & Haider, M. (2015). Beyond the hype: Big data concepts, methods, and analytics. *International Journal of Information Management, 35*(2), 137–144. doi:10.1016/j.ijinfomgt.2014.10.007

Ganji, M. F., & Abadeh, M. S. (2011). A fuzzy classification system based on Ant Colony Optimization for diabetes disease diagnosis. *Expert Systems with Applications, 38*(12), 14650–14659. doi:10.1016/j.eswa.2011.05.018

Garg, P., Rani, R., & Miglani, S. (2015). Mining professional's data from Linkedin. In *Proceedings of the 2015 Fifth International Conference on Advances in Computing and Communications (ICACC), IEEE* (pp. 98-101). 10.1109/ICACC.2015.35

Garnett, T., Appleby, M. C., Balmford, A., Bateman, I. J., Benton, T. G., Bloomer, P., Burlingame, B., Dawkins, M., Dolan, L., Fraser, D., Herrero, M., Hoffmann, I., Smith, P., Thornton, P. K., Toulmin, C., Vermeulen, S. J., & Godfray, H. C. J. (2013). Sustainable intensification in agriculture: Premises and policies. *Science, 341*(6141), 33–34. doi:10.1126cience.1234485 PMID:23828927

Gaston, K. J., & O'Neill, M. A. (2004). Automated species identification: Why not? *Philosophical Transactions of the Royal Society of London. Series B, Biological Sciences, 359*(1444), 655–667. doi:10.1098/rstb.2003.1442 PMID:15253351

Gbenga, E., Stephen, J., Chiroma, H., Olusola, A., & Emmanuel, O. (2019). *Heliyon Machine learning for email spam filtering : review, approaches and open research problems.* doi:10.1016/j.heliyon.2019.e01802

Georga. (2013). Multivariate Prediction of Subcutaneous Glucose Concentration in Type 1 Diabetes Patients Based on Support Vector Regression. *IEEE Journal of Biomedical and Health Informatics, 17*(1).

Georga, E. I. (2015). Online Prediction of Glucose Concentration in Type 1 Diabetes Using Extreme Learning Machines. *International Conference,* 3262-3265. 10.1109/EMBC.2015.7319088

Ghasemaghaei, M., Ebrahimi, S., & Hassanein, K. (2018). Data analytics competency for improving firm decision making performance. *The Journal of Strategic Information Systems*, *27*(1), 101–113. doi:10.1016/j.jsis.2017.10.001

Ghazinour, Matwin, & Sokolova. (2016). Yourprivacyprotector, A recommender system for privacy settings in social networks. *Int. J. Secur. Priv. Trust Manag.*, *2*(4).

Ghiassi, M., & Lee, S. (2018). A domain transferable lexicon set for Twitter sentiment analysis using a supervised machine learning approach. *Expert Systems with Applications*, *106*, 197–216. doi:10.1016/j.eswa.2018.04.006

Goëau, H., Bonnet, P., Joly, A., Bakić, V., Barbe, J., Yahiaoui, I., ... Molino, J. F. (2013, October). Pl@ntnet mobile app. In *Proceedings of the 21st ACM international conference on Multimedia* (pp. 423-424). ACM. 10.1145/2502081.2502251

Gonçalves, G. R., Ferreira, A. A., de Assis, G. T., & Tavares, A. I. (2014). Gathering alumni information from a web social network. In *Proceedings of the Web Congress (LA-WEB), 2014 9th Latin American, IEEE* (pp. 100-108). 10.1109/LAWeb.2014.17

Gopal, A., Reddy, S. P., & Gayatri, V. (2012, December). Classification of selected medicinal plants leaf using image processing. In *2012 International Conference on Machine Vision and Image Processing (MVIP)* (pp. 5-8). IEEE. 10.1109/MVIP.2012.6428747

Gorla, N., & Lam, Y. W. (2004). Who should work with whom? Building effective software project teams. *Communications of the ACM*, *47*(6), 79–82. doi:10.1145/990680.990684

Grispos, G., Storer, T., & Bradley, W. (2011). A comparison of forensic evidence recovery techniques for a windows mobile smart phone. *Digital Investigation*, *8*(1), 23–36. doi:10.1016/j.diin.2011.05.016

Gudivada, V. N. (2017). Data Analytics: Fundamentals. In M. Chowdhury, A. Apon, & K. Dey (Eds.), Data Analytics for Intelligent Transportation Systems (pp. 33-45). Elsevier.

Guo, Y. (2012). Using Bayes Network for Prediction of Type-2 Diabetes. *The 7th International Conference for Internet Technology and Secured Transactions (ICITST-2012)*.

Gupta, M., Rastogi, R., Chaturvedi, D. K., Satya, S., Verma, H., Singhal, P., & Singh, A. (2019). Comparative Study of Trends Observed During Different Medications by Subjects under EMG & GSR Biofeedback. *ICSMSIC-2019*, 748-756. https://www.ijitee.org/download/volume-8-issue-6S/

Guzman, E., Azócar, D., & Li, Y. (2014). Sentiment analysis of commit comments in github: An empirical study. In *Proceedings of the 11th Working Conference on Mining Software Repositories, ACM* (pp. 352-355). 10.1145/2597073.2597118

Hall, P., Marron, J. S., & Neeman, A. (2005). Geometric representation of high dimension, low sample size data. *Journal of the Royal Statistical Society. Series B, Statistical Methodology*, *67*(3), 427–444. doi:10.1111/j.1467-9868.2005.00510.x

Hanneman & Riddle. (2005). *Introduction to Social Network Methods*. Academic Press.

Hanneman, R. A., & Riddle, M. (2005). *Introduction to Social Network Methods*. Academic Press.

Hansen, D., Shneiderman, B., & Smith, M. A. (2010). *Analyzing Social Media Networks with NodeXL: Insights from a Connected World*. Morgan Kaufmann.

Haralick, R. M., & Shapiro, L. G. (1992). *Computer and robot vision* (Vol. 1). Addison-wesley.

Hastie, T., Tibshirani, R., & Friedman, J. (2016). *The Elements of Statistical Learning Data Mining, Inference, and Prediction*. Springer.

Ha-Thuc, V., Xu, Y., Kanduri, S. P., Wu, X., Dialani, V., & Yan, Y., ... Sinha, S. (2016). Search by ideal candidates: Next generation of talent search at Linkedin. In *Proceedings of the 25th International Conference Companion on World Wide Web, International World Wide Web Conferences Steering Committee* (pp. 195-198). 10.1145/2872518.2890549

Ha-Thuc, V., Venkataraman, G., Rodriguez, M., Sinha, S., Sundaram, S., & Guo, L. (2015). Personalized expertise search at linkedin. In *Proceedings of the 2015 IEEE International Conference on Big Data (Big Data)* (pp. 1238-1247). 10.1109/BigData.2015.7363878

Haykin, S. (2009). *Neural Networks and Learning Machines* (3rd ed.). Prentice Hall.

He & Chu. (2010). *A Social Network-Based Recommender System.* SNRS.

Hesketh, T., & Zhu, W. X. (1997). Health in China: traditional Chinese medicine: one country, two systems. *BMJ (Clinical Research Ed.), 315*(7100), 115–117. doi:10.1136/bmj.315.7100.115 PMID:9240055

Hinton, G. E., Osindero, S., & Teh, Y. W. (2006). A fast learning algorithm for deep belief nets. *Neural Computation, 18*(7), 1527–1554. doi:10.1162/neco.2006.18.7.1527 PMID:16764513

Hodgson, E. (2020). *K-Means Clustering And Why It's Good For Business.* Retrieved 07 12, 2020, from dotactiv.com: https://www.dotactiv.com/blog/why-k-means-clustering-is-good-for-business

Holsapple, C., Lee-Post, A., & Pakath, R. (2014). A unified foundation for business analytics. *Decision Support Systems, 64*, 130–141. doi:10.1016/j.dss.2014.05.013

Hsu, C.-C., Lee, Y.-C., Lu, P.-E., Lu, S.-S., Lai, H.-T., Huang, C.-C., ... Su, W.-T. (2017). Social Media Prediction Based on Residual Learning and Random Forest. *Proceedings of the 2017 ACM on Multimedia Conference - MM '17.* doi:10.1145/3123266.3127894

Hu, X., Tang, L., Tang, J., & Liu, H. (2013). Exploiting social relations for sentiment analysis in microblogging. *Proceedings of the sixth ACM international conference on Web search and data mining - WSDM '13*, 537. 10.1145/2433396.2433465

Hwang, W., Kim, T., Ramanathan, M., & Zhang, A. (2008). Bridging centrality: Graph mining from element level to group level. In *Proceedings of the 14th ACM SIGKDD International Conference on Knowledge Discovery and Data Mining, ACM* (pp. 336-344). 10.1145/1401890.1401934

Ibrahim, Sabri, & Mangshor. (2018). Leaf Recognition using Texture Features for Herbal Plant Identification. *Indonesian Journal of Electrical Engineering and Computer Science, 9*(1).

Introducing workplace by Facebook. (2016, October 10). Retrieved from https://newsroom.fb.com/news/2016/10/introducing-workplace-by-facebook

Iyan, M., Yeni, H., & Hartono, W. S. (2013). *The Identification of Medicinal Plants based on Fractal using Fuzzy C-Means Clustering.* Central Library of Bogor Agricultural University. https://repository.ipb.ac.id/handle/123456789/57517

Janani, R., & Gopal, A. (2013, September). Identification of selected medicinal plant leaves using image features and ANN. In *2013 international conference on advanced electronic systems (ICAES)* (pp. 238-242). IEEE.

Jansen, S. (2018). *Hands-On Machine Learning for Algorithmic Trading: Design and implement investment strategies based on smart algorithms that learn from data using Python.* Packt Publishing.

Javier, L., Villalba, G., Lucila, A., Orozco, S., Rosales, J., & Hernandez-castro, J. (2017). A PRNU-based counter-forensic method to manipulate smartphone image source identification techniques. *Future Generation Computer Systems, 76*, 418–427. doi:10.1016/j.future.2016.11.007

Jha, V. (2017). *Random Forest – Supervised classification machine learning algorithm.* Retrieved 8 24, 2019, from https://www.techleer.com: https://www.techleer.com/articles/107-random-forest-supervised-classification-machine-learning-algorithm/

Jiang, L., Cheng, Y., Yang, L., Li, J., Yan, H., & Wang, X. (2019). A trust-based collaborative filtering algorithm for E-commerce recommendation system. *Journal of Ambient Intelligence and Humanized Computing, 10*(8), 3023–3034. doi:10.100712652-018-0928-7

Jiang, S., Rho, S., Chen, B.-W., Du, X., & Zhao, D. (2015, June). Face hallucination and recognition in social network services. *The Journal of Supercomputing, 71*(6), 2035–2049. doi:10.100711227-014-1257-z

Jones, G. M., Geoferla, L. A., & Winster, S. G. (2020). *A Heuristic Research on Detecting Suspicious Malware Pattern in Mobile Environment.* Academic Press.

Jones, G. M., & Winster, S. G. (2017). Forensics Analysis On Smart Phones Using Mobile Forensics Tools. *International Journal of Computational Intelligence Research, 13*(8), 1859–1869.

Joshi, P. (2017). *Artificial intelligence with python.* Packt Publishing Ltd.

Jothi, N. (2015). Data mining in healthcare. *Procedia Computer Science, 72,* 306–313. doi:10.1016/j.procs.2015.12.145

Juozenaite, I. (2018). *Application of machine learning techniques for solving real world business problems: the case study-target marketing of insurance policies (Project Work presented as partial requirement for obtaining the Master's degree in Information Management).* Academic Press.

Jurgovsky, J., Granitzer, M., Ziegler, K., Calabretto, S., Portier, P., He-guelton, L., & Caelen, O. (2018). Sequence classification for credit-card fraud detection. *Expert Systems with Applications, 100,* 234–245. doi:10.1016/j.eswa.2018.01.037

Jurka, T. (2018, March 29). *A Look Behind the AI that Powers LinkedIn's Feed: Sifting through Billions of Conversations to Create Personalized News Feeds for Hundreds of Millions of Members.* Retrieved from https://engineering.linkedin.com/blog/2018/03/a-look-behind-the-ai-that-powers-linkedins-feed--sifting-through

K. K., D., & Vinod, S. (2018). Crime analysis in India using data mining techniques. *International Journal of Engineering & Technology, 7*(2.6), 253. doi:10.14419/ijet.v7i2.6.10779

Kadir, A., Nugroho, L. E., Susanto, A., & Santosa, P. I. (2013). *Leaf classification using shape, color, and texture features.* arXiv preprint arXiv:1401.4447

Kahramanli, H., & Allahverdi, N. (2008). Design of a hybrid system for the diabetes and heart diseases. *Expert Systems with Applications, 35*(1-2), 82–89. doi:10.1016/j.eswa.2007.06.004

Kaisler, S., Armour, F., Espinosa, J. A., & Money, W. (2013). Big Data: Issues and Challenges Moving Forward. *2013 46th Hawaii International Conference on System Sciences,* 995–1004. 10.1109/HICSS.2013.645

Kalyoncu, C., & Toygar, Ö. (2015). Geometric leaf classification. *Computer Vision and Image Understanding, 133,* 102–109. doi:10.1016/j.cviu.2014.11.001

Kamil, M. (2016, June 3). *Introducing Premium Insights: Keeping you in the know on companies you care about.* Retrieved from https://blog.linkedin.com/2016/06/02/introducing-premium-insights-keeping-you-in-the-know

Kan, H. X., Jin, L., & Zhou, F. L. (2017). Classification of medicinal plant leaf image based on multi-feature extraction. *Pattern Recognition and Image Analysis, 27*(3), 581–587. doi:10.1134/S105466181703018X

Karie, N. M., Kebande, V. R., & Venter, H. S. (2019). Forensic Science International : Synergy Diverging deep learning cognitive computing techniques into cyber forensics. *Forensic Science International: Synergy, 1*, 61–67. doi:10.1016/j.fsisyn.2019.03.006 PMID:32411955

Karthikeyan, P., Selvi, S. T., Neeraja, G., Deepika, R., Vincent, A., & Abinaya, V. (2017). *Prevention of shilling attack in recommender systems using discrete wavelet transform and support vector machine.* Paper presented at the 2016 Eighth International Conference on Advanced Computing (ICoAC). 10.1109/ICoAC.2017.7951753

Karunamoorthi, K., Jegajeevanram, K., Vijayalakshmi, J., & Mengistie, E. (2013). Traditional Medicinal Plants: A Source of Phytotherapeutic Modality in Resource-Constrained Health Care Settings. *Journal of Evidence-Based Complementary & Alternative Medicine, 18*(1), 67–74. doi:10.1177/2156587212460241

Katzir, Z., & Elovici, Y. (2018). *Quantifying the resilience of machine learning classifiers used for cyber security.* doi:10.1016/j.eswa.2017.09.053

Kaushik, R., Apoorva Chandra, S., Mallya, D., Chaitanya, J. N. V. K., & Kamath, S. S. (2016). *Sociopedia: An Interactive System for Event Detection and Trend Analysis for Twitter Data.* Springer India.

Kellengere Shankarnarayan, V., & Ramakrishna, H. (2020, September). Paradigm change in Indian agricultural practices using Big Data: Challenges and opportunities from field to plate. *Information Processing in Agriculture, 7*(3), 355–368. Advance online publication. doi:10.1016/j.inpa.2020.01.001

Khalid, O., Khan, M. U. S., Khan, S. U., & Zomaya, A. Y. (2014). OmniSuggest: A Ubiquitous Cloud-Based Context-Aware Recommendation System for Mobile Social Networks. *IEEE Transactions on Services Computing, 7*(3), 401–414. doi:10.1109/TSC.2013.53

Kikuchi, H., Yoshiuchi, K., Yamamoto, Y., Komaki, G., & Akabayashi, A. (2012). Diurnal variation of tension-type headache intensity and exacerbation: An investigation using computerized ecological momentary assessment. *Biopsychosoc Med, 6*(18). doi: . doi:10.1186/1751-0759-6-18.Page-11,12

Kiran, D. & Mina, M. (2018). Internet of Things for Healthcare: A Review. *International Journal of Advanced in Management, Technology and Engineering Sciences.*

Kolaczyk, E. D., & Csárdi, G. (2014). *Statistical Analysis of Network Data with R.* Springer. doi:10.1007/978-1-4939-0983-4

Kolog, E. A., Montero, C. S., & Toivonen, T. (2018). Using Machine Learning for Sentiment and Social Influence Analysis in Text. *Advances in Intelligent Systems and Computing*, 453–463. doi:10.1007/978-3-319-73450-7_43

Kossinets, G. & Watts. (2006). Empirical analysis of an evolving social network. *Science, 311*(5757), 88–90.

Kossinets, G., & Watts, D. J. (2006). Empirical Analysis of an Evolving Social Network. Science, 311(5757), 88–90. doi:10.1126cience.1116869

Kotsiantis, S. B., Zaharakis, I., & Pintelas, P. (2007). Supervised machine learning: A review of classification techniques. *Emerging Artificial Intelligence Applications in Computer Engineering*, 3-24.

Kramer, S. B., Reganold, J. P., Glover, J. D., Bohannan, B. J. M., & Mooney, H. A. (2006). Reduced Nitrate Leaching and Enhanced Denitrifier Activity and Efficiency in Organically Fertilised Soils. *Proceedings of the National Academy of Sciences of the United States of America, 103*(12), 4522–4527. doi:10.1073/pnas.0600359103 PMID:16537377

Kumar, A. (2018). *Naive Bayesian Model.* Retrieved 8 24, 2019, from www.acadgild.com: https://acadgild.com/blog/naive-bayesian-model

Kumar, N. (2019, May 9). *Advantages and Disadvantages of Linear Regression in Machine Learning*. Retrieved July 9, 2020, from The Professionals Point: http://theprofessionalspoint.blogspot.com/2019/05/advantages-and-disadvantages-of-linear.html

Kumar, Pandey, & Rana. (2008). Production and Marketing of Potato in Banaskanthao District of Gujarat. *Indian Journal of Agriculture Marketing, 22*(1).

Kumar, E. S., & Talasila, V. (2014, April). Leaf features based approach for automated identification of medicinal plants. In *2014 International Conference on Communication and Signal Processing* (pp. 210-214). IEEE. 10.1109/ICCSP.2014.6949830

Kumar, N., Belhumeur, P. N., Biswas, A., Jacobs, D. W., Kress, W. J., Lopez, I. C., & Soares, J. V. (2012, October). Leafsnap: A computer vision system for automatic plant species identification. In *European Conference on Computer Vision* (pp. 502-516). Springer. 10.1007/978-3-642-33709-3_36

Kumar, P., Kumar, V., & Thakur, R. S. (2019). A new approach for rating prediction system using collaborative filtering. *Iran Journal of Computer Science, 2*(2), 81–87.

Kumar, P., & Thakur, R. S. (2018). Recommendation system techniques and related issues: A survey. *International Journal of Information Technology, 10*(4), 495–501.

Kumar, P., & Thakur, R. S. (2020). Liver disorder detection using variable-neighbor weighted fuzzy K nearest neighbor approach. *Multimedia Tools and Applications*, •••, 1–21.

Kumar, R. (2017). *Machine Learning and Cognition in Enterprises: Business Intelligence Transformed*. Apress. doi:10.1007/978-1-4842-3069-5

Kurka, Godoy, & Von Zuben. (2015). *Online Social Network Analysis: A Survey of Research Applications in Computer Science*. Academic Press.

Kyoung, J. K. (2003). Financial time series forecasting using support vector machines. *Neurocomputing, 55*(1-2), 307–319. doi:10.1016/S0925-2312(03)00372-2

Lakshmiprabha, K. E., & Govindaraju, C. (2019). Hydroponic-based smart irrigation system using Internet of Things. *International Journal of Communication Systems*, e4071. doi:10.1002/dac.4071

Lal, D., & Singh, N. (2010). Mass multiplication of Celastrus paniculatus Willd: An important medicinal plant under in vitro conditions via nodal segments. *International Journal of Biodeversity and Conservation, 2*(6), 140–145.

Lan, Y., Chen, S., & Bradley, K. F. (2017). Current status and future trends of precision agricultural aviation technologies. *International Journal of Agricultural and Biological Engineering, 10*(3), 1–17.

Lavanya & Srinivasan. (2018). A survey on agriculture and greenhouse monitoring using IoT and WSN. *International Journal of Engineering & Technology, 7*(2.33), 673-677.

Lee & Kim. (2016). Identification of Type 2 Diabetes Risk Factors Using Phenotypes Consisting of Anthropometry and Triglycerides based on Machine Learning. *IEEE Journal of Biomedical and Health Informatics, 20*(1).

Lee, K. F., & Hon, H. W. (1989). Speaker-independent phone recognition using hidden Markov models. *IEEE Transactions on Audio, Speech, and Language Processing, 37*(11), 1641–1648.

Le, H.-S., Oparin, I., Allauzen, A., Gauvain, J.-L., & Yvon, F. (2013). Structured Output Layer Neural Network Language Models for Speech Recognition. *IEEE Transactions on Audio, Speech, and Language Processing, 21*(1), 195–204.

Levien, R. (2009). Attack-resistant trust metrics. In *Computing with Social Trust* (pp. 121–132). Springer. doi:10.1007/978-1-84800-356-9_5

Li, C., Ma, X., Jiang, B., Li, X., Zhang, X., Liu, X., . . . Zhu, Z. (2017). *Deep speaker: an end-to-end neural speaker embedding system.* arXiv preprint arXiv:1705.02304

Li, H., Xu, X., Liu, C., Ren, T., & Wu, K. (n.d.). *A Machine Learning Approach To Prevent Malicious Calls Over Telephony Networks.* Academic Press.

Li, D., Chen, C., Lv, Q., Shang, L., Zhao, Y., Lu, T., & Gu, N. (2016). An algorithm for efficient privacy-preserving item-based collaborative filtering. *Future Generation Computer Systems, 55,* 311–320. doi:10.1016/j.future.2014.11.003

Liew, S. W., Fazlida, N., Sani, M., Abdullah, M. T., Yaakob, R., & Sharum, M. Y. (2019). An effective security alert mechanism for real-time phishing tweet detection on Twitter. *Computers & Security, 83,* 201–207. doi:10.1016/j.cose.2019.02.004

Li, H., Ma, B., & Lee, C.-H. (2007). A Vector Space Modeling Approach to Spoken Language Identification. *IEEE Transactions on Audio, Speech, and Language Processing, 15*(1), 271–284. doi:10.1109/TASL.2006.876860

Li, L., Zheng, G., Peltsverger, S., & Zhang, C. (2016). Career trajectory analysis of information technology alumni: A Linkedin perspective. In *Proceedings of the 17th Annual Conference on Information Technology Education, ACM* (pp. 2-6). 10.1145/2978192.2978221

List of best 25 mobile apps used for mental and physical health. (n.d.). https://www.psycom.net/25-best-mental-health-apps

Little, R. J., & Rubin, D. B. (2002). *Statistical analysis with missing data.* John Wiley & Sons. doi:10.1002/9781119013563

Liu, L., Vernica, R., Hassan, T., & Damera Venkata, N. (2019). Using text mining for personalization and recommendation for an enriched hybrid learning experience. *Computational Intelligence, 35*(2), 336–370. doi:10.1111/coin.12201

Li, Y. M., & Li, T. Y. (2013). Deriving market intelligence from microblogs. *Decision Support Systems, 55*(1), 206–217. doi:10.1016/j.dss.2013.01.023

Logesh, R., & Subramaniyaswamy, V. (2019). *Exploring hybrid recommender systems for personalized travel applications. In Cognitive informatics and soft computing.* Springer.

Lops, P., De Gemmis, M., Semeraro, G., Narducci, F., & Musto, C. (2011). Leveraging the Linkedin social network data for extracting content-based user profiles. In *Proceedings of the fifth ACM Conference on Recommender Systems* (pp. 293-296). 10.1145/2043932.2043986

Mackay. (2013). Information and the transformation of sociology: Interactivity and social media monitoring. *Commun. Capital Critique (London), 11*(1), 117–126.

Magid, L. (2013, May 1). *What is snapchat and why do kids love it and parents fear it? (Updated).* Retrieved from https://www.forbes.com/sites/larrymagid/2013/05/01/what-is-snapchat-and-why-do-kids-love-it-and-parents-fear-it

Mahdikhanlou, K., & Ebrahimnezhad, H. (2014, May). Plant leaf classification using centroid distance and axis of least inertia method. In *2014 22nd Iranian conference on electrical engineering (ICEE)* (pp. 1690-1694). IEEE. 10.1109/IranianCEE.2014.6999810

Mainetti, L., Patrono, L., & Stefanizzi, M. L. (2016). An Internet of sport architecture based on emerging enabling technologies. *Computer and Energy Science (SpliTech) International Multidisciplinary Conference on,* 1-6. 10.1109/SpliTech.2016.7555928

Malik, F. (2018). *Machine Learning Algorithms Comparison*. Retrieved 7 12, 2020, from FinTechExplained: https://medium.com/fintechexplained/machine-learning-algorithm-comparison-f14ce372b855

Manfred, B. (2007). Current Developments and Future Chllenges of Coordination in Pervasive Environments. *16th IEEE International workshops on Enabling Technologies: Infrastructure for Collaborative Enterprises, 51 – 55*, doi:10.1109/WIRELESSVITAE.2011.5940920

Manojkumar, P., Surya, C. M., & Varun, P. Gopi. (2017). Identification of Ayurvedic Medicinal Plants by Image Processing of Leaf Samples. *Third International Conference on Research in Computational Intelligence and Communication Networks (ICRCICN).*

Maria Jones, G., Godfrey Winster, S., & Santhosh Kumar, S. V. N. (2019). *Analysis of mobile environment for ensuring cyber-security in IoT-based digital forensics* (Vol. 900). Advances in Intelligent Systems and Computing. doi:10.1007/978-981-13-3600-3_14

Mariappan & Zhou. (n.d.). A Threat of Farmers' Suicide and the Opportunity in Organic Farming for Sustainable Agricultural Development in India. *Sustainability 2019*. doi:10.3390u11082400

Mårtensson, P., & Bild, M. (2016). *Teaching and learning at business schools: Transforming business education*. Taylor & Francis. doi:10.4324/9781315611907

McCrae, R. R., & Costa, P. T. Jr. (1989). Reinterpreting the Myers-Briggs type indicator from the perspective of the five-factor model of personality. *Journal of Personality, 57*(1), 17–40. doi:10.1111/j.1467-6494.1989.tb00759.x PMID:2709300

McCranie. (2015). *Dyads and Triads, Reciprocity and Transitivity. In Interuniversity Consortium for Political and Social Research (ICPSR)*. University of Michigan.

Meenakshi & Singh. (2008). Post Harvest Losses in Fruits and vegetables in Himachal Pradesh. *Indian Journal of Agriculture Marketing, 22*(1).

Méndez, J. R., Cotos-yañez, T. R., & Ruano-ordás, D. (2019). A new semantic-based feature selection method for spam filtering. *Applied Soft Computing, 76*, 89–104. doi:10.1016/j.asoc.2018.12.008

Meredith, S. (2018, April 10). *Facebook-Cambridge Analytica: A timeline of the data hijacking scandal*. Retrieved from https://www.cnbc.com/2018/04/10/facebook-cambridge-analytica-a-timeline-of-the-data-hijacking-scandal.html

Miller, M. (2016, August 17). *To get a job, use your weak ties*. Retrieved from https://www.forbes.com/sites/nextavenue/2016/08/17/to-get-a-job-use-your-weak-ties

Mishra, B. B., & Nayak, K. C. (2004). Organic farming for sustainable agriculture. *Orissa Review, 10*, 42–45.

Mo & Li. (2015). Research of Big Data Based on the Views of Technology and Application. *Am. J. Ind. Bus. Manag., 5*(4), 192–197.

Mohamed, A., Dahl, G. E., & Hinton, G. E. (2009). Deep belief networks for phone recognition. *NIPS Workshop on Deep Learning for Speech Recognition and Related Applications.*

Mohamed, A., Dahl, G. E., & Hinton, G. E. (2012). Acoustic Modeling Using Deep Belief Networks. *Transactions on Audio, Speech, and Language Processing, 20*(1), 14–22. doi:10.1109/TASL.2011.2109382

Mohammed, M., Badruddin, M., & Mohammed, B. (2017). *Machine learning: algorithms and applications*. CRC.

Mohapatra, H. P., & Rath, S. P. (2005). *In vitro studies of Bacopa monnieri—an important medicinal plant with reference to its biochemical variations*. Academic Press.

Mohler, G. (2014). Marked point process hotspot maps for homicide and gun crime prediction in Chicago. *International Journal of Forecasting, 30*(3), 491–497. doi:10.1016/j.ijforecast.2014.01.004

Mondal, S., & Bours, P. (2018). Journal of Information Security and Applications A continuous combination of security & forensics for mobile devices. *Journal of Information Security and Applications, 40*, 63–77. doi:10.1016/j.jisa.2018.03.001

Morphy, E. (2018). *What Is a Neural Network and How Are Businesses Using Them?* Retrieved 8 24, 2019, from CMSWire: https://www.cmswire.com/digital-experience/what-is-a-neural-network-and-how-are-businesses-using-it/

Mo, Z., & Li, Y. (2015). Research of big data based on the views of technology and application. *Am. J. Ind. Bus. Management., 05*(04), 192–197. doi:10.4236/ajibm.2015.54021

Muller, A. C., & Guido, S. (2017). *Introduction to machine learning with Python: a guide for data scientists.* O'Reilly Media.

Mustapha, F. A. (2017). Monitoring of Pesticide Residues in Commonly Used Fruits and Vegetables in Kuwait. *International Journal of Environmental Research and Public Health, 2017*(14), 833. doi:10.3390/ijerph14080833

Nami, S., & Shajari, M. (2018). Cost-sensitive payment card fraud detection based on dynamic random forest and k-nearest neighbors. *Expert Systems with Applications, 110*, 381–392. doi:10.1016/j.eswa.2018.06.011

Namisiko, P., & Aballo, M. (2013). Current Status of e-Agriculture and Global Trends: A Survey Conducted in TransNzoia County, Kenya. *International Journal of Scientific Research (Ahmedabad, India), 2*(7).

Nandwani, D. (Ed.). (2016). *Organic Farming for Sustainable Agriculture.* Springer. doi:10.1007/978-3-319-26803-3

Narula, G. (2019, May 19). *Machine Learning Algorithms for Business Applications – Complete Guide.* Retrieved July 7, 2020, from https://emerj.com/: https://emerj.com/ai-sector-overviews/machine-learning-algorithms-for-business-applications-complete-guide/

Newman, J., & Cox, S. (2012). Language Identification Using Visual Features. *IEEE Transactions on Audio, Speech, and Language Processing, 20*(7), 1936–1947. doi:10.1109/TASL.2012.2191956

Newman, M. E. J. (2003). The structure and function of complex networks. *SIAM Review, 45*(2), 167–256. doi:10.1137/S003614450342480

Nguyen, G., Minh, B., Tran, D., & Hluchy, L. (2018). Data & Knowledge Engineering A heuristics approach to mine behavioural data logs in mobile malware detection system. *Data & Knowledge Engineering, 115*(January), 129–151. doi:10.1016/j.datak.2018.03.002

Nithiyanandhan, K., & Reddy, T. B. (2017). Analysis of the Medicinal Leaves by using Image Processing Techniques and ANN. *International Journal of Advanced Research in Computer Science, 8*(5).

NMPB & FRLHT. (n.d.). http://www.medicinalplants.in/aboutfrlhtdb

Oakley, P. (2014, July 13). *Turn off LinkedIn Broadcasts when you change your profile and other automatic updates.* Retrieved from https://www.linkedin.com/pulse/20140713162507-3188984-turn-off-linkedin-broadcasts-when-you-change-your-profile-and-other-automatic-updates/

Oliveira, T. H. M., Painho, M., Santos, V., Sian, O., & Barriguinha, A. (2014). Development of an agricultural management information system based on open-source solutions. *Procedia Technology, 16*, 342–354. doi:10.1016/j.protcy.2014.10.100

Onuwa, Eneji, Itodo, & Sha'Ato. (2017). Determination of Pesticide Residues in Edible Crops and Soil from University of Agriculture Makurdi Farm Nigeria Department of Chemistry. *Asian Journal of Physical and Chemical Sciences, 3*(3), 1-17.

Papadopoulos, S., Troncy, R., Mezaris, V., Huet, B., & Kompatsiaris, I. (2011). Social Event Detection at MediaEval 2011: Challenges, Dataset and Evaluation. *MediaEval 2011 Workshop.*

Patwardhan, B., Warude, D., Pushpangadan, P., & Bhatt, N. (2005). Ayurveda and traditional Chinese medicine: A comparative overview. *Evidence-Based Complementary and Alternative Medicine, 2*(4), 465–473. doi:10.1093/ecam/neh140 PMID:16322803

Pavate & Ansari. (2015). Risk Prediction of Disease Complications in Type 2 Diabetes Patients Using Soft Computing Techniques. *Fifth International Conference on Advances in Computing and Communications.*

Pentland. (2016). *Reinventing society in the wake of big data.* Available: https://www.edge.org/conversation/alex_sandy_pentland-reinventing-society-in-the-wake-of-big-data

Perez, S. (2019, January 30). *It's time to pay serious attention to TikTok.* Retrieved from https://techcrunch.com/2019/01/29/its-time-to-pay-serious-attention-to-tiktok

Peri, C., & Ho, B. (2011). *Sams teach yourself the Twitter API in 24 hours.* Pearson Education.

Polat, K., Güneş, S., & Arslan, A. (2008). A cascade learning system for classification of diabetes disease: Generalized Discriminant Analysis and Least Square Support Vector Machine. *Expert Systems with Applications, 34*(1), 482–487. doi:10.1016/j.eswa.2006.09.012

Poria, S., Cambria, E., Howard, N., Huang, G.-B., & Hussain, A. (2016). Fusing audio, visual and textual clues for sentiment analysis from multimodal content. *Neurocomputing, 174*, 50–59. doi:10.1016/j.neucom.2015.01.095

Pradhan & Mohapa. (2015). E-agriculture: A Golden Opportunity for Indian Farmers. *An International Journal Research and Development, A Management Review, 4*(1).

Prasad, B. R., & Agarwal, S. (2016). Comparative study of big data computing and storage tools: A review. *International Journal of Database Theory and Application, 9*(1), 45–66. doi:10.14257/ijdta.2016.9.1.05

Prom-on, S., & Ranong, S. N. (2016). DOM: A big data analytics framework for mining Thai public opinions. In R. Buyya (Ed.), Big Data: Principles and Paradigms. Morgan Kaufmann.

Prom-on, S., Ranong, S. N., Jenviriyakul, P., Wongkaew, T., Saetiew, N., & Achalakul, T. (2016). *DOM: A big data analytics framework for mining Thai public opinions.* In R. Buyya (Ed.), *Big Data: Principles and Paradigms* (pp. 339–355). Morgan Kaufmann.

Pundkar, S.V. (2014). *Study of Various Techniques for Medicinal Plant Identification.* Academic Press.

Pushpa, B. R., Anand, C., & Nambiar, P. M. (2016). Ayurvedic plant species recognition using statistical parameters on leaf images. *International Journal of Applied Engineering Research, 11*(7), 5142–5147.

PyCharm. (n.d.). https://en.wikipedia.org/wiki/PyCharm

Qazi, N., & William, W. B. L. (2019). *An interactive human centered data science approach towards crime pattern analysis.* doi:10.1016/j.ipm.2019.102066

Rahman, M. N., Esmailpour, A., & Zhao, J. (2016). Machine learning with big data an efficient electricity generation forecasting system. *Big Data Research*, 9-15.

Rahmani, M. E., Amine, A., & Hamou, R. M. (2016). Supervised Machine Learning for Plants Identification Based on Images of Their Leaves. *International Journal of Agricultural and Environmental Information Systems, 7*(4), 17–31. doi:10.4018/IJAEIS.2016100102

Rastogi, R., Chaturvedi, D. K., Satya, S., Arora, N., & Chauhan, S. (2018). An Optimized Biofeedback Therapy for Chronic TTH between Electromyography and Galvanic Skin Resistance Biofeedback on Audio, Visual and Audio Visual Modes on Various Medical Symptoms. *National Conference on 3rd MDNCPDR-2018 at DEI.*

Rastogi, R., Chaturvedi, D. K., Satya, S., Arora, N., Singhal, P., & Gulati, M. (2018). Statistical Resultant Analysis of Spiritual & Psychosomatic Stress Survey on Various Human Personality Indicators. *The International Conference Proceedings of ICCI 2018.* 10.1007/978-981-13-8222-2_25

Rastogi, R., Chaturvedi, D. K., Satya, S., Arora, N., Yadav, V., Chauhan, S., & Sharma, P. (2018). SF-36 Scores Analysis for EMG and GSR Therapy on Audio, Visual and Audio Visual Modes for Chronic TTH. Proceedings of the ICCIDA-2018.

Rastogi, R., Chaturvedi, D. K., Satya, S., Arora, N., Sirohi, H., Singh, M., Verma, P., & Singh, V. (2018). *Which One is Best: Electromyography Biofeedback Efficacy Analysis on Audio, Visual and Audio-Visual Modes for Chronic TTH on Different Characteristics. In Proceedings of ICCIIoT- 2018, 14-15 December 2018 at NIT Agartala.* Elsevier. https://ssrn.com/abstract=3354375

Rau. (2016). Development of a web-based liver cancer prediction model for type II diabetes patients by using an artificial neural network. *Computer Methods and Programs in Biomedicine, 125,* 58–65.

Ricci, F., Rokach, L., & Shapira, B. (2015). *Recommender systems: introduction and challenges. In Recommender systems handbook.* Springer. doi:10.1007/978-1-4899-7637-6

Richthammer, C., Weber, M., & Pernul, G. (2017). Reputation-enhanced recommender systems. In *Proceedings of the IFIP International Conference on Trust Management,* (pp. 163-179). Springer.

Roberson. (2008). *Nature's Pharmacy, Our Treasure Chest: Why We Must Conserve Our Natural Heritage. A Native Plant Conservation Campaign Report.* Academic Press.

Rodriguez, S. (2017, August 14). *U.S. judge says LinkedIn cannot block startup from public profile data.* Retrieved from https://www.reuters.com/article/us-microsoft-linkedin-ruling-idUSKCN1AU2BV

Rosenbaum, E. (2019, April 3). *IBM artificial intelligence can predict with 95% accuracy which workers are about to quit their jobs.* https://www.cnbc.com/2019/04/03/ibm-ai-can-predict-with-95-percent-accuracy-which-employees-will-quit.html

Roslansky, R. (2014, February 19). *The definitive professional publishing platform.* Retrieved from https://blog.linkedin.com/2014/02/19/the-definitive-professional-publishing-platform

Roslansky, R. (2016, September 22). *Introducing LinkedIn Learning, a better way to develop skills and talent.* Retrieved from https://learning.linkedin.com/blog/whats-new/launching-linkedin-learning

Roy, P., & Das, P. K. (2011). Language Identification of Indian Languages Based on Gaussian Mixture Models. *International Journal on Wisdom Based Computing, 1*(3), 54–59.

Ryman-tubb, N. F., Krause, P., & Garn, W. (2018). Engineering Applications of Artificial Intelligence How Artificial Intelligence and machine learning research impacts payment card fraud detection : A survey and industry benchmark. *Engineering Applications of Artificial Intelligence, 76*(November), 130–157. doi:10.1016/j.engappai.2018.07.008

Sabarinaand & Priya. (2015). Lowering data dimensionality in big data for the benefit of precision agriculture. *International Conference on Intelligent Computing, Communication & Convergence.*

Saeid, M., Rezvan, M., & Barekatain, M. (2018). Machine learning for internet of things data analysis : A survey. *Digital Communications and Networks, 4*(3), 161–175. doi:10.1016/j.dcan.2017.10.002

Saez-Trumper, D., Comarela, G., Almeida, V., Baeza-Yates, R., & Benevenuto, F. (2012). Finding trendsetters in information networks. *Proceedings of the 18th ACM SIGKDD international conference on Knowledge discovery and data mining - KDD '12*, 1014. 10.1145/2339530.2339691

Sai Jayaram, A. K. V., Ramasubramanian, V., & Sreenivas, T. V. (2003). Language identification using parallel sub-word recognition. *IEEE Int. Conf. on Acoustics, Speech, and Signal Proc, 1*, 32-37.

Saini, H., Rastogi, R., Chaturvedi, D. K., Satya, S., Arora, N., Gupta, M., & Verma, H. (2019). An Optimized Biofeedback EMG and GSR Biofeedback Therapy for Chronic TTH on SF-36 Scores of Different MMBD Modes on Various Medical Symptoms. In Hybrid Machine Intelligence for Medical Image Analysis. Springer Nature Singapore Pte Ltd. doi:10.1007/978-981-13-8930-6_8

Saini, H., Rastogi, R., Chaturvedi, D. K., Satya, S., Arora, N., Verma, H., & Mehlyan, K. (2018). *Comparative Efficacy Analysis of Electromyography and Galvanic Skin Resistance Biofeedback on Audio Mode for Chronic TTH on Various Indicators. In Proceedings of ICCIIoT- 018*. Elsevier. https://ssrn.com/abstract=3354371

Salgueiro, J. R., & Kivshar, Y. S. (2016). Optimization of Biased PT-Symmetric Plasmonic Directional Couplers. *Selected Topics in Quantum Electronics IEEE Journal of, 22*(5), 60–66. doi:10.1109/JSTQE.2016.2555283

Samir, Zanjala, & Talmaleb. (2016). Medicine Reminder and Monitoring System for Secure Health Using IOT, ICISP2015. *Procedia Computer Science*, 471–476. doi:10.1016/j.procs.2016.02.090

Sana & Jaya. (2015). Ayurvedic Herb Detection Using Image Processing. *International Journal of Computer Science and Information Technology Research, 3*(4).

Santhi, S., & Raja Sekar, J. (2013). An Automatic Language Identification Using Audio Features. *International Journal of Emerging Technology and Advanced Engineering, 3*(1), 358–364.

Santos, A. C. S. G., Menezes, T. P., & Hora, H. R. M. (2014). Análise do perfil de aluno e egresso de cursos técnicos por meio de data mining: Estudo de caso no Instituto Federal Fluminense. *Tear: Revista de Educação. Ciência e Tecnologia, 3*(1), 1–24. doi:10.35819/tear.v3.n1.a1828

Sathwik, T., Yasaswini, R., Venkatesh, R., & Gopal, A. (2013, July). Classification of selected medicinal plant leaves using texture analysis. In *2013 Fourth International Conference on Computing, Communications and Networking Technologies (ICCCNT)* (pp. 1-6). IEEE. 10.1109/ICCCNT.2013.6726793

Satya, S., Rastogi, R., Chaturvedi, D. K., Arora, N., Singh, P., & Vyas, P. (2018). Statistical Analysis for Effect of Positive Thinking on Stress Management and Creative Problem Solving for Adolescents. *Proceedings of the 12th INDIA-Com*, 245-251.

Satya, S., Arora, N., Trivedi, P., Singh, A., Sharma, A., Singh, A., Rastogi, R., & Chaturvedi, D. K. (2019). *Intelligent Analysis for Personality Detection on Various Indicators by Clinical Reliable Psychological TTH and Stress Surveys. In Proceedings of CIPR 2019 at Indian Institute of Engineering Science and Technology*. Springer.

Seals, C. D., Clanton, K., Agarwal, R., Doswell, F., & Thomas, C. M. (2008). Lifelong learning: Becoming computer savvy at a later age. *Educational Gerontology, 34*(12), 1055–1069. doi:10.1080/03601270802290185

Senbagavalli, T., & Arasu, G. T. (2016, August). Opinion Mining for Cardiovascular Disease using Decision Tree based Feature Selection. *Asian Journal of Research in Social Sciences and Humanities, 6*(8), 891–897. doi:10.5958/2249-7315.2016.00658.4

Sengupta, S. (2019). Machine Learning. Packt Publishing.

Shankararaman, V., & Gottipati, S. (2016). Mapping information systems student skills to industry skills framework. In *Proceedings of the Global Engineering Education Conference (EDUCON), IEEE* (pp. 248-253). 10.1109/EDUCON.2016.7474561

Shapero, D. (2016, October 6). *Now you Can Privately Signal to Recruiters You're Open to New Job Opportunities.* Retrieved from https://blog.linkedin.com/2016/10/06/now-you-can-privately-signal-to-recruiters-youre-open-to-new-job

Sharma, S., Rastogi, R., Chaturvedi, D. K., Bansal, A., & Agrawal, A. (2018). Audio Visual EMG & GSR Biofeedback Analysis for Effect of Spiritual Techniques on Human Behavior and Psychic Challenges. *Proceedings of the 12th INDIACom*, 252-258.

Sharma, R., Mithas, S., & Kankanhalli, A. (2014). Transforming decision-making processes: A research agenda for understanding the impact of business analytics on organisations. *European Journal of Information Systems*, *23*(4), 433–441. doi:10.1057/ejis.2014.17

Sharma, S., & Thokchom, R. (2014). A review on endangered medicinal plants of India and their conservation. *Journal of Crop and Weed*, *10*(2), 205–218.

Shubham, B., Isha, M., & Saranya, S. S. (2018), Smart Healthcare Monitoring Using IOT. *International Journal of Applied Engineering Research, 13*(15), 11984-11989. http://www.ripublication.com

Siddique, N., & Adeli, H. (2013). *Introduction to Computational Intelligence. In Computational Intelligence: Synergies of Fuzzy Logic, Neural Networks and Evolutionary Computing.* John Wiley & Sons Ltd.

Silva, P. R., & Brandão, W. C. (2015). Arppa: Mining professional profiles from Linkedin using association rules. In *Proceedings of the 7th International Conference on Information, Process, and Knowledge Management (eKnow 2015), Lisbon, Portugal, February 22, 2015, International Academy, Research, and Industry Association* (pp. 72-77). Academic Press.

Simon, D., Gilles, G., & Jean-Jacques, V. (2009). The Web of Things: Interconnecting Devices with high usability and performance. *ICESS*, 323 – 330. https://hal.inria.fr/inria-00390615

Singh, D., Leavline, E., Muthukrishnan, S., & Yuvaraj, R. (2018). Machine Learning based Business Forecasting. *I.J. Information Engineering and Electronic Business*, 40-51.

Singh, A., Rastogi, R., Chaturvedi, D. K., Satya, S., Arora, N., Sharma, A., & Singh, A. (2019). Intelligent Personality Analysis on Indicators in IoT-MMBD Enabled Environment. In *Multimedia Big Data Computing for IoT Applications: Concepts, Paradigms, and Solutions.* Springer. Advance online publication. doi:10.1007/978-981-13-8759-3_7

Singhal, P., Rastogi, R., Chaturvedi, D. K., Satya, S., Arora, N., Gupta, M., Singhal, P., & Gulati, M. (2019). Statistical Analysis of Exponential and Polynomial Models of EMG & GSR Biofeedback for Correlation between Subjects Medications Movement & Medication Scores. *ICSMSIC-2019*, 625-635. https://www.ijitee.org/download/volume-8-issue-6S/

Singh, K., Chander, R., & Kapoor, N. K. (1997). Guggulsterone, a potent hypolipidaemic, prevents oxidation of low density lipoprotein. *Phytotherapy Research: An International Journal Devoted to Medical and Scientific Research on Plants and Plant Products, 11*(4), 291–294. doi:10.1002/(SICI)1099-1573(199706)11:4<291::AID-PTR96>3.0.CO;2-R

Singh, L. P. (1992). *Economics of Tobacco Cultivation, Production and Exchange.* Deep and Deep Publications.

Singh, N. R., & Singh, M. S. (2009). Wild medicinal plants of Manipur included in the red list. *Asian Agri-History*, *13*(3), 221–225.

Skeels, M. M., & Grudin, J. (2009). When social networks cross boundaries: A case study of workplace use of Facebook and Linkedin. In *Proceedings of the ACM 2009 International Conference on Supporting Group Work, ACM* (pp. 95-104). 10.1145/1531674.1531689

Solis, B., Li, C., & Szymanski, J. (2014). The 2014 state of digital transformation. *Altimeter Group, 1*(1), 1–33.

Soryani, M., & Minaei, B. (2011). Social networks research aspects: A vast and fast survey focused on the issue of privacy in social network sites. *International Journal of Computational Science, 8*(3), 363–373.

Stoltzfus, J. (2020). *How might companies use random forest models for predictions.* Retrieved July 7, 2020, from https://www.techopedia.com/: https://www.techopedia.com/how-might-companies-use-random-forest-models-for-predictions/7/32995

Sufian, H., Faraz, I. K., & Bilal, H. (2019). Understanding Security Requirements and Challenges in Internet of Things (IoT). *RE:view*. Advance online publication. doi:10.1155/2019/9629381

Sukhadeve, A. (2017). *Introduction to Logistic Regression.* Retrieved 8 20, 2019, from www.analyticsinsight.net: https://www.analyticsinsight.net/introduction-to-logistic-regression/

Sun, J. (2009). Functional Link Artificial Neural Network-based Disease Gene Prediction. *Proceedings of International Joint Conference on Neural Networks.* 10.1109/IJCNN.2009.5178639

Tajbakhsh, M. S., & Solouk, V. (2014). Semantic geolocation friend recommendation system: Linkedin user case. In *Proceedings of the 2014 6th Conference on Information and Knowledge Technology (IKT), IEEE* (pp. 158-162). 10.1109/IKT.2014.7030351

Tam, P.W. (2016). The government answers apple in the iPhonecase. *The New York Times.* Available: https://www.nytimes.com/2016/03/12/technology/the-government-answers-apple-in-the-iphone-case.html?ribbon-ad-idx=4&rref=technology&module=Ribbon&version=origin&region=Header&action=click&contentCollection=Technology&pgtype=articleover&_r=0

Tam. (2016). The Government Answers Apple in the iPhone Case. *The New York Times.* Available: http://www.nytimes.com/2016/03/12/technology/the- government-answers-apple-in-the-iphone-case.html?ribbon-ad-idx=4&rref=technology&module=Ribbon&version=origin&region=Header&action=click&contentCo llection=Technology&pgtype=artic leover&_r=0

Tang, J. L., Liu, B. Y., & Ma, K. W. (2008). Traditional chinese medicine. *Lancet, 372*(9654), 1938–1940. doi:10.1016/S0140-6736(08)61354-9 PMID:18930523

Tantawy, R. Y., Farouk, Z., Mohamed, S., & Yousef, A. H. (2014). *Using professional social networking as an innovative method for data extraction: The ICT Alumni Index case study.* arXiv preprint arXiv:1410.1348.

Thiel, Kötter, Michael, Silipo, & Winters. (2012). *Creating Usable Customer Intelligence from Social Media Data: Network Analytics meets Text Mining.* Academic Press.

Tian, L., Meng, Q., Wang, L., & Dong, J. (2014). A study on crop growth environment control system. *International Journal of Control and Automation, 7*(9), 357–374. doi:10.14257/ijca.2014.7.9.31

Torres-Carrasquillo, P. A., Reynolds, D. A., Deller, J. R. Jr, Singer, E., Greene, R. J., & Kohler, M. A. (2002). Language identification using Gaussian Mixture Model Tokenization. *IEEE Int. Conf. on Acoustics, Speech, and Signal Proc.* 10.1109/ICASSP.2002.1005850

Tota, K., Rayabarapu, N., Moosa, S., Talla, V., Bhyravbhatla, B., & Rao, S. (2013). InDiaMed: A comprehensive database of Indian medicinal plants for diabetes. *Bioinformation, 9*(7), 378–380. doi:10.6026/97320630009378 PMID:23750084

Trachtenberg, A. (2015, February 12). *Changes to our developer program.* Retrieved from https://developer.linkedin.com/blog/posts/2015/developer-program-changes

Tucker, C. S., Behoora, I., Nembhard, H. B., Lewis, M., Sterling, N. W., & Huang, X. (2015). Machine Learning Classification Of Medication Adherence In Patients With Movement Disorders Using Non-Wearable Sensors. *Computers in Biology and Medicine*, *66*, 120–134. doi:10.1016/j.compbiomed.2015.08.012 PMID:26406881

Ueda, N., Nakano, R., Ghahramani, Z., & Hinton, G. (2000). SMEM Algorithm for Mixture Models. *Neural Computation*, *12*(9), 2109–2128. doi:10.1162/089976600300015088 PMID:10976141

van de Kerkhof, van Persiea, Noorbergena, Schoutenb, & Ghauharalic. (2015). Spatio-temporal analysis of remote sensing and field measurements for smart farming. *Spatial Statistics 2015: Emerging Patterns.*

van Evert, Fountas, Jakovetic, Crnojevic, Travlos, & Kempenaar. (n.d.). Big Data for weed control and crop protection. *Weed Research*. Doi:10.1111/wre.12255

Varian, H. (2014). Big Data: New Trick for Econometrics. *The Journal of Economic Perspectives*, *28*(2), 3–28. doi:10.1257/jep.28.2.3

Vavliakis, K. N., Tzima, F. A., & Mitkas, P. A. (2012). Event Detection via LDA for the MediaEval2012 SED Task. *MediaEval 2012 Workshop.*

Ved, Sureshchandra, Barve, Srinivas, Sangeetha, Ravikumar, Kartikeyan, Kulkarni, Kumar, Venugopal, Somashekhar, Sumanth, Begum, Rani, Surekha, & Desale. (2016). *FRLHT's ENVIS Centre on Medicinal Plants.* Academic Press.

Venkataraman, D., & Mangayarkarasi, N. (2016, December). Computer vision based feature extraction of leaves for identification of medicinal values of plants. In *2016 IEEE International Conference on Computational Intelligence and Computing Research (ICCIC)* (pp. 1-5). IEEE. 10.1109/ICCIC.2016.7919637

Vesset, D. (2018a). *Descriptive analytics 101: What happened?* Retrieved 5 24, 2019, from Analytics for all: https://www.ibm.com/blogs/business-analytics/descriptive-analytics-101-what-happened/

Vesset, D. (2018b). *Diagnostic analytics 101: Why did it happen?* Retrieved 8 24, 2019, from Analytics for all: https://www.ibm.com/blogs/business-analytics/diagnostic-analytics-101-why-did-it-happen/

Vesset, D. (2018c). *Predictive analytics 101: What will happen next?* Retrieved 8 24, 2019, from Analytics for all: https://www.ibm.com/blogs/business-analytics/predictive-analytics-101-will-happen-next/

Vesset, D. (2018d). *Prescriptive analytics 101: What should be done about it?* Retrieved 8 24, 2019, from Analytics for all: https://www.ibm.com/blogs/business-analytics/prescriptive-analytics-done/

Violent Crime - Crime in the United States 2009. (n.d.). Retrieved March 14, 2020, from https://www2.fbi.gov/ucr/cius2009/offenses/violent_crime/index.html

Vishwakarma, A. C., & Solanki, R. (2018). Analysing Credit Risk using Statistical and Machine Learning Techniques. *International Journal of Engineering Science and Computing*, *8*(6), 18397–18404.

Vlahos, G. E. (2004). Ferratt and Knoepfle, The use of computer based information systems by German managers to support decision-making, inf. *Manage*, *41*(6), 763–779.

Vyas, P., Rastogi, R., Chaturvedi, D. K., Arora, N., Trivedi, P., & Singh, P. (2018). Study on Efficacy of Electromyography and Electroencephalography Biofeedback with Mindful Meditation on Mental health of Youths. *Proceedings of the 12th INDIA-Com*, 84-89.

Wakefield, K. (2019). *A guide to machine learning algorithms and their applications.* Retrieved from https://www.sas.com/en_gb/insights/articles/analytics/machine-learning-algorithms.html

Wäldchen, J., & Mäder, P. (2018). Plant species identification using computer vision techniques: A systematic literature review. *Archives of Computational Methods in Engineering, 25*(2), 507–543. doi:10.100711831-016-9206-z PMID:29962832

Wamba, S. F., Gunasekaran, A., Akter, S., Ren, S. J., Dubey, R., & Childe, S. J. (2017). Big data analytics and firm performance: Effects of dynamic capabilities. *Journal of Business Research, 70*, 356–365. doi:10.1016/j.jbusres.2016.08.009

Wang, J., Zhang, Y., Posse, C., & Bhasin, A. (2013). Is it time for a career switch? In *Proceedings of the 22nd international conference on World Wide Web, ACM* (pp. 1377-1388). 10.1145/2488388.2488509

Wei, R., Sunny, X., & Liu, X. (2019). Telematics and Informatics Examining the perceptual and behavioral effects of mobile internet fraud : A social network approach. *Telematics and Informatics, 41*(April), 103–113. doi:10.1016/j.tele.2019.04.002

White, C. (2015, June 25). *Don't knock millennials until you try their recruiting ideas.* Retrieved from https://business.linkedin.com/talent-solutions/blog/2015/06/dont-knock-millennials-until-you-try-their-recruiting-ideas

Wimmer, H., & Powell, L. M. (2015). A comparison of open source tools for data science. *Proceedings of the Conference on Information Systems Applied Research, 8*, 4–12.

Witt. (2005). *Data Analysis in Speech Applications* (Vol. 1). AVIOS.

Witten & Hall. (2011). *Data mining: Practical machine learning tools & techniques.* Google.

Wong & Sridharan. (2001). Fusion of Output Scores on Language identification System. *Workshop on Multilingual Speech and Language Processing.*

Woodard, J. D. (2016). Data Science and Management for Large Scale Empirical Applications in Agricultural and Applied Economics Research. *Applied Economic Perspectives and Policy, 38*(3), 373–388. doi:10.1093/aepp/ppw009

World Health Organization. (2002). *WHO traditional medicine strategy 2002-2005.* Geneva: World Health Organization. https://www.who.int/medicines/library/trm/trm_strat_eng.pdf

World Health Organization. (2008, December). W*HO Traditional Medicine, Fact Sheet No 134, Technical report.* WHO.

World Health Organization. (2013). *The WHO Traditional Medicine (TM) Strategy 2014–2023.* WHO. https://www.who.int/iris/bitstream/10665/92455/1/9789241506090_eng.pdf?ua=1

Wu, D., Schaefer, D., & Rosen, D. W. (2013). Cloud-based design and manufacturing systems: A social network analysis. *ICED13: 19th International Conference on Engineering Design.*

Wu, S. G., Bao, F. S., Xu, E. Y., Wang, Y. X., Chang, Y. F., & Xiang, Q. L. (2007, December). A leaf recognition algorithm for plant classification using probabilistic neural network. In *2007 IEEE international symposium on signal processing and information technology* (pp. 11-16). IEEE.

Xue-Hui. (2013). Comparison of three data mining models for predicting diabetes or prediabetes by risk factors. *Kaohsiung Journal of Medical Sciences, 29*, 93-99.

Xun, L. S., Gottipati, S., & Shankararaman, V. (2015). Text-mining approach for verifying alignment of information systems curriculum with industry skills. In *Proceedings of the 2015 International Conference on Information Technology Based Higher Education and Training (ITHET), IEEE* (pp. 1-6). IEEE.

Xu, Y., Li, Z., Gupta, A., Bugdayci, A., & Bhasin, A. (2014). Modeling professional similarity by mining professional career trajectories. In *Proceedings of the 20th ACM SIGKDD international conference on Knowledge discovery and data mining* (pp. 1945-1954). 10.1145/2623330.2623368

Yadav, K., & Singh, N. (2011). In vitro propagation and biochemical analysis of field established wood apple (Aegle marmelos L.). *Analele Universitatii din Oradea. Fascicula Biologie, 18*(1).

Yadav, K., Singh, N., & Aggarwal, A. (2011). Influence of arbuscular mycorrhizal (AM) fungi on survival and development of micropropagated Acorus calamus L. during acclimatization. *Agricultural Technology (Thailand), 7*(3), 775–781.

Yadav, S., Timbadia, M., Yadav, A., Vishwakarma, R., & Yadav, N. (2017). Crime pattern detection, analysis & prediction. *Proceedings of the International Conference on Electronics, Communication and Aerospace Technology, ICECA 2017,* 225–230. 10.1109/ICECA.2017.8203676

Yang, C., Huang, Q., Li, Z., Liu, K., & Hu, F. (2017). Big Data and cloud computing: Innovation opportunities and challenges. *International Journal of Digital Earth, 10*(1), 13–53. doi:10.1080/17538947.2016.1239771

Yeh, Y. (2016, October 19). *Rethinking endorsements so you always look your best.* Retrieved from https://blog.linkedin.com/2016/10/19/rethinking-endorsements-LinkedIn-features

Yiu, T. (2019). *Understanding Random Forest.* Retrieved 8 2019, from https://towardsdatascience.com/understanding-random-forest-58381e0602d2>

Yousef, A., & Charkari, N. M. (2015). SFM: A Novel Sequence-Based Fusion Method For Disease Genes Identification And Prioritization. *Journal of Theoretical Biology, 383,* 12–19. doi:10.1016/j.jtbi.2015.07.010 PMID:26209022

Yu, A. (2016, April 18). *Introducing the LinkedIn Students App: Helping Soon-to-Be College Graduates Conquer Their Job Search.* Retrieved from https://blog.linkedin.com/2016/04/18/introducing-the-linkedin-students-app--helping-soon-to-be-colleg

Yu, L., & Liu, H. (2004). Efficient feature selection via analysis of relevance and redundancy. *Journal of Machine Learning Research, 5,* 1205–1224.

Yu, Y., Lin, H., Meng, J., & Zhao, Z. (2016, June). Visual and Textual Sentiment Analysis of a Microblog Using Deep Convolutional Neural Networks. *Algorithms, 9*(2), 41. doi:10.3390/a9020041

Zakrasek, N. (2017, November 15). *New tools to make your job search simpler.* Retrieved from https://www.blog.google/products/search/new-tools-make-your-job-search-simpler

Zangooei, M. H., Habibi, J., & Alizadehsani, R. (2014). Disease Diagnosis with a hybrid method SVR using NSGA-II. *Neurocomputing, 136,* 14–29. doi:10.1016/j.neucom.2014.01.042

Zantalis, F., Koulouras, G., Karabetsos, S., & Kandris, D. (2019). *A Review of Machine Learning and IoT in Smart Transportation.* Future Internet. doi:10.3390/fi11040094

Zecchin. (2012). Neural Network Incorporating Meal Information Improves Accuracy of Short-Time Prediction of Glucose Concentration. *IEEE Transactions on Biomedical Engineering, 59*(6).

Zeng, D., Chen, H., Lusch, R., & Li, S. H. (2010). Social media analytics and intelligence. *IEEE Intelligent Systems, 25*(6), 13–16. doi:10.1109/MIS.2010.151

Zhang, Y., Abbas, H., & Sun, Y. (2019). Smart e-commerce integration with recommender systems. *Electronic Markets, 29*(2), 219–220. doi:10.100712525-019-00346-x

Zhao, R., Yan, R., Chen, Z., Mao, K., Wang, P., & Gao, R. X. (2019). Deep learning and its applications to machine health monitoring. *Mechanical Systems and Signal Processing, 115,* 213–237. doi:10.1016/j.ymssp.2018.05.050

Zhe, Y., Qihao, Z., Lei, L., Kan Z., & Wei, X. (2016). *An IOT-Cloud based wearable ECG monitoring system for smart healthcare.* Doi:10.1007/S10916-016-0644-9

ZhilbertTafa. (2015). An Intelligent System for Diabetes Prediction. *4ᵗʰ Mediterranean Conference on Embedded Computing MECO – 2015*, 378-382.

Zhou, D., Chen, L., & He, Y. (2015). An unsupervised framework of exploring events on twitter: filtering, extraction and categorization. *Proceedings of the Twenty-Ninth AAAI Conference on Artificial Intelligence.*

Zhou, W., Wen, J., Xiong, Q., Gao, M., & Zeng, J. (2016). SVM-TIA a shilling attack detection method based on SVM and target item analysis in recommender systems. *Neurocomputing, 210*, 197–205. doi:10.1016/j.neucom.2015.12.137

Zhu, T., Ren, Y., Zhou, W., Rong, J., & Xiong, P. (2014). An effective privacy preserving algorithm for neighborhood-based collaborative filtering. *Future Generation Computer Systems, 36*, 142–155. doi:10.1016/j.future.2013.07.019

Ziani, A., Azizi, N., Schwab, D., Aldwairi, M., Chekkai, N., Zenakhra, D., & Cheriguene, S. (2017). *Recommender system through sentiment analysis.* Academic Press.

Zide, J., Elman, B., & Shahani-Denning, C. (2014). Linkedin and recruitment: How profiles differ across occupations. *Employee Relations, 36*(5), 583–604. doi:10.1108/ER-07-2013-0086

Zissman, M. (1996). Comparison of four approaches to automatic language identification of telephone speech. *IEEE Transactions on Audio, Speech, and Language Processing, 4*(1), 31–34. doi:10.1109/TSA.1996.481450

Zissman, M. A., & Berkling, K. M. (2001). Automatic language identification. *Speech Communication, 35*(1), 115–124. doi:10.1016/S0167-6393(00)00099-6

Zue, V. W., & Hazen, T. J. (1997). *Automatic Language Identification Using a Segment-Based Approach.* Proceeding Eurospeech. doi:10.1121/1.418211

Zufferey, D., Hofer, T., Hennebert, J., Schumacher, M., Ingold, R., & Bromuri, S. (2015). Performance Comparison Of Multi-Label Learning Algorithms On Clinical Data For Chronic Diseases. *Computers in Biology and Medicine, 65*, 34–43. doi:10.1016/j.compbiomed.2015.07.017 PMID:26275389

About the Contributors

V. Sathiyamoorthi is currently working as an Associate Professor in Computer Science and Engineering Department at Sona College of Technology, Salem, Tamil Nadu, India. He was born on June 21, 1983, at Omalur in Salem District, Tamil Nadu, India. He received his Bachelor of Engineering degree in Information Technology from Periyar University, Salem with First Class. He obtained his Master of Engineering degree in Computer Science and Engineering from Anna University, Chennai with Distinction and secured 30th University Rank.He received his Ph.D degree from Anna University, Chennai in Web Mining. His areas of specialization include Web Usage Mining, Data Structures, Design and Analysis of Algorithm and Operating System. He has published five papers in International Journals and eight papers in various National and International conferences. He has also participated in various National level Workshops and Seminars conducted by various reputed institutions.

Atilla Elci is full professor in the Software Engineering Department, Hasan Kalyoncu University, Turkey. He retired as full professor and chairman, Aksaray University (2012-2017). Served at Purdue, METU, Haliç, Başkent, EMU, Toros, SDÜ, and Aksaray. His pro practice includes ITU as chief technical advisor (1985-97) and IT&T Pvt Ltd as owner, Turkey (1997-2003). He has organized/served for committees of numerous international conferences. He has organized IEEE COMPSAC & ESAS since 2006, SIN Confs since 2007; and, IJRCS Symposiums 2008-9. He has published extensively; edited Semantic Agent Systems (Springer, 2011), Theory and Practice of Cryptography Solutions for Secure Information Systems (2013), Handbook of Applied Learning Theory and Design in Modern Education (2016), Metacognition and Successful Learning Strategies in Higher Education (2017), Comptemporary Perspectives on Web-Based Systems (May 2018), and Faculty Development for Digital Teaching and Learning (May 2019) all by IGI Global, and the procs SIN Confs by ACM, ESAS by IEEE CS. He serves IEEE COMPSAC since 2005, track chair (2008-2015), Standing Committee Member since 2014. He is an assoc editor of Expert Systems and board member of other journals. BSEE METU, Ankara (1970), M.Sc. & Ph.D. in Computer Sciences, Purdue Univ, USA (1973, 1975). His research and experience encompass web semantics, agent-based systems, robotics, machine learning, knowledge representation and ontology, information security, and educational technology.

* * *

Taushif Anwar is a Ph.D. scholar in the Department computer science, School of Engineering & Technology at Pondicherry University, Pondicherry, India. He received MCA degree from, Punjab Technical University and BCA degree from Jamia Hamdard University, New Delhi, India. His research interests include the area of Recommender System, Data Mining and Machine Learning.

Namratha Birudaraju has been qualified in M.Tech (CSE) and MBA (HR). Has 10 years of academic experience. Published research papers in various International journals,Scopus indexed journals and book chapter in IGI global. Interested research areas are Big Data, data mining, Cloud computing and networks.

D. K. Chaturvedi is working in Dept. of Elect. Engg, Faculty of Engg, D.E.I., Dayalbagh, Agra since 1989. Presently he is Professor. He did his B.E. from Govt. Engineering College Ujjain, M.P. then he did his M.Tech. and Ph.D. from D.E.I. Dayalbagh. He is gold medalist and received Young Scientists Fellowship from DST, Government of India in 2001-2002 for post doctorial research at Univ. of Calgary, Canada. Also, he had research collaboration with different organizations at national and international level. He is the Fellow - The Institution of Engineers (India), Fellow - Aeronautical Society of India, Fellow - IETE, Sr. Member IEEE, USA and Member of many National and International professional bodies such as IET, U.K., ISTE, Delhi, ISCE, Roorkee, IIIE, Mumbai and SSI etc. The IEE, U.K. recognized his work in the area of Power System Stabilizer and awarded honorary membership to him in 2006. He did many R&D projects of MHRD, UGC, AICTE etc. and consultancy projects of DRDO. He contributed in the national mission of ICT of Govt. of India as Virtual Power Lab Developer. He has guided 10 Ph.Ds., 65 M.Tech. Dissertations and published more than 300 International and National Papers. He has chaired and Co-Chaired many International and National Conferences. He is referee of many International Journals including IEE Proceedings and IEEE Transactions. He is Head of Dept. of Footwear Technology, Convener, Faculty Training and Placement Cell, and Advisor, IEI Students' Chapter (Elect. Engg.), D.E.I. Dayalbagh, Agra.

Calin Constantinov has a Bachelor of Computer Engineering degree and a Master of Software Engineering degree from the University of Craiova. He is currently a PhD Candidate in the area of Social Data Analysis. Along with accumulating 4 years of teaching experience, he has been working in the industry for 8 years and is now leading Digital Innovation teams. As a Certified Neo4j Professional, he is using Graph Databases for most of his work and research. Key focuses include untangling multidimensional data and interpreting patterns within highly-connected structures.

S. Godfrey Winster is working in the Department of Computer Science and Engineering at SRM Institute of Science and Technology, Kattankulathur, India. He has 18 years of teaching experience in various reputed engineering colleges in Chennai. He received his BE in Computer Science and Engineering from the University of Madras in 2002 and Master's degree in Computer Science and Engineering from Sathyabama University in 2006. He received his Doctorate in Web Mining from Anna University and his research interest includes web mining, semantic web, Cloud Computing, Big Data Analytics and social networking. He has published various research papers in international journals and conferences.

Bollipelly Pruthviraj Goud is working as an Assistant Professor in the Department of Information Technology, Anurag Group of Institutions (CVSR).

Md Imran Hussain is an MTech student of Computer Science and Engineering at the Department of Computer Science, Pondicherry University, India. He received a Bachelor of Technology, program at Bengal Institute of Technology And Management, Maulana Abul Kalam Azad University of Technology, West Bengal, India in 2016. His research interest areas are Machine Learning and Deep Learning.

Anitha J. received her Bachelors degree in Computer Science and Engineering from Bangalore University, Masters degree in Computer Science and Engineering and PhD degree from Anna University, Chennai, India in the area of Knowledge based Systems. She is currently working as Professor & Head of Department, Department of Computer Science and Engineering, R V Institute of Technology and Management, India. She has 50 publications in International and National conferences, 30 publications in National journals and International Journals and 3 book chapters. She has four patents filed to her credit and has worked on few funded projects. She has also published two books on C Programming and Operating Systems. She is a life Member of ISTE and CSI. Her research interest includes bioinformatics, machine learning, image processing, Internet of Things and Knowledge based systems.

G. Maria Jones, Research Scholar in computer science and engineering department at Saveetha Engineering College, Chennai, India. She carries out her research activities since 2018. Her research activities involve digital forensics, Machine Learning and malware propagation.

Kalaivani Karuppiah received her M.E in Computer Science and Engineering from the Anna University, Chennai, India in 2015. She is working as an Assistant Professor in the Department of Computer Science and Engineering at the P.S.N.A. College of Engineering and Technology, Dindigul, India. She has totally 5 years of teaching experience. She is member of various professional societies like ISTE and IAENG. Her research interests include qualified M.E in CSE teaching from PSNACET as an Assistant Professor, Her professional interests focus on Data Mining, Image Processing. She is a member of the Indian Society for Technical Education . She is active in publishing a variety of papers in national/International Conference and journal for about 16.Also Participated in various workshops and seminar.

Kalangi Praveen Kumar is working as an Assistant Professor in the Department of Information Technology, Anurag Group of Institutions, Hyderabad.

Senbagavalli M. is an Associate professor in the Department of Information Technology at Alliance University – Bangalore from May 2018.she has received Bachelor's degree in Information Technology from Periyar University in 2004 and Master's degree in Computer Science and Engineering from Anna University in the year 2009 and Ph.D. in Computer Science and Engineering from Anna University, Chennai in the year 2017. Her research interests include Data Science and Networking. She has published some papers in National and International Journals. She is an Editorial Board Member in International Journal of Research Review in Engineering and Management and Journal of Trading, Economics and Business and Reviewer in Springer Nature.

Sujaritha M. was born in Thiyagaduram, Villupuram District, TamilNadu, India, in 1973. She received her A.M.I.E degree in Computer Science and Engineering in the year 2000 from Institution of Engineers (India). She was awarded Suman Sharma prize award for securing second highest mark in AMIE amongst women students in the year 1994. She received M.E. degree from Bharathiar University at Government College of Technology Coimbatore during 2003. She has secured GATE scholarship during her P.G. course. She completed her Ph.D degree in Anna University, Chennai, under the guidance of Dr.S.Annadurai in the year 2011. She has sixteen years of teaching experience and ten years of research experience in the field of Computer Vision, Image Processing and Soft Computing. Currently she is serving as Professor at Sri Krishna College of Engineering and Technology, Coimbatore. She has visited Malaysia to present her research papers and Chair a session in an International Conference. She has completed two research projects funded by Government of India. She is currently involved in Women Entrepreneurship Development project sponsored by Department of Science and Technology, Government of India. She has published fifteen research papers in International Journals, more than thirty research papers in National and International Conferences. She is guiding three research scholars in the field of internet of things in agriculture. She has mentored a team in Smart India Hackathon 2019 and gave a solution for an ISRO problem and won first prize.

Mihai L. Mocanu received his Ph.D. degree from the University of Craiova, Romania, in 1999. He was a Visiting Research Scholar and consultant for software development for image-guided surgery projects with the Imaging Science and Information Systems (ISIS) Center, Department of Radiology, Georgetown University, Washington D.C., U.S.A., from 2001 to 2002. He is currently Full Professor and PhD Supervisor within the Department of Computers and Information Technology, and Vice-Dean of the School of Control and Computers, since 2016. He has authored/coauthored 10 books and more than 150 papers published in journals or conference proceedings, and was a lead researcher/ director for more than 20 research contracts. His research interests include parallel computing, data analysis and modeling, (discrete event) systems simulation, computational (medical) imaging, advanced software design methods and software engineering (UML, agile methodologies).

Durgadevi Mullaivanan is currently pursuing her Ph.D. in the Department of Computer Science and Engineering at Pondicherry Engineering College, Puducherry, India. She obtained her M.Tech in Network and Internet and Engineering in 2015 from the Department of Computer Science, Pondicherry University, Puducherry, India. She has done her B.Tech in Computer Science and Engineering in 2013 from Manakula Vinayagar Institute Of Technology, Pondicherry University, Puducherry, India.. Currently, she is working in the fields of Data Mining, and Evolutionary Computing.

Kağan Okatan received his Ph.D. degree from Okan University Business Administration (English) with his PhD thesis titled 'Effects of Internal and External Innovation Capacity on Innovation Success'. He received his Master's degree from Information Technology Department of Bahçeşehir University and completed his higher education in Marmara University Sales Management and Anadolu University Business Administration programs. He had worked as a banker at Pamukbank T.A. since 1998 until August 2001. He established a wide range of customer communications in branch banking including daily transactions, loans, individual and private portfolio customer representation, individual marketing and sales units. After completing his master's degree, he started to work in the Billing and Income Assurance Department of Telsim Mobil Telecommunications. In the following years, he worked as Application Analyst, Senior Application Manager and Pricing Applications Manager and lastly Transformation Programmes Senior Project Manager at Vodafone Telecommunications. He continues his professional career as an Assistant Professor at the Department of International Trade Department at Istanbul Kültür University.

Madhumathy Perumal is working as Associate Professor has completed engineering from Anna University and ME (gold medalist) from VMU and PhD from Anna University. She has 12 years of teaching experience. Area of interest includes Computer networks, Wireless Communication, Internet of Things, Mobile Communication. Has published 60 papers in international and national journal / conferences. Life member of ISTE. Reviewer for IEEE, IET, Springer and ELSEVIER. Published an Indian Patent.

Venkatesh R. received his M.E in Computer Science and Engineering from Anna University Chennai in India, in 2007 and Ph.D. in Information and Communication engineering in 2010 at Alagappa University, Karaikudi. Currently, he is working as a Professor in the Department of Information Technology in PSNA College of Engineering and Technology, Dindigul, India. He has totally twenty years of teaching experience which includes 11 years of research experience. He has published 20 papers in International journals, 2 papers in National journals, and presented 22 papers at International conferences and 10 papers at National conferences. His research interests include Biometrics, Artificial intelligence, Compiler design, Neural Networks, Soft computing, Network security and Networks. He has co-authored a book entitled ''Compiler Design'' published by Yes Dee Publishing.

Kalpana Ramanujam is currently working as Professor in Dept. of CSE at Pondicherry Engineering College. She completed Bachelor of Technology in Computer Science from Pondicherry Engineering College, during 1992-96. She completed Master of Technology in Computer Science from Pondicherry University in 1998. As a Professor she teaches UG and PG students and supervises Doctoral research. She has a teaching experience of 20 years in PEC. She has published 75 research papers in International conferences/Journals with high impact factor. Her area of interest includes Parallel and Distributed Systems &Computing, Algorithm design and Optimization.

A. Prasanth Rao is currently working as a Professor, in the Dept. of Information Technology, Anurag group of institutions, Hyderabad. Total 15 years of Experience in teaching and 9 years in industry. Completed Doctorate from JNTU-H, Hyderabad. Research domains are IOT, Cloud Computing and Information Security and published 30 paper in journals.

Rohit Rastogi received his B.E. degree in Computer Science and Engineering from C.C.S.Univ. Meerut in 2003, the M.E. degree in Computer Science from NITTTR-Chandigarh (National Institute of Technical Teachers Training and Research-affiliated to MHRD, Govt. of India), Punjab Univ. Chandigarh in 2010. Currently he is pursuing his Ph.D. In computer science from Dayalbagh Educational Institute, Agra under renowned professor of Electrical Engineering Dr. D.K. Chaturvedi in area of spiritual consciousness. Dr. Santosh Satya of IIT-Delhi and dr. Navneet Arora of IIT-Roorkee have happily consented him to co supervise. He is also working presently with Dr. Piyush Trivedi of DSVV Hardwar, India in center of Scientific spirituality. He is a Associate Professor of CSE Dept. in ABES Engineering. College, Ghaziabad (U.P.-India), affiliated to Dr. A.P. J. Abdul Kalam Technical Univ. Lucknow (earlier Uttar Pradesh Tech. University). Also, He is preparing some interesting algorithms on Swarm Intelligence approaches like PSO, ACO and BCO etc. Rohit Rastogi is involved actively with Vichaar Krnati Abhiyaan and strongly believe that transformation starts within self.

Sudheer Reddy is working as Professor in Dept. of Information Technology, Anurag Group of Institutions, Hyderabad.

Sravan Kumar S. is working as an Assistant Professor in Dept. of Information Technology, Anurag group of institutions (CVSR), Hyderabad.

Roopashree S. pursuing PhD from Visveswaraya Technical University, Belagavi, India. Research area includes Machine Learning and Computer Vision. Received degrees, M.Tech in Computer Science and Engineering from Visveswaraya Technical University, Belagavi and Bachelor of Engineering in Computer Science and Engineering from Mysore University, Karnataka, India. Currently working as Assistant Professor in Department of Computer Science and Engineering, School of Engineering, Dayananda Sagar University. Published an Indian Patent in Machine Learning and Image Processing. She has worked as Assistant Professor in reputed engineering college for seven years and as a software developer for four years in MNC company under embedded systems and PLM platform. Life member of Computer Society of India and a graduate student member of IEEE. She has two Indian patents to her credit. She has published in International and National Journals / Conferences. Area of interest includes Machine Learning, Computer Vision, Image Processing, Internet of Things, Deep Leaning and Pattern Recognition.

Jesudas T. is a Professor and Head of the Department of Mechatronics Engineering at Mahendra Engineering College (Autonomous) – Namakkal from August 2014. He has received Bachelor's degree in Mechanical Engineering from Madras University in 1996 and a Master's degree in Computer Integrated Manufacturing from Anna University, Chennai in 2006, and Ph.D. in Mechanical Engineering from Anna University, Chennai in the year 2012. His research interests include Traditional and Non-Traditional Machining, Robotics and Machine Vision and image processing. He has published so many papers in National and International Journals. He chaired and served in many international conferences and workshops. He also owns two patents. He is an Editorial Board Member in Indian Journals, International Journal of Research Review in Engineering and Management, and Reviewer in Elsevier and Springer Nature. He is a member of the Board of Study for the Mechatronics Department at Mahendra Engineering College from 2014 to till now. He served as an Assessor in PMKVY Assessment Process for Solar Pump Technician, Green House Fitter and Organic Grower in 2017, 2018 respectively. Dr.Jesudas Thangaraju has received many awards which include the "Innovative Academician of the Year 2019" from the Centre for Education Growth and Research (CEGR) held on 18th April 2019 at New Delhi and the "National Leadership Excellence Award 2019-Young Scientist of the Year Award" from Integrated Chambers of Commerce and Industry held on 27th July 2019 at New Delhi and "Innovative & Dedicated Technological Researcher Award", from the Society of Innovative Educationalist & Scientific Research Professional, Chennai. In associated with Innovative Scientific Research Professionals Malaysia held in 2018 at Malaysia and "Certificate of Reviewing", in July 2016 from Precision Engineering, Elsevier, Science Direct and "Certificate of Outstanding Contribution in Reviewing", in January 2017 from Precision Engineering Elsevier, Science Direct.

Uma V. is presently working as an Assistant Professor in Department computer science at Pondicherry University, Pondicherry, India. She did her Ph.D and M.Tech (computer science) from Pondicherry University, Pondicherry, India. Her research interests include Distributed Computing Systems, Artificial Intelligence, Knowledge Representation and Reasoning, Data Mining.

D. Sudaroli Vijayakumar is an Assistant Professor in the Department of Computer Science at PES University. She holds B.E in computer science and M.tech in Digital Communication and Networking. Her research interests span on finding machine learning-based solutions in various domains ranging from software testing, wireless networks, etc. She is a cisco certified professional and was a cross-functional trainer. She holds fast tracker, let's clone you awards. She is a fellow of IAENG, Analytics Society, and CSI.

Index

Ensure Quality Research is Introduced to the Academic Community

Become an IGI Global Reviewer for Authored Book Projects

Premier Reference Source

Emerging GIS Applications for Emergency and Disaster Management

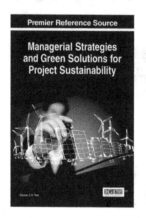

Premier Reference Source

Managerial Strategies and Green Solutions for Project Sustainability

Premier Reference Source

Comparative Approaches to Using R and Python for Statistical Data Analysis

Premier Reference Source

Solutions for High-Touch Communications in a High-Tech World

The overall success of an authored book project is dependent on quality and timely reviews.

In this competitive age of scholarly publishing, constructive and timely feedback significantly expedites the turnaround time of manuscripts from submission to acceptance, allowing the publication and discovery of forward-thinking research at a much more expeditious rate. Several IGI Global authored book projects are currently seeking highly-qualified experts in the field to fill vacancies on their respective editorial review boards:

Applications and Inquiries may be sent to:
development@igi-global.com

Applicants must have a doctorate (or an equivalent degree) as well as publishing and reviewing experience. Reviewers are asked to complete the open-ended evaluation questions with as much detail as possible in a timely, collegial, and constructive manner. All reviewers' tenures run for one-year terms on the editorial review boards and are expected to complete at least three reviews per term. Upon successful completion of this term, reviewers can be considered for an additional term.

If you have a colleague that may be interested in this opportunity, we encourage you to share this information with them.

IGI Global Proudly Partners With eContent Pro International

Receive a 25% Discount on all Editorial Services

Editorial Services

IGI Global expects all final manuscripts submitted for publication to be in their final form. This means they must be reviewed, revised, and professionally copy edited prior to their final submission. Not only does this support with accelerating the publication process, but it also ensures that the highest quality scholarly work can be disseminated.

English Language Copy Editing

Let eContent Pro International's expert copy editors perform edits on your manuscript to resolve spelling, punctuaion, grammar, syntax, flow, formatting issues and more.

Scientific and Scholarly Editing

Allow colleagues in your research area to examine the content of your manuscript and provide you with valuable feedback and suggestions before submission.

Figure, Table, Chart & Equation Conversions

Do you have poor quality figures? Do you need visual elements in your manuscript created or converted? A design expert can help!

Translation

Need your documjent translated into English? eContent Pro International's expert translators are fluent in English and more than 40 different languages.

Hear What Your Colleagues are Saying About Editorial Services Supported by IGI Global

"The service was very fast, very thorough, and very helpful in ensuring our chapter meets the criteria and requirements of the book's editors. I was quite impressed and happy with your service."

– Prof. Tom Brinthaupt,
Middle Tennessee State University, USA

"I found the work actually spectacular. The editing, formatting, and other checks were very thorough. The turnaround time was great as well. I will definitely use eContent Pro in the future."

– Nickanor Amwata, Lecturer,
University of Kurdistan Hawler, Iraq

"I was impressed that it was done timely, and wherever the content was not clear for the reader, the paper was improved with better readability for the audience."

– Prof. James Chilembwe,
Mzuzu University, Malawi

Email: customerservice@econtentpro.com   **www.igi-global.com/editorial-service-partners**

IGI Global's Transformative Open Access (OA) Model:
How to Turn Your University Library's Database Acquisitions Into a Source of OA Funding

In response to the OA movement and well in advance of Plan S, IGI Global, early last year, unveiled their OA Fee Waiver (Read & Publish) Initiative.

Under this initiative, librarians who invest in IGI Global's InfoSci-Books (5,300+ reference books) and/or InfoSci-Journals (185+ scholarly journals) databases will be able to subsidize their patron's OA article processing charges (APC) when their work is submitted and accepted (after the peer review process) into an IGI Global journal. *See website for details.

How Does it Work?

1. When a library subscribes or perpetually purchases IGI Global's InfoSci-Databases and/or their discipline/subject-focused subsets, IGI Global will match the library's investment with a fund of equal value to go toward subsidizing the OA article processing charges (APCs) for their patrons.

   Researchers: **Be sure to recommend the InfoSci-Books and InfoSci-Journals to take advantage of this initiative.**

2. When a student, faculty, or staff member submits a paper and it is accepted (following the peer review) into one of IGI Global's 185+ scholarly journals, the author will have the option to have their paper published under a traditional publishing model or as OA.

3. When the author chooses to have their paper published under OA, IGI Global will notify them of the OA Fee Waiver (Read and Publish) Initiative. If the author decides they would like to take advantage of this initiative, IGI Global will deduct the US$ 2,000 APC from the created fund.

4. This fund will be offered on an annual basis and will renew as the subscription is renewed for each year thereafter. IGI Global will manage the fund and award the APC waivers unless the librarian has a preference as to how the funds should be managed.

Hear From the Experts on This Initiative:

"I'm very happy to have been able to make one of my recent research contributions, "Visualizing the Social Media Conversations of a National Information Technology Professional Association" featured in the *International Journal of Human Capital and Information Technology Professionals*, freely available along with having access to the valuable resources found within IGI Global's InfoSci-Journals database."

– **Prof. Stuart Palmer**,
Deakin University, Australia

Printed in the United States
By Bookmasters